Donated
To The Library by

Dr. Charles W. Sydnor, Jr
18th President
Emory & Henry College
1984-1992
Class of 1965

ROUGH RIDERS

*Colonel Theodore Roosevelt. (520.3-004, Theodore Roosevelt
Collection, Houghton Library, Harvard University.)*

ROUGH RIDERS

THEODORE ROOSEVELT,
His Cowboy Regiment, and the
Immortal Charge Up San Juan Hill

MARK LEE GARDNER

WILLIAM MORROW

An Imprint of HarperCollins*Publishers*

HarperCollins books may be purchased for educational, business, or sales promotional use. For information, please e-mail the Special Markets Department at SPsales@harpercollins.com.

FIRST EDITION

Designed by Ralph Fowler

Library of Congress Cataloging-in-Publication Data has been applied for.

ISBN 978-0-06-231208-2

16 17 18 19 20   OV/RRD   10 9 8 7 6 5 4 3 2 1

To Ronald Kil
Artist—Hunter—Friend

*To those who never soldiered in war times there is
a halo that is inviting, but to those who have, there
is no halo. It only comes with the years afterward
when all things are softened as into a dream.*

CAPTAIN ROBERT B. HUSTON, ROUGH RIDERS

*I suppose that war always does bring out what
is highest and lowest in human nature.*

THEODORE ROOSEVELT

CONTENTS

ALSO BY MARK LEE GARDNER

*To Hell on a Fast Horse: The Untold Story
of Billy the Kid and Pat Garrett*

*Shot All to Hell: Jesse James, the Northfield Raid,
and the Wild West's Greatest Escape*

ROUGH RIDERS

PROLOGUE

Wednesday, January 10, 1906
The White House

President Theodore Roosevelt is all smiles as he moves about and briskly shakes hands with the several guests gathered in his private office and the adjoining cabinet room. The president's favorite and overused exclamations punctuate the conversation: "Bully!" "By George!" and the drawn-out "Deeelighted!"

Among those present today are Secretary of War William Howard Taft, U.S. Army Chief of Staff Lieutenant General Adna R. Chaffee, and Surgeon General Presley Marion Rixey. Also in the small crowd are several army and navy officers—all in full dress uniform—members of the legislative council of the American Medical Association, and a collection of newspaper correspondents.

This is a very special day because the president has gathered these men to witness the presentation of a Medal of Honor. This is the first time a Medal of Honor ceremony has taken place in the White House, the first time since the nation's highest military honor was created during the Civil War that a president of the United States has personally presented. In all previous years, Medals of Honor simply came in the mail.

Roosevelt believed that medal recipients deserved more. As commander in chief, he issued an order on September 20, 1905, requiring that medals be conferred in person by the president "with formal and impressive ceremonies." Roosevelt's wish, according to a newspaper report, was "to increase the value of the Medal of Honor as much as possible, and to make it as rare and as precious as the Victoria Cross."

In an interesting but fitting coincidence, the man being honored this day, Captain James Robb Church, performed his acts of valor while serving as assistant surgeon under Roosevelt in the First United States Volunteer Cavalry, widely known as the Rough Riders. At the Battle of Las Guásimas, Cuba, on June 24, 1898, Church had risked his life time and again treating wounded troopers on the firing line. No less than five times, he had lifted a Rough Rider on his back and carried him to the rear, all the while being exposed to the enemy's highly accurate Mauser rifles.

On three previous occasions, Captain Church had been formally recommended for this recognition, the first coming less than a year after his gallantry in Cuba, but for some reason, the recommendations languished at the War Department. Roosevelt was even under the impression that Church had received the medal seven years ago, until his close friend and former commander of the Rough Riders, Major General Leonard Wood, told him otherwise. The president wants today's precedent-setting ceremony to make up for that long delay.

To begin, the portly Secretary Taft presents Captain Church to the president, and the room is completely silent as Taft reads from the recommendations that describe Church's heroics. Roosevelt proudly looks on; in his hand is a morocco case that holds the medal. Once Taft finishes, Roosevelt turns to Church and speaks directly to him, but for all to hear:

> There is no distinction which confers greater honor upon any
> American in military or civil life than this—the one honor coveted
> above all others, by every man in the military service of the United
> States. It was my good fortune as colonel of the regiment in which you

*served to be an eyewitness to your gallantry and to bear testimony to
it by letter to the proper authorities, stating the reasons why I deemed
that you were entitled to the Medal of Honor. I wish to state, Mr.
Secretary, that the letters I wrote were written before I was president.
Since I was president, I have held no communication whatsoever with
the military authorities on the subject.*

Roosevelt, with another big smile, presents the morocco case to the
captain.

"Captain Church," he says warmly, "there could be no greater plea-
sure than that I now experience in handing to my old comrade and
friend this Medal of Honor."

The president firmly shakes Church's hand and pulls him close,
and in a softer voice but still loud enough for all to hear, says, "There
is no greater comradeship than that which comes from having lived
in the trenches together."

Church, overtaken by emotion, is speechless. He bows respectfully to Roosevelt, and it is both eloquent and touching. The president wanted to make the Medal of Honor presentation impressive and
memorable, and he has succeeded beyond all expectations.

Although there were many American heroes in Cuba during the
summer of 1898—and many who did not survive that short war—
Captain Church is the only Rough Rider to receive the medal. Yet
another former Rough Rider is in this room, and he too should be
wearing it. This man had been recommended for it by all his commanding officers, and several eyewitnesses testified to his actions
above and beyond the call of duty. But because of pettiness, resent-
ment, and, undoubtedly, some jealousy, the War Department had
denied giving it to him.

This man is none other than the president. And having never received the medal he earned under a hot Cuban sun is among his greatest disappointments.

But Roosevelt is somewhat vindicated as he presents the coveted decoration to Captain Church. Both men know it. They share the truth of an experience that only those who were there can truly know. As part of a ragtag regiment of southwestern cowpunchers, Oklahoma Indians, Ivy League football stars, and champion polo players, they had faced death boldly and defeated the enemy.

They had been Rough Riders.

Chapter One

Some Turn of Fortune

I think I smell war in the air.

FREDERIC REMINGTON

Frank Brito rode through the darkness, his cow pony's shod hooves making a slow, steady clopping on the hard dirt. Occasionally there would be a sudden scraping sound when its hooves struck a rocky outcropping, or a jolt to the rider when the pony stepped into a small ditch or arroyo.

Brito was riding through the rough country between Silver City, New Mexico Territory, and the mining town of Pinos Altos ("tall pines"), where his parents lived. It was now nearly midnight, and he was dog tired: he had been in the saddle for hours. But he was almost home, just a few more miles.

The twenty-one-year-old Brito had been born at Pinos Altos. His parents, natives of Mexico, were of Yaqui Indian heritage. His father, Santiago, had worked various gold claims at Pinos Altos since long before Frank's birth. As a young man, Frank had set type in the small office of the weekly *Pinos Altos Miner,* and he had grown up to be a handsome fellow, standing five feet eight inches tall with a dark complexion like his parents, coal black hair, and striking blue eyes.

That spring of 1898, Frank had been pulling in a dollar a day as a cowpuncher for southwestern New Mexico's Circle Bar outfit. But he had received a message from his father to come back to Pinos Altos immediately. His father knew Frank was a ten-hour horseback ride from home, so Frank knew he wouldn't have sent for him unless it was something important. Finally, as Frank's pony neared the old place, he could see that the house was all lit up, oil lamps glowing in every room. Frank's first thought was not a good one: surely someone must have died.

Santiago Brito had been waiting anxiously for his son. When he heard Frank's pony approach the house, he came out onto the porch. Before Frank could slide out of the saddle, Santiago told him that the United States had declared war against Spain. He had gotten the news from nearby Fort Bayard, so there was no doubt about it. More important, Santiago had learned that the government had authorized a volunteer regiment to be composed of cowboys and crack shots from the western territories. Santiago told his son that first thing in the morning, he and his older brother, Joe, were going to ride to Silver City and enlist.

"In those days," Frank would recall decades later, "you didn't talk back to your father, so we did it."

This war with Spain was no surprise to Assistant Secretary of the Navy Theodore Roosevelt. For months, he had been doing everything in his power—not always with the direct knowledge or approval of the secretary—to make the navy ready for the great conflict he was certain was coming. And he also let it be known that he had no intention of observing the war from afar. Crazy as it sounded—and more than a few did think Roosevelt was crazy—this lightning-rod bureaucrat intended to go where the bullets were flying. He had been waiting for a war, any war, his entire adult life, and now that it was here, *nothing* was going to keep him from the battlefield.

Many would blame Roosevelt's outsized martial spirit on the family's supposed stain of his father not taking up arms in the Civil War. Theodore Senior was a staunch Lincoln Republican married to a staunch southern patriot from Georgia, and rather than deepen the divide within his family by becoming a Yankee soldier, he had paid a substitute to serve in his place (an option many well-off men in the North took advantage of). Theodore Junior would later write, "I had always felt that if there were a serious war I wished to be in a position to explain to my children why I did take part in it, and not why I did not take part in it."

But Roosevelt's war fever was actually due to America's fever for war, or at least its long glorification of all things military. The Civil War had erupted just three years after Roosevelt's birth in a New York City brownstone, and that terrible conflict had exerted a strong influence on a most impressionable boy. Two of his uncles on his mother's side served in the Confederate navy, and little Theodore witnessed his mother, aunt, and grandmother pack small boxes of necessities destined for the wrong side of federal lines (surreptitiously, of course, while Theodore Senior was away).

Nearly everything about the Civil War seemed glorious to a boy far removed from the actual fighting. The best and most popular songs of the day were martial songs, from the rousing "The Battle Cry of Freedom" and the poignant "Just Before the Battle, Mother" to the tragic "The Vacant Chair." The oversized pages of *Harper's Weekly* and *Frank Leslie's Illustrated Newspaper* were chock-full of spectacularly detailed engravings of saber-wielding cavalrymen at full gallop, smoke-belching cannons, and corpse-strewn battlefields. And there were the dignified portraits of the war's many heroes, both North and South: Grant, Sherman, Sheridan, Lee, Jackson, Stuart, and the like.

After the Civil War, veterans were showered with adulation for the rest of their lives. The erecting of commemorative monuments and markers on numerous battlefields became a minor industry. And there were the Fourth of July parades, the reunions, and, for many, high political office. In the United States, the quickest way to fame and votes at election time had always been the winning of laurels on the battlefield.

No wonder young men born too late for the great Civil War hoped they would be given their own chance to prove themselves, in their own war, on their own fields of valor. Theodore Roosevelt clearly was one of these.

In 1882, as if his job as New York State's youngest assemblyman wasn't enough of a responsibility, he joined the New York National Guard, eventually rising to the rank of captain. But the Guard mostly set up camps and drilled, which was a lot like *playing* soldier. No enemy. No thrill of battle. No glory.

Then, in the summer of 1886, Roosevelt sniffed an opportunity to get into a real fight. At the time, he was cattle ranching in the Badlands of Dakota Territory. Roosevelt was one of a number of well-to-do young easterners who were drawn to the Wild West for its business opportunities—and adventure. As a passionate hunter, the Little Missouri River country was appealing to him with its last small herds of buffalo, as well as deer, elk, and even bighorn sheep. "It was a land of vast silent spaces," he wrote, "of lonely rivers, and of plains where the wild game stared at the passing horseman."

And it was an escape. Roosevelt had lost his first wife, Alice, and his mother on the same cold February day in 1884, his wife to Bright's disease after giving birth to their daughter, his mother to typhoid fever. Roosevelt had met and fallen in love with Alice while a student at Harvard; they had been married less than three years. The page in Roosevelt's diary for February 14, the date of those two tragic losses, contains only a black "X" and the words, "The light has gone out of my life." For Roosevelt, the long days on a working cattle ranch and his numerous hunting excursions helped him push away the sadness and reinvigorate himself.

But during his brief career as a rancher, Roosevelt never completely cut his ties to the East or its politics, and his blood rose when he read the newspaper reports of growing tension between the United States and Mexico over the false imprisonment of an American newspaper editor in El Paso del Norte, Mexico. The United States was demanding his release, and Mexico was refusing. Texans called for war, and rumors swirled of troops mobilizing on both sides of the border.

Roosevelt dashed off a letter to Secretary of War William Endicott on August 10, 1886, "offering to raise some companies of horse riflemen out here in the event of trouble with Mexico." He confided to friend Henry Cabot Lodge, "I haven't the least idea there will be any trouble; but as my chance of doing anything in the future worth doing seems to grow considerably smaller, I intend to grasp at every opportunity that turns up." Alas, diplomacy prevailed, and Mexico released its prisoner after a three-day trial. "If a war had come off," Roosevelt fantasized to Lodge, "I would surely have had behind me as utterly reckless a set of desperadoes, as ever sat in the saddle."

Roosevelt had always had this something "worth doing" close in his mind. But nine more years would pass before he saw another opportunity to do anything about it. That moment came in 1895 as Spain was fighting a new insurrection in Cuba. On March 8, a Spanish gunboat spotted the American mail ship *Alliança* as it steamed past Cuba's east coast and fired upon it repeatedly. Spain knew the Cuban rebels were receiving supplies from vessels sailing from Florida, but the *Alliança* was six miles out to sea, and it was traveling north, away from Cuba. Fortunately, the *Alliança* was the faster ship and quickly outran the gunboat. The United States demanded an apology; Spain wasn't forthcoming with one.

By this time, the thirty-six-year-old Roosevelt was back in the government in Washington and serving in Grover Cleveland's administration as a U.S. Civil Service commissioner. He turned not to the secretary of war, however, but to New York governor Levi P. Morton. In a March 19 letter to the governor, Roosevelt jotted this postscript, which he marked "Private":

In the very improbable event of a war with Spain I am going to beg
you with all my power to do me the greatest favor possible; get me a
position in New York's quota of the force sent out. Remember, I make
application now. I was three years captain in the 8th Regiment N. Y.
State militia, and I must have a commission in the force that goes to
Cuba! But of course there won't be any war.

Roosevelt was right. There wouldn't be any war, not now, but
Americans had become sympathetic with Cuba's struggle for independence, fueled in part by the yellow press's graphic accounts of
"cruel wrongs" and "barbarities" committed against the Cubans by
the Spanish government. Spain was the last Old World country with
colonies in the New World and, as such, was a "weak and decadent"
relic, according to Roosevelt.

"I am a quietly rampant 'Cuba Libre' man," he wrote his sister
Anna Roosevelt Cowles on January 2, 1897:

I doubt whether the Cubans would do very well in the line of
self-government; but anything would be better than continuance
of Spanish rule. I believe that [President] Cleveland ought now
to recognize Cuba's independence and interfere; sending our fleet
promptly to Havana. There would not in my opinion be very serious
fighting; and what loss we encountered would be thrice over repaid
by the ultimate results of our action.

Three months after sharing his not-so-quiet views with his sister,
Roosevelt accepted the appointment of assistant secretary of the navy
in the new administration of President William McKinley. It was
an ideal position for the author of *The Naval War of 1812*, which was
published in 1882 and was the first of his many books. But more important, the secretaryship made him an insider, privy to the administration's every move—or lack thereof, much to his vexation—in its
increasingly strained relations with Spain.

Roosevelt's new status in the nation's capital added to his already impressive circle of prominent friends and acquaintances: navy and army
men, journalists, more politicians, entrepreneurs, scientists, and so
on. Some he found stimulating, others not; some of like mind, others
not. One he found both remarkably stimulating and of like mind was
thirty-six-year-old army surgeon Captain Leonard Wood, who served
as personal physician for McKinley (and his seizure-suffering wife)
and for the secretary of war and his family.

Roosevelt and Wood first met at a Washington dinner party in June
1897 and quickly became fast friends. It didn't hurt that Wood was a
fellow Harvard man and an excellent football player, but Roosevelt
was most impressed by Wood's experiences chasing the Chiricahua
Apache leader Geronimo eleven years earlier.

Wood had asked for and received the command of an infantry detachment that was lacking an officer and led it for several weeks in
pursuit of Geronimo and his followers. One night, he volunteered to
ride alone through seventy miles of Apache land to deliver important dispatches. By the end of the campaign, Wood had covered thousands of miles of mountain and desert country in northern Mexico
and southern Arizona, much of it on foot and in temperatures at times
exceeding one hundred degrees. His courage and gallantry during the
campaign would earn him the Medal of Honor.

Not surprisingly, the blue-eyed medico was an outstanding speci-
men of manhood, standing five feet ten inches tall (an inch taller than
Roosevelt) with a "superb chest." His long, serious face matched his
disposition. Roosevelt chum Owen Wister observed that the captain
"was inclined to be silent, inclined to be grave." In this way, he was
the opposite of Roosevelt. Nevertheless, Wood and the assistant secretary were each highly competitive, and they shared a near-sadistic
passion for testing the limits of the human body.

Roosevelt had been a puny, sickly child plagued by terrifying asthma attacks. One day, when he was about eleven, Roosevelt's father said, "Theodore, you have the mind but you have not the body, and without the help of the body the mind cannot go as far as it should. You must *make* your body. It is hard drudgery to make one's body, but I know you will do it."

Demonstrating the indomitable spirit that would be his trademark as an adult, the young Roosevelt spent hours upon hours pulling himself up between horizontal bars in the home's open-air gym, fully equipped and paid for by his father. Roosevelt's sister Corinne would never forget seeing her brother hanging from the bars, "widening his chest by regular, monotonous motion." After two years of this "drudgery," the young man took up boxing. The subsequent transformation in Roosevelt's body and health was nothing short of phenomenal.

Roosevelt's "real tastes were for the rougher and hardier forms of exercise," remembered Wood. He "always loved to gather a party of men who felt equal to a bit of hard work and give them a thorough try-out, which generally resulted in using them up pretty badly. . . . His excellent endurance, his aptness in rough, hard climbing, and especially his ability to take his followers and generally outlast them on hard walks and runs ending in a dash up a fissure in a ledge where one had to be able to chin the edge and swing up or confess defeat by going around, all these demonstrated that he had built up a condition of unusual physical fitness."

Most afternoons Roosevelt and Wood could be found boxing, wrestling, fencing, or playing football (tackle, of course). But Wood was becoming tired of Washington, and like Roosevelt, he desperately wanted a field command if war came. He even told Roosevelt he was considering returning to the West and maybe starting a ranch. Roosevelt urged his friend to wait just a little longer. War with Spain, he told him emphatically as only Roosevelt could, was not far off.

Then, in the early morning darkness of February 16, 1898, lights went on in home after home in Washington and soon the White House, where President McKinley was awakened to the horrid news that the battleship USS *Maine* had exploded in Havana Harbor. "Many wounded, and doubtless more killed and drowned," the initial report read.

The explosion, the result of the ship's powder magazine igniting, rocked Havana, breaking windows in several houses and leaving the *Maine* a twisted carcass of steel. The final death toll was a staggering 266 officers and men.

The *Maine* had been sent to Cuba just three weeks earlier, after anti-American demonstrations in pro-Spain Havana threatened U.S. citizens and property there. Although the battleship's visit to the Cuban capital was meant to be friendly, it was still provocative under the circumstances.

Many in the United States instantly suspected that Spain had orchestrated the tragedy. Headlines like the one in Washington's *Evening Times,* published well before any solid details could reach the States, were typical: "Blown Up by Spain, Every Evidence That the Maine Was Torpedoed." The newspaper added beneath it, "Two Hundred and Fifty American Sailors the Food of Sharks."

Wreckage of the USS Maine *in Havana Harbor. Photo by John C. Hemment. (Author's Collection.)*

And Roosevelt was just as quick to lay blame, writing confidentially to a young Harvard friend the same day, "The *Maine* was sunk by an act of dirty treachery on the part of the Spaniards."

The navy ordered an investigation to determine what caused the explosion, but this would take a few weeks to complete. In the meantime, when Roosevelt wasn't providing Secretary of the Navy John D. Long with endless recommendations about preparing the navy for war, he and Wood feverishly tried to position themselves to be a part of any invading force once war came. Roosevelt wrote to New York State's adjutant general three times about his desire to serve.

"I don't want to be in an office during war," he wrote on March 9, "I want to be at the front. . . . If I were in New York City, I think I could raise a regiment of volunteers in short order. . . . I have a man who rendered most gallant service with the regular Army against the Apaches, whom I should very much like to bring in with me if I could raise a regiment. . . . Have you any idea how quickly I could get uniforms, arms, etc.?"

One week later, Roosevelt, Wood, and McKinley's secretary, John Addison Porter, dined with Senator Redfield Proctor at Washington's Metropolitan Club. Proctor had recently returned from Cuba and could not stop talking about the shocking conditions he had seen. In those areas in revolt, which was most of the island, Spain's military governor had forcefully moved all Cubans from their rural homes and relocated them to larger towns. To keep these Cubans (known as *reconcentrados*) in, and the insurgents out, the governor had surrounded the towns with trenches, barbed wire, and blockhouses, making them virtual prison yards. In the last few months, Proctor said, two hundred thousand *reconcentrados* had died from starvation and disease.

The atrocities Proctor described were a preview of a speech he would give before the Senate the next day. That speech, quoted at length on the front pages of numerous newspapers, "aroused a spirit of hot indignation throughout the nation," remembered Wood, "and a determination to terminate these conditions."

"[W]e might have ignored cruelty and oppression, had they been further off," explained Owen Wister years later, "as it was, we began to feel it our duty in the name of liberty and humanity to help the weak little neighbor, and also to abate the nuisance."

Just eleven days after Proctor's chilling report, the country was again filled with indignation—and a seething desire for vengeance. The navy's board of inquiry on the *Maine* disaster concluded that the battleship "was destroyed by the explosion of a submarine mine." Although the board could not identify who was responsible for the mine, nearly all Americans, and particularly the yellow press, further convicted Spain.

President McKinley was now facing intense pressure to intervene in Cuba, and among those pushing him were Roosevelt and Wood. McKinley half fondly referred to them as the "war party." During Wood's daily visits to attend to Mrs. McKinley, the president jokingly greeted the surgeon with, "Well, have you and Theodore declared war yet?"

Wood usually replied, "No, Mr. President, we have not, but we think you should take steps in that direction, sir."

Those steps, uneasy ones to be sure, officially began on April 11. In a message to Congress, McKinley asked for authorization to end the hostilities between the Cuban insurgents and the Spanish government and to establish a new, stable government for the island, using the force of American arms if necessary. Few believed that Spain would acquiesce without the use of force, though McKinley, a Civil War veteran who dreaded the suffering and death that war would bring, still had hope of avoiding armed conflict.

"The President still feebly is painfully trying for peace," an exasperated Roosevelt jotted in his pocket diary on April 16. "His weakness and vacillation are even more ludicrous than painful."

Congress vacillated a little as well, but on April 19, it passed a joint resolution demanding that Spain get out of Cuba once and for all. It also empowered the president to use "the entire land and naval force of the United States" to make it so. Spain responded by declaring war on April 23, and Congress followed with its own formal war declaration two days later. Now came the critical work of forming not only a war strategy but quickly mobilizing an invasion force.

"I have the Navy in good shape," Roosevelt scrawled in his diary. "But the army is awful. The War Dept. is in utter confusion."

"I want to introduce you to my personal friend, Dr. Leonard Wood," began Roosevelt's short letter to Massachusetts governor Roger Wolcott. "He is an intimate friend of mine, and one of the best fellows, as well as one of the best officers that I know. He wants to go as a field officer in one of the Massachusetts regiments."

Written on April 16, more than a week before the declaration of war, it was one of several glowing letters Wood had asked others to send to the governor of his home state, including one from the secretary of war, Russell Alger. But even with these high-powered recommendations, plus his status as a Medal of Honor recipient, Wood was essentially told to get in line. As Roosevelt later recalled, at least ten men clamored for each potential officer's commission.

The extremely well-connected Roosevelt was having no easier time when he asked for a spot for himself and Wood in the Seventy-First Regiment, New York National Guard. Roosevelt also pressed General Fitzhugh Lee (formerly the consul-general at Havana) to appoint him as an officer on the general's staff, when it became known that Lee would be given some type of command. Roosevelt's maneuverings became so commonly known that a false story went over the wires on April 17, claiming that Roosevelt had just resigned his secretaryship to join Lee. The general promptly denied making any promises.

The situation was getting more desperate by the day. Then, on April 22, Congress passed a bill to temporarily increase the military, including a provision for three thousand volunteers ("possessing special qualifications") from the country at large. This provision was added by a Wyoming senator who believed the army would benefit from some regiments composed of cowboys and "mountaineers" from out west.

The American cowboy was thought to be a natural-born, crack-shot fighting man by a public fed on shoot-'em-up dime novels and thrilling performances from Buffalo Bill's Congress of Rough Riders of the World. (Newspapers reported that Cody was raising his own regiment of cowboys and Indians to fight in Cuba.) Some within the military shared that view, romantic as it was.

"I believe that the 'cow boys,' so called, are the very best material for cavalry service in Cuba, or anywhere else, for that matter," opined Major William M. Wallace of the Second U.S. Cavalry. "They are necessarily young men and thorough horsemen: the spirit that put them into the saddle to start with is apparent all the time. . . . No man who is not a daring fellow can be a good cow boy."

Roosevelt knew quite a bit about cowboys, too, and Secretary of War Russell Alger was as aware of this as he was of Roosevelt's desire to take part in the coming campaign—Roosevelt had made that annoyingly clear. So, on Saturday, April 23, Alger called Roosevelt into his office. The three thousand "at large" volunteers, he told him, would be divided into three regiments of mounted riflemen to be recruited in the western territories. Would Roosevelt accept command of one of these regiments?

Alger's offer came as a surprise to Roosevelt, but it was now his turn to surprise Alger. He couldn't accept, at least not the colonelcy. After six weeks in the field, Roosevelt explained, he would have no qualms about leading a regiment. But the war might be over by then. And as rapidly as things were moving right now, the organizing and outfitting of a new regiment, as well as Roosevelt's own military education, would best be served with an experienced officer at the reins. That man, Roosevelt told him, was Leonard Wood. If Alger would appoint Captain Wood the regiment's colonel, Roosevelt would happily accept the lieutenant colonelcy, the second in command.

Roosevelt's refusal of the colonelcy came across to Alger as pure stupidity. Take the command, Alger insisted, and he would appoint

Wood lieutenant colonel. As for organizing the regiment and getting it into fighting trim, it was simple: just order Wood to do the work. But Roosevelt strongly objected.

"I did not wish to rise on any man's shoulders," Roosevelt wrote later—he refused "to hold any position where any one else did the work."

Alger was flabbergasted. Roosevelt's ego was substantial, but here the secretary was handing him a colonelcy, his own regiment, a chance to grab all the glory, and Roosevelt wouldn't take it. Not only that, Roosevelt was urging another man in his stead. The secretary ended the meeting cordially, saying he would seriously consider Roosevelt's request.

The next day, Roosevelt fired off a letter to his ranch foreman in Billings County, North Dakota: "It may be that I am going to Cuba." If so, he continued, he might come there to raise a company of volunteers. "I shall telegraph you at once when anything is decided. As yet it is all in the dark, and I may not be able to go [to Cuba]. I have been anxious to strike for the last six months."

But in just twenty-four hours, the darkness evaporated. On Monday morning, April 25, Alger informed Roosevelt that he would appoint Wood colonel of the regiment. Roosevelt then agreed to accept the appointment as lieutenant colonel. Until the regiment was recruited, however, he would continue to fulfill his duties as assistant secretary of the navy, at which time he would resign.

It's doubtful that any other man in Washington that morning was as giddy as thirty-nine-year-old Theodore Roosevelt, but some of the wives in the administration were appalled at what they saw as his outright selfishness, and they confronted him about it.

"Mr. Roosevelt, you have six children, the youngest a few months old and the eldest not yet in the teens," one said. "While the country is full of young men who have no such responsibilities and are eager to enlist, you have no right to leave the burden upon your wife of the care, support and bringing up of that family."

In truth, it was much more of a burden upon Mrs. Roosevelt than these women knew. Theodore Roosevelt had married Edith Carow, a childhood playmate, nearly three years after the death of his first wife. Edith gave him five children, four boys and a girl. On March 7, she'd undergone a dangerous surgery to drain an internal abscess, from which she was still recuperating. On top of this, their eldest boy, ten-year-old Ted, was fighting a mysterious illness. Their conditions were so serious that Roosevelt wondered if either would fully recover.

Still, that did not sway Roosevelt's resolve. "I have done as much as any one to bring on this war," he told the ladies, "because I believed it must come, and the sooner the better, and now that the war is declared, I have no right to ask others to do the fighting and stay at home myself."

Years later, he would confide to an aide, "I know now that I would have turned from my wife's deathbed to have answered that call." It was his "one chance to cut my little notch on the stick that stands as a measuring rod in every family."

The administration wives were far from the only ones dismayed at Roosevelt's actions. Privately, his boss, Secretary Long, strongly disapproved. Writing in his diary the same day Roosevelt accepted Alger's offer, Long commented that his subordinate was a "man of unbounded energy and force. He thinks he is following his highest ideal, whereas, in fact, as without exception every one of his friends advises him, he is acting like a fool."

Yet Long had to admit there might be something to this foolishness. "[H]ow absurd all this will sound," he wrote, "if, by some turn of fortune, he should accomplish some great thing and strike a very high mark."

Getting a command was one thing. Getting that command recruited, fully outfitted, and then setting soldiers on Cuba's beaches with the army's first wave was going to be a near-Herculean task. To begin with, the Ordnance and Quartermaster Departments were sure to see a mad rush for weapons, uniforms, and accoutrements, some of

which were in short supply. And moving the recruits from rendezvous points in the far western territories to a single location where
they could be organized and trained would take time, as would purchasing hundreds of cavalry mounts.

And of course, once they got to Cuba, Wood and Roosevelt's regiment would be jockeying for a place along with Regular Army units,
state National Guard units, and the other two cowboy regiments. If,
as Roosevelt expected, the war was short, many of the volunteer units
would never see action. Any trifling delay or snafu could knock theirs
out of the hunt.

But the two friends started with a decided advantage. First, they
were, for the moment, both in Washington, close to the army personnel they would need to call upon for their various wants. Second,
they were Roosevelt and Wood. Their close relationships in the administration, from the president on down, had already gotten them
their own command. And with the War Department now in a fren-
zied state, Secretary Russell Alger was more than happy to give them
a free hand.

"Go right ahead and don't let me hear a word from you until your
regiment is raised," he told Wood. "When your requisition and other
papers are ready, bring them to me to sign, and I'll sign them." No
other regimental officers had anything close to that kind of free hand.

Wood promptly planted himself in the secretary of war's office,
where he sent and answered a flurry of telegrams concerning the raising of the 780 men authorized for his regiment. Under the secretary's
name, he asked the governor of New Mexico Territory for four troops,
and two from the Arizona Territory. Oklahoma Territory, one troop.
And when officials from the Indian Territory (present-day eastern
Oklahoma) complained that they were not included in the call for volunteers, they were asked to contribute two troops.

The regiment's military designation was the First U.S. Volunteer
Cavalry, but within days, the press was calling it "Roosevelt's Rough
Riders."

"The newspapers keep talking about Roosevelt's Regiment," a

friend wrote Wood. "Give the reporters a bit of discipline & have things called by the right name."

But Wood didn't mind that his lieutenant colonel was getting all the attention. And there was nothing he could have done about it, anyway. "This only goes to show," observed one newspaper in a biting tone, "that wherever Roosevelt rides is the head of the parade."

Clever journalists coined other nicknames for the cowboy regiment—"Teddy's Terrors," "Teddy's Toughs," "Roosey's Red Hot Roarers," and the ghastly "Rooseveltians"—but Rough Riders stuck.

Officially, the recruits were supposed to be "frontiersmen possessing special qualifications as horsemen and marksmen." But Roosevelt was quick to tell the press that the recruits did not have to be cowpunchers, even though these "at large" volunteer units were being referred to as "cowboy regiments." Above all else, he said, they must be good men: "Desperate characters and reckless mountaineers and plainsmen will not be enlisted."

And it went without saying that no black men would be enlisted, even if they were sure enough cowboys. At this time, and for decades to come, the U.S. Army was segregated.

Roosevelt emphasized that he didn't want men who were looking for some kind of outdoor soiree. "If anyone is going into the regiment with the idea that it is to be a hippodrome, he is making an error," he said pointedly. "If there is any fighting, this regiment is going to be in it. That is what it is for."

Western governors were eager to send men Roosevelt's way, and some of them took an active role in soliciting specific recruits. New Mexico governor Miguel Otero designated Santa Fe as the rendezvous point for the territory's four troops, "because I want to personally inspect every man that leaves." He assured the secretary of war that "only A-1 men would be accepted."

One of the A-1 men Otero had in mind was famed lawman Pat Garrett, the slayer of Billy the Kid. But the forty-seven-year-old Garrett, sheriff of Doña Ana County, was in the midst of a manhunt for the murderers of a prominent local prosecutor; it was not a good time to go to Cuba. And the lawman already had enough notoriety to last a lifetime and beyond.

Even with Garrett unavailable, Otero would have no problem finding other eminent citizens to serve. A larger concern for the governor were rumors that some of New Mexico's "Hispanos," who made up more than two-thirds of the territory's population, sympathized with Spain. These rumors, according to Otero, had been "started for some selfish motive by some individuals." He wished to assure the secretary of war that New Mexico's Hispanos "are all extremely anxious to go to the front. All their sympathies are entirely with the United States and Cuba, and against Spain." Moreover, Otero pointed out that the territory's bilingual men would be particularly valuable during an invasion of a Spanish-speaking country.

In reality, when New Mexico gathered its quota of recruits in Santa Fe, only about five percent of them were of Spanish descent. Oddly, Otero would later claim that he purposely limited the number of native New Mexicans accepted. In a May 3 letter, he admitted that "I did not like to include a great number of native citizens, because I have lived here long enough to know that the 'cow-boy' generally does not get along any too well with the New Mexican, as during the Civil War New Mexico furnished 9,500 federal troops who did the principal fighting against the Texas troops, and the border cow-boys look on us still with just a little disfavor."

Actually, animosity between New Mexicans and Texicans dated back to before the U.S.-Mexican War, but whether it was because of this or some other reason, the New Mexico contingent would count only a handful of men of Spanish descent. Just one Rough Rider officer was a Hispano: Captain Maximiliano Luna. The twenty-seven-year-old Luna, a former county sheriff, was a rising star in the territory's Republican Party and a member of New Mexico's legislative assembly.

Another criticism the governor and others had to manage was that the recruits weren't the real deal; that is, they weren't true "rough riders." A newspaper article labeled Luna's troop a bunch of "tenderfoot cowboys" and doubted that many of them would be accepted into the regiment. However, this slander came from the *Albuquerque Democrat*, which was naturally hostile to Otero's Republican administration—hardly an unbiased observation.

Then there was the unnamed New Mexico man who told the *New York World*, "Roosevelt's cowboy regiment is liable to be a fake." He claimed the men were not being recruited in cowboy country but in railroad towns. "Probably not 10 percent of the men recruited ever were cowboys in their lives," he said, "and I doubt if one-fourth of them ever rode a horse."

This same criticism cropped up in Arizona as well. "The members of this so-called 'cowboy' regiment seem to have been recruited from the sort of cowboys that ranges up and down Washington Street, Phoenix," complained one Arizona newspaper. "Many of them are not horsemen in the mildest construction, and as crack marksmen have yet to distinguish themselves."

Indeed, Captain James McClintock, himself a newspaper journalist, admitted that in his Arizona troop, "the working cowboy is not materializing very rapidly." Nevertheless, a good many of the men had "graduated as cowboys," he argued, and they were expert horsemen. And, echoing Roosevelt's criteria for the recruits, McClintock added: "The character of the men enlisting is of the very highest kind morally and intellectually. They come from among the very best people of Phoenix and will be a great credit to the territory."

The men rushing to sign up did represent all manner of society. They were miners, lawyers, stenographers, actors, printers, carpenters, saddlemakers, electricians, barbers, jewelers, bakers, railroad workers, schoolteachers, painters, and, to be sure, cowboys. Twenty-four-year-old George Hamner was a night telegrapher with the Atchison, Topeka & Santa Fe Railway at Wagon Mound, New Mexico, when he caught the fever to enlist, although he almost caught it too late. On May 5, he sent a telegram to New Mexico's adjutant general, Henry B. Hersey, who had been appointed major of the New Mexico Rough Riders:

Wagon Mound N.M. May 5
H. B. Hersey,
Adjt Genl

Any chance to get in cavalry now? Answer collect.

Geo Hamner

Hersey's reply came back forty-six minutes later:

Santa Fe 5/5
Geo. Hamner
Wagon Mound NM

If you are first class horseman and shot and ready to face anything and can take today's train for Santa Fe Come Otherwise do not come.

Hersey Major

Hamner jumped on the next train for Santa Fe and became a member of Maximiliano Luna's troop. In a letter to his girlfriend in Virginia, Hamner explained his reason for enlisting, and it had nothing to do with liberating the Cubans: "I am fighting, or going to fight, to avenge the *Maine*. And 'Remember the *Maine*' is our war cry!" Most of the recruits had the same motivation. A special train carrying prospective Rough Riders from northeastern New Mexico sported large banners the length of each Pullman car. One banner proclaimed in huge letters, "WE REMEMBER THE MAINE."

Some men, though, had other pressing reasons for wanting to go to Cuba. According to one Rough Rider, certain of his comrades had joined because they had either skipped bail, were wanted for horse stealing, or, worse, had killed someone. That was indeed true of Oklahoma outlaw Jim Cook, a member of the notorious "Cook Gang," led by his brother Bill. Jim had escaped from the Cherokee National Penitentiary in Tahlequah, Indian Territory, during the previous winter, where he had served half of an eight-year manslaughter sentence. The

A crowd sends off Rough Rider recruits from the depot at Las Vegas, New Mexico Territory. (Courtesy of the City of Las Vegas Museum and Rough Rider Memorial Collection.)

twenty-three-year-old fugitive became a member of Troop L, which was raised at Muskogee. He even used his real name.

Another wanted man who joined up was later startled and crestfallen to bump into the Arizona lawman who'd been on his trail. The two men's names are unknown, but the story of their encounter was told again and again:

"Well," the wanted man said, "you've got me at last."

"How do you mean I've got you?" the lawman said.

"Why you have. You came for me, didn't you?"

"I didn't come for you," said the lawman. "I'm here to fight under Roosevelt same as you are. I don't know you except as a soldier."

"You mean you're not my enemy anymore?"

"No sir, I haven't any enemies now but Spaniards."

"And you ain't goin' to give me up?"

"Not in a hundred years! There's my hand on it, comrade."

On Wednesday, May 4, Leonard Wood called at the White House
to see the president one last time. The two took a long walk on the
White House grounds, and Wood briefed McKinley on his dizzying
efforts of the last few days to raise and equip the Rough Riders. The
surgeon was pleased that he had been able to secure Model 1896 Krag-
Jorgensen carbines for his men. They were standard issue for the Regular cavalry, and having the same firearms increased the odds that
his regiment would be brigaded with the Regulars. This was critical
because the Regulars would likely see most of the action in a brief
conflict.

Moreover, the Krag-Jorgensen fired a .30-40 round using smokeless
powder. This meant that his men would not have to wave away a
cloud of white smoke after pulling the gun's trigger, unlike the National Guard units, which were equipped with older guns using blackpowder cartridges. It also meant that their positions would not be
revealed to the enemy by the telltale puffs of gunsmoke.

For sidearms, Wood had ordered the time-tested and nearly inde-
structible Model 1873 Colt Single Action Army revolver. It had a five-
and-a-half-inch barrel, making it easy to get the gun in and out of
its holster, and it fired a .45-caliber cartridge, which could punch a
good-sized hole in just about anything close up. Another advantage
was that most westerners either owned a Colt of their own or were
at the very least thoroughly familiar with it. As Roosevelt put it, the
men were "armed with what might be called their natural weapon,
the revolver."

Of course, cavalrymen were famous for carrying sabers, but it
would take precious time to train the men to use them efficiently,
and the cavalry saber probably wasn't very practical considering the
mostly unbroken horses that would be purchased for the troops. For
the first week or so, a rodeo could break out any minute with these
semiwild mounts; the recruits didn't need long, pointy blades thrown
into the mix.

Instead of sabers, Wood wanted machetes, the same kind that were used in the Cuban sugar fields—and were being carried by the Cuban insurgents. One eyewitness to the machete's use in combat reported "that almost every one struck at all is struck on the side and back of the neck. The blow almost severs the head from the body." It turned out these "Cuban" machetes were made by the Collins Co. of Hartford, Connecticut, and Wood directed that they be purchased there for the Rough Riders.

As for uniforms, Wood was told flatly by the quartermaster general that none were to be had. But the quartermaster general was referring to the army's standard blue wool uniform. Wood didn't want those; the stifling Cuban jungle was going to be torture enough. He wanted the Model 1884 fatigue uniform made of brown canvas. Those were available, he was told, although the shirts would have to be the regulation dark blue wool flannel pullover. There were plenty of those, too, and, as one Rough Rider remembered, they were "hotter than hell."

Wood told the president he had selected San Antonio, Texas, as the rendezvous for his troops. The home of the Alamo was the location of Fort Sam Houston and the San Antonio Arsenal, where they could draw what supplies were available, even if they were likely to be rather antiquated. Additionally, San Antonio was surrounded by horse country, and it was not far from Gulf of Mexico ports where the regiment could board a transport for Cuba.

Wood was due to depart for San Antonio that same day. He told McKinley that Roosevelt would remain in Washington for a few days longer, to stay on top of the requisitions and to tidy up any loose ends in the Navy Department.

When the two men ended up back at the White House, they said good-bye. And with a salute to his commander in chief, Wood was off to Texas and, he hoped, the chance for his and Roosevelt's cowboys to strike a blow for the *Maine*.

Chapter Two

East Meets West

*Theodore has a great hold on them, and before long
he will be able to do anything he likes with them.*

ROBERT MUNRO FERGUSON, TROOP K

While Leonard Wood traveled in comfort on a train bound for San Antonio, Theodore Roosevelt nearly wore out his shoes tramping back and forth between the secretary of war's office and the offices of various army bureau chiefs attempting to expedite Wood's requisitions for arms, uniforms, and equipage. Unfortunately for Roosevelt, many of these bureau chiefs did not share his sense of urgency. They were, he wrote later, "for the most part elderly incompetents, whose idea was to do their routine duties in such a way as to escape the censure of routine bureaucratic superiors and to avoid a Congressional investigation. They had not the slightest conception of preparing the army for war."

Time and again, one of these bureau chiefs would find some trivial irregularity with a Wood requisition, whereupon Roosevelt would go straight to the secretary of war and get an order approving the requisition. "Oh, dear!" exclaimed one chief who kept getting overruled, "I had this office running in such good shape—and then along came the war and upset everything!"

When Roosevelt wasn't battling the army bureaucracy, he faced piles of applications from men begging for a place in the Rough Riders, which he had already overenlisted. Those applications would eventually number more than six thousand—the secretary of war had allotted the regiment only 780. "We haven't room for another man, unless some of those we have get out," Roosevelt told a reporter. "But they won't. They aren't that kind." All those applications, though, made Roosevelt swell with pride: "By George, our young Americans are all right yet."

Just a day after proclaiming the regiment full, Roosevelt was elated to learn that the number of recruits allotted the Rough Riders had been raised to one thousand, although this good news would not help the men whose applications spilled over Roosevelt's desk. It did, however, help the New York clubmen, Ivy Leaguers, and assorted friends Roosevelt had already promised a spot in the regiment, ignoring that they clearly were not from the "western territories."

Among these were Woodbury Kane, champion yachtsman, former Harvard football player, and schoolmate of Roosevelt; David "Dade" Goodrich, son of the rubber manufacturer and captain of Harvard's varsity boat crew; Sumner Gerard, Harvard law student and former captain of Yale's track team; Reginald Ronalds, Yale football star and son of London socialite (and Arthur Sullivan mistress) Mary Frances Ronalds; Craig Wadsworth, legendary steeplechase rider and former Harvard football player; and Robert Munro Ferguson, of Scotland, former aide-de-camp to the governor general of Canada and a Roosevelt ranch partner.

Roosevelt's office was frequently crowded with groups of men he had offered a place in the regiment. On one such ocassion, an excited recruit let out a war whoop in the corridor, prompting his companions to join him. The shouts echoed through the halls of the State, War, and Navy Building, and clerks jumped up from their desks and ran to see what the commotion was, only to find Roosevelt surrounded by a throng of his rowdy men. He appeared to be enjoying it.

On May 5, thirty-one prospective Rough Riders called on Roosevelt.

They included several of the New York "millionaire recruits," as some
newspapers called them, three former New York City mounted police-
men who had served under Roosevelt when he was on the police
board, fifteen Harvard and Yale men, and even a few real cowboys.
Before officially accepting them into the regiment, Roosevelt gave
them the requisite line-in-the-sand speech:

> Gentlemen: You have now reached the last point. If any of
> you do not mean business, let him say so now. An hour from
> now it will be too late to break out. Once in, you've got to see
> it through. You've got to perform without flinching whatever
> duty is assigned to you, regardless of the difficulty or danger
> attending it.
>
> If it is garrison duty, you must attend to it. If it is meeting the
> fever, you must be willing. If it is the closest kind of fighting,
> you must be anxious for it.
>
> You must know how to ride, how to shoot, how to live in
> the open. Absolute obedience to every command is your first
> lesson. No matter what comes you mustn't squeal.
>
> Think it over, and if any man wishes to withdraw he will be
> gladly excused, for hundreds are ready to take his place.

The next day, Adjutant General Henry Corbin swore in Roosevelt
as lieutenant colonel of the First U.S. Volunteer Cavalry. The short
ceremony took place in Corbin's office and was witnessed by several
prominent army officers, senators, and representatives, as well as several newspaper reporters. At the conclusion, Roosevelt was all smiles
as he received congratulatory handshakes and backslaps.

Shortly before his swearing in, Roosevelt had undergone a physical examination given by the army's surgeon general. No one was
surprised that Washington's most physically fit man passed easily,
although the surgeon general had conveniently ignored Roosevelt's
need of eyeglasses to see. An old hunting companion claimed that
Roosevelt "could not recognize his best friend at a distance of ten feet
without them."

On May 9, Roosevelt wrote to Leonard Wood in San Antonio with an update on their requisitions. His constant pestering had made him a real nuisance to the quartermaster general and the chief of the Bureau of Ordnance, but everything was now on its way, though from widely scattered points. The Krag-Jorgensen carbines and Colt revolvers were coming from the Springfield Armory in Massachusetts; the uniforms from the St. Louis Arsenal in Missouri; horse equipment and cavalry equipment from the Rock Island Arsenal in Illinois; and carbine cartridges (80,000) from the Frankford Arsenal in Philadelphia.

Adding considerably to Roosevelt's anxiety was current talk that the army was within days of launching its invasion of Cuba. If so, the Rough Riders would likely ship out from Galveston, and he was concerned that they wouldn't be ready in time. And he was even more nervous about his own prospects. "I suppose you will be keeping me here for several days longer," Roosevelt continued to Wood, "but there is one thing, old man, you mustn't do, and that is run any risk of having me left when the regiment starts to Cuba. Of course I know you wouldn't do it intentionally, but remember that at any cost, I must have a chance to get with you before you start."

Finally, on the night of Thursday, May 12, Roosevelt was able to board a train in Washington for San Antonio. But no matter how fast the telegraph poles flashed past his Pullman window, the train wasn't going nearly fast enough. "It will be bitter," he wrote his sister Corinne, "if we don't get to Cuba."

The Rough Riders were already the most famous outfit in the U.S. Army, but when the first contingents arrived at San Antonio's "International" fairgrounds, the regiment's headquarters and camp, they found they had no uniforms, no weapons, no tents, no blankets, and no horses. What they did have were plenty of curious townsfolk, and that turned out to be something of a circus.

Naturally, many of those gazing upon the enlisted men had expected to see the wild and woolly West in the flesh. There were a few, though, who did not think all that highly of the "wild" part. "Yes, they are characters," someone in the crowd was overheard to proclaim. "They shoot first and investigate afterwards."

The officers and men of the Rough Riders tried to dispel such fictions. Captain William "Buckey" O'Neill of Prescott, Arizona, told a San Antonio newspaperman: "There are no outcasts and no desperadoes in the Arizona Column." Another trooper chimed in: "We are not long-haired roughs like some people expect to see."

But the crowds weren't disappointed because mixed in with the town boys from Phoenix, Albuquerque, and Santa Fe were some colorful broncobusters exactly like they were hoping for. Fairly typical was twenty-seven-year-old New Mexico cowboy Alvin C. Ash. Standing more than six feet tall and weighing 210 taut pounds, the man had never in his life worn a shirt with a collar. And he refused to wear white shirts; more particularly, stiff white dress shirts.

"Once when I was about twenty-one, I had a notion I wanted to dress up," he told a writer, "so I got half a dozen white shirts. I put one of 'em on, and wore it a couple of hours, but I couldn't stand it. I had to give the whole lot away, and I've never had a white shirt since."

As Ash was telling his story, the writer noticed a peculiar scar in the Rough Rider's left palm and asked him about it.

"Oh, that is nothing," the blue-eyed Ash said matter-of-factly. "That's something I got in a little mix-up. . . . I caught a Greaser's six-shooter by the muzzle, and he bored my hand. Guess he'd fixed me if I hadn't stopped him. Had his gun up against my belly."

Just as big a draw as the Rough Riders was the mascot brought by the Arizona troopers: a six-month-old mountain lion. The animal had been lassoed near Prescott, then purportedly won in a poker game, and finally borrowed and brought to San Antonio with the troopers. "[H]e has been looked at and admired by thousands," Trooper Thomas Laine wrote the cougar's owner. "[H]e is getting quite tame; the boys had him all over the yard; he plays like a kitten and is getting fat, the boys feeding and watering him all the time. We have been trying to make him eat hard tack, but he don't like it, but hope, before long, to give him a good square meal of Spanish liver." "He" was actually a "she," and the Arizona boys had named the mountain lion Josephine.

The New Mexico contingent brought their own mascot—a "gifted dog, which has been making railroad trips all over the West for years," or so one newspaper claimed. Trooper George Hamner said the scruffy lapdog had been snatched when their train stopped at Hutchinson, Kansas. The dog's name was said to be Salisbury but was quickly changed to Cuba. Poor Cuba didn't get nearly the attention from the crowds Josephine did, except when the two mascots played together, making quite a show rolling and jumping in the dirt. A third mascot, which showed up later, was a golden eagle from New Mexico named Teddy.

On May 9 and 10, most of the college men and millionaire recruits arrived.

The train carrying twenty-one-year-old Harvard student J. Ogden Wells and eleven of his classmates pulled into San Antonio at noon on May 9, but their first order of business was not reporting at the Rough Rider camp. As Wells recorded in his diary, their first stop was San Antonio's finest hotel, the Menger, situated downtown on Alamo Plaza.

There they enjoyed a nice dinner (one dollar each), after which, they "took leave of civilization," as Wells phrased it, and stepped on the city's electric trolley that would take them the three miles to the camp.

The Rough Riders at the fairgrounds had been tipped off that the Harvard men were in town and gathered quickly when they heard the trolley's bell. As Wells and the others passed through the gate, cheers and shouts erupted for these "college boys," who quickly found themselves surrounded by two hundred jostling troopers, each one wanting to shake their hands. Wells later wrote that these southwestern Rough Riders were "a splendid set of men . . . tall and sinewy, with resolute, weather-beaten faces and eyes that look a man straight in the face without flinching."

The millionaire recruits, mostly New Yorkers, also dined at the

Menger before beginning their lives as cavalrymen. They showed up at camp wearing new sombreros and blue flannel shirts, causing a San Antonio newspaper to comment that they could easily be mistaken for genuine westerners "at a distance of several blocks." Unlike most of the Rough Riders, they carried valises with clean linens, razors, soap, and choice cigarettes. The same newspaper, in another joke at the expense of the "Fifth Avenue boys," suggested that "there were also a few hand mirrors in the valises."

Twenty-nine-year-old William Tiffany, grandson of Commodore Matthew Perry and the secretary and treasurer of a New York railway supply manufacturer, didn't appreciate the humor or the attention. When a photographer asked for a picture of Tiffany and some of the other New Yorkers, Tiffany angrily waved him off.

"What do you want the picture for? One of those horrible newspapers?" he asked. "It's an outrage the way newspapers are treating us. . . . Why don't they let us alone? We came down here to fight, and we don't want all this nonsense. There ought to be some law against it."

The *San Antonio Daily Express*, which reported Tiffany's outburst, apparently took offense and made him out to be a spoiled rich boy, reporting on how dissatisfied he was with the camp food and his "distress" that he wouldn't be able to have a hot bath.

But the western Rough Riders took much more kindly to the easterners. Arthur F. Cosby, a twenty-six-year-old New York lawyer and Harvard grad, wrote his father that the western men he encountered "seem to like the New Yorkers, say they are 'all right.' I have heard one or two complain of them but not seriously—they all say the New Yorkers are 'gentlemen' and plucky."

The easterners earned the respect of the other men by willingly following orders and cheerfully undertaking a variety of chores, be it digging a ditch or hauling hay for the horses. Colonel Wood kept an eye on the college boys and clubmen and wrote to his wife, Louise, "You would smile to see the New York swells sleeping on the ground and on the floor of the pavilion we have without blankets and doing kitchen police for a troop of New Mexico cowboys, all working together and as chummy as can be."

The fairgrounds had been selected as the Rough Riders' camp because there was room for the hundreds of tents for the officers and men, and the adjacent Riverside Park (named for the San Antonio) had open space for the mounted drills. But Fort Sam Houston, located a few miles north of downtown, barely had enough tents on hand for the regiment's officers. Until the Rough Riders' "dog tents" arrived, the enlisted men had spread out in the large Exposition Building and the adjacent grandstand.

The lack of blankets, which, like everything else, were in transit, forced nearly all the Rough Riders to be "chummy." The few blankets that could be scrounged up, some of which were saddle blankets and pads borrowed from the civilian mule packers, each had to be shared by two or three men. Some troopers chose to sleep in the hay stacked next to the Exposition Building while others lucky enough to have blankets (the Harvard boys had come prepared with their own rubber ones) grabbed armfuls of hay to place under them.

With several troops of young men together in one large hall, it wasn't easy to get a good night's rest. Sergeant Royal A. Prentice, a twenty-one-year-old New Mexico stenographer, recalled the first raucous night. He had been asleep just a short time when a shoe came flying out of the darkness and thumped his head. He bolted upright in pain, grabbed the shoe, and flung it in the direction he thought it had come from. Instead, it struck another sleeping Rough Rider, and within seconds, hundreds of shoes—and everything else within reach—were arcing back and forth in the large room. One tired trooper lamented in a letter home, "it is almost hell to get the boys to settle down to sleep."

Lieutenant Colonel Theodore Roosevelt stepped off his train at San Antonio at 7:30 A.M. on Sunday, May 15. His new tan uniform with bright yellow standing collar had hardly a crease and stood out sharply in the morning sun. It was one of several he had custom ordered from Brooks Brothers of New York. Army officers were responsible for purchasing their own uniforms, horses, saddles, and weapons, and that suited Roosevelt just fine. Brooks Brothers was his haberdasher of choice, and they had a history of making uniforms dating back to the War of 1812. Their tailors had made his cavalry uniforms out of the new lightweight khaki material the army had only recently adopted.

Close behind Roosevelt was his black valet, Marshall, a veteran of the Ninth Cavalry, carrying several bags. They took a carriage to the Menger, where Roosevelt had breakfast. Later that morning, Colonel Wood and Major George Dunn came to escort Roosevelt to the camp. The forty-two-year-old Dunn was a Washington lawyer who had received his commission through the influence of President McKinley. In announcing his appointment as a major in the Rough Riders, the newspapers noted Dunn's recent position as "master of the hounds" for the exclusive Chevy Chase Hunt Club. Roosevelt's own view, which he recorded in his diary, was that Dunn was "a bit slick."

Roosevelt's wall tent stood next to Wood's. The regiment's quartermaster and adjutant, First Lieutenant Tom Hall, was temporarily bunking there and would now have to change quarters. Roosevelt did not like the idea of putting an officer out of a tent, however, and insisted it was plenty big enough for the both of them. Hall suddenly found himself "tenting with the most remarkable man I ever met."

While Marshall unpacked and organized, Roosevelt got right to work, meeting with the regiment's several officers and conquering a pile of letters—some 250—that had stacked up for him in the camp post office. Many of these letters were more requests from young men seeking appointments as officers in the regiment, or letters of recommendation from the applicants' influential friends. They were too late.

Several callers, acquaintances and prominent locals, dropped in on the lieutenant colonel, but they were a minor distraction compared to the record crowds of visitors to the camp that Sunday afternoon and

Colonel Leonard Wood and staff at San Antonio. Wood and Roosevelt
are wearing their khaki uniforms. Regimental Adjutant Tom Hall
stands in the center, fourth from the right. (560.3-016, Theodore
Roosevelt Collection, Houghton Library, Harvard University.)

evening. Roosevelt was a celebrity unlike anyone San Antonio had seen in a long time. The *San Antonio Daily Express* fawned over him:

> *Theodore Roosevelt is only about 35 years old but he has been a*
> *Western plainsman, a New York business man, a reformer, a*
> *politician, an author and several other things. But above all he is an*
> *American gentleman and a patriot. He will doubtless have a bright*
> *place in history as the man who resigned the comfortable, lucrative*
> *and distinguished position of Assistant Secretary of the Navy to go*
> *to the thick of battle. . . . He possesses an independent fortune, but he*
> *really has no use for it. He is essentially a man of action. . . . He is*
> *shrewd, resourceful and courageous and is capable of both planning*
> *campaigns in a masterly manner and carrying out his plans.*

Approximately ten thousand people flooded through the fairgrounds that day, poking about here and there, asking countless questions of the men, most hoping to catch a glimpse of the famed lieutenant colonel of the Rough Riders.

The enlisted men actually relished the attention, especially because the majority of the visitors were young ladies. It also gave them opportunities to be ornery, if not outright mean. Whenever a curious black boy was spotted, a shout was raised and several troopers instantly began chasing the poor lad, threatening to scalp him.

Each Sunday afternoon, Riverside Park hosted a popular concert by Professor Carl Beck's Military Band, and following this day's performance, the portly bandleader marched his musicians to the Rough Riders' camp and formed them in a circle around Roosevelt's tent. With a wave of his baton, a rousing serenade commenced, the band "playing patriotic airs as they were never played before." This, of course, instantly drew the enlisted men, and after the music stopped, they began shouting for a speech from Roosevelt.

He stepped out of his tent, smiled at the crowd, thanked the men for the warm welcome, and told them what everyone who could read a newspaper already knew, that "the eyes of the entire civilized world were on them, and that they were expected to do what no others would do."

"I expect you to acquit yourselves creditably," he continued, "and I know I will not be disappointed. When we get to Cuba and get at the Spaniards, I want your watchword, my men, to be 'Remember the *Maine*,' and you shall avenge the *Maine*. We are expected to fight, and that we must do!"

His final words were met with wild cheers from the men, and Beck, sensing the moment, quickly got the attention of his musicians and started them playing "Yankee Doodle." The men whooped and hollered even louder.

For many of the Rough Riders, this was their first exposure to Roosevelt, an intense and animated speaker who feared no audience. Later that evening, in talking over their impressions of the lieutenant colonel, one trooper said, "He looks as though he was there with the goods, only I don't like the way he skins his teeth back when he talks to a fellow."

Roosevelt made no effort to hide his inexperience as a cavalry officer. He was often seen in camp holding the thick cavalry drill manual and loudly practicing various commands, completely oblivious to the troopers just steps away. His boyish enthusiasm for any task was contagious, and he talked down to no man—unless he deserved it. A journalist put it best: Roosevelt "was the greatest 'mixer' among the people that this country has ever produced, or probably ever will produce." He was at ease with kings and cowboys, presidents and paupers.

And his time as a rancher in the Badlands had made Roosevelt comfortable with many of the frontier types who formed the regiment. He had gone west years ago as a spectacle-wearing dude with expensive guns and a silver-mounted hunting knife made by Tiffany & Co., but he surprised everyone who made the mistake of taking him for just another tenderfoot from the East.

Three fun-loving cowboys had made that mistake one day in 1883 in the small settlement of Medora, Dakota Territory. Roosevelt, then just twenty-four years old, had stepped into a store to buy some postage stamps when the cowboys rushed up to Roosevelt's horse, took off its saddle and bridle, and led the animal out of sight. They then put the saddle and bridle on a mean bronc named White-faced Kid, which looked nearly identical to Roosevelt's mount.

As the cowboys eagerly watched from a hiding spot, Roosevelt walked out of the store and casually pulled himself up into the saddle. In an instant, White-faced Kid hunched his back and flipped Roosevelt into the dirt. Hearing the commotion, the store owner came out and asked if he was hurt.

"Not a bit of it," Roosevelt said.

Roosevelt picked himself up, grabbed the saddle horn again, put his foot in the stirrup, and swung his leg up over the saddle. This time, the Kid didn't wait for Roosevelt to get seated. The bronc shot its rear legs out and bucked its rider over its head. Roosevelt did a somersault and landed with a thud, breaking his spectacles.

The cowboys ran up, unable to contain their laughter as they helped a stunned Roosevelt to his feet and dusted him off. Roosevelt paid them no mind, however, saying only, "It's too bad I broke my glasses," as he limped into the store.

Just as the cowboys were about to switch the horses back, Roosevelt came out again wearing a new pair of glasses he'd fetched from his bag. He headed straight for White-faced Kid.

Roosevelt jumped into the saddle, got both his feet in the stirrups, and clamped his knees onto the bronc's sides. The Kid leaped forward and broke into a gallop, horse and rider speedily disappearing down the road. The cowboys weren't laughing now; they were worried about the tenderfoot. Chances were, the dude was going to end up with a broken neck. A minute later, though, the Kid came galloping back through the dust, a grinning Roosevelt firmly in the saddle. Roosevelt let out a whoop as he pulled on the reins and halted in front of the cowboys, whose jaws were nearly touching the ground. This tenderfoot could not only ride a horse, but he had grit. "We took a shine to him from that very day," recalled one of the tricksters.

Roosevelt just as quickly won over the men of the Rough Riders. Trooper Kenneth Robinson, a Scotsman and cousin by marriage to Roosevelt's sister Corinne, observed: "The men always do their best [drilling] when he is out. He would be amused indeed if he heard some of the adjectives and terms applied to him, meant to be most complimentary but hardly fit for publication."

Trooper Alvin C. Ash stayed far away from those salty adjectives in writing to his mother about Roosevelt. He simply said that the lieutenant colonel was "the most magnetic man I ever saw."

Uniforms and gear had begun arriving a couple of days before Roosevelt, although in a haphazard manner. One day the men would get gloves and mess pans. The next it would be rubber ponchos and cotton undershirts, and so on. Three troops went for days without knives and forks and did the best they could with their fingers or whatever they could scavenge to make do.

Blankets finally showed up on May 13, and the brown canvas uniforms were issued the next day, each man receiving coat and trousers, canvas leggings, one pair of socks, one pair of shoes, and the western-looking Model 1889 campaign hat (underdrawers and wool shirts were still in transit). As each trooper stepped up to receive his uniform, an officer took a quick look at the man, called out a size, and a bundle was forthwith shoved into the trooper's hands. The officer usually guessed the man's size correctly, but sometimes he guessed wrong, and soon a line formed of men with coats they could swim in or hats that fell down to their ears.

The day the blue wool overshirts were issued, one Phoenix trooper found a surprise in his. In a "secret place," perhaps in one of the pockets, was a card bearing the name and address of a Cincinnati woman. Not only that, but the woman had penned a note offering marriage to whomever received the shirt. The trooper was not opposed to the idea but thought he better exchange photographs first.

An item of apparel that was not army issue but became a Rough Rider signature was the bandanna. Probably some cowpunchers decided they couldn't part with their silk bandannas and simply wore them with their uniforms. It was the perfect touch for a body of cowboy cavalry, and soon troopers were taking the trolley downtown to buy bandannas. Roosevelt sported a blue bandanna with white polka dots, as did many of his men.

The coveted Krags and Colt revolvers were distributed to the men on May 19 and 20, and the troopers admiringly ran their hands over the carbines' wood stocks, worked the bolt actions, and sighted down the barrels. But it was the arrival of two menacing-looking machine guns that caused the biggest stir in camp. Manufactured by Colt of Hartford, Connecticut, the same company that made the regiment's revolvers, these gas-fired, belt-fed automatic weapons were gifts courtesy of the millionaire recruits. One of the guns had been purchased by two older sisters of Woodbury Kane. The cost of the second had been split among New Yorkers Joseph Stevens, William Tiffany, and one or two others.

*Gun detail for the Colt machine guns, San Antonio. William Tiffany, who helped
pay for one of the guns, is holding the machine gun on the right. The trumpeter
is Emilio Cassi, a native of Monaco and veteran of the French Foreign Legion.
(560.3-014, Theodore Roosevelt Collection, Houghton Library, Harvard University.)*

An excited Roosevelt ordered that the machine guns be set up
behind his tent, and as officers and men gathered round, many of
whom had never seen a rapid-fire gun, he explained exactly how they
worked. Each gun could fire five hundred rounds in a minute flat,
and at three thousand yards, the bullets would "tear human beings
to pieces." The Colts came with ten thousand rounds of ammunition,
which Colonel Wood pointed out wasn't nearly enough for the coming
campaign. A further complication was that the guns did not fire the
same cartridge as the Krag-Jorgensens, instead taking a 7 x 57 mm—
the same round used in a Spanish Mauser.

Wood thought for a second and said, "All right, we'll capture the
ammunition for them from the Spaniards."

Everyone, Roosevelt especially, was anxious to see the guns fired, so both guns, 115 pounds each with their heavy tripods, were carried a short distance to the San Antonio River. Kane got behind one gun and an agent of the Colt company got behind the other. The ammunition belts were fed into the magazines, the cocking levers jerked back, and the two men pulled the triggers simultaneously. A steady *pop-pop-pop-pop-pop-pop-pop-pop* spewed from the guns as plumes of water sprayed up from the river and chunks of mud from the opposite bank flew into the air. The guns didn't jam once.

Kane, who had earned a sergeant's stripes only a week earlier, was promptly promoted to first lieutenant and placed in command of the machine guns, and several of his New York chums were assigned to his gun detail, including Tiffany and Stevens. They were the envy of the regiment.

The Winchester Repeating Arms Company, of New Haven, Connecticut, not to be outdone by its Hartford rival, also shipped a weapon to San Antonio, but it was not intended for the regiment as a whole. It was a gift for the regiment's lieutenant colonel, a Model 1895 Winchester lever-action carbine specially made for Roosevelt. It sported a nickel steel barrel and English walnut stock with a saddle ring mounted on the left of the receiver. Most important, it was chambered for the .30-40 round, the same used for the Krags. The local Winchester dealer and several San Antonio citizens made the presentation at Roosevelt's tent.

Roosevelt had made no secret of his admiration for Winchester's lever-action repeaters. He especially liked the Model 1895, which, in the right hands, was capable of getting off two to three shots per second. "I may not shoot well," Roosevelt had said once, "but I know how to shoot often." Surprised and pleased, he thanked the gentlemen and promised to use the Winchester to avenge the *Maine*.

Each day, horses for the troopers had been driven into camp in bunches of twenty-five and thirty from Fort Sam Houston, where they were being inspected and purchased. Officers either bought their horses locally or had their own horses shipped to them by rail (these latter were generally the finest horseflesh in camp). Roosevelt purchased two mounts at San Antonio, a bay called Little Texas and a larger horse his servant Marshall christened Rain-in-the-Face, after the famed Lakota chief. They had cost Roosevelt $50 each, which was a bargain. Some officers paid as much as $125 for their mounts.

The public notice from the Quartermaster's Department called for horses that were "well broken to saddle," but according to Oklahoma broncobuster Bill McGinty, the horses purchased "hadn't been broke but once if that." The first time the troopers were given the order "Mount," at least three hundred horses began to buck, throwing riders left and right. "By the time the dust cleared," recalled McGinty, "them eastern boys were scattered all over Texas."

Even getting the horses to form a line was a challenge. The "horses hadn't the slightest idea of what was wanted," remembered Royal A. Prentice. "Some of the horses seemed to think we were getting ready for a race while others considered it a free-for-all and proceeded to pitch, bite, strike and kick at everything near them." In the early

Roosevelt's valet and former Buffalo Soldier, Marshall,
holds Little Texas. (R560.3.EL61-022, Theodore Roosevelt
Collection, Houghton Library, Harvard University.)

going, the antics of the rough range stock were costing the regiment about a man a day, "knocked clean out."

Several easterners wisely hired the more experienced bronc riders in the regiment to "take some of the devilishness" out of their mounts. One Arizona cowboy was accepting money in advance for a guarantee that a horse would get ridden. There was just not enough time to ride all the wild broncs the New Yorkers were turning over to him.

In addition to getting cavalrymen and cavalry horses to cooperate with each other, the horses had to be trained to ignore gunfire—or at least put up with it. Otherwise, the first time a shell exploded on the battlefield, there would be another bucking exhibition. To accomplish this, the troopers stood in formation, holding their mounts by the halter straps while the noncommissioned officers galloped around them on horseback firing their Colts in the air as fast as they could pull back the hammers. The first time they did this, they got a stampede worse than anything seen on a cattle drive. Frightened horses and men thundered away in a cloud of dust, while the few troopers who were able to hold on to the halter straps frantically tried to pull themselves up as they were being dragged.

During a break in these exercises, some of the troopers motioned for their comrades to look at what Roosevelt was doing with Little Texas. "He was riding a high-spirited horse, full of action, this day," recalled Corporal David Hughes, "and he put him through all the paces, jumps and quick turns and would 'set' his horse in the shortest kind of space."

Once most of the horses had been distributed to the troops, regimental drill took place daily, and it was hardly any time at all before Roosevelt and his men were able to see real progress. One Harvard undergrad described the exhilarating mounted drills for family back home:

> *Six hundred horses galloping in column of fours is a fine wave of power. The dust lifts up so thick it is like a fog, and you can barely see the next man ahead. Half-blinded, wet with sweat, and the horses on both sides rubbing against your legs, you go tearing, galloping on.*

Then suddenly through the white wall of dust you see the haunches of
the horses ahead sink down and a hand shoot upward with the fingers
spread apart. There is a quick jam, a creaking and rubbing of leather,
and they're off again.

At the end of a particularly hot and sticky afternoon, Roosevelt was leading one of the squadrons (four troops) back to the fairgrounds when he abruptly ordered a halt just outside the gate. They had stopped in front of a recently established beer garden.

"Captains will dismount their troops, and the men can go in and drink all the beer they want," Roosevelt said loudly, "which I will pay for." Then, glaring through his spectacles, he added, "But if any man drinks more beer than is good for him, I will cinch him!"

The grateful troopers followed orders, and as Royal A. Prentice recalled, "Nectar never tasted as good as that beer."

It did not take long for Colonel Wood to learn of Roosevelt's gener-

Rough Riders drilling in the San Antonio dust. (R560.3.D83-010, Theodore
Roosevelt Collection, Houghton Library, Harvard University.)

osity (it was even reported in the local newspaper). Wood understood that his lieutenant colonel only meant to reward the men for a particularly good drill, but he could not have an officer putting on a beer fest for the enlisted men, no matter how well intended.

That evening at the officers' mess, Wood casually brought up the subject of officers drinking with their men and made it clear that he strongly disapproved. He ended the discussion by coldly stating, "[O]f course an officer who would go out with a large batch of men and drink with them [is] quite unfit to hold a commission."

Roosevelt was mortified but didn't say a word. Shortly after dinner, however, Wood heard Roosevelt's quick steps approaching his tent.

"I would like to speak with the colonel," Roosevelt said through the canvas.

Wood invited a crestfallen Roosevelt to come in.

"I wish to tell you, sir, that I took the squadron, without thinking of this question of officers drinking with their men, and I gave them all a schooner of beer. I wish to say, sir, that I agree with what you said. I consider myself the damnedest ass within ten miles of this camp. Good night."

A few days later, the owners of the beer garden presented two barrels of beer to one of the troops, but the troop's captain knew any alcohol had to be approved by the commanding officer before it could be brought into camp. Wood was briefly away, leaving Roosevelt in command. The moment the captain brought up the gift, Roosevelt threw up his hands and stopped him in midsentence.

"Nothing doing," Roosevelt said. "Beer is a subject I do not want to hear about."

Daily at noon, the men were given approximately one hour to rest before mess call, but instead, most of the men lined up to apply for a pass to leave camp that evening. The passes had to be obtained from the regimental adjutant, Tom Hall, who didn't make the process easy. Lieutenant Hall was a West Point graduate, a former officer in the Tenth Cavalry, and a published author of fiction and poetry. He was also the true definition of a martinet, instructing the men on the proper way to approach and enter his tent and always finding trifling reasons to upbraid them. The thirty-five-year-old adjutant soon became hated.

Those troopers who received passes hopped on the trolley later in the day and rode it to downtown San Antonio. Some of these men were anxious to pick up money wired from home, and as the regiment had no sutler (a civilian merchant attached to an army unit or post), there were always necessities to buy in town. One trooper's shopping list included a pound of Durham tobacco, cigarette papers, four bandannas, six pairs of socks, pocket watch, pocketknife, toothbrush and powder, soap, three towels, writing paper and envelopes, stamps, and one pencil.

There was also sightseeing, of course, and the Alamo mission was high on every trooper's list. Nearly all the Rough Riders visited the historic shrine at one time or another. Most of the men had enlisted in a patriotic fervor, and the place where Davy Crockett, Jim Bowie, William Travis, and the other Alamo defenders died for Texas independence in 1836 only amplified those feelings.

The men found plenty of other things to do in town. After exploring the Alamo, Rough Rider Ben Colbert, a Chickasaw Indian whose great-grandfather had fought with Andrew Jackson at the Battle of New Orleans, walked to a phonograph parlor a short distance away on Houston Street and asked to listen to a new cylinder recording. His pick was John Philip Sousa's "The Stars and Stripes Forever," performed by Sousa's Grand Concert Band.

Some Rough Riders used their passes to cool off with a dip at Scholz's Natatorium, a popular indoor swimming pool. And a meal at a good restaurant, or one of the chili stands, was always a welcome substitute for the predictable army rations of bacon, beef, beans, and potatoes, which weren't always of the best quality or sufficient quantity. The groundskeeper for the fairgrounds actually opened a small dining establishment in his residence, which sat near the entrance to

Oklahoma Chickasaw Indian Ben Colbert.
(Author's Collection.)

the park, and it quickly became a favorite mealtime hangout of the millionaire recruits. They nicknamed it the Waldorf-Astoria.

San Antonio's saloons and gambling halls were another Rough Rider magnet—and a source of frustration for the regiment's officers. Only about twenty passes were issued per troop each day, but two to three times as many men were requesting them. Consequently, each night dozens of Rough Riders without passes slipped through the fence around the fairgrounds and jumped on the trolley for downtown. An evening of carousing didn't make for the best soldiers in the morning. One captain wondered out loud if all the men reporting to him ill were "really sick or just tired."

Eventually, the saloons and gambling dens—and the hack drivers who transported the men back to camp after the trolley stopped running at night—cleaned the western boys out of their funds. This helped somewhat with the problem of the men sneaking away from camp: it was hard to drink and gamble when you were broke.

On the afternoon of May 20, the Rough Riders finally moved out of the Exposition Building and grandstand into several hundred "dog tents." A simple, two-piece affair, each tent was designed for two men. The tents offered little relief from the stifling heat, as they had been erected out in the open with no shade. "The perspiration simply rolls all the time, and the dust flies," wrote Arthur F. Cosby. One of the cowpunchers, though, welcomed the change. He said he hadn't slept in a house in six years before spreading his bedroll in the Exposition Building and was more than happy to get outdoors again.

Mess call for supper was at 6:00 P.M., and the meal was often followed by a baseball game. Then, as the sun sank and men gathered in small groups to talk and joke and sip coffee, music began to float over the camp. "Several glee clubs have been formed," wrote one trooper, "and there are dozens of banjo players in the camp, and among them are some really talented musicians." With all that music, but no ladies to dance with, some Rough Riders put on stag dances, kicking up their heels and the dust until a bugle sounded "Taps" at 9:00 P.M.

Despite their varied backgrounds, the men had bonded wonderfully. "They are now all brothers," wrote a visitor to the camp, "and the millionaire from New York could be seen at San Antonio borrowing tobacco just as natural as the cowboy borrows a gun."

Wood and Roosevelt were surprised and delighted with how the regiment had come together and how rapidly the drills with the entire regiment, now more than nine hundred officers and men, were improving. Wood wrote to President McKinley that the regiment's progress was "simply astounding," and he hoped the president would get a chance to see what "a most exceptionally fine body of men" they were. Roosevelt also wrote to the president from San Antonio, and with typical zeal, he declared, "I really think that the rank and file

Roosevelt with two of his men in front of the historic Mission Concepción, San Antonio. (Author's Collection.)

of this regiment is better than you would find in any other regiment anywhere."

Although Wood and Roosevelt were indeed proud of the Rough Riders, their letters also served as not-so-subtle attempts to put the regiment on an equal footing with any Regulars about to embark for Cuba. "We are ready now to leave at any moment," Roosevelt insisted in his letter, "and we earnestly hope we will be put into Cuba with the very first troops; the sooner the better."

In truth, Wood and Roosevelt were not entirely happy with some of the Rough Rider officers. They were either political appointees, or had been elected by the men—which was standard procedure with volunteer regiments—and as a result, there was bound to be, in the words of Wood, "a few weak sisters." By May 25, Roosevelt, who rarely changed his mind after forming a first impression of someone, had decided that Major Dunn was "a pitiful failure."

But there were several standouts among the officers too. Forty-eight-year-old Alexander Brodie, the senior major and commander of the Arizona contingent, was a grizzled, tough-as-nails former cavalry officer who had campaigned against the Apaches in Arizona Territory in the 1870s. A West Point graduate (twenty-seventh in his class), he had also organized the First Regiment Arizona National Guard and served as its first colonel. If anyone knew the cavalry drill regulations inside out, he did. Second Lieutenant Thomas Rynning, himself a former Indian fighter in the Regular Army, judged Brodie "one of the finest soldiers I've ever known."

New Mexico's William H. H. Llewellyn, the forty-five-year-old captain of Troop G, was a prominent Las Cruces politician and attorney whose career included stints as a gold miner, a newspaper reporter, a deputy U.S. marshal, and an Indian agent. Standing six feet tall, he carried the scars of four bullet wounds from scrapes with Apaches and outlaws. An associate described him as one of a rare breed of men "so used to gunfire that they can inhale the smoke without choking." Along with Sheriff Pat Garrett, Llewellyn was one of the first individuals Governor Otero thought of when seeking officers for the New Mexico troops.

Twenty-six-year-old Allyn K. Capron, a lieutenant in the famed Seventh U.S. Cavalry, had been in charge of the captive Chiricahua Apaches of Geronimo's band at Fort Sill, Oklahoma Territory, when the call for volunteers came. Getting a temporary leave of absence, he was ordered to examine and muster in the Rough Rider recruits from the Oklahoma and Indian Territories. After enlisting the last of the Indian Territory's 170 men, the recruits elected him captain of Troop L. Colonel Wood had actually offered Capron the position of regimental adjutant, but Capron declined because it would "take him out of the line of promotion."

The blood of heroes flowed through Capron's veins. His grandfather, Captain Erastus Allyn Capron, died leading a charge in the Battle of Churubusco during the U.S.-Mexican War. His father, Allyn

Senior, was a West Point grad currently serving as a captain in the Fifth Artillery. Roosevelt found the dashingly handsome Capron "tall and lithe, a remarkable boxer and walker, a first-class rider and shot, with yellow hair and piercing blue eyes." Roosevelt was endlessly fascinated by the cavalryman's tales of often dangerous dealings with the Apaches, as well as Capron's mastery of Indian sign language.

But the officer Roosevelt seemed to connect with most, other than Wood, was Captain William Owen "Buckey" O'Neill of Troop A. The thirty-eight-year-old O'Neill gave his occupation as lawyer when enlisting, but that was only one facet of an incredible career. Beginning in 1879, he had worked for a string of Arizona Territory newspapers (including the famed *Tombstone Epitaph*), had been a court reporter, a probate judge, a county sheriff, a school superintendent, a territorial adjutant general, and, finally, the mayor of Prescott. In the midst of these endeavors, O'Neill wheeled and dealed in mining and real estate, becoming a wealthy man in the process.

A frontier highbrow as well, O'Neill frequently quoted Robert Browning, Walt Whitman, and Percy Bysshe Shelley, much to Roosevelt's delight. And he penned realistic short stories set in Arizona Territory that appeared in the *San Francisco Chronicle* and *San Francisco Examiner*. What really excited Roosevelt, though, were O'Neill's true-life experiences as the sheriff of Yavapai County, like the time O'Neill had his horse shot out from under him while chasing a band of train robbers. The Arizonan came across to Roosevelt as "a wild, reckless fellow, soft spoken, and of dauntless courage and boundless ambition."

With men such as these, Roosevelt's boasting about the rank and file of the Rough Riders was understandable, but real proof would only come when the regiment faced Spanish guns for the first time. And whether or not they would get that chance was still anybody's guess. Already, Commodore George Dewey, in command of the navy's Asiatic Squadron (an appointment Roosevelt had helped Dewey secure), had defeated Spain's Pacific Squadron in the Battle of Manila

*William "Buckey" O'Neill as sheriff of Yavapai County,
Arizona Territory. (560.3-115, Theodore Roosevelt
Collection, Houghton Library, Harvard University.)*

Bay on May 1. It was a stunning victory that demonstrated the superiority of the U.S. Navy over Spain's aging fleet. This war, Roosevelt knew, couldn't last long.

———

"Tonight the citizens of San Antonio will show their appreciation of Colonels Wood and Roosevelt and their Rough Riders by tendering them a concert in Riverside park," reported the *San Antonio Daily Light* of May 24. Professor Beck had prepared a program that included a fantasia titled "Cavalry Charge" arranged especially for the regiment. Beck told the newspaper that his piece depicted the charging of cavalry against enemy infantry, the melee of battle (with booming artillery), followed by the infantry fleeing the battlefield and the cavalry in hot pursuit. Special effects would be produced by anvil and cannon firing.

The concert started promptly at 8:30 P.M., and the crowd, according to the *Light,* was "one of the largest ever congregated in the park." Beck's "Cavalry Charge" came up third in the lengthy program, with everyone—adults, children, and Rough Riders—anxious to hear the promised pyrotechnics. It was definitely a rousing piece, and as the music got faster and louder, several band members held up pistols and fired blank cartridges into the air. Suddenly a Rough Rider jumped up and shouted, "Help him out, boys!" No further encouragement was needed as several men drew their revolvers and began blasting away.

Women shrieked and covered the ears of their crying children. Some ran away dragging the little ones behind them. Horses hitched to the one-hundred-plus carriages reared and pulled on their tethers. Luckily, no one was hurt during the ensuing panic, and the Rough Riders' officers quickly got their men under control.

Those "persons who never heard the whirr of lead before had a chance to hear it last night," reported the *Light*. A shaken Professor Beck said, "I was in the Franco-Prussian War and saw some hot times, but I was as uneasy last night as I ever was in battle."

But the town's competing daily, the *San Antonio Daily Express,* claimed that no live rounds were used, and the panic described by the *Light* did not happen. And Adjutant Hall later wrote that all revolvers and carbines were under guard in camp, and no ammunition had yet been issued to the men. Hall blamed the incident on town rowdies.

Whatever the truth, Royal A. Prentice judged Beck's "Cavalry Charge" "one of the finest things I ever heard."

Chapter Three

A Perfect Welter of Confusion

War! Why, it is an advertisement to foreigners
of our absolutely unprepared condition.

COL. LEONARD WOOD

Startling news disrupted the Rough Rider camp the morning of May 26: a Rough Rider was dead. Irad Cochran Jr., just nineteen years old, had been running drills a few days earlier when he was thrown from his horse and struck the ground headfirst. Within hours, a high fever set in—bacterial meningitis—and he was taken to the post hospital at Fort Sam Houston, where he died.

Cochran's funeral was held the next day. At the conclusion of the service, seven Rough Riders raised their carbines in unison as the entire regiment looked on in silence, their heads bared. They faced the black casket containing Cochran's body in full dress uniform.

The honor guard fired three sharp volleys. The regimental bugler played "Taps." Then, members of the deceased man's company, Troop E, escorted the casket out of the fairgrounds and to a waiting horse-drawn hearse, which carried the casket to the railroad depot.

Cochran's body would be shipped over the Southern Pacific to his grieving parents in Las Vegas, New Mexico.

For Cochran to die like this, bucked off a horse, something nearly every trooper had experienced and walked away from, was particularly unsettling for his comrades. The young man died without having seen Cuba, robbed of his chance to strike a blow for the *Maine*. Cochran had died without glory.

Yet by that evening, his tragic end would be a distant, if unpleasant, memory. As his casket rode in a baggage car destined for New Mexico, a War Department clerk in Washington, D.C., tapped out a telegram with new orders for Colonel Wood. Those orders arrived at camp headquarters at 6:00 P.M. Wood smiled as he silently read the telegram. The regiment was to leave San Antonio immediately for Tampa, Florida, and report to Major General William Shafter, commander of the Fifth Army Corps. Because of its closeness to Havana, Tampa had been chosen as the debarkation point for the invasion of Cuba.

Wood handed the telegram to Roosevelt, who quickly scanned it. He looked at Wood with first shock and then joy, then embraced his friend. After less than three weeks of training, they were heading off to war.

"Colonel Wood is exactly what we expected, an indefatigable worker, constantly on the move and one of the most efficient officers I ever knew," reported Major Hersey to New Mexico's governor Otero. Wood was also unflappable and virtually unreadable—he possessed a poker face, according to one trooper. The colonel would need all those traits to get the Rough Riders from Texas to Florida.

The first problem was that the regiment was still not yet completely outfitted. Some men were waiting for the simplest of things, such as the crossed saber insignia for their hats, while others were still without the Krag-Jorgensen carbines. And no one seemed to know what had happened to the shipment of machetes. Roosevelt chalked this up to the general incompetence he saw everywhere in Washington. "They express us stuff we don't need, and send us rifles by slow freight!" he complained in his diary.

Adjutant Tom Hall suspected at least some of the delays were a backlash against the regiment's sudden popularity. The newspapers had not done the Rough Riders any favors by publishing article after article about them and profile after profile on Roosevelt, who was partly to blame—he could always be counted upon for a lively interview. When Regular Army officers saw themselves and their units so suddenly and completely overshadowed by a new regiment of volunteers, they could not help but feel some jealousy and contempt.

Whatever the reason for the delays of the supplies, Wood was not about to let that keep his regiment out of the coming campaign. He now downplayed the importance of the machetes, saying they were heavy and cumbersome and that they would only be used for cutting brush anyway. His men could do without them.

Both Wood and Roosevelt were determined to have the regiment on its way by Sunday night, and that gave them just forty-eight hours to pack up everything and load it onto railroad cars. That is, if the Southern Pacific could get them the needed engines and cars.

In addition to the officers and men, there were 960 horses and 192 pack mules, and 40 civilian mule packers. If they loaded twenty horses per stock car, which was the norm, the regiment would need forty-eight cars for the cavalry mounts alone. There was also the regiment's provisions, tentage, saddles, bridles, ammunition crates, and fodder for the horses and mules.

By Sunday morning, however, the Southern Pacific was ready for them. Officers barked orders as men collapsed tents, rolled blankets, and saddled horses. Once the order came to move out, the brown canvas-uniformed troopers pulled themselves up in their saddles and began the hour-long ride from the fairgrounds to the Union Stock Yards, where dozens of railroad cars waited. The day had already become ungodly hot, and the long column of cavalry and supply wagons kicked up a suffocating dust cloud.

Once at the stockyards, the loading lasted all day and into the night. The regiment would eventually fill seven trains, the first leaving at 2:00 P.M., its steam whistle shrieking and Rough Riders cheering as it rolled out of the yard. The last section left the following morning. Each chugging locomotive pulled eight stock cars, three passenger coaches, five freight cars, and a Pullman car for officers.

Inside the coaches, it was wall-to-wall troopers with no relief from the heat. Even the breeze coming through the open windows was hot. To make matters worse, the troopers soon discovered that the water coolers in each passenger car didn't hold nearly enough water for so many men. Nonetheless, parched or not, they were finally off.

The troopers killed the hours on the train writing letters to family, playing card games, and singing. Cowboy ballads and rousing Civil War songs—"John Brown's Body" was a favorite—were sung so loudly that they drowned out the rumble of the iron wheels and clacking of the tracks. The officers tended to have slightly different musical tastes. In one of the Pullmans, they could be heard singing "Mandalay," Rudyard Kipling's ballad about a British soldier pining for his lover left behind in India.

And there were a few little ditties the Rough Riders composed themselves, such as:

> *How well we remember that year of ninety-eight,*
> *When the cowboys rode out of the West.*
> *The Spaniards sent a cannon-ball a-whizzing through the air*
> *That struck Roosevelt in the breast.*
> *Then up jumped Teddy;*
> *Says he, I am not dead;*
> *I'm sure they would not kill me if they could!*
> *Oh, those good old days of ninety-eight,*
> *When we fit for Colonel Wood—*
> *When we fit for Colonel Wood, by Gawd,*
> *When we fit for Colonel Wood,*
> *Those good old days of ninety-eight, when we fit for Colonel Wood.*

Yet of all the musical numbers in the Rough Riders' repertoire, the one that became the regiment's anthem was the toe-tapping ragtime song "A Hot Time in the Old Town," first published in 1896. Professor Beck's oompah band had performed this number several times for the Rough Riders, and not only was it quite catchy, but the song's signature line, "There'll be a hot time in the old town, tonight!," seemed to capture perfectly the spirit of their San Antonio adventures—and what they intended to do to the Spaniards once they got to Cuba.

News of the trains carrying the famed Rough Riders preceded them, and large crowds gathered in each town on the line. Young women passed the men flowers, love notes, magazines, fried chicken, pies, and watermelons. In return, the ladies often asked for—and got—shiny brass buttons yanked from the men's uniform coats. Even army hardtack (a large cracker) became a cherished souvenir.

Ben Colbert, the Oklahoma Chickasaw, thanked his lucky stars he was part of Troop F, the same one that also included John Avery McIlhenny, one of the millionaire recruits. McIlhenny was the son of the creator of Tabasco sauce, and when the Rough Rider train stopped in McIlhenny's hometown of New Iberia, Louisiana, his mother was waiting with a feast she had put together with the town's citizens: two long lunch baskets, five kegs of beer, and two demijohns of champagne.

But the best was still to come. Thousands greeted the trains as they pulled into the station at New Orleans. "There were cheers, music, beautiful women, many colored lights, etc.," Private Guy Le Sturgeon told his mother in a letter, "also bananas, cigarettes, cigars, tobacco, ham sandwiches, deviled crab, fried fish, etc." One jolly merchant even handed out large palm leaf fans to each trooper. "Never did I see such an ovation," declared Le Sturgeon.

Colonel Wood saw something more. Everywhere he looked, men, women, and children were smiling and waving small American flags. "All the cost of this war is amply repaid by seeing the old flag as one sees it today in the South," he wrote his wife. "We are indeed once more a united country."

Twenty-three-year-old Yale grad Theodore Miller frantically pushed through the crowds at the New Orleans depot hoping that all the commotion was indeed for the Rough Riders and not one of the many other troop trains heading for Florida. Miller had left New York on May 28 after receiving a wire from his boyhood friend, Second Lieutenant David Goodrich, telling him that he could still get into the regiment—vacancies were always coming up due to illness (one man got the measles), and there had even been a few deserters. But Miller would have to come immediately.

Miller's decision to enlist had troubled his family, especially his mother. Theodore's older brother, John, had decided to join the navy, and now her youngest child was about to go off to war. She pleaded with her son to reconsider, but his mind had been made up for some time. The reasons he expressed were uncannily similar to those of another Theodore.

"[W]hat I want to do is get into the 'scrap,'" Miller wrote his family, "and be able to do something worth doing. . . . This has always been a dream of my life, and now that America is about to engage in war, and there is a possibility of my getting into it, it seems still a dream for me to realize."

Miller's urge to "do something worth doing" came naturally. His father, Lewis Miller, was a wealthy inventor and manufacturer of agricultural equipment. A noted philanthropist as well, he had cofounded in 1874 the Chautauqua movement, summer camps that fostered adult education with lectures and entertainment. Theodore Miller's brother-in-law was an inventor, too: Thomas Alva Edison.

Miller had purchased train tickets to San Antonio, but upon entering Texas, he learned the Rough Riders were on their way to Tampa, so he changed trains at Dallas, hoping to catch up with the regiment in New Orleans. Although the Rough Rider trains were arriving in New Orleans at various times on May 31, each train had to remain there several hours so that the horses in the stock cars could be unloaded and taken to nearby pens for water, feed, and a little rest. With such long delays, Miller would easily catch up to them, but knowing that did not make him any less anxious. It was "a chase for a prize I greatly coveted," he wrote.

Finally, Miller spotted the prize: "I almost yelled for joy when I saw the yellow canvas suits, and the soldierly appearance of many men getting on and off the cars, for I felt sure I had caught the Rough Riders."

Miller was not the only young man to join the regiment in New Orleans. Robert Wrenn, William Larned, and Edward Burke also arrived direct from New York hoping to become Rough Riders. Wrenn and Larned happened to be the country's top tennis players; the twenty-four-year-old Wrenn (Harvard '95) had four U.S. singles championships under his belt and was the reigning co-World No. 1 player. Burke, twenty-five years old, was a polo-playing member of the exclusive New York Athletic Club.

The new recruits easily passed their physical examinations and were assigned to one of the baggage cars. They would not be mustered into the service and get their uniforms until the regiment reassembled again at Tampa. Thus, Miller entered the car wearing a derby hat and dress suit and carrying a valise, but the boys warmly welcomed him and the others. Their train pulled out at 2:30 P.M., with everyone hollering over and over,

> Rough! Tough! We're the stuff!
> We're the scrappers; never get enough! W-h-o-o-e-e!

The troop trains were now on the Louisville & Nashville line, which hugged the coast through Mississippi and part of Alabama. Most of the Rough Riders thought this a strange, exotic land. The sweet smell of magnolias, in full bloom, wafted through the cars. Spanish moss dripped off the cypress trees. The swamps with water lilies and tall reeds were "grandly picturesque." But not the alligators: "They are mean looking individuals," Royal A. Prentice observed in his diary.

For Theodore Miller, the glimpses of African American culture he got from the big open door of the baggage car—the scattered forty-acres-and-a-mule farms and black musicians playing banjo, fiddle, and bones at the different railroad stations—were completely new to him. Such sights brought back memories of what he had read as a child in *Uncle Tom's Cabin*.

Each train had its share of mischief makers. "Nothing is sacred," Guy Le Sturgeon admitted to his mother. "No law goes unbroken that we can break." While passing through a sleepy Alabama burg, one of the cowboy troopers looked up ahead and spied a young hog rooting in the mud near the tracks. The cowboy quickly unfurled his lariat and began swinging a big loop above his head. The train must have been traveling at least twenty miles per hour, but as the cowboy's car came up alongside the hog, he flicked his wrist and sent the loop, quick as lightning, directly at the unsuspecting animal.

It could not have been a more perfect toss. The cowboy jerked the lariat tight, and the terrified animal squealed incessantly as it bounced and slid alongside the moving train. As his fellow Rough Riders cheered and laughed, the cowboy grunted and pulled the poor animal up and into the railroad car. The hog became the mascot of Troop H, at least temporarily.

As the Rough Riders approached Florida, some of the officers thought it would be appropriate to sing Stephen Foster's "Old Folks at Home" when their train crossed the Suwannee River. They cooled to the idea, though, when they realized they would cross the river long before sunup. Not Troop F's First Lieutenant Horace Weakley. "He had strong ideas on the subject of 'fitting occasions,'" recalled one of the officers.

Weakley somehow kept himself awake, and just before they reached the famed river, he whooped and shook his fellow officers out of their slumbers. He was initially met with some strong cursing, but Weakley soon had all of them singing, "Way down upon de Swanee Ribber, far, far away. . . ."

The American army assembling at Tampa was fast approaching thirty thousand men. The camps of the several regiments, mostly Regulars, stretched for miles. The Rough Riders' lead train halted in a jumble of railroad cars and locomotives two miles from the Tampa depot on the evening of June 2. Colonel Wood had wired headquarters earlier in the day, giving his approximate arrival time, but as he looked up and down the tracks, not a soul was to be seen.

With a train full of hungry troopers and horses that needed to be watered and fed, Wood had no interest in waiting around to see if someone showed up, so he walked into town. What he saw there was distressing. Tampa was "in a most frightful mix," Wood wrote his wife. "Streets packed with soldiers and a foot deep in real beach sand. Confusion, confusion, confusion."

Headquarters was at the opulent Moorish-styled Tampa Bay Hotel, which was filled with generals, foreign attachés, journalists, and officers' wives. Here Wood located Major General Commander Nelson A. Miles and Major General William Shafter of the Fifth Army Corps. After a brief talk, they decided it was too late to take the Rough Riders to the campsite selected for them. Instead, they instructed Wood to back his train up to some nearby stock corrals, unload the horses and mules, and make a temporary camp. Someone would show him to his designated camp in the morning.

Unloading and watering the stock took the usual several hours, and as the other Rough Rider trains were steadily coming in, few troopers got any sleep. Nevertheless, at 6:00 the next morning, Wood had the men in their saddles and on their way to the new campsite.

Roosevelt, who traveled with the last sections, arrived later that morning, but there was another train behind him that had been inexplicably sidetracked eighteen miles from Tampa. Captain George Curry, Troop H, had charge of this train and tried to make contact with Colonel Wood for instructions, but with the bedlam that was Tampa, no one knew where to locate the colonel.

Finally, after sitting on the tracks for eighteen long hours, Curry asked the engineer and conductor to move the train to a small stockyard with water two miles away so he could tend to his suffering horses. The pair refused, saying they were following orders from the railroad. The thirty-seven-year-old Curry, a prominent southern New Mexico Democrat and businessman, was used to getting his way— or else. In early May, while escorting recruits to Santa Fe, he had punched out a restaurant manager who refused to accept a voucher for their meals.

There were several former railroad employees in Curry's troop, so he arrested the engineer and conductor and hijacked their train. While the horses were watered and fed at the stockyards, Curry had his men unload the saddles. He next ordered his troopers to saddle the horses and mount up. Leaving a small guard with the train to protect their gear and provisions, he led the remainder of his command to Tampa.

Curry needed to report to an officer, and unfortunately the first he found was the Fifth Army Corps's adjutant general, who was shocked when Curry told him he had commandeered the train. Calling the captain's action "arbitrary," the adjutant general wrote a stern note to Colonel Wood recommending that Curry be reprimanded strongly.

After Curry and his men found the Rough Riders' camp, he went alone to regimental headquarters. Wood was away, and Roosevelt was in command. The lieutenant colonel silently read the adjutant general's note. Then he read it out loud to Curry, who braced himself for some kind of tongue-lashing.

Instead, Roosevelt calmly laid the letter on his desk and looked straight into Curry's eyes.

"Captain Curry," Roosevelt said, "why the hell did you wait eighteen hours?"

The Rough Rider camp was located a mile west of the Tampa Bay Hotel, in a broad sand flat surrounded by a scattering of tall pines. The tents were laid out in streets with picket lines for the horses running along each row of tents. Having the horses so close drew swarms of ugly flies. But there always seemed to be a breeze, even during the hottest part of the day, and it cooled down at night.

The "'boys' are delighted to find Tampa pleasanter than San Antonio instead of worse, as they expected," Private Arthur F. Cosby wrote his mother. "The greatest relief is to be away from that perfectly horrible dust."

Wood had reorganized the regiment at San Antonio, cutting down the number of enlisted men in each of the four New Mexico troops and creating a new company with the surplus. That meant the Rough Riders now consisted of twelve troops, which were divided into three squadrons. The first squadron contained three Arizona troops, A, B, and C, and the Oklahoma Territory troop, D. The New Mexico troops, E, F, G, and H, made up the second squadron. In the third squadron, troops I and K were men from all over the country, while troops L and M came from Indian Territory.

Several of the millionaire recruits ended up in K, which earned it the rather unflattering name "silk stocking troop." But easterners made up only about half of this troop. Roosevelt family friend Robert Munro Ferguson, recently promoted sergeant, wrote to Roosevelt's sister Corinne that K "has a large number of first rate cowpunchers and sheriffs drafted into it. . . . We are more or less intelligent and are looked to as the possible crack troop." The other troops would have taken issue with Ferguson's claim, but Troop K did have the two Colt machine guns.

For the first thirty-six hours in Tampa, the horses were rested and the men drilled on foot. It took nearly that much time to find out what had happened to their provisions and baggage. In trying to relieve the congestion from all the arriving trains, railroad employees had unloaded cars wherever they could and as quickly as they could. But even after the men located the provisions, they couldn't find army wagons to haul the supplies to camp. Until all this got sorted out, Roosevelt, Wood, and Major Brodie paid out of their own pockets to get rations for the men.

Another, more maddening worry was news from headquarters that only a portion of the regiment would sail with the first fleet to Cuba—and it might be as few as four troops. Even more, the Rough Riders would go and fight as infantry. They were to be "dough boys," Guy Le Sturgeon wrote his mother. The reason for this was that there were not nearly enough transports (steamships) in Tampa Bay for Shafter's army, let alone the thousands of cavalry mounts. So only the general, field, and staff officers' horses, and the mules for the pack trains and wagons, would go with the first expedition. The remaining Rough Riders and all their horses would wait for the next fleet to assemble.

This news sent Roosevelt into a panic; if eight troops were left behind, he would have to stay as their commanding officer. By the time more transports were brought in, the war in Cuba could be over—and it probably would be. Roosevelt declared to one of his lieutenants that he absolutely would not remain in Tampa. He was going to Cuba, he fumed, even if he had to take a reduced rank of lieutenant or captain.

Roosevelt did not have to do anything drastic yet, as a final decision was still to come. In the meantime, the Rough Riders were the main attraction at Tampa, as they had been in San Antonio. One person described them as "the lions of the camp." But some locals, including the Tampa mayor, were initially leery of those lions—they had read about the concert gone awry in San Antonio and other shenanigans. "They were afraid of us. How absurd!" commented one of the men.

Imagining that after the Rough Riders received their army pay, they would go on a wild drunken spree through their town, a group of Tampa citizens submitted a petition requesting the money be withheld until the men were well out to sea. The army paymaster rejected their petition, but the citizens had nothing to worry about. In another snafu, the paymaster ran out of cash before he got to the Rough Riders. The men would not be paid off until the night before they left for Cuba.

The usual mob of journalists flocked to the Rough Riders. The "photograph fiends" snapped pictures of the men "standing, sitting and lying down, awake and sleeping, eating, chewing, smoking,

*Regimental ride near Tampa. (R560.3.Em3-026, Theodore Roosevelt
Collection, Houghton Library, Harvard University.)*

talking, walking, riding, washing, shaving, and I know not what,"
remembered an officer. And it wasn't just still pictures. A cameraman
for the Edison Kinetoscope Company filmed the Rough Riders on
horseback as they cantered past him, guidons fluttering in the wind.

Several visitors to the camp requested special exhibitions of horsemanship and pistol shooting, but Roosevelt was not about to put
on what would essentially be a Wild West show. He politely denied
their requests, saying it was "contrary to the regulations." The large
number of sightseers became so disruptive to the mounted drills that
Wood implemented a new policy: all visitors to the camp were required to have a pass. No women were to be allowed unless by special
permission.

Frederic Remington, the famed illustrator and Roosevelt friend,
was somewhat miffed when he was forced to get a pass. Never, he said,
in his years of visiting western military posts and sketching soldiers in
the field had he been required to have a pass to visit a camp of Amer-

ican soldiers. And he was even less happy after being admitted. Like most every other visitor, he expected to find a bunch of mustachioed gunslingers. He should have known better.

"Why, you are nothing but a lot of cavalrymen!" he exclaimed. The Rough Riders took that as a supreme compliment.

On June 6, military attachés from England, France, Germany, Russia, and Japan came from the Tampa Bay Hotel to watch the regiment go through the mounted drill. Afterward, Wood and Roosevelt basked in the praise the attachés showered on them. "[T]hey had heard of the peculiar idea of this regiment and wanted to see us," Wood wrote his wife. "Both the English and German [attachés] said it was the most soldierly camp and the best-looking one, regular or vol., which they had seen."

Yet as "soldierly" as they appeared, the Rough Riders often had their own take on regulations. One evening about midnight, the officer of the guard approached the camp sentry. As was proper, the sentry shouted, "Halt, who goes there?"

"Officer of the guard."

"Advance, officer of the guard, and be recognized," said the sentry.

But the sentry's command was wrong, for the officer was carrying a sword, and a sentry was not supposed to let an armed man approach him.

"Don't you see that I have a sword in my hand?" asked the officer.

"Yes."

"Well, what are you going to do about it?"

"Oh, pshaw!" said the sentry. "I'm not afraid of your sword!"

Edith Roosevelt, who had made a wonderful recovery from her March surgery, arrived in Tampa by train from Sagamore Hill, the Roosevelt home near Oyster Bay, on the night of June 4. It was her last opportunity to see Theodore again before he left for combat. She was one of just two or three women allowed to visit the Rough Riders camp (a female journalist justly threw a fit but to no avail).

"It has been a real holiday to have darling mother here," Theodore Roosevelt wrote their children. "I brought her out to the camp, and she saw it all—the men drilling, the tents in long company streets, the horses being taken to water, my little horse Texas, the colonel and the majors, and finally the mountain lion and the jolly little dog Cuba, who had several fights while she looked on."

Roosevelt stayed with Edith at the Tampa Bay Hotel during her visit. The five-hundred-room resort—"so enormous that the walk from the rotunda to the dining-room helps one to an appetite," a correspondent observed—seemed more like a military-themed country club. One evening, the Roosevelts dined with close friends and fellow Rough Riders Robert Munro Ferguson and Kenneth Robinson. The Regular Army officers in the room were shocked at what they considered a scandalous breach of military etiquette: Ferguson was a sergeant and Robinson a private. It only added to their general contempt for volunteers—and they weren't inclined to like the Rough Riders anyway. But Roosevelt didn't care what they thought. To a fault, he was loyal to friends.

A number of other Rough Riders—those who were well heeled—also partook of the hotel's high-class amenities. Theodore Miller, the tennis players Wrenn and Larned, and their friend Burke rented rooms and swam in the hotel's pool with Frederic Remington. Several of the clubmen took baths in journalist Richard Harding Davis's tub. Arthur F. Cosby, who wrote his mother that the camp food was "not good," joined his fellow swells for an occasional "bully dinner" in town.

The tennis players and Burke had been assigned to Troop A, an Arizona troop, and their failure to embrace camp life did not go unnoticed by their western comrades.

"Them dudes will have to get themselves into shape," a Troop A sergeant complained to a reporter. "They live by themselves, take their meals at hotels, and rather feel their oats. I think that the boys will bring 'em down soon if they don't change a little."

The boys didn't have time. Word came on the sixth that the Rough

Riders should prepare to move at a moment's notice. But it was still uncertain who would go and who would stay. Finally, after an "awful morning" of worrying, Roosevelt learned that eight troops, and not four, would be going to Cuba. Each of the eight would be limited to seventy men, which meant those troops selected would still have to leave behind ten or more individuals. The men were not happy with this news, but Roosevelt felt as if he had been granted a lifesaving reprieve—he would now go as one of the two squadron commanders.

Although Roosevelt could finally relax, the rest of the regiment remained as anxious as ever while Colonel Wood tried to determine which four troops to leave behind. Private Guy Le Sturgeon expressed the feelings of every Rough Rider when he wrote his mother, "What would be the good of being a soldier if I must stay here and groom horses for six months?"

For the most part, Wood had a good idea which troops he wanted with him, but he had a hard time deciding between two New Mexico troops, so he called their captains, George Curry and Maximiliano Luna, to his tent.

"I am sorry I cannot take you both," Wood told them, "but I must leave one troop of your squadron here."

"Colonel," Luna pleaded, "I must beg you to make it possible for me to fight in Cuba. I like to feel that I am representing the Spanish-speaking peoples of New Mexico. We are loyal to the United States. I want to fight to prove it."

Naturally, Curry wanted his men to go just as badly. There was a tense silence as the two captains looked to the colonel. Finally, Captain Allyn Capron, standing nearby, suggested they flip a coin. Curry and Luna quickly agreed. Wood fished out a silver quarter and tossed it in the air. Luna won.

Along with Luna's Troop F, Wood chose troops A, B, D, E, G, K, and L. "Everybody was excited," Theodore Miller observed, "and we heard the cheers from the different troops as they received their orders."

Those same cheers were gut-wrenching for the men designated to remain behind. In a bitter irony, although Private Guy Le Sturgeon was a member of Luna's Troop F, he was among the men detailed to remain behind in order to get the troop down to seventy. Also among those who got the bad news was Frank Brito, the young New Mexico cowboy who had ridden all night to reach his parents' home in Pinos Altos and been instructed by his father to sign up for the Rough Riders. Colonel Wood assured him and the others that they would be joining him in Cuba as soon as possible.

"We were too angry to hear him," Brito recalled, "and if we had, I doubt we'd have believed him. We had come a long way together and being left out at the last minute was not something any of us had counted on."

Some of the late-joining members of the lucky troops, such as Miller and the tennis players, were not completely outfitted. Unless they could come up with weapons and accoutrements, they would be stuck with the other unfortunates.

Miller remembered seeing a stray carbine that belonged to one of the troopers who was staying with the horses. He quickly fetched it and went to see his captain. But just as he did, the carbine's owner appeared and claimed it. This soldier then began begging the captain to let him go with the troop. The captain consented, and Miller watched as the man jumped and shouted with joy.

Devastated, Miller rushed away from his comrades and broke down and cried. He was not the only Rough Rider in tears that day, and he was in no better shape early the next morning when his captain walked up to him carrying a carbine and a cartridge belt. The captain thrust the Krag and the belt into a stunned Miller's hands. It turned out a trooper had fallen asleep during guard duty the night before, and the captain immediately thought of a more deserving young man. Miller was going to Cuba.

Incredibly, so were the two tennis players and Burke, although they had a bit more pull than Miller. Robert Wrenn's weapon came courtesy of Lieutenant Colonel Roosevelt. It was the Model 1895 saddle carbine presented to Roosevelt by the Winchester Repeating Arms

Company in San Antonio. Now Wrenn would be the one who would use it to avenge the *Maine*.

Denied their horses, the Rough Riders had to figure out how to carry their gear on their backs—and they had to adapt to this quickly. An infantryman arrived in the camp to demonstrate. First, one-half of the dog tent was spread out on the ground, then the trooper's blanket spread on top of that. A rubber poncho, change of underwear, socks, razors, quinine pills (for malarial fevers), and any extra bandannas were placed on the blanket and the whole thing was rolled up, bent into a horseshoe shape, and tied at the ends. The pack was then slipped over the trooper's head, the top of the horseshoe resting on the left shoulder and the ends under the right arm.

A tin cup hung from a hook on the wide cartridge belt (filled with 125 rounds of ammunition), and a haversack slung over the shoulder carried each soldier's tin mess kit. An especially important accoutrement, a canvas-covered canteen, also hung from the belt. Missing from the belt was a leather holster, for the Colt revolvers and their ammunition were deemed to be too much extra weight. Only the officers were allowed to bring along their sidearms. The same with the much-touted machetes. They were later issued to the detail assigned to the Colt machine guns, but no one else got them.

As the men packed their gear, Roosevelt inventoried his own essential items for the campaign. Marshall, his valet, organized while Roosevelt checked and double-checked. Knowing that there would be no possibility of replacing his eyeglasses in Cuba, Roosevelt had ordered a dozen pairs before leaving Washington. Not the pince-nez style he preferred, but the more traditional metal frames with earpieces that snuggly hooked around the ears. Not even a hurricane could knock them off.

Roosevelt stashed eyeglasses everywhere so he would have an extra pair always close in case of an emergency: a pair was sewed inside the new Stetson he had purchased in San Antonio, another pair was sewed in his shirt, two pairs were in his saddlebags, and so on. He was the quintessential Boy Scout before there was such a thing as a Boy Scout.

For a sidearm, Roosevelt carried a revolver like no other in the entire invasion force. A Colt New Navy Model 1892 in .38 caliber, it had been salvaged from the wreck of the *Maine* and presented to him by his brother-in-law, William S. Cowles, a navy captain. Roosevelt's handsome German-made officer's saber, with sharkskin-wrapped hilt, had been a gift from some of the employees at the Navy Department.

He also carried with him, in one of his large tunic pockets, a slim leather-covered booklet that was stamped in gilt on the front cover with the word *Diary*. Because of its small size (no bigger than a checkbook), his entries were necessarily brief, but there was always enough room to vent his frustration at the army's bungling.

"No plans; no staff officers; no instructions to us," he scrawled under June 6. "Each officer finds out for himself & takes his chances."

The following day, Colonel Wood was directed to have his eight troops at a certain railroad siding by midnight, where they would board a train to take them the nine miles to the harbor. It was a bright, moonlit evening, and Wood had no trouble getting his men to the siding on time, but there was no train for them. Standing in formation, they waited, and they waited. Finally, at 3:00 A.M., Wood was told to move to another siding. Once there, officers up and down the line shouted, "At rest."

"We were in columns of four," Arthur F. Cosby wrote his mother, "and I assure you that every man fell on the ground literally in his tracks, with his roll around him, and fell asleep. It is too absurd to think of our sleeping that way, gun in hand, but we did and slept well."

The sun came up and still no train. The men were famished, but there were no rations to be had. Several troopers wandered over to a nearby regiment to bum breakfast; others actually woke up families at private residences to ask for food. All the while, a fuming Wood and Roosevelt tried to get answers about how they would be traveling to the Tampa Bay pier.

About 6:00 A.M., they sighted a train slowly approaching the siding, but it turned out to be a train of empty coal cars. It wasn't what they had been promised, but it would do. Wood got the train stopped, told the engineer he now had a load of Rough Riders to haul, and ordered his officers to get the men and supplies on board.

Soon they were chugging down the tracks, the coal dust swirling inside the open cars and getting in every man's eyes and clothes. Wood and Roosevelt, along with several officers, rode in the caboose, which was now the front of the train as it backed toward Port Tampa. Just before reaching their destination, though, the train pulled off on a sidetrack to let a passenger train pass—by railroad rules, passenger trains took priority over coal trains.

This particular passenger train happened to be carrying the Seventy-First New York Volunteers, and as they came alongside the coal cars, the New Yorkers spotted the brown canvas uniforms and realized they were looking at Rough Riders—Roosevelt's Rough Riders. As they neared the caboose, the men in the first cars began yelling: "Hallo Teddy!" "Speech! Speech!" "We want Teddy Roosevelt! We want Teddy Roosevelt!" "Show us your teeth, Teddy!" Each car in succession joined in the cheers until a thousand men were all chanting in unison "We—Want—Teddy—Roosevelt!"

Roosevelt never appeared, but the New Yorkers gave the Rough Riders a much-needed laugh.

The tracks stretched out onto the mile-long pier, and as the coal train approached the bay, Wood and Roosevelt saw the jam of dozens of railroad cars and the big steamships lined up taking on men and supplies. Thousands of soldiers crowded the narrow strip of land between the trains and the transports, some men standing in formation and others knotted in groups.

In a repeat of their arrival in Tampa, no one met the Rough Riders at the pier to tell them where to go or which transport was theirs.

Loading of the Fifth Army Corps at the Tampa Bay pier. (R560.3.EL64-049,
Theodore Roosevelt Collection, Houghton Library, Harvard University.)

Wood and Roosevelt pushed through the throngs looking for someone in charge and were relieved when they finally found Generals
Shafter, commander of the expedition, and Miles, the senior officer in
the U.S. Army. If anyone would know, they would.

But they didn't. All Shafter and Miles could tell the colonels was
that if they didn't locate their transport soon, they would not be
able to accompany the expedition. This naturally sent shock waves
through Roosevelt, who was determined to use any means possible,
devious or otherwise, to get his men on a boat.

After some time, the pair located the depot quartermaster, the man
responsible for allotting transports. But it turned out that he had failed
to allot a transport for the Rough Riders, which brought a string of
choice words from Roosevelt. The quartermaster nervously shuffled
through his notes and assigned the Rough Riders to the *Yucatan*, waiting out in the channel for a place at the pier. He advised the colonels

to board the ship immediately or they might lose their spot. What he didn't tell them was that the ship had already been allotted to the Seventy-First New York, the regiment whose train had passed them that morning.

Stepping out of the quartermaster's office, Wood spotted a small motorboat and promptly commandeered it. As he sped out to take possession of the *Yucatan*, Roosevelt walked back to the men. After going only a short distance, he learned that not only had their transport been previously assigned to the New Yorkers, but to the Second U.S. Infantry as well. The Seventy-First New York alone had more men than the ship could comfortably hold. Roosevelt broke into a run.

He was definitely showing his teeth as he raced up to his waiting men and began barking orders. Roosevelt left part of the regiment to guard the train with their supplies and double-quicked the remainder to the gangway where the *Yucatan* was to dock. The Seventy-First arrived just after the Rough Riders, but Roosevelt had so many of his men crowded around the gangway that no one else could get close. When the Seventy-First's colonel tried anyway, Roosevelt refused to allow his men to board.

Next, the commanding officer of the Second U.S. Infantry, who outranked Roosevelt, sent orders for the Rough Riders to move aside and allow his regiment to take possession. Roosevelt scribbled an evasive reply, stalling for time as the *Yucatan* slowly approached.

Seeing Wood at the ship's bow, Roosevelt began yelling—and Wood yelled back.

"What he was saying I had no idea," Roosevelt recalled, "but he was evidently speaking, and on my own responsibility, I translated it into directions to hold the gangway, and so informed the regulars that I was under orders of my superior and of a ranking officer—to my great regret, etc., etc.—could not give way as they desired."

There was a long delay in attaching the gangway. All the while, the men stood in the scorching sun—"100 in the shade," according to trooper Ben Colbert. The moment the gangway was secured, Roosevelt hurried his men aboard.

Looking down from the ship's rail, Roosevelt saw two men standing on the gangplank with a hand-cranked motion picture camera on a tripod. The men had hoped to get on board with the Seventy-First until Roosevelt turned the regiment away.

"What are you young men up to?" he shouted.

"We are the Vitagraph Company, Colonel Roosevelt, and we are going to Cuba to take moving pictures," replied the cameraman, Albert E. Smith.

"I can't take care of a regiment but I might be able to handle two more," Roosevelt said, waving them on board. Any camera had an almost hypnotic effect on Roosevelt, Smith recalled, and this day his "zeal for publicity was alive and roaring."

Rough Riders on board the transport Yucatan. *(R560.3.Em3-030, Theodore Roosevelt Collection, Houghton Library, Harvard University.)*

Now that Roosevelt had seized a transport, the next task was to retrieve the supplies and the rest of the men. They were about a mile away, and the supplies, including the heavy machine guns, were piled on the ground—a general had ordered the coal train removed. With no wagon in sight, most of the Rough Riders who had just gotten on the boat were ordered off to help fetch the provisions.

It was a grueling job. "Almost died under weight of a bag of coffee," wrote Theodore Miller. "Never worked so hard in my life." With all their marching of the last several hours, a few jokers started referring to the Rough Riders as Wood's Weary Walkers.

By 6:00 P.M., the regiment's supplies were loaded. Wood had permitted four companies of the Second Infantry and its brass band to board, so in total, there were 940 men crammed into the *Yucatan*, which had berths for only 714. The officers' horses, including Roosevelt's Little Texas and Rain-in-the-Face, were in the hold of another boat.

Finally, with all on board excited, relieved, and dog tired, the *Yucatan* pulled away from the pier. The Second Infantry's band raised their instruments and began playing "A Hot Time in the Old Town." The Rough Riders answered with cowboy yelps. And as the drums banged and cymbals crashed, an optimistic Ben Colbert and his comrades changed the song's words to "there'll be a hot time in Cuba next week."

Chapter Four

Cuba at Last

*I am going to Cuba; I will take all the chances of meeting
death by yellow fever, smallpox or by a Spanish bullet
just to see the Spanish flag once on a battlefield.*

THEODORE ROOSEVELT

Wednesday afternoon, June 8
Port Tampa, Florida

Major General William Shafter and his staff pushed through the
throngs of soldiers on the pier, albeit slowly. The general in charge
of the Cuban expedition was sixty-two years old, weighed more than
three hundred pounds, and suffered from gout, which made it difficult for him to walk. How he would handle Cuba's tropical climate
and rough terrain was anybody's guess, but to those observing the
panting general on the pier, it didn't look good.

Shafter had wanted to sail out of the bay at daylight. Yet the problems with the overwhelmed railroad and the utter chaos at the port,
which he had done very little to alleviate, made that impossible. He
was now on his way to board the transport *Seguranca*, which was ready
to take its place with the other ships gradually assembling in the bay.

Before he reached the *Seguranca*'s gangway, however, a messenger ran up to Shafter and thrust an urgent telegram in his hand. It was from the War Department:

> *Wait until you get further orders before you sail. Answer quick.*
>
> R. A. Alger
> Secretary of War

Shafter and his aides did an about-face and headed for the nearest shade. The general dictated a reply to Alger:

> *Message received. Vessels are in the stream, but will be able to stop them before reaching the Gulf.*
>
> *Shafter,*
> *Major-General*

It wasn't until later that night that Shafter learned why his mission had been abruptly halted. What was believed to be a Spanish armored cruiser and a torpedo-boat destroyer had been sighted just off the north coast of Cuba, in the Nicholas Channel. If that were true, they were certainly there to attack the American transports. The navy needed time to bring in more warships to escort the convoy.

Although it would now be a few days before the convoy could sail, Shafter decided to keep his army on the ships, most of which were anchored out in the bay, and that included the *Yucatan*. If he were to disembark his men and establish camps near the port, it would take as many as three days to get men and equipment loaded again once orders came to proceed. But life on the transports was not going to be pleasant, and each day that passed brought the army that much closer to Cuba's dreaded "yellow fever season." Both yellow fever and malaria were spread by mosquitoes, but this wasn't known in 1898. What was known was that fever cases spiked in Cuba during the summer.

Yellow fever, called the "black vomit" because those infected vomited blood, was often fatal.

The *Yucatan's* decks were so jam-packed that there was no room for drills or any kind of exercise for the troopers. The officers were essentially confined to their cabins, as it was futile to step out and try to navigate through the mass of soldiers. The lower hold, where several companies were quartered, was just as tight. Roosevelt compared it to the Black Hole of Calcutta.

There was very little for the men to do. The Second Infantry band bravely performed two concerts a day in the sweltering heat, often accompanied by the howls of the mascot Cuba, the only one of the regimental mascots taken on board. At other times, the Rough Riders joined in singing their favorite songs. Music seemed to always liven things up, at least temporarily.

Swimming was allowed near the ship in the mornings and evenings, although there was a constant worry about sharks. Consequently, the men swam in squads while other troopers kept watch on the main deck, carbines at the ready.

During one morning swim, Royal A. Prentice suddenly heard the lookouts shouting "Shark!" Then he heard the buzzing of bullets overhead followed a split second later by the cracks of the carbines. "I thought it was a joke," he recalled, "until happening to look up at the bridge I saw the Ship's Captain yelling and swinging his arms directing us to come quickly. You may be sure right then the world's swimming record for speed was broken."

If the swells in the regiment were less than fond of the camp food in Tampa, they were even more aghast at the rations on the ship. Meals were always the same: canned beef that was stringy and tasteless (one trooper called it "salt-horse"), canned beans, canned tomatoes, hardtack, and coffee. And the water didn't taste good. At least one Harvard man didn't have to drink the water because he had smuggled aboard several bottles of champagne.

Charles Knoblauch of Troop E, a member of the New York Stock

Exchange, finally had had enough one day. He was by far the best swimmer in the regiment, so he jumped off the ship and swam the half mile to shore, sharks be damned. There he had a fine dinner, smoked a cigarette, and then swam back to the *Yucatan*.

The rest of the Rough Riders chose a much less extreme method of supplementing their rations, what Arthur F. Cosby described as " 'rustling' extras." By that he meant trying to buy or trade for little niceties like lemons, ice, sandwiches, cookies, and pies.

Soldiers could get those things in two ways. One was to bribe the ship's cooks. The other was to be lucky enough to be assigned to a detail going ashore or placing an order with some trooper in the detail. Quite a few men made tidy profits on the goodies they purchased at the Port Tampa grocery stores and numerous temporary booths. Five New Mexico troopers each pitched in $5 and bought canned fruit, pickles, hams, bread, cigars, tobacco, and cocoa, among other things. When they got back to the *Yucatan,* they sold enough of their plunder to make their money back and still had four small hams, pickles, and mustard for their own mess.

Writing letters home and making diary entries was another time killer, although there was little new to report as the days dragged on. Roosevelt, a prolific letter writer, filled his friends and family in on his indignation and criticisms of those in charge.

"I suppose it is simply the ordinary fortune of war for the most irritating delays to happen," Roosevelt wrote his sister Corinne on June 12, "but it seems to me that the people at Washington are inexcusable for putting us aboard ship and then keeping us crowded to suffocation on this transport for six days in Tampa harbor in a semitropical sun. . . . [T]he interminable delays and the vacillation and utter absence of efficient organization are really discouraging."

Arthur F. Cosby wrote his mother that even the army veterans and hardened cowpunchers, men who had "roughed it all of their lives," were complaining: "It is bad enough anyway to go to Cuba in such boats, but to lie around day after day beforehand is trying."

Then it came. On Sunday afternoon, June 12, Secretary of War Alger finally ordered the expedition to sail. It turned out that the "Spanish gunboats" had actually belonged to the Americans.

The Rough Riders learned of Alger's orders the following morning, causing more than a few to jump for joy, but Roosevelt outshone them all. "When Colonel Roosevelt heard the news he could not restrain himself and entertained us all by giving an impromptu war dance," wrote J. Ogden Wells.

The next twenty-four hours were taken up with loading late-arriving supplies and getting the thirty-two transports in their formation of three long columns and poised at the mouth of the bay. To the great relief of every Rough Rider, two companies of the Second Infantry were taken off the *Yucatan* and placed on another transport. There had simply been too many men, and the departure of the approximately two hundred soldiers with their gear freed up some much-needed space on the ship. The Rough Riders got another break when it turned out that the Second's regimental band was not one of the companies to go.

About an hour before sunset on Monday, the transports steamed toward their positions. Suddenly several Rough Riders began shouting and pointing up ahead. The *Yucatan* appeared to be bearing down on the transport *Matteawan*, which was at anchor and waiting for a pilot. As the *Yucatan* closed to one hundred and fifty yards of the *Matteawan*, its captain blew a long blast on the boat's whistle. The *Yucatan*'s anchor dropped and splashed into the ocean while water boiled at the stern from the reversing of the ship's engines.

Most of the Rough Riders knew that the *Yucatan*'s bow held several hundred pounds of a nitroglycerin-based explosive for a pneumatic dynamite gun, an odd-looking artillery piece assigned to the Rough Riders at the last minute. The troopers had lugged crate after crate of its ammunition into the hold. If the *Yucatan* slammed into the *Matteawan*, the entire ship might erupt in a fiery ball, and it was going to be close. At the last moment, the *Yucatan* came to a halt. Less than six feet separated the two hulls, and several men from each ship leaned far over the rails and stretched out their arms in an effort to shake hands.

After a few minutes, the *Yucatan* weighed anchor and slowly steamed past the *Matteawan*. It was later learned that a serious problem had occurred with the ship's steering apparatus.

About 3:00 P.M. on June 14, the flotilla finally sailed out into the Gulf. Mounted in front of the captain's cabin on the *Yucatan* were the two Colt machine guns. The dynamite gun was also installed on the deck. If the convoy was attacked, the Rough Riders weren't going down without a fight.

With the navy escort, water tenders, and other small craft, the convoy numbered forty-eight vessels; more gunboats were waiting for them off Key West. The transports carried 819 officers and 16,058 enlisted men. There were also 272 teamsters and packers, 107 stevedores, and 30 civilian clerks. More than 2,000 horses and mules kicked and snorted in the various ships' holds.

Eleven foreign attachés in full military regalia traveled with the expedition, looking like peacocks with their gold braids and glistening medals. Also in full force was the press with eighty-nine war correspondents. Among these writers and artists were such notables as Richard Harding Davis, Caspar Whitney, John Fox Jr., Frank Norris, Frederic Remington, and Howard Chandler Christy. "I expect to make myself rich on this campaign," Davis had written his family.

At least two newspapers chartered their own boats. William Randolph Hearst, owner of the *New York Journal*, sailed on the *Sylvia*, which was set up with a darkroom for his photographer, while the *New York World* chartered a tug named *Three Friends*. Stephen Crane, already internationally renowned for his novel *The Red Badge of Courage*, was on the latter.

Roosevelt was much more at ease now that the expedition was under way, and he could enjoy the ocean's beauty and ponder possibilities. "Today we are steaming southward through a sapphire sea, wind-rippled, under an almost cloudless sky," he wrote his wife on June 15.

Last evening we stood up on the bridge and watched the red sun sink
and the lights blaze up on the ship, for miles ahead and astern, while
the band played piece after piece, from the "Star Spangled Banner"
at which we all rose and stood uncovered, to "The Girl I Left Behind
Me."—But it is a great historical expedition, and I thrill to feel that
I am part of it. If we fail, of course we share the fate of all who do
fail, but if we are allowed to succeed (for certainly we shall succeed,
if allowed) we have scored the first great triumph in what will be a
world movement.

Roosevelt's "world movement," the beginning of the end, he hoped, of Old World dominance, would start at Santiago de Cuba. With a population of between forty and fifty thousand, Santiago was Cuba's second-largest city, after Havana. Founded by Spaniards in 1515, the city fronted a picturesque bay, five miles long, on the island's southeast coast. It was 688 miles, as the crow flies, from Tampa.

Santiago had not been part of the original invasion plan. That plan, conceived in early May, called for a landing of the Fifth Corps at Mariel, on Cuba's north coast. From there, Shafter's army would move east and take Havana, which American warships were already blockading. But on May 29, the War Department learned that Spain's Atlantic battle squadron under Admiral Pascual Cervera was holed up in Santiago's harbor.

Cervera's fleet was a critical target. Until its capture or destruction, it would be a looming threat to any military operations in the Caribbean and even to cities on the U.S. coast. But as long as Cervera remained in Santiago's harbor, he was virtually untouchable. The landlocked bay was surrounded by high bluffs with gun batteries and fortifications, and the only access to the harbor, a winding channel just 220 yards wide at its narrowest point, was laced with submarine mines. All this made it much too risky for American battleships to enter the harbor and engage the Spaniards.

The U.S. Navy's North Atlantic Squadron under Rear Admiral

William T. Sampson would blockade the bay to keep Cervera from escaping, but to root out the Spanish squadron, the navy would need the help of the army. Shafter's task, then, was to assault Santiago by land and capture its Spanish garrison. With the fall of Santiago, Cervera's warships in the bay would be doomed.

Because several of Shafter's transports were slow-going, well-past-their-prime sidewheelers, the convoy traveled at a pedestrian seven knots. At that rate, the voyage around the eastern tip of Cuba and then west along the island's south coast toward Santiago might take a week. That was far too long for the men of Troop A to put up with an accordion that one man in the troop had purchased before leaving Tampa. He'd never even played one before, and his pitiful efforts to teach himself were absolutely painful. One day, when the owner wasn't looking, his squeezebox was mercifully given a burial at sea.

Twice a day, the Rough Riders drilled on deck in infantry tactics and in the use of their carbines: position and aiming, estimating distance, and rapid firing. Captain Capron conducted a school for the

Captain Allyn K. Capron, Troop L.
(Author's Collection.)

regiment's officers, and he made it clear he did not always agree with the army manual, particularly its comments about what to do "in case of retreat." He warned the officers that the very thought of a possible retreat would eat at the men's minds and lead to disastrous consequences.

"If you go into action you want to win," he said forcefully. "I have heard officers say in the presence of their men that soldiers cannot live in the face of a direct fire from the modern rifle. You had better impress upon your men that the only way for them is to charge through, and to charge through it quickly."

Roosevelt let it be known how much he approved of this, as he was becoming even more impressed with the captain of Troop L. He considered him the best soldier in the regiment. "Capron's training and temper fitted him to do great work in war," Roosevelt wrote later, "and he looked forward with eager confidence to what the future held, for he was sure that for him it held either triumph or death."

The Rough Riders could withstand the pitching and spinning of the meanest bronc and hold on to their breakfasts, but the rolling of the *Yucatan* on the open sea was a different animal entirely. Many became so seasick they had to stop eating because nothing would stay down. The days spent waiting in Tampa Bay had depleted the rations on board the ships, but with some men not eating, there was plenty of food for the ones who did fancy a meal. As the troopers gradually got over their nausea, however, getting enough to eat became the most serious challenge of the voyage.

Royal A. Prentice recalled that a can of tomatoes, a can of peaches, and a can of milk, along with all the tasteless hardtack they could stomach, would be issued to a squad of eight men. "The cans were opened and passed around the squad," he wrote, "and each man took a spoonful from the can as it passed, AND NO MORE!"

The ship's cooks continued to sell food on the sly, but the prices they charged, which were eyebrow-raising high to start with, soon became outrageous. Theodore Miller believed the ship's baker made $200 the first day out. The New Yorkers "simply poured money into the kitchen," he wrote in his diary. And for a time, the swells finagled their way into the dining room after the officers were finished with their meal.

"One not having experienced it can hardly realize how we begged for food," wrote Miller, "and even stole a cracker or piece of bread from passing waiters." Some men were so desperate for real nourishment they paid the dining room steward to sneak them the scraps from the officers' plates. Arthur F. Cosby could see that the food shortage, combined with the heat, was weakening the regiment. "All the men have lost flesh at the most astonishing rate," he told a friend. How Wood and Roosevelt could not have known about the lack of sufficient rations is a puzzle.

On June 17, as the *Yucatan* steamed southeast through the Nicholas Channel, the Rough Riders could finally see the Cuban mainland off the starboard side. About noon, the troopers on the decks were able to spot in the distance a small sailboat slicing through the blue sea, coming closer and closer. It had a flag streaming from its mast that was so large it seemed to dwarf the boat underneath it. It was soon apparent that the flag was one flown by the *insurrectos,* known as *La Estrella Solitaria,* the Lone Star flag. As the small craft swung near, the three Cubans inside stood up and cheered the Stars and Stripes flying from the *Yucatan.* They joyously waved their hats from side to side and fired their guns in the air as the transport steamed past. The Cubans were a reminder to the Rough Riders that this war was about much more than avenging the *Maine.* For the men in the sailboat, and the thousands more fighting Spanish soldiers on the island, it was Cuba Libre!

"At night we looked at the new stars, and hailed the Southern Cross when at last we raised it above the horizon," Roosevelt recalled. Many of those nights stargazing from the *Yucatan* he spent alongside Captain

Buckey O'Neill, the gregarious former mayor of Prescott, Arizona. Their discussions were deep, philosophical. Roosevelt remembered that O'Neill liked to talk about "the mysteries which lie behind courage, and fear, and love, behind animal hatred, and animal lust for the pleasures that have tangible shape."

O'Neill had accomplished much in his thirty-eight years, yet, like Roosevelt, he believed the one thing missing could only be found in the din of battle. "If, by risking his life, no matter how great the risk, he could gain high military distinction, he was bent on gaining it," Roosevelt wrote. "He had taken so many chances when death lay on the hazard, that he felt the odds were now against him; but, said he, 'Who would not risk his life for a star?'"

O'Neill was referring to a promotion, a general's star. But if death found him instead, he was prepared for that, too. Before leaving his home, O'Neill had taken out two life insurance policies with the New York Life Insurance Company worth $10,000, paying the extra "war premium." He had also made sure that the Mutual Life Insurance Company of New York would honor an existing policy he held. Whatever happened, his wife would be taken care of.

Shafter knew where on the island they were going to strike, but he was keeping those orders secret from the officers and men aboard the transports. But once the *Yucatan* entered the Windward Passage and turned south to round Cape Maisí, all the Rough Riders were convinced it would be Santiago. By Monday, June 20, they could see the jagged, barren mountains rising up from Cuba's shore. Colonel Wood marveled at their beauty and said they reminded him of the ranges he had traversed in Arizona and Sonora, Mexico. Roosevelt thought they looked like mountains he had seen in Montana.

As Wood and Roosevelt gazed at the coast, J. Ogden Wells lay on the hurricane deck sunning with other troopers. He thought for a moment of the day's date and suddenly realized that if he had not enlisted, he would be taking his final exams at Harvard on this very day.

Wells had no regrets, however. "I feel that I am where I ought to be," he jotted in his diary, "and although the life is a hard one, I would not return to college if I could for I could not then be true to my ideal."

About midday, the *Yucatan*, the transport *City of Washington*, and their escort caught up with some of the fleet off Guantánamo Bay (recently captured by U.S. Marines) and continued steaming west until some fifteen miles from Santiago. Early the next morning, June 21, it began to rain; a good-sized storm was brewing. Worried that a severe gale could potentially drive the ship too close to the shore, the *Yucatan's* captain took his boat farther out to sea. Those Rough Riders brave enough to stick their heads out from under cover watched a serpentine white column form over the ocean and reach skyward—a waterspout. As the men looked on in awe, a small funnel dropped down on each side of it. The *Yucatan* and the other transports gave the ominous weather phenomenon a wide berth.

Late that afternoon, the Rough Riders got their first view of the famed Castillo del Morro, an imposing seventeenth-century fortification guarding the mouth of Santiago Bay. Rear Admiral Sampson wanted Shafter to attack this fortress and another one across the outlet. If these two defenses could be captured, the navy would be able to remove the submarine mines unmolested. Shafter wisely declined; his orders were to take Santiago's garrison, not throw men against stone ramparts.

After consulting with General Calixto Garcia of the *insurrectos*, Shafter decided to land most of his army, including the Rough Riders, at the small village of Daiquirí, about fifteen miles east of Santiago Bay. Prior to the landing, Sampson's warships would shell the shoreline and village, where an American mining company had a small dock and a high pier for offloading iron ore. A Cuban force of one thousand men would circle in from the east to cut off the escape of the Spanish soldiers.

The night before the landing seemed the perfect time for some of the Rough Riders to get their revenge on the extortionists among the *Yucatan's* cooks. Having salivated for two weeks over what was in the

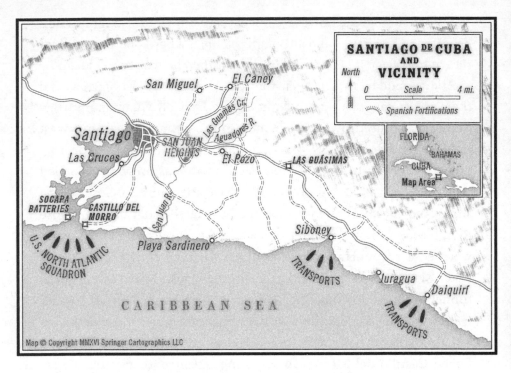

ship's galley, they secretly forced their way in. A few of the troopers were old hands at chuck-wagon cooking and knew how to turn out a decent biscuit. So bags of flour were slit open, dough prepared, and in no time at all, plump biscuits were in the oven. The pans kept coming all through the night, and as the men had also found large cans of "imitation" preserves, the famished troopers stuffed themselves on biscuits and jelly.

Reveille sounded at 3:30 A.M. on June 22. In the hour before breakfast, the Rough Riders gathered their gear and checked weapons and ammunition. Orders called for each man to carry his blanket roll with shelter tent and poncho, a haversack with three days' field rations, a full canteen, and one hundred cartridges. Including his Krag-Jorgensen, a trooper would be carrying at least sixty pounds.

The landing operation was to commence at daybreak, but that came and went and the transports were just then moving in on Daiquirí. About 8:00 A.M., the men of the *Yucatan* crowded on deck and heard the booming of gunboats shelling the coast several miles to the west. This was a feint, to deceive the Spaniards as to the actual landing place. Then, at 9:40 A.M., the bombardment of Daiquirí began.

"The valleys sent back the reports of the guns in long, thundering echoes that reverberated again and again," observed J. Ogden Wells, "and the mountainside began at once to spurt up geysers of earth and branches of broken bushes. The blockhouse [one of several] was demolished, and the thatched shacks were soon bright bonfires. It was the grandest sight I ever witnessed, and I could hardly realize that the shots were fired in anger and that the warships were searching for hidden batteries." In the middle of the navy's fireworks, Ben Colbert scribbled in his diary. The whole regiment, he wrote, was whistling "A Hot Time in the Old Town." After thirty minutes, the big guns fell silent. A line of several small boats, filled with men of the Eighth Infantry, steadily made its way to the shore. But before they reached the dock, mounted *insurrectos* galloped down the beach waving a large Cuban flag. Daiquirí was secure. In fact, the few hundred Spanish defenders had evacuated early that morning. The fires seen from the transports had actually been set by the retreating Spaniards.

The landing of the rest of the army was just as disorganized as its boarding in Tampa. There were not nearly enough landing boats to go around, even after borrowing the tenders of the warships, and although Shafter had set up in advance the order in which each unit was to disembark, it was not working out that way. Further complicating things was Daiquirí's tiny dock (twenty-five by forty feet). Partially burned by the Spaniards, who also removed most of its planks, it could handle only a few boats at a time. Roosevelt waited and fumed.

Shortly before noon, the USS *Vixen*, a converted yacht, steamed near the *Yucatan*. Its captain, Lieutenant Alexander Sharp Jr., hailed Roosevelt, who instantly recognized Sharp as his aide in the Navy Department. Roosevelt had gotten Sharp his position on the *Vixen*.

When the lieutenant offered to help get the Rough Riders landed, Roosevelt and Wood quickly boarded the yacht. There, Sharp told them his black Cuban pilot could guide the *Yucatan* to within a few hundred yards of the shore. Wood and Roosevelt did not have to think twice; the pilot was put aboard the *Yucatan*. Meanwhile, the *Vixen* delivered Wood, Roosevelt, and other officers to the dock.

With the Cuban at the wheel, the *Yucatan* gained a good mile and a half from where it had been waiting, dropping its anchor very near the dock as promised. Roosevelt recalled that when the captains of the other transports saw what the *Yucatan* was doing, they fell in behind "like a flock of sheep."

"In theory it was out of our turn," Roosevelt admitted later, "but if we had not disembarked then, Heaven only knows when our turn would have come, and we did not intend to be out of the fighting if we could help it."

Transferring the Rough Riders from the *Yucatan* to the wharf was not nearly so easy. The recent storms had caused a heavy swell. Hardly noticeable on the big transports, it was treacherous at the dock, the water rising and dropping six to ten feet at a time and sometimes breaking over it. When a landing boat arrived alongside, the officers and men on board waited for the water to reach its highest point, when they would quickly fling their carbines, sabers, haversacks, and blanket-roll packs up on the dock before the boat dropped down again. When the next wave came, they leaped for the waiting arms of their comrades, who pulled them onto the dock.

None of the Rough Riders failed to make the jump, but plenty of carbines, revolvers, bugles, canteens, and hats did. As the carbines were irreplaceable, Charles Knoblauch and a few others stripped down and spent the afternoon diving from the dock and retrieving the weapons and other equipment from the sea floor.

Roosevelt and O'Neill remained at the dock to assist not only the Rough Riders but the other regiments coming in. O'Neill was just steps away when two black troopers, Buffalo Soldiers, of the Tenth

Cavalry slipped on the wet planking as they made their jump and fell into the churning water between the boat and the dock. Their heavy ammunition belts quickly pulled them down. The Arizona captain dived in fully clothed to save them; Knoblauch jumped right behind him. After several tense seconds, the two Rough Riders came up for air and then dived again—and again. It was as if the sea had swallowed the black soldiers. Their bodies washed up on the beach the next morning, the Fifth Corps's first casualties.

As boatload after boatload of troopers came in, their small crafts bobbing and pitching in the blue surf, three Rough Riders were already struggling up a steep, rocky hill overlooking Daiquirí. They carried a large silk American flag rolled on a long wooden pole. The flag had been hand-stitched in Phoenix by members of the Woman's Relief Corps and presented to the Arizona squadron by the governor. The ladies had not been able to get a proper cord and tassels in time so they had substituted long red, white, and blue ribbons.

Daiquirí's highest blockhouse stood on the hill's summit, some three hundred feet above the beach. Although the navy had done its best to destroy it, when the dust had cleared, it was still very much intact. The Rough Riders slowly made their way toward this blockhouse, while soldiers below and on the transports carefully watched their progress. After about thirty minutes, the troopers reached the crest, where they were soon joined by three other men. One man unfurled the flag and began waving it while another was seen climbing the blockhouse's steep tin roof. Suddenly, the flag appeared at the top of the blockhouse, flying straight out from the pole.

Troop B's Captain James McClintock was one of those watching as the flag began flapping in the wind. The distance made it difficult to tell what flag it was—until he spotted the fluttering ribbons. "Yell, you Arizona men," he shouted, "that's our flag!"

The Rough Riders yelled—as did the rest of the army. One of the bands began playing "My Country, 'Tis of Thee," and soon the air was filled with the steam whistles of the transports and warships and the firing of carbines and revolvers.

That afternoon, members of the Rough Riders met up with the *insurrectos,* who greeted them warmly and handed them coconuts and cigarettes. When the troopers tried to pay, their money was refused. "No! No! We are brothers," the Cubans told them, "what is ours is yours, take all you wish." The Rough Riders gave them hardtack in exchange, which the Cubans were happy to get. One woman from the village, leading three children, went from trooper to trooper, asking for hardtack. In the folds of her dress she had collected nearly a hundred of the hard crackers.

This was the Rough Riders' first good look at the Cuban fighting force, and although their opinions varied, most were not impressed. More than a few were appalled. "They were a motley looking crowd," J. Ogden Wells wrote in his diary, "big, black fellows with shiny bodies, most of them only half clad and some nearly naked." To Roosevelt, the Cubans were "a crew of as utter tatterdemalions as human eyes ever looked on armed with every kind of rifle in all stages of dilapidation. It was evident, at a glance, that they would be no use in serious fighting."

What the Rough Riders failed to consider was that the *insurrectos* had not been underfed for only two weeks, as they had been; these freedom fighters had been suffering from a lack of nutrition for years. They did not have a true commissary, and they had largely been forced to live off the land. And there was no such thing as a quartermaster. The jungle chewed up clothing of any kind, and it was no wonder theirs was in tatters or nonexistent. And for them, clothing was not easily replaced.

But a few Rough Riders were able to see beyond the Cubans' appearance. After noting their shortcomings, including that there were a number of young boys in their ranks, one Arizona trooper observed that they were "all imbued with confidence and are therefore good soldiers." And Tom Hall, the regiment's adjutant, pointed out

A typical Cuban insurrecto. *Note the condition of his clothing.*
(Author's Collection.)

that "after all, they kept three hundred thousand Spaniards guessing for three years—no slight achievement."

The Rough Riders, five hundred and sixty strong, set up their camp a few hundred yards from the shore, just in back of the village. Thick jungle grew on one side of the camp, and a stagnant pool of water lined with palm trees bordered the other. To their immediate front, the Tenth Cavalry was busy making its camp. The Tenth was one of two black cavalry regiments in Shafter's army, the other being the

Ninth. There were also two black infantry regiments, the Twenty-Fourth and the Twenty-Fifth. The Spaniards would call them *Yankees ahumados*: smoked Yankees.

Back in Florida, these Buffalo Soldiers were not allowed to wash where white men washed or drink where white men drank. If a black barber had white customers, they couldn't get a shave. And they certainly weren't allowed to enjoy the dining rooms at the Tampa Bay Hotel. Things were going to be a little different in Cuba, for everyone.

Colonel Wood instructed the men not to put up their dog tents but to sleep that night on their packs with their carbines at their side. There was still plenty of daylight left, though, so the Rough Riders explored the village, went for swims in the ocean, and thought about supper. Royal A. Prentice, of Troop E, was lucky enough to catch an old hen and, along with some sweet bell peppers, made chicken soup. It was a welcome change from the rations on the transport, but try as they might, he and his squad mates couldn't chew the tough meat from the old bird and spit it out. Others were content with their hardtack, beans, and coffee—and coconuts, which were an added treat.

As the men gradually settled down for the night, some sat cross-legged near the fires writing letters home and making diary entries. Ben Colbert, reflecting on the days he and the men of Troop F had spent at sea, wrote, "I may some day forget the *Maine* but I shall *never* forget the *Yucatan*."

Most of the Rough Riders were able to sleep well that first night in Cuba. Despite the dampness, the ground was a welcome soft bed after sleeping on the hard wooden deck of the transport.

Sometime during the night, Royal A. Prentice awoke to feel something heavy moving over his body. Startled, he stopped breathing. The crewmembers on the transport had warned him, and anyone else they could corral, about man-crushing boa constrictors that were so prevalent on this island—as were the giant, coconut-throwing monkeys. Prentice's bunkie, who had been lightly sleeping, woke up when Prentice's breathing stopped. He asked Prentice what was the matter.

"At that time," Prentice recalled, "the weight lifted, and I told him a snake at least thirty feet long had just crawled over me." The bunkie started to laugh—until he felt something begin to crawl over him. He let out a yell, and both men jumped to their feet.

Their comrades raced over with matches and quickly discovered the "snake": a large land crab. After a little cursing, everyone stumbled back to their places.

The men woke on the morning of June 23 to a heavy dew and clear skies. There were still some six thousand of Shafter's men to land. While the boats went back and forth between the transports and the dock, those Rough Riders without any immediate orders began improving their camp. Some Cubans showed them how to make a simple covering, or lean-to, from palm leaves and foliage, and soon there were dozens of jungle shelters scattered about the camp. The men even built a palm-thatched bower for Wood and Roosevelt's headquarters.

The morning also saw the offloading of the horses and mules, which consisted of shoving the frightened animals out the side hatches of the transports. One after another, they plunged into the surf, not sure which way to swim. The animals milled about in circles; some swam out to sea. Finally, a few of the mule skinners on the beach began ringing small bells. Pack mules were trained to follow a bell mare, and they swam toward the sound. Once a few of the mules made it onto the beach and were herded together, most of the other animals in the water were able to see them and swam to the same place. Many of the horses had to be tethered together and towed close to the shore.

Roosevelt's two horses were not pushed out the side but were brought up from the ship's hold using a hoist, just like cargo. Roosevelt watched anxiously from the dock as Rain-in-the-Face, a large band around his belly, was slowly raised by a cable. Once the horse was high enough to clear the side of the ship, the spar with its dangling steed was swung out over the water. As Rain-in-the-Face was lowered, however, a vicious wave crashed against him, flipping him into the churning surf. The dazed animal, unable to recover, drowned before anything could be done.

Albert E. Smith, the cameraman with the Vitagraph Company, vividly remembered the lieutenant colonel's reaction: "Roosevelt, snorting like a bull, split the air with one blasphemy after another to the indescribable terror of the young crewmen."

These crewmen, realizing the next horse, Little Texas, was Roosevelt's as well, became all nerves. "With the greatest care, they banded the horse," recalled Smith. "Before each pull at the hoist, opinions were exchanged and judgments rendered, until it seemed that if the animal did not collapse from the strain of sheer suspension it would surely die from starvation."

"Stop that goddamned animal torture!" Roosevelt shouted, which did nothing for the crewmen's nerves, nor did it cause them to increase their overly cautious pace. Finally, Little Texas was lowered into the water, and the band around its belly released. All watched as the horse swam safely to shore. The crewmen were happy not to be in Roosevelt's steely glaze and let out a long sigh of relief.

At 1:00 P.M., just as the Rough Riders got the camp to their liking, Wood received orders to be ready to move at a moment's notice. Siboney, on the coast eight and a half miles to the west, had been occupied that morning by infantry under Major General Henry Lawton. Three miles beyond the village, Cubans under General Demetrio Castillo Duany had fought a brief skirmish with the retreating Spanish rearguard. Nine Cubans had been wounded, one mortally. Major General Joseph Wheeler, commander of Shafter's Cavalry Division, sensed a much bigger fight was near, and he was going to make damn sure his cavalry was in it.

Thirty-three years before, Wheeler had led a cavalry corps in the Civil War, but then he had worn a coat of Confederate gray. They had called him "Fightin' Joe." When the Spanish-American War broke out, he was sixty-one years old and a member of Congress from Alabama, but he anxiously sought a commission, and McKinley gave it to him. The quintessence of a reunited North and South, Wheeler was short, only five feet two inches tall, and looked older than he was with his white beard and balding head, but Roosevelt thought him "a regular game-cock."

At 1:30, the order came to start the Rough Riders on the road to Siboney. The troopers hurriedly knocked down their shelters and stamped out fires, clipped on their thick ammunition belts, and slipped on haversacks and packs.

Some of the mules were still on the transports, so the Rough Riders were only allotted eighteen for provisions and ammunition—the regiment had had close to two hundred when it arrived in Tampa. Wood refused to give the chief surgeon, Henry La Motte, a pack animal for his two medical cases, and when La Motte made the mistake of saying he didn't want to go without them, Wood ordered him to stay behind. La Motte's assistant surgeon, First Lieutenant James Robb Church, a former Princeton football standout, and his stewards would march with the regiment, packing what medical supplies they could on their backs. (After the regiment left, La Motte scrounged up two mules. So that he would have one to ride, he removed from their backs baggage and bedding belonging to several officers, including Roosevelt.)

The situation was so desperate that Wood told the mule skinners to use one of his two saddle horses, a thoroughbred Kentucky mare, to haul the headquarters mess kit. Roosevelt was particularly distressed. A good amount of the regiment's equipment was still in the *Yucatan's* hold, including most of the saddles. There was no saddle for Little Texas, and the *Yucatan* was now out of reach. Roosevelt's "wrath was boiling, and his grief was heart-breaking," recalled war correspondent Edward Marshall. Marshall came to the rescue and loaned his own saddle to Roosevelt. Back in Tampa, Shafter had refused to allow the journalists' horses on the transports, but Marshall had already carried his saddle aboard his ship.

The march began at about 3:00 P.M., and the day had become a scorcher. The men had spent two weeks on the transport with hardly any exercise and inadequate rations, and they were understandably soft. And quite a few of them had still not gotten their "land legs" back.

A good number of the Rough Riders had lived most of their lives on a saddle bronc, so being afoot was already a challenge in itself. Oklahoma cowpuncher Bill McGinty, a favorite of the regiment, was one of these. "McGinty is a little bow-legged red-headed man who looks stupid," Arthur F. Cosby wrote his mother. "He cannot drill, he cannot keep step in marching, but put him on a horse and he is a wonder. He has had his head completely shaved and looks funnier than ever." As McGinty struggled to keep up, even he admitted he was "a better stepper on horseback than on foot."

The "road" to Siboney was really just a mountain path, and it was hardly that in places. The column started out four men abreast, but, as the jungle closed in, it changed to two abreast, and before long, the men were trudging along in single file.

As the afternoon wore on, they strained under the weight of their blanket-roll packs, which caught on the overhanging limbs and brush, causing many a trooper to lose his balance and tumble to the ground. When the men came to a clearing, the sun bore down like a furnace, and their packs seemed to get heavier and heavier. "At last we could stand it no longer," wrote J. Ogden Wells, "and we began to throw away our blankets; after the blankets went cans of meat, then our coats and underclothes until some only had their guns and ammunition left, for these were essentials."

At some point in the march, Roosevelt looked at his plodding men and pulled on Little Texas's reins. "Boys," he said, "this won't do; I'm going to walk with you." He slid off his horse and led it the rest of the way.

Five hours after leaving Daiquirí, the regiment marched through Siboney. A squadron each of the First and Tenth Cavalries came up behind them. More than a few Rough Riders noticed that the campsite selected for the cavalry was far beyond that of the infantry division. "It was then we realized we had been racing," wrote J. Ogden Wells, "racing to get ahead of Lawton and his infantry."

Shafter intended for Lawton and Wheeler to remain in the vicinity of Siboney, at least until he could land the rest of his men, horses, and mules, as well as his supplies. And he had clearly designated Lawton's division to be in the lead. Wheeler decided to take a broad view of Shafter's orders. And with Shafter on the *Seguranca*, Wheeler was the senior officer at the front. The enemy was less than four miles away, and his dismounted cavalry was now perfectly poised to strike the first blow. Fightin' Joe had not come all the way to Cuba to sit and wait.

At about 9:00 P.M., Brigadier General Samuel B. M. Young, commander of Wheeler's Second Brigade, which included the Rough Riders, summoned Wood. Young had just come from a meeting with General Wheeler at the home of General Duany. Duany had drawn the Americans a map that showed the position of the Spaniards when his Cubans had attacked them that morning. The place was named for the bushy trees that grew there: Las Guásimas. Duany believed the enemy had at least fifteen hundred men, but they could have been reinforced since that morning. Young told Wood that Wheeler had issued orders to march on the Spaniards at daylight.

Wood walked back to his camp to find Roosevelt. Several Rough Riders were gathered around fires drying their uniforms, which had become soaked with sweat during the march. But then a typical tropical rainstorm had cut loose just before they had finished supper, pouring down steadily for well over an hour.

It was nearly midnight, and Roosevelt was trying to get some sleep when Wood nudged him awake. Roosevelt listened eagerly as Wood went over the plan of attack. As they talked in low voices, they noticed Captain Capron standing alone at the headquarters fire, which had pots of coffee and food. The two colonels joined Capron and gave him the welcome news as they ate.

Capron, hardly able to contain his excitement, requested that his Troop L have the forward position in the morning, and Wood gladly gave it to him. They would be marching through thick jungle, and that would give the Spaniards an advantage. With Capron, his best officer, in the lead, Wood felt confident the advance would be as safe as possible.

Wood later recalled: "We decided that nothing should be said of the advance to the other officers or men, as I feared it would prevent their getting a sound sleep. . . . In this matter, Capron agreed with me, and just as I was leaving said, 'Well, even if we don't sleep tonight, there will be a great many of us who will get a long sleep before tomorrow night.'"

Chapter Five

Vultures Overhead

*The day that Roosevelt can go into battle with
them will likely be the happiest of his life.*

CHICAGO TRIBUNE

Friday, June 24, 1898
Rough Rider camp outside Siboney

A bugle sounded reveille well before sunup. "It was dark as pitch," wrote J. Ogden Wells, "and it seemed as if I had hardly closed my eyes."

Their shoulders aching and legs stiff and sore, the men slowly got up from the wet ground and stretched and groaned. After a quick breakfast, the men who had not tossed their packs during the march of the day before went through them and got rid of everything but the most essential items. They now knew what to expect from a long jungle tramp, and some even split their blankets in half to lighten their loads.

But whatever attention they were giving their fatigue and soreness was offset by their anticipation of meeting the enemy. That morning Wood told a few men that today they would "smell powder," and his words had raced through the regiment. When some troopers asked

Roosevelt about it, he flashed his teeth and promised they would have some "fun" within two hours.

The troopers assembled for roll call, which found the ranks a little thinned out—a number of men had not yet recovered from their exertions of the previous day. As each enlisted man's name was methodically called in the different troops, Wood and Roosevelt tended to their mounts and made sure the saddle cinches were tight. At 6:00 A.M., Wood gave the order to move out.

Correspondents Richard Harding Davis and Edward Marshall were sticking close to the head of column that morning. The thirty-four-year-old Davis, tall and masculine, wrote for the *New York Herald* and *Scribner's Magazine*. He was also a Roosevelt chum. As an author himself, the lieutenant colonel enjoyed the company of well-known and like-minded writers, and Davis was the most celebrated war correspondent of the day. Marshall, twenty-eight years old, was employed by Hearst's *New York Journal*. Stephen Crane of the *World* and two others barely got onshore in time at Siboney to catch the tail end of the regiment. They were all keenly aware that stories about the Rough Riders sold papers.

The regiment followed a rough trail for more than six hundred feet up the steep ridge behind their camp, climbing over jagged limestone rocks and sometimes having to grab on to shrubs to pull themselves up. Wood and Roosevelt had no choice but to lead their horses. At least a half dozen times, the men were forced to stop to catch their breath; a few fell out and went no farther. Finally reaching the ridge's summit, they were rewarded with a spectacular view of Siboney and its blue-green inlet full of transports, far below them.

"Delicate bugle calls floated softly up to us like blasts from fairy trumpets," wrote Edward Marshall, "and the squalor of the Cuban town at our feet was gilded into glory by the morning sun."

Here on the ridge top, the Rough Riders met up with several of General Lawton's infantrymen, who had been stationed there as pickets the night before to guard against a Spanish attack. "The information had leaked out that we were advancing against the enemy and

Roosevelt and war correspondent Richard Harding Davis.
(Author's Collection.)

soon going to have a fight," recalled Colonel Wood, "and as we passed these troops all sorts of good wishes were showered upon us."

As the Rough Riders marched forward, they were now on a lush rolling tableland with large palms and beautiful flowering vines that formed a canopy above them. A thick undergrowth of tall grasses with occasional cactus and yucca crowded each side of the trail, the yucca's long, thin pointed leaves earning it a name that now seemed particularly appropriate: "Spanish Bayonet." Roosevelt was an accomplished naturalist, and he marveled at the many jungle birdsongs he heard, recognizing several, from the common mourning dove to the brush cuckoo.

Occasionally the men would break out of the trees into a small glade, the green foliage appearing almost fluorescent in the direct sunlight. To the east, they could glimpse the treetops sloping down to a valley about a mile away. Down in that valley, screened from view by the jungle, marched four troops each of the Tenth and First U.S. Cavalries—464 men—with three Hotchkiss mountain guns. This column was under General Young's command.

The valley road Young's men traveled and the lesser-used ridge trail over where the Rough Riders marched paralleled each other for approximately four miles until they joined near where the valley road (the main route to Santiago) went over a pass in the hills. This place was Las Guásimas. If all went according to plan, Young would attack the enemy from the front while Wood hit their flank, the two assaults preferably coming at the same time. It seemed fairly straightforward, but it would be impossible for Young and Wood to communicate with each other on the march, and there were many unknowns. Would the Spaniards be where they expected them? How strong were they? It would be, as Young later characterized the two American columns, a "reconnaissance in force."

Today was Captain Allyn Capron's twenty-seventh birthday, and as promised, his Troop L, approximately sixty men, marched in the lead, most of the time in single file due to the heavy jungle. Six point guards with two Cuban guides carefully scouted two hundred yards in advance of the rest of his troop.

Suddenly, Capron's men encountered two soldiers of the Twenty-Second U.S. Infantry, scouts for General Lawton, quickly coming down the trail.

"Boys, the Spaniards are ahead of us," one of the scouts said, explaining that they had heard the enemy soldiers working on their entrenchments during the night.

A few minutes later, one of Capron's point men came back and told the captain they had come across the body of a Cuban, presumably killed in the fight of the day before. More important, they believed they had spotted a blockhouse. Capron called a halt and then hurried down the trail to find Wood, who was riding two hundred yards behind Troop L.

Wood, wondering why the column had stopped, was trotting his horse toward the front when he saw Capron approaching. He calmly listened to the captain's report, and as Capron returned to the head of the column, Wood gave the order "Silence in the ranks," which in itself was hardly silent as it passed from troop to troop behind him. Then came "Load chambers and magazines," and the men flipped open the box magazines of their Krags, dropped in five cartridges, and worked the carbines' bolts to chamber rounds, the clinking of the cartridges and the sharp metallic clicks of the bolt actions echoing up and down the trail.

There was a long pause as the men waited for the next order. Already tired and hot, many sat down on the ground and started fanning themselves with their hats. The sweat glistened on their faces; some of them slowly chewed on long blades of grass. The men "were totally unconcerned," a surprised Roosevelt recalled, "and I do not think they realized that any fighting was at hand." He was amused to overhear one group "discussing in low murmurs, not the Spaniards, but the conduct of a certain cowpuncher in quitting work on a ranch and starting a saloon in some New Mexican town."

Roosevelt, leaning on Little Texas, began chatting with Edward Marshall about a luncheon they had attended at the Astor House in New York. As they spoke, Roosevelt glanced over at the strands of barbed wire on the ground—wire fencing lined each side of the trail here. He walked over and picked up an end and studied it carefully.

"Great Scott!" Roosevelt said. "This wire has been cut today."

"What makes you think so?" Marshall asked.

"The end is bright and there has been enough dew, even since sunrise, to put a light rust on it, had it not been lately cut."

Wood had gone to the front of the column a second time and

returned when Roosevelt approached him with a concern he had just then received from the chief surgeon.

"Colonel," he said, saluting, "Doctor La Motte reports that the pace is too fast for the men, and that over fifty have fallen out from exhaustion."

"I have no time to bother with sick men now," Wood snapped.

Roosevelt, surprised by Wood's tone, replied, "I merely repeated what the surgeon reported to me."

"I have no time for them now," Wood tried to explain, this time less sharply. "I mean that we are in sight of the enemy."

Wood gave orders to deploy the troops on each side of the trail and to prepare to advance. Roosevelt was to take the right wing, and Major Alexander Brodie, the old Indian fighter, the left. With the stragglers and a detachment left on the coast, the regiment numbered less than five hundred men.

Meanwhile, Troop L's point guard with their Cuban guides moved forward slowly and cautiously. Capron followed several yards behind, and the rest of Troop L was farther back still. The calls of the mourning doves now sounded oddly different and more frequent.

The trail crested a knoll and led the point guard down a long slope. It was nearly impossible to make out anything in the thick foliage, although the men could see down the trail and occasionally through small breaks in the trees. Then they saw them: Spanish soldiers with their distinctive, sombrero-like straw hats were standing about three hundred yards away. The troopers dropped to the ground on each side of the path. Someone noticed their Cuban guides had disappeared.

Twenty-three-year-old Tom Isbell, part Cherokee Indian and son of a deputy U.S. marshal, crawled ahead until he was only sixty yards from the Spaniards. He drew a bead on one who was standing away from the others and pulled the trigger. The carbine cracked and Isbell saw the Spaniard's gun fly up in the air and the man topple over. Isbell quickly worked the Krag's bolt and ejected the brass shell casing and put it in his pocket—a souvenir of the first kill of the war. A second later, the Spaniards answered, or as Isbell described it, "hell opened."

A storm of bullets zipped through the brush, one passing through Isbell's neck. "I don't know how many shots were fired at me," Isbell said later, "but it seemed to me the entire Spanish army was shooting right at me."

At the sound of the gunfire, Wood, dismounted now, walked quickly forward, listening intently to make sure the shots were coming from enemy rifles. Satisfied that they were, he continued with his deployment. The Rough Riders then advanced on the double-quick. Alternately, as each troop reached Wood and Roosevelt, they were directed off to one side of the path or the other. Troops F, D, and E were sent to the left while G, K, and A went to the right.

Wood was as stone-faced as ever while Roosevelt was on fire with excitement. He "jumped up and down, literally, I mean, with emotions evidently divided between joy and a tendency to run," remembered Edward Marshall. As the second troop of Roosevelt's wing filed through the opening in the barbed-wire fence, he joined it, his orderly close behind leading Little Texas.

Marshall watched Roosevelt slip into the jungle and later remained convinced that he had witnessed a moment of incredible transformation. For when Roosevelt stepped through that fence, "he became the most magnificent soldier I have ever seen," Marshall wrote. "It was as if that barbed-wire strand had formed a dividing line in his life, and that when he stepped across it he left behind him in the bridle path all those unadmirable and conspicuous traits which have so often caused him to be justly criticized in civic life."

But Roosevelt had little idea where he was leading his men—or where they were leading him. He could hear the gunfire, which was increasing at a frightful rate, but he could only see a few feet ahead of him in the dense undergrowth. Even when he could see a distance, the Spanish Mausers used smokeless powder, so there was nothing to give away their positions.

Suddenly bullets began punching holes in the palm leaves and striking tree limbs, splattering like rain. The 173-grain Mauser bullets traveled at 2,296 feet per second and made a sound, according to journalist Marshall, "like 'zzzzz-eu.' It begins low, goes up high, and then drops, and stops suddenly on the 'eu.' "

Roosevelt jerked his head around to see who the Spaniards were shooting at. "Then it dawned on us," he recalled, "that we were the target."

A bullet struck a palm next to Little Texas, the bark splinters causing the horse to pitch and buck against the tree. Roosevelt's orderly, holding tight to the reins, was able to calm the animal, but a visibly worried Roosevelt ran up to Little Texas and hurriedly undid the buckle on the saddlebag nearest the palm.

"They haven't hurt the nag, Sir," said the orderly.

"I know," Roosevelt snapped, "but blast 'em, they've smashed my specs!"

Roosevelt told the orderly to stay put with his horse; he wouldn't need the mount. He then ordered his wing to face left and, except for those men held in reserve, deploy in a skirmish line.

This fight would be nothing like those old Currier and Ives prints from the Civil War, with lines of men, shoulders pressing close to shoulders. For years now, the tactics against very accurate modern rifles called for soldiers on a firing line to be placed at intervals of three to six yards—less chance of a stray bullet finding a mark if there was open space between the men.

"Scatter out to the right there, quick, you!" Roosevelt shouted as he moved his men forward. "Scatter to the left; look alive, look alive!"

The men of both wings had stepped into a hornets' nest. With great cunning, the Spaniards had established their positions in a large V, which gave them command of both sides of the trail, overlapping the Rough Riders' flanks. The ridge trail may have been the lesser traveled of the two routes, but that's where the Spaniards had chosen to wait. And the most dangerous place that day in the jungle, at least during the fight's first minutes, was the V's point—where Tom Isbell had opened hell.

Captain Capron had started to deploy his troop on both sides of the trail when the shooting began, and he was now in the face of the direct enemy fire he had described in his officers' school on the *Yucatan*. He would be damned if he was going to retreat, but it would be suicide for his single troop to attempt to push through the enemy line. The Spaniards were entrenched and had two machine guns that were spewing lead across wide swaths of jungle. All Capron could do was hold his ground until the rest of the regiment could come up in support.

Capron, his Model 1892 Colt revolver in his hand, ordered his men to lie down or find cover. But Capron stood fearlessly in the trail, all five feet eleven inches of him, as Mauser bullets made the jungle air sing around him. Twenty-one-year-old Sergeant Dillwyn Bell stood next to his captain.

"Give me your gun a minute," Capron said to Bell, at the same time holstering his Colt.

Bell handed Capron his Krag, and then Capron knelt down into a prone position, took careful aim, and fired. A Spaniard crumpled. Capron chambered another round and fired again. Another Spaniard dropped in the trench. Bell picked up a carbine from a dead comrade and began shooting as well.

Tom Isbell, just a few yards from Capron and Bell and slowly bleeding from the wound in his neck, was firing too. And he began taking more hits. A bullet tore into his left thumb, followed by another striking his right side, near the hip, which passed cleanly through. A few minutes later, a bullet pierced a different spot in his neck and lodged against bone. Some of these wounds felt like pinpricks; others Isbell didn't notice until he saw the blood. But he would not leave his position, and over the next several minutes, he was hit three more times: in the left hand, a gash to his head, and yet again in the neck. He held his position until he began to feel faint from loss of blood.

It seemed to the men of Troop L that they were fighting the battle all by themselves. There was no sign of support from the other troops. Suddenly Capron felt a sting in his left shoulder, and his body stiffened. A Mauser bullet had traveled through his torso and exited from his abdomen. Capron, still conscious, guessed the wound was mortal. A few of his men rushed up to him and wanted to carry him to the rear, but he turned them away.

"Let me see it out, I want to see it all," Capron said. "I'd sooner lie here."

Ed Culver, of Muskogee, Indian Territory, had been part of the point guard with Isbell and was lying with his head near the edge of the trail, his body stretched across it. Sergeant Hamilton Fish Jr., six feet two and three-quarter inches tall and the grandson of former Secretary of State Hamilton Fish, ran up to Culver and jokingly said, "Old boy, you've got a good place."

"I have got a good place," a smiling Culver replied.

Fish and Culver, one a society boy and the other a cowboy, had become buddies after Fish transferred to Troop L back in Tampa, just before the regiment left for Cuba. Both men were proud to be in Capron's troop. Only the day before, Fish had written his mother about the captain, saying, "I would follow him to hell."

Fish plopped down in the grass a foot from Culver and began firing his Krag. "The sun was just bilin' down on us," remembered Culver. "The Spaniards was pepperin' us from each side."

Fish had just gotten off his second shot when he felt the bullet punch into his left side. It made a loud sound like a slap. Fish gasped and then shouted, "I am wounded, I am wounded!"

"And I am killed!" blurted Culver.

Fish turned to look at Culver and then struggled to lift himself on his left elbow.

"The same bullet hit both of us," Fish said. "Give me your canteen, old boy."

Culver passed him the canteen and promptly fainted. When Culver came to, Fish was smiling at him.

"You're all right, old boy," Fish said.

"Sergeant, are you hit hard?" Culver asked.

When Fish didn't answer, Culver reached over and took off his hat. Fish was gone.

The bullet that struck Fish had exited his right side and entered Culver's breast, above the heart, but Culver would survive.

With Capron down, the command of Troop L fell to First Lieutenant John R. Thomas, who walked up and down the line, making sure the men were at their proper distances. But just twenty minutes after Capron fell, a bullet smashed into Thomas's leg, spinning him to the ground. By this time, Wood had brought Troop B up in support, and he saw Thomas go down. He spurred his horse toward the lieutenant, who was grasping his leg. Wood dismounted and told Thomas to take the horse and ride to the rear. But Thomas refused to leave the line. Besides, Thomas said, the boys needed to see their colonel up on his horse in plain sight.

Wood did just that, and even when dismounted, he walked on the side of his horse (named Charles Augustus) facing the enemy trenches—it would be cowardly to use his mount as a shield. In the more open places, the Spaniards could not help but see Wood, and they expended rounds upon rounds of ammunition attempting to strike the colonel.

"The volley firing of the enemy was like clockwork, rapid and of a degree of excellence I have never heard in our service, even in practice," Wood recalled. The bullets were cutting the leaves so that they "were falling like flakes of snow." One Rough Rider said that "if we had been hit as often with bullets as we were with leaves there would have been nothing left of us."

Several men cursed as the bullets buzzed around them.

"Don't swear—shoot!" Wood barked.

Wood's steely nerve this day earned him the nickname The Icebox. Behind that cool façade, though, Wood was cursing himself for not having taken out a $100,000 life insurance policy before leaving home.

———————

"There they are, Colonel; look over there." Richard Harding Davis was standing next to Roosevelt and pointing across a valley to the right. "I can see their hats near that glade."

Roosevelt squinted. He could hear booming farther to the right, the Hotchkiss battery of the Tenth Cavalry. General Young's column had been engaged for some time now.

Roosevelt brought up his binoculars. After a minute, he made out the figures Davis was pointing to and called over four of the regiment's best shots. Roosevelt gave the men an estimate of the range and watched as they flipped up their carbines' ladder sights and adjusted the notched crosspieces. The men fired, the 220-grain bullets of their Krags slicing through the air at two thousand feet per second.

Roosevelt carefully studied the Spaniards for any reaction to the shots, but he saw none. The aim was obviously low. Roosevelt had the men raise their sights' crosspieces and fire again. Still nothing. Again they adjusted the sights as more troopers came up to give it a try. Now Roosevelt saw several Spaniards jump from their positions and run to another spot. The Rough Riders had the range.

The skirmish line slowly advanced, with the men moving from bush to bush and tree trunk to tree trunk, firing at each halt. But the palm trees were little protection, and the Mauser bullets had no trouble punching through the soft, green wood. Roosevelt was standing behind one tree, his head slightly off to the side observing the action, when a bullet slammed into the trunk, sending wood splinters and dust flying into his left eye and ear. Roosevelt rubbed his eye and face until the sting went away, then peered again to the front.

It didn't take long for the Americans' gunfire to drive the Spaniards from their positions and into the cover of the jungle. Soon Roosevelt saw another body of men cross the glade from the right, following the same route as the retreating Spaniards. From a distance, he wasn't able to tell if these were Cuban allies, who were supposed to be attached to Young's column, or if they were more retreating enemy soldiers. Roosevelt ordered his men to hold their fire, and they watched as the figures disappeared on the other side of the glade.

The shooting was beginning to die down now, at least on this part of the field, and after a few minutes, Roosevelt spotted another force very near where he had seen the possible Cubans. He gazed through his binoculars and recognized the black troopers of the Tenth Cavalry. As Roosevelt later learned, the "Cubans" had indeed been Spanish soldiers, who were falling back from the advance of these Regulars.

"I don't know what kind of cavalry they make," one Rough Rider remarked afterward about the black troopers, "but they are a glorious success as infantrymen. There can be no better soldiers in the world, and yet I used to doubt whether the negro could fight with as much dash as the white man."

Wood had instructed Roosevelt to link his wing with General Young's left. Now Roosevelt could see Young's men, but it was a question of whether or not Young's troopers recognized the Rough Riders. Corporal Fredrik Kloumann Lie, a twenty-six-year-old native of Norway, grabbed Troop K's guidon, climbed a nearby tree, and began waving the red-and-white flag back and forth in long sweeps. This, of course, drew the fire of the Spaniards, but Lie continued to wave the guidon until he saw a trooper of the Tenth wave a guidon back at him.

Having connected his skirmish line, thin as it was, with Young, Roosevelt was anxious to find Wood. He was still unsure of the location of the main body of the Spanish army, nor had he received any additional orders. "I was in a mood to cordially welcome guidance," he wrote later, "for it was most bewildering to fight an enemy whom one so rarely saw."

After ordering Troop G, the New Mexico boys under Captain Llewellyn, to follow him, Roosevelt began a fast walk toward the ridge trail, the last place he had seen Wood. Heavy gunfire was coming from that direction. As he pushed through the brush and vines, he regretted wearing the saber that had been presented to him by his friends in the Navy Department. The sword was intended for a cavalryman on horseback, but with Roosevelt on foot, it kept getting between his legs.

Roosevelt reached the trail and turned toward the front, passing the dead and wounded of Troop L, including Hamilton Fish, faceup, his eyes glazed over. He kept moving while the New Mexicans fanned out to the left of the trail. He finally saw Wood up ahead, coolly strolling along the skirmish line leading Charles Augustus. It was a miracle, he thought, that neither Wood nor his horse had received even a scratch.

Wood gave Roosevelt a quick briefing. Not only was Capron mortally wounded, but Troop L's second in command, Lieutenant Thomas, was also out of the fight. Wood had brought up Captain James McClintock's Arizona troop to support Capron's men, but they had hardly deployed on the line when McClintock collapsed with two ugly wounds in his left ankle. They could sorely use their Colt machine guns right now, but the damn packers had skedaddled when the shooting started, leaving the mules with the guns to wander off into the jungle.

As the two talked, Major Brodie came up cradling his left arm. He was indignant about being wounded and refused to leave the line, but it was obvious he was in great pain. When Brodie began to stagger from lightheadedness, Wood forced him to go to the rear. Roosevelt would have to take charge of Brodie's left wing. Go to the extreme left of the line and find the enemy's flank, Wood told Roosevelt, then press forward.

The regiment's hospital stewards had erected makeshift shelters on the trail, in the few places that were level and clear, to serve as a field hospital. The first patient had come on his own two feet: Tom Isbell. He had so many wounds and was covered with so much blood he looked like he had been blasted with a shotgun. But with little more than borrowed bandannas, the stewards patched him up and decided he was able to walk back to Siboney. When Isbell left, one of the attendants remarked, "[I]t isn't fair to call that man one case; he ought to count as a dozen!"

Another man covered with blood that morning was Assistant Surgeon James Robb Church, though none of it was his own. Wood thought he "looked like a butcher." The thirty-one-year-old Church would periodically disappear down the trail and come back with a wounded soldier on his back, the soldier often weighing more than the surgeon. The hike between the front lines and the dressing station was several hundred yards, and the sticky heat was intense, yet Church retrieved five men in this way.

It was risky enough for a surgeon to be near the skirmish line, but Church, who stood more than six feet tall, was frequently on it and even in advance of it, kneeling beside a downed man while his comrades were lying flat on the ground, the Mauser bullets buzzing all around them. And what made Church's actions even more remarkable was that he always seemed to have a grin on his face.

Assistant Surgeon James Robb Church. (R560.3.EL61-027a, Theodore Roosevelt Collection, Houghton Library, Harvard University.)

Rarely did any of the Rough Riders want to leave the fight. When several of the men picked up Lieutenant Thomas of Troop L with a blanket litter, he began thrashing and screaming:

"You're taking me to the front, aren't you? You said you would. They've killed my captain—do you understand? They've killed Captain Capron. The son of a bitch Mexicans! They've killed my captain."

The men carried Thomas toward the rear but assured him they were going to the firing line. All the while, Thomas's blood dripped from the soaked blanket to the grass below, leaving a trail behind them. Then the twenty-two-year old lieutenant became agitated again. He could hear the firing, and it was getting more distant. He violently grabbed at the wrists of the litter bearers.

"For God's sake, take me to the front!" he said. "Do you hear me, I order you; damn you, I order—We must give them hell. They've killed Capron. They've killed my captain."

Fortunately for the men carrying him, and Thomas too, he soon lost consciousness from the heat and blood loss.

George Roland of Troop G, a cowboy from New Mexico, had been struck in the side by a Spanish bullet, but he paid no mind to it and continued to blast away with his Krag. Roosevelt, who was nearby, saw the blood and asked Roland about the wound. Roland answered that it was hardly nothing. Roosevelt, unsatisfied, ordered Roland to come closer. Not only was there an ugly wound, but the bullet had broken at least one of Roland's ribs. Roosevelt ordered him to the hospital.

"After some grumbling he went," Roosevelt recalled, "but fifteen minutes later, he was back on the firing line again and said he could not find the hospital—which I doubted." Roosevelt gave up and let him stay.

Then there were those Rough Riders whom no surgeon could save. Henry Haefner, a miner from Gallup, New Mexico, dropped when a Mauser bullet punched through his hip, traveling across his body through his bowels. It was a mortal wound, but death would come slowly. Two troopers grabbed Haefner's arms and dragged him to a tree, where he propped himself up and asked for his canteen and his rifle. As the line moved forward, Roosevelt would look back and see Haefner methodically firing his Krag, reloading, and firing again.

Richard Harding Davis came upon a slim, clean-shaven trooper stretched out behind a rock. There was a small hole in the center of the soldier's forehead, about two inches above the eyes, but his chest "was heaving with short, hoarse noises." Davis knelt down, took some water from his canteen, and washed the wound and found where it exited at the back of the head. He tried to pour some water into the boy's mouth, but the water rolled off his clenched teeth.

Davis reached into the trooper's blouse pocket and pulled out a thin book—a copy of the New Testament, published by the American Bible Society two years earlier. He flipped it open. Scribbled in pencil on the endpapers was "Tilden Dawson, Nevada, Mo."

"It's no use," came a voice from behind Davis. The journalist turned around to see another young soldier standing in the trail.

"[T]he surgeon has seen him," the soldier said. "He says he is just the same as dead. He is my bunkie; we only met two weeks ago at San Antonio; but he and me had got to be such good friends—But there's nothing I can do now."

The bunkie sat down and began to cry. Davis moved on toward the sound of the guns.

Back on the skirmish line, Wood walked up on a trooper who had been shot through the chest. Blood completely soaked the young man's clothes, but he was somehow still conscious. When he saw his commander, he pulled himself up against a tree and slowly reached out his hand.

"Colonel," he said, "I have only a minute. Can you shake hands and say goodbye?"

Roosevelt found the jungle nearly as thick on the left side of the line as it was on the right, but his men were able to catch occasional glimpses of the enemy through the brush and trees. Richard Harding Davis recalled that the Rough Riders moved forward in "quick, desperate rushes . . . sometimes the ground gained was no more than a man covers in sliding for a base. At other times half a troop would rise and race forward and then burrow deep in the hot grass and fire."

Troop F was at the far end of Roosevelt's left wing, and its men had become too scattered. When it appeared the Spaniards were moving to cut them off from the rest of the line, a Troop F officer yelled, "By the right flank, double time!" Troopers John Winter and William Erwin heard the order and started running to the right, Erwin a little in the lead. Winter and Erwin, both of San Antonio, had met for the first time as Rough Riders and had become close. They had been fighting together most of the morning.

Winter's eyes were on the ground as the two ran past several wounded comrades. The instant Winter looked up at Erwin running ahead of him, a spray of blood splattered his face. "[T]he breath left my body for the moment," Winter later wrote his father, "as the whole top of his head flew up in the air, his skull blown to atoms by an explosive bullet. He fell heavily with a thud, and I ran on past his body, but I knew at last the meaning of the phrase, 'The Art of War.'"

Steadily, the troopers forced the Spanish line back, but each time the enemy retreated, they withdrew just a short distance to another defensive position. As Wood described it in a letter to his wife, the Rough Riders were "beating them back from rock fort to rock fort."

The left wing under Roosevelt had now advanced to where the men could see across a large open area to an old Bacardi rum distillery that included a number of red-tiled buildings. Several Spanish infantrymen were firing from there.

Roosevelt grabbed a Krag from one of his wounded troopers, raised it to his shoulder, and began to shoot. One of the New York Rough Riders looked at Roosevelt, turned to a buddy, and said, "And yet, by jing, a couple o' years ago, we people in New York didn't think Teddy knew enough to review a parade of cops!" He was referring to Roosevelt's time as a New York City police commissioner.

Roosevelt feared he was getting separated from Wood on the right, so he halted his skirmishers five hundred yards from the distillery. The men poured gunfire into the buildings, feverishly working the bolts of their carbines after each shot. Fortunately, the enemy's return fire was high, going over the heads of the Rough Riders.

Roosevelt was worried about his men; he could see they were exhausted. Most had long ago shed their packs and haversacks. Then, over the gunfire, Roosevelt could hear cheering in Wood's direction. That could only mean that Wood's troopers were charging.

"I sprang up and ordered the men to rush the buildings ahead of us," Roosevelt recalled later. "They came forward with a will."

The enemy began running, too—toward Santiago. "The Spaniards naturally could not believe that this thin line [of Rough Riders] which suddenly broke out of the bushes and from behind trees and came cheering out into the hot sunlight in full view, was the entire fighting force against it," explained Richard Harding Davis. "They supposed the regiment was coming close on its heels."

On the other side of the battlefield, the Spaniards were fleeing in front of General Young's force of Buffalo Soldiers and white Regulars—although a few snipers remained behind to pick off any trooper they could spot. Spry old General Wheeler climbed a tree to see if he could spot where these bullets were coming from. "I see them," he soon shouted to his anxious staff below, "they are running, the damn Yankees—no, no, I mean the Spaniards—are running away!"

Roosevelt and his men easily took the vacated buildings to their front. And now the sounds of battle abruptly ceased—no more buzzing Mauser bullets or rhythmic machine-gun fire. Roosevelt again became momentarily confused: "I had not the faintest idea what had happened: whether the fight was over; or whether this was merely a lull in the fight; or where the Spaniards were; or whether we might be attacked again; or whether we ought ourselves to attack somebody somewhere else."

As the men walked in and around the buildings, they stepped on large piles of Mauser shell casings and empty stripper clips. These clips, which held five cartridges each, allowed for extremely fast loading of the bolt-action Mausers, much faster than the Krags, and they explained the extraordinarily heavy firing that had plagued the Rough Riders.

Some troopers had advanced beyond the buildings and into the jungle. Roosevelt ordered the bugler to sound recall. Then he sent several men as pickets to stand watch to their left and out to their front. Another detail went after water—at least twelve men had collapsed from heat exhaustion and dehydration after the last charge.

A few of the boys of Troop E, mostly New Mexicans, thought they were being smart when, early that morning before the march, they had discovered a hogshead of rum near camp and decided to fill their canteens with this native alcohol. They realized their mistake too late, for "the extreme heat created a terrific thirst which the fiery rum would not alleviate," remembered Royal A. Prentice, "and the first call of every wounded man was for water."

As Roosevelt consulted with his officers and rattled off more orders, a trooper came up and reported that Colonel Wood had been killed. This news was a shock, but it was no surprise. Roosevelt had seen with his own eyes how Wood had brazenly exposed himself to the enemy fire. He assumed the report was true, which meant that he now commanded the regiment. After making certain the left wing was in good shape, he started walking briskly toward the right side of the line to see for himself the condition of the other troops. That's when he bumped into a living and breathing Leonard Wood.

The report of Wood's death had come from the regimental adjutant. Tom Hall had panicked when he thought he saw Wood collapse on the firing line. It was actually the journalist Edward Marshall he saw go down (Marshall and Wood were said to be wearing similar shirts), but Hall did not rush to the side of the man he believed was his fallen commander. Instead, he fled back over the trail to Siboney, reporting that Wood had been killed and that he had been ordered to bring up reinforcements. Hall even claimed to have Wood's dying message to his wife.

"Our Adjutant, Hall, apparently retreated," Arthur Cosby wrote his mother, "but he always was hated & we will get him out of the regiment. He is a bully."

Wood confirmed what Roosevelt now suspected: the fight was over. It had lasted roughly two hours and twenty minutes, the first shots coming at approximately 7:20 A.M. With sweltering heat and the confusion of the dense jungle, it had seemed like an eternity for many of the men, and yet it wasn't even close to noon. Regardless of the battle's duration, the Rough Riders were far too played out to pursue the retreating Spaniards. They would make camp near the battlefield, with the next few hours devoted to finding all of their dead and wounded.

As Roosevelt and Wood talked, reinforcements from Siboney appeared, all greatly disappointed that they had missed the first land battle of the campaign. "Every one says it was a wonderfully gallant and brilliant action, etc., etc.," Wood wrote to his wife.

The most gallant of the Rough Riders that day died just after the battle ended. "Have we won?" Captain Capron asked in a faint voice. When told yes, he replied, "Well, I'm glad. It was a good fight." A moment later, he was dead.

It was remarkable how quickly the vultures found the battle's casualties as the hot sun did its work on dead flesh, although this did make it easier to locate the bodies. The birds got to a boy from Troop A before his body could be recovered, and the carrion feeders did what they did to all the corpses: they pecked and tore at the eyes, face, and blood-soaked wounds. Captain Buckey O'Neill viewed the body momentarily with Roosevelt when it was brought in.

"Colonel," O'Neill said reflectively, "isn't it Whitman who says of vultures that 'they pluck the eyes of princes and tear the flesh of kings'?"

Roosevelt, probably the best-read man in Cuba, was stumped, but he knew it wasn't Whitman. Later, Roosevelt concluded that O'Neill must have been thinking of Ezekiel: "Speak unto every feathered fowl. . . . Ye shall eat the flesh of the mighty, and drink the blood of the princes of the earth."

Journalists, some arriving too late for the battle, converged on the Rough Riders, eager to take photos and gather information for their stories. Burr McIntosh, working for *Leslie's Weekly*, was anxious to see the body of Hamilton Fish. He found it lying next to the body of another trooper, Fish's hobnailed boots sticking far out from the army blanket that covered him.

"My first impulse was to steal a picture of the face while no one was looking," the correspondent admitted later, "but I didn't, and am glad of it. However, I removed the blanket from his face for a few brief seconds. There was no sign of pain, only the faint suggestion of the old smile of victory, which I had so often seen."

In 1874, Hamilton Fish's grandfather had used diplomacy as secretary of state to prevent a war with Spain after Spanish authorities had captured and executed several Americans who were transporting Cuban insurrectionists (known as the *Virginius* Affair). Now that man's grandson had died in a war with Spain. The night before his death, young Fish had fretted about what the future might hold. "It would be just my luck," he said, "to be put out of the way in the first scrap, and not see any of the war."

Burr McIntosh resisted the impulse to photograph Fish's face, but he did snap a picture of the two bodies stretched out in the grass, staking his claim to a distasteful scoop: having the "first picture taken after death."

Stephen Crane learned from a trooper that his friend Edward Marshall was "all shot to hell" and found him at the field hospital.

"Hello, Marshall! In hard luck, old man?"

"Yes, I'm done for," Marshall said.

"Nonsense! You're all right, old boy. What can I do for you?"

"Well, you might file my dispatches. I don't mean file 'em ahead of your own, old man—but just file 'em if you find it handy."

Marshall, whose spine had been splintered by a Mauser bullet, had somehow written his report on the fight between moments of intense

Hamilton Fish—the last photo taken of him in his life.
(Author's Collection.)

agony and unconsciousness. Crane not only carried Marshall's dispatch the several miles to the coast and cabled it to the *Journal*, a competing newspaper, but he arranged to have a stretcher sent to the wounded journalist, then walked back to the field hospital to help bring Marshall in the next day.

Most of the war correspondents in Cuba carried some type of sidearm. Marshall and Richard Harding Davis were no exception, but they were the exception when it came to participating in a battle. An excited Marshall was seen firing his revolver several times at the Spanish lines, even though they were well out of range at six hundred yards. Davis, who had lost many hours of sleep over turning down an offered captain's commission, borrowed a Krag and joined in the final charge.

"I knew every other one of them [the Rough Riders], had played football, and all that sort of thing, with them," Davis explained in a letter to his family, "so I thought as an American I ought to help." He ended up firing about twenty rounds in the charge.

In an even more unusual exception, both Marshall and Davis received special commendations in Wood's official report, and General Wheeler endorsed them. Roosevelt actually told Davis he would make him a captain in the regiment any time he wanted it. But no such accolades were given to the two men from the Vitagraph Company. After the wood cabinet of their moving picture camera was splintered by two Mauser bullets, they abruptly decided they had all the footage they needed.

"It appeared to be foolish to go on . . . shooting pictures out in the open, calling to Rough Riders to stand up so that we might get a better shot," explained cameraman Albert E. Smith. "You couldn't operate an old-fashioned tripod camera from a belly position." It was decided that "Vitagraph would retreat," so they hurriedly packed their camera and jumped on the next boat to the States.

Sometime in the afternoon following the fight, two Cubans captured a Spanish captain near the Rough Rider camp (some said he was a spy). The man was brought to Wood and questioned. "We can't understand Americans," the Spaniard is reported to have said. "Cubans run when we shoot; Americans crowd upon our firing line and shoot like hell!" He also told Wood that they would surrender Santiago if the Americans would let them keep their weapons and the warships blockaded in Santiago's harbor.

The interrogation completed, Wood let the Cubans have their prisoner. The *insurrectos* marched him across the road and promptly chopped off his head. "In battle with the Cubans, the Spanish take no prisoners, and, to make it more emphatic, neither do the Cubans," a trooper wrote in a letter home.

That night, the men gathered around their different messes with emotions running between elation for their victory and deep sadness for the loss of friends—eight Rough Riders had been killed and more than forty were wounded. One of the men of Troop L, known for his sweet tenor voice, began to sing "The Vacant Chair," probably the saddest song to come out of the Civil War. "It was enough to choke a man up," one trooper remembered.

Not far from camp, a guard kept watch over the bodies of the fallen, lined up in a row along the trail. Out of the darkness, a solitary figure approached the guard. He was wearing the uniform of a captain of artillery and looked to be in his early fifties. He asked to see the body of Captain Capron, explaining that he was Captain Allyn Capron of the First U.S. Artillery. He was there to see his son's body.

The guard watched as the senior Capron pulled back the blanket covering his son's face. The veteran artilleryman then snapped to attention, his body perfectly erect for several seconds. Next, his right hand came up sharply to his forehead in a salute. Then, without saying a word, Captain Capron turned and walked back down the trail.

Chapter Six

Road to Santiago

I put myself in the way of things happening, and they happened.

THEODORE ROOSEVELT

The Rough Riders buried their dead the next morning, all except Captain Capron, whose body was taken to the coast and interred in a temporary grave overlooking the ocean. The mass grave at Las Guásimas was a long trench, its bottom lined with fresh guinea grass. In it, seven bodies lay side by side, their feet pointing to the east. Over the top was placed a lush blanket of palm leaves. Funeral call came at 10:00 A.M.

Harper's Weekly correspondent John Fox Jr. had arrived too late for the battle, but he was there to witness the funeral: "At the head of the trench stood the chaplain; around it, the comrades of the dead; along the road straggled a band of patient ragged Cubans, and approaching from Santiago a band of starving women and children for whom the soldiers gave their lives. No man could ask a braver end, a more generous cause, or a kindlier grave."

The regiment's chaplain read from the Bible, after which the Rough Riders joined in singing "Nearer, My God, to Thee." Shovelfuls of dirt were tossed on the palm leaves. Chief Trumpeter Emilio Cassi stepped forward and played "Taps," and then came a concluding prayer.

As these teary-eyed men stood silent that morning, their heads bowed, newspaper typesetters across the United States stood in front of the keyboards to their linotype machines typing the stories of the American victory—and casualties—at Las Guásimas for the day's afternoon and evening editions. These stories, as well as all military communications, came via telegraphic dispatches sent from Guantánamo Bay, where an undersea cable ran from there to the island of Haiti. From Haiti, another cable ran direct to New York City, fifteen hundred miles away. Transmission time from Cuba to the United States was roughly twenty minutes.

It was no surprise that the news reports gave the Rough Riders much of the glory, even though the First and Tenth Cavalries under General Young fought equally as hard against the Spaniards entrenched on the valley road. Appearing on the front pages of the *San Francisco Call* and the *Kansas City Journal* was a portrait not of Young or Leonard Wood, but of the Rough Riders' second in command: Theodore Roosevelt.

Yet it was also the Rough Riders who received the lion's share of the criticism, and of that there was plenty, spouted by Regular Army officers and several journalists. Stephen Crane, who walked at the rear of the Rough Rider column when the fight erupted, had particularly harsh words, writing in his June 25 dispatch that "Lieut. Col. Roosevelt's Rough Riders, who were ambushed yesterday, advanced at daylight without any particular plan of action as to how to strike the enemy. The men marched noisily through the narrow road in the woods, talking volubly, when suddenly they struck the Spanish lines." Although Crane praised the men's grit under fire, he blamed the regiment's heavy losses on "the remarkably wrong idea of how the Spanish bushwhack. It was simply a gallant blunder."

The claim that their regiment had been ambushed grated on Wood and Roosevelt, although many Rough Riders wrote letters home in the battle's aftermath saying just that (even Roosevelt devotee Richard Harding Davis painted Las Guásimas as an ambush). Quickly, though, the word became taboo. One Regular Army officer recalled that for a couple of days after the battle, the wounded and sick Rough Riders coming into Siboney all said "they had been ambushed. On the second or third day, however, the same men denied most emphatically that they had been ambushed."

Wood and Roosevelt were both adamant that they had not been surprised. Not only had Wood learned where he would find the Spaniards in his meeting with General Young (who had been shown a map of the enemy's location), but Captain Capron had alerted Wood immediately upon spotting the Spaniards, which had prompted Wood to begin deploying his regiment. It was "a plain standup fight that the Americans knew was coming in plenty of time to avoid it if they wanted to, which they didn't," a bristly Major Brodie told a reporter.

But even though Wood had a very good idea where he would run into the Spaniards, he had no clue about the placement of their lines until it was too late. That wicked V was like walking into the jaws of a trap. A Rough Rider described it in a letter to his mother: "The Spanish let our advance guard march into their midst. . . . The Spaniards were along the side of the trail we were marching in and knew right where we were, but we could not see them on account of the underbrush. There were Spaniards on our front and on [our] right and left flank. They poured a crossfire into us and a fire from straight in front." That sure sounded like an ambush.

Another controversy swirled around the size of the Spanish force at Las Guásimas. The first reports, which came from Cubans and Spanish military documents scattered behind, indicated that the number was around four thousand. The Rough Riders instantly embraced that figure because they were convinced that those hellacious volleys could only have come from thousands of Spanish Mausers. But soon the figure was reduced to two thousand, and then twelve hundred, and there were some who claimed it was no more than six hundred. The correct number was 2,078, but only 1,500 of them had actually participated in the battle.

The small number of men engaged on both sides, as well as the fight's relatively short duration, led some to say it was nothing more than a skirmish. Edward Marshall, whose wound to his spine would cripple him for life, had a short answer for that: "[I]f it was a skirmish, then I wish never to see a battle."

The victory's importance was also questioned, especially when it was later learned that the Spanish force at Las Guásimas had already been ordered to withdraw to the defenses of Santiago, and that it had only been putting up a rearguard action to strike a quick blow on the advancing Americans. According to *Leslie's* correspondent Burr McIntosh, the American victory's primary accomplishment was to get certain officers in the Cavalry Division noticed in the newspapers before anyone else in Shafter's army. Capron, Fish, and the others had died, he angrily declared, all because of General Wheeler's "greed."

The chair of the House Committee on Military Affairs, John A. T. Hull, was outraged by these negative accounts and was quick to condemn the Rough Riders' leaders. Without any firsthand knowledge whatsoever, Hull told a group of reporters in the War Department that "it seems to me Cols. Wood and Roosevelt needlessly led their men into the ambush. . . . It looks like a case of thoughtless, reckless, and impetuous disregard of orders, in which several brave men lost their lives, when there was no occasion for the sacrifice."

Hull didn't know what he was talking about, and most Americans ignored his grandstanding. They were more of a mind with journalist Fox: "The fight was a perfect exhibition of dauntless courage. So let critical lips be dumb."

That dauntless courage did prove one thing—that this regiment of Ivy Leaguers and cowpunchers wasn't just a bunch of pretty boys, that they were capable of withstanding a withering fire as well as any battle-hardened veterans.

"I had often wondered what my feelings would be when the firing began, and bullets were whistling all around," Troop F's Sam Weller wrote his parents. "As it was an experience I had never had, I could hardly imagine just how it would affect me. Now I know how it _did_ affect me. I can say truthfully that I was never less excited nor more composed. The whistling shot seemed to steady my nerve instead of shake it."

Las Guásimas also gave the American army tremendous confidence. "It proved to the men that they could whip the Spaniards if they could get at them," wrote the Fifth Corps's commander, General Shafter. The Spaniards may have been ordered to retreat, but in the end, they had been routed. It was clear from the valuable things they hastily abandoned—wagonloads of ammunition, provisions, clothing, and a number of their dead—that their withdrawal had been anything but orderly.

Above all, though, the Rough Riders got to see how Wood and Roosevelt handled themselves—and their men—during the stress of battle, and their admiration for the colonels had only strengthened.

"Wood sauntered around and looked quite at home," wrote a soldier from Troop D. "Roosevelt stood beside me in the hottest fire and seemed as cool as a cucumber."

Fred Herrig was a cowboy who had traveled all the way from Montana to serve under Roosevelt. Thirty-six years old and a native of Lorraine, France, he had first met Roosevelt fifteen years earlier in Medora, Dakota Territory. Herrig remembered Roosevelt looking like a kid with his eyeglasses and little brown mustache. He "did look too nice for anything," Herrig recalled.

Herrig eventually worked for Roosevelt on his Little Missouri ranches, and the two formed a fast friendship, hunting together many times for deer and bighorn sheep. Herrig especially liked to tell the story of their last hunt, in which Roosevelt killed a magnificent bighorn ram at four hundred yards. It was late November and bitterly cold, and by the time they got back to the ranch with the trophy, it was after midnight and both men's ears were frostbitten. But the next day, as Herrig ran his fingers gingerly over his ears, Roosevelt flashed his famous grin and said, "We can get new skin on our ears, but we'll never get another ram like that one."

When Herrig received a telegram from Roosevelt, telling him to go to San Antonio and join the Rough Riders, Herrig grabbed what he'd need and went straight there. He became a member of Troop K and was very proud when he was selected as a gunner for one of the Colt machine guns. After the Las Guásimas fight, several small detachments from the different troops were sent out to look for the missing mules that still had the Colt guns strapped to their backs. Herrig saw it as a matter of personal pride that he was among those chosen to find them because Roosevelt had talked him up to all the officers as a first-rate hunter.

Toward dusk, he came upon two sets of mule tracks going down a ravine. It was too late to trail them, so he returned to camp without saying a word and went to sleep. He woke the next morning at 3:00 A.M. and started back for the battlefield—there were some skilled trackers from Indian Territory among the Rough Riders looking for the mules as well, and he wanted to get a good head start.

Herrig carefully followed the mule tracks as they wound through the jungle. He finally caught up to them twelve hours later, the Colt guns on their backs. With the mules in tow, Herrig arrived in camp at dusk. He marched straight to headquarters, and when Roosevelt saw him, there was that big smile again. Roosevelt turned to Colonel Wood and said, "Didn't I tell you, didn't I tell you, Wood, Fred would find those guns?"

Roosevelt had another reason to smile when his personal bundle, the one the chief surgeon had thrown off the mule at Daiquirí, arrived in camp with a supply train. It held his extra clothing and small necessities—he hadn't taken off his clothes for four days. And there hadn't been a moment when his uniform wasn't soaked with rain, dew, or sweat.

"I am personally in excellent health," he assured Edith in a June 27 letter, "in spite of having been obliged for the week since I landed, to violate all the rules for health which I was told I must observe."

The Rough Riders had moved their camp two miles nearer Santiago and close to General Lawton's division, except Lawton was now in the advance position as Shafter originally intended. Shafter was pleased about the victory at Las Guásimas, but he had given General Wheeler very clear instructions not to bring on another fight just yet.

The dog tents were clustered along the Aguadores River, a beautiful, clear stream that rippled over large rocks. The campground was marshy, but at least the men were away from the rank smell of death at Las Guásimas. From a hill next to camp, they could see the quaint-looking rooftops of Santiago approximately six miles away, as well as a glimpse of their future: Spanish blockhouses.

The men had erected a temporary Rough Riders headquarters— a shelter made from a canvas wagon cover—near the overhanging limbs of a large mango tree. The merry bunch that gathered there included the British and German attachés and journalists Caspar Whitney of *Harper's Weekly* and Davis, who shared Roosevelt's tent. More than one trooper urged his parents to watch for Davis's articles. He is "our friend," Sam Weller wrote, "so his accounts will do us full justice."

Unlike their meals on the *Yucatan*, the officers' fare now consisted solely of hardtack, bacon, and coffee. For a time, there was no sugar for the coffee, and they soon ran out of salt, but Wood and Roosevelt declared they would not eat anything that was not part of the men's rations. And those rations never failed to be short and irregular. For the rest of the campaign, said one officer, the regiment "lived literally from hand to mouth."

Roosevelt knew there were stacks of provisions sitting on the beach at Siboney, just waiting for transportation. One morning, he rounded up about forty men and marched to the coast to see what he could bring back. After checking with a commissary clerk, Roosevelt began looking through the piles and came across several large sacks of dried beans—eleven hundred pounds, in fact. But the commissary clerk said the beans were only for the officers' mess. Roosevelt thought a minute, looked at the pile of beans and then looked back at the clerk. With a serious face, Roosevelt requested eleven hundred pounds of beans—for the officers' mess.

"Why, Colonel," said the surprised clerk, "your officers can't eat 1,100 pounds of beans."

"You don't know what appetites my officers have," Roosevelt said.

Roosevelt got his beans, but the clerk warned him that the army might charge them to his salary. Roosevelt didn't care; it wasn't the first time he had to dip into his own pocket for his boys. "[L]ast evening we got some beans," Roosevelt wrote Edith, "and oh! what a feast we had, and how we enjoyed it."

Out of necessity, the troopers became fairly creative with their cooking. The daily coffee ration consisted of two spoonfuls of Arbuckles' whole beans, but there was no coffee grinder. The men had used the butts of their Colt revolvers back in Tampa, but, except for the officers, they had been ordered to leave their Colts behind before departing for Cuba. George Hamner, the railroad telegrapher, took a dried coconut shell and cut a hole in one end. He put the beans in the shell and then pounded them with a small pestle he had carved. It worked surprisingly well and became known as "Hamner's coffee mill."

When it came to the bacon and hardtack, the usual preparation was to fry the bacon first and then fry the hardtack in the bacon grease. But Troop F's McCurdy brothers came up with a recipe that called for soaking four of the hard crackers in water until they turned into a gooey dough. To this they added salt, mixed in a little coffee, and then fried the glob in the bacon grease. The finishing touch was a little sugar on top. The brothers also added sugar to fresh mangoes and boiled the fruit down until it was the consistency of applesauce. When stewed in this way, one trooper thought it tasted like canned peaches.

Mangoes were not for everyone. It gave many men cramps and diarrhea, and even though it was a mainstay of the Cubans, some regiments' officers and surgeons cautioned their men to avoid it. The Rough Riders' surgeons initially said it was okay to eat the mangoes but then changed their minds, believing that the plentiful fruit might serve as a carrier for yellow fever (the discovery that mosquitoes transmitted the yellow fever virus would not occur for another two years). By then, many troopers had already become addicted and, growing extremely tired of half rations of bacon and hardtack, were willing to risk it. One of these was Troop F's Guy M. Lisk.

Lisk, a schoolteacher in civilian life, stood just over six feet tall and was the spitting image of Abraham Lincoln. The Rough Riders, always ready to bestow a nickname, started calling him "Abe." When "Abe" got to Cuba, he simply couldn't get enough mangoes; he would eat a hatful at one sitting. So his nickname was promptly revised: he became "Mango Abe."

Limes were also abundant, and the men were encouraged to eat them, whether ripe or not. When there was sugar, many a tin cup sloshed with cool limeade. "The juice of this fruit," wrote an officer with the Tenth Cavalry, "was the most palatable thing that passed my lips in Cuba."

The mundane rations, as well as their shortage, would have been much easier to put up with if only there had been plenty of tobacco. Whether it was pipes, cigars, or hand-rolled cigarettes, a good many Rough Riders were heavy smokers. As Richard Harding Davis explained it, "With a pipe the soldier can kill hunger, he can forget that he is wet and exhausted and sick with the heat, he can steady his nerves against the roof of bullets when they pass continually overhead."

But for a stretch of four days there was no tobacco in camp, and the men suffered through nicotine withdrawal. They got headaches, became nervous, and couldn't sleep. If someone came back from Siboney with an extra plug of tobacco, it sold for two dollars instead of the usual eight cents. Some troopers became so desperate they concocted their own "tobacco" out of dried horse droppings, grass, roots, and tea.

The biggest concern, though, was drinking water. The men were instructed to boil their water, but all they had to boil it in was their tin cups, and when they were on the move, there was no time for boiling. Besides, no one wanted to carry around a canteen full of warm water. In their camp next to the Aguadores, the men were not allowed to bathe, shave, wash clothes, or clean dishes in the stream, and guards were posted all along the stream to make sure of it. As there were more than a dozen regiments camped above and below the Rough Riders, it was critical not to pollute the water for those downstream. Of course, when the tropical downpours came, the filth of the camps washed straight into the river.

"It rains every day at three o'clock for an hour and such rain you never guessed," wrote Davis. "It is three inches high for an hour. Then we all go out naked and dig trenches to get it out of the way." The trail running next to the different camps—the main road to Santiago— became a stream of mud. Footwear never dried out and was soon ruined. Even worse, the Krags began to rust, which caused a frantic search for oil.

The troopers always felt grimy and sticky; personal cleanliness was practically impossible. In order to get a long-overdue scrubbing, George Hamner dug a hole the size of his haversack, emptied his haversack nearby, placed the open haversack in the hole, and then made several trips to the stream with his tin cup to fill the haversack with water, keeping the sides apart with sticks. He could now take a sponge bath, and the hot sun dried out his haversack in minutes afterward. An officer of the Tenth dug an even larger hole and lined it with his rubber overcoat, creating a temporary tub, but he also had only his tin cup to fill it. Nevertheless, it was wonderful to feel clean.

When the men weren't on fatigue or guard duty, or assigned to a scouting party, they scrounged for paper to write letters home. At times, writing paper was so scarce that they resorted to scribbling on the brown paper that came wrapped around the hardtack or on empty pillboxes that once contained quinine. Following Las Guásimas, they filled their letters with details of the battle and what they had seen of it. Some troopers stuffed battlefield souvenirs into the envelopes with their letters. Arthur Cosby mailed his parents labels from enemy ammunition packages and even a Spanish military document.

A few troopers accused the Spaniards of violating the rules of international warfare by using "explosive bullets." "These are powder filled steel or lead balls which burst on contact or after traveling a certain distance," Sam Weller informed his parents. "They make a terrible wound. . . . The explosive bullets fooled us during the fight. We heard their cracking like rifle shots all round us and could not understand it. For a while those of us on the firing line thought our own men in the rear were shooting at us by mistake."

Some of the wounds seen by Weller and his comrades were indeed grisly, but they were not the result of explosive bullets. The Mauser rounds contained a hard lead core that was jacketed with cast steel covered with a nickel copper alloy. This was confirmed by army surgeons and even Roosevelt. "The Mauser bullets themselves made a small clean hole," Roosevelt wrote, "with the result that the wound healed in a most astonishing manner. One or two of our men who were shot in the head had the skull blown open, but elsewhere the wounds from the minute steel-coated bullet, with its very high velocity, were certainly nothing like as serious as those made by the old large-caliber, low-power rifle."

In addition to their battle experiences, the Rough Riders wrote about camp life and of the exotic land and climate they had been thrust into—the "garden spot of Cuba and a finer country I never saw," claimed one ebullient trooper. And invariably, they asked for news. "Have seen no newspapers for 15 days," wrote Arthur Cosby, "nor received any mail for a long time." Sam Weller wrote on June 29 that he was "nearly wild to hear from home. The last letter I received was just as we were leaving Port Tampa. That was two & a half weeks ago—though I have passed through so much since then it seems so many months or years."

The troopers also wrote to reassure loved ones they were okay, though they felt compelled to remind them there was no guarantee they were coming back. "If I go under," wrote one Rough Rider, "let my faults be buried with me."

Between supper and the sounding of "Taps" at 9:00 P.M., there was the usual singing and storytelling. In the distance, the bands of the different regiments could be heard playing through their repertoires of martial tunes. Roosevelt recalled that when a band got to "The Star-Spangled Banner," "all, officers and men alike, stood with heads uncovered, wherever they were, until the last strains of the anthem died away in the hot sunset air."

Later, as it got dark, numerous small yellow lights floated out of the mist like magic, slowly moving through the air, becoming brighter as they got closer. These were the Cuban endemic firefly. Ben Colbert, the Chickasaw, wrote in his diary that they were as big as June bugs, and gave "a light as large as a lantern." They reminded him of home.

Theodore Miller was walking from the field hospital back to camp with another trooper when they came upon a regiment of Cuban fighters. "They seem greatly pleased to see all these U.S. soldiers," Miller wrote in his diary, "and there is a twinkle in every eye as you look at them. Cuba Libre is their call, and they smiled all over when we shouted that at them."

Unfortunately, the Rough Riders were fast losing their camaraderie with the Cubans. Eight hundred Cubans had been promised to General Young, but they didn't show up until the fight was over. "The Cuban insurgents so far have been nearly useless," Arthur Cosby wrote his mother. "They did not give us proper warning or we should never have been caught in that ambuscade. They are a dirty, tattered, picturesque lot of negroes."

Another problem was theft by the Cubans. The Rough Riders had thrown off their packs and haversacks during the battle, but before they could return to retrieve their things, several Cubans had rifled through them and taken the rations. Most of the troopers were forced to go without food until midnight, when a pack train arrived. The Cubans were surely starved for rations themselves, but the Rough Riders, who had just experienced a brutal day in the jungle marching and fighting, were not happy. Wood soon gave strict orders to keep all Cubans out of the camp due to their pilfering.

"[T]here is no specious intercourse between the Cubans and the

Americans," observed Stephen Crane. "Each hold largely to their own people and go their own ways."

Every day, soldiers and pack trains slogged over the mucky trail that ran by camp. Squads of Rough Riders with picks and shovels, along with men from other regiments, worked in the brutal heat to widen the road and remove large boulders so the supply wagons and artillery batteries could pass. One of those batteries was commanded by Captain Capron's father, and they made their camp just across the road.

Two representatives from the Rough Riders carried the personal effects of Captain Capron to his father's tent. They wished to express the sympathy of the entire regiment for his loss. They also intended to tell the father about a novel raffle Captain Buckey O'Neill had come up with for Capron's horse. O'Neill planned to raise a good deal of money for Capron's widow and, in the end, present her with the horse as well. But in what became a very awkward visit, the senior Capron refused to accept his son's belongings. He was angry and bitter and wanted no reminders.

On June 28, a Tuesday, General Shafter and staff rode past the Rough Rider camp. For those troopers who had not yet seen the Fifth Corps commander, his huge bulk was something to behold. J. Ogden Wells recorded in his diary that the general "looked like he could carry the mule better than the mule could carry him."

Roosevelt was by no means an admirer of General Shafter—the incompetence and mismanagement he had seen thus far was "maddening"—but Richard Harding Davis despised the commander. Shafter had offended Davis during the landing at Daiquirí, when the journalist asked to go ashore with the first boats. Shafter had refused, explaining that he didn't want reporters in the way in case the Spaniards put up a resistance. But Davis persisted. He said he was not just any reporter but a "descriptive writer." "I do not care a damn what you are," Shafter snapped. "I'll treat all of you alike."

The day before Shafter's appearance at the Rough Rider camp, scouting parties—and correspondent Davis—spotted some ominous-

*Major General William Shafter and staff, photographed
by John C. Hemment. (Author's Collection.)*

looking activity to the west on Los Cerros del Río San Juan, the north-south hills overlooking Santiago. The Americans named the hills San Juan Heights. An occasional ranch house or villa was visible there, the buildings abandoned long ago but since fortified by the Spaniards. The most distinctive of these was located on a long, grassy ridge that would become known as San Juan Hill. Davis thought the building looked like a Chinese pagoda. Near this blockhouse, a long scar began taking shape on the hillside: the Spaniards were digging trenches and rifle pits, and their straw sombreros could be seen bobbing up and down.

As daily reports of this came back, Davis and several of his officer friends wondered why Shafter did nothing to disrupt their efforts, such as direct some of his artillery to make the hillside a little lively for the trench diggers. Actually, Shafter had hoped he could advance against the Spanish defenses on June 28, but he was preoccupied with the landing of supplies and reinforcements at Siboney and getting them to the front. Considering the victory at Las Guásimas, he likely believed the Spaniards would be easily defeated regardless of when he launched his attack. Just days before, Shafter had boasted to a photographer on board the *Seguranca* that he "would make a very short campaign of it."

Nevertheless, the men worried about those trenches and wondered how they would forcibly take them in the face of Spanish Mausers and machine guns. A Rough Rider with one of the scouting parties wrote his parents that "chances are we will have a desperate fight to take the place." Roosevelt would later explain that a "generation had passed since the Civil War and most men had forgotten how formidable entrenchments were, and did not realize the immense resisting power of even small blockhouses when attacked by infantry, unsupported or not properly supported by artillery."

Shafter, a Medal of Honor–winning Civil War veteran, surely had vivid recollections of that conflict. Even so, the Spaniards on San Juan Heights were left unmolested as he readied the Fifth Corps for a major assault.

Davis would later describe and criticize this, along with numerous other matters relating to Shafter's handling of the campaign. "If [Brigadier General Adna] Chaffee or Lawton, who are the finest type of officers I ever saw, were in command," Davis wrote his father on June 29, "we would have been fighting every day and would probably have been in by this time."

J. Ogden Wells noticed more activity than usual on the road next to camp. It was Thursday morning, June 30. "Everything is moving towards the front," he scribbled in his diary. "Mule train after mule train is being pushed forward with supplies and ammunition, and it looks as if a heavy battle is expected. The men are all eager for the struggle and will not need much urging."

About 3:00 P.M., a staff officer rode up to Rough Riders headquarters with orders for the regiment to move out in an hour. He also informed Wood and Roosevelt that General Wheeler and General Young were down with fever. Wood was to take command of Young's Second Brigade. That left Roosevelt in sole command of the Rough Riders. Most everyone expected he would command the regiment sooner or later, but getting the regiment like this, before a major engagement, was uncannily fortuitous.

Bugles sounded as the men hurriedly took down their shelter tents and rolled their blankets. Lines formed for the issuing of three days' rations. At some point, Roosevelt caught sight of blue-eyed George Roland, the trooper who had received the bullet in his ribs at Las Guásimas. Roosevelt had allowed Roland to continue fighting that day, but after the battle, he had ordered the cowboy to the temporary hospital at Siboney.

Roland complied and was duly admitted to the hospital, but the

New Mexico cowboy George Roland, Troop G. (R560.3.EL61-033, Theodore Roosevelt Collection, Houghton Library, Harvard University.)

doctors took one look at his nasty wound and made arrangements to put him on the hospital ship so that he could receive proper treatment in the States. Their mistake was telling Roland this, and he slipped out the window the first chance he got and walked the six miles to camp carrying his heavy pack and carbine. Once again, Roosevelt couldn't bear to turn him away, and let him join the other men.

The Rough Riders had only enough mules to transport the Colt machine guns and the pneumatic dynamite gun (the dynamite gun had missed out on the action at Las Guásimas because it arrived too late at Siboney). Whatever the men could not pack on their backs had to be left behind. This included the officers' baggage.

The officers formed the regiment into column alongside the road and waited—and waited some more. General Shafter's marching orders were received by many of his regiments at nearly the same time with no attempt to stagger their advance. Consequently, the road, which was no more than ten feet wide, became a clogged river of thousands of plodding men. Finally, after what seemed like hours, Roosevelt was able to get his regiment onto the road behind the First and Tenth Cavalries, but his troubles were far from over.

"Every few minutes there would be a stoppage in front," Roosevelt recalled, "and at the halt I would make the men sit or lie down beside the track, loosening their packs. The heat was intense as we passed through the still, close jungle, which formed a wall on either hand."

Up ahead of the column, a large egg-shaped object never before seen in Cuba slowly rose above the trees. As the Rough Riders studied this curiosity, it rose higher until they saw, suspended beneath it, a basket holding two men. It was the Signal Corps's observation balloon, and Roosevelt was not impressed. To him it was "an experimental toy" and completely unnecessary, for one could just as easily reconnoiter the Spanish positions from the hilltops as from the balloon. And the balloon's operation required many men and several wagons to haul the needed apparatus. "If, instead of this, they had been employed in bringing beans to the front for the soldiers," Roosevelt wrote, "the result would have been in every way infinitely better."

The shadows deepened as the afternoon turned into evening and still the Rough Riders marched; or, in reality, stood, squatted, sat, and sometimes walked. In the darkness, Royal A. Prentice slipped in the mud and fell under Roosevelt's Little Texas. A comrade shouted a warning as Prentice struggled to pull himself up: "Look out, Colonel, a man has fallen under your horse!"

"Don't worry," Roosevelt answered calmly, "no horse will step on a Rough Rider."

About 9:00 P.M., the regiment reached El Pozo, a prominent hill approximately a mile and a half east of the San Juan blockhouse and next to the Siboney-Santiago road. Roosevelt led his column off the road to the left and toward the hill's summit, where there was an abandoned sugar plantation. Wood was there pointing out the camping spots assigned to the cavalry's First Brigade. The Rough Riders threw off their packs and collapsed upon the ground. One trooper wrote in his diary that they had marched six miles. The actual distance as the crow flies was less than two, but the heat, mud, and walking with full packs, Krags, ammunition, and canteens had been exhausting.

There were to be no fires and no bugle calls, nothing to alert the enemy to their position. Roosevelt and Wood spread their saddle blankets on the grass and slept under their raincoats. Or at least tried to sleep. "I suppose that, excepting among hardened veterans, there is always a certain feeling of uneasy excitement the night before the battle," Roosevelt wrote.

At some point during the evening, he got up and made a round of his regiment's sentries, the stars shining brightly in a clear sky just as they had those nights on the deck of the *Yucatan* when he was with Buckey O'Neill. Perhaps O'Neill would earn his star tomorrow.

Reveille was at 4:00 A.M., the officers of each troop shaking their men awake. Before roll call came an hour and a half later, they dug into their rations—more hardtack, but they ate it up. The next meal probably wouldn't be anytime soon.

Roll call had just been completed when the men's attention was drawn to the rumbling sounds of wheels and rattling metal. Looking in the direction of the commotion, they saw the artillery battery of Captain George S. Grimes—four breech-loading 3.2-inch guns—racing up El Pozo hill. "It was a fine sight," wrote Roosevelt, "to see the great horses straining under the lash as they whirled the guns up the hill and into position."

Roosevelt had received nothing in the way of orders for his regiment. What he did know was that General Lawton's infantry division of more than six thousand men was to begin the day's fighting by attacking a village three miles to the north called El Caney. Garrisoned by approximately five hundred Spanish soldiers, the village was on the Santiago-Guantánamo road, over which the Spaniards might bring reinforcements. In enemy hands, El Caney would be a threat to Shafter's right flank and rear when he made his assault on San Juan Heights, so it was important that El Caney fall first.

Once Lawton's division took El Caney (Lawton told Shafter the village would be his in two hours), he was to march his force southwest and join on the right Shafter's remaining two divisions now waiting near El Pozo hill. These were the infantry division of Brigadier General Jacob Kent and Wheeler's dismounted cavalry, under Brigadier General Samuel Sumner due to Wheeler's illness. All three divisions were then to advance on San Juan Heights.

At 7:30 A.M., the Rough Riders heard the booming of artillery that signaled the beginning of the bombardment of El Caney. About thirty minutes later, Captain Grimes shouted, "No. 1 . . . load! . . . prime! . . . fire!"

A giant plume of white smoke belched from the crest of El Pozo—the American artillery used black powder. Grimes's orders were repeated for each gun in the battery. Several officers and men of various regiments, eager to see the fireworks, abandoned their units and hurried to where the foreign attachés and correspondents were glassing the distant green slopes from behind the guns.

Grimes's men fired at least a dozen rounds without getting a response from the Spaniards on San Juan Hill, which led some of the Rough Riders to believe the battle was practically won. Colonel Wood knew better and remarked to Roosevelt that it would be a good idea to move the brigade because any return fire that was directed at Grimes's battery could just as easily harm his men.

Not far away, Ben Colbert had been sitting on the ground with his diary open as Grimes's battery fired on the defenses near the San Juan blockhouse: "I was quietly writing a few notes and thinking what a fine place I had to protect myself. I was just thinking 'just watch us lick 'em' when bang went a shell just over us."

Several Cubans were watching from the tiled roof of one of the abandoned buildings when that first shrapnel shell, timed to explode just above them, sprayed bullets and jagged metal straight into their midst, killing and maiming. They "all collapsed and disappeared," remembered a Rough Rider. "They seemed to curl up into little balls and roll in every direction."

The Cubans weren't the only ones running for cover. Pudgy Frederic Remington was running, too, dragging his horse behind him. "It was thoroughly evident that the Spaniards had the range of everything in the country," Remington observed. "They had studied it out."

They also had the assistance of the clouds of blackpowder smoke that floated above Grimes's battery. The Spaniards were firing smokeless powder, which made their batteries nearly impossible to spot.

Roosevelt and Wood sprinted for their horses, and just as Roosevelt pulled himself up onto Little Texas, a fragment from an exploding shell struck his right wrist, causing an awful bump and some bleeding. "That's the first one," he muttered. "They'll have to do better than that next time."

It could have been much worse. One man was on the ground with blood gushing from the stump of his leg. Others were motionless, dead. Roosevelt yelled at the Rough Riders to follow him behind the crest of the hill, and they came pell-mell, finally halting in some thick underbrush. Here they waited in a jumbled mass far to the left of the guns as the artillerymen dueled it out. After about a half hour, the firing ceased.

Like Ben Colbert, Theodore Miller was never without his small diary. He mostly intended his daily entries for the enjoyment of his parents. Miller was writing in it when Roosevelt and his officers began sorting out the different troops and putting the regiment into a column of fours.

"Must stop," he scribbled. "Now in line. Good-bye; will send this. Please excuse mistakes, for I have written in a hurry."

Miller stuffed the notebook and small pencil into his pocket and shouldered his Krag. Then he heard an officer shout, "Forward!" Bugles sounding, Miller and his comrades swiftly marched below Grimes's battery and turned onto the narrow and muddy Siboney-Santiago road.

Roosevelt, taut and eager, rode at the front of his regiment. Up ahead, in the distance, loomed San Juan Heights under a clear blue sky.

Chapter Seven

A Bully Fight

Sound, sound the clarion, fill the fife!
Throughout the sensual world proclaim,
One crowded hour of glorious life
Is worth an age without a name.

THOMAS OSBERT MORDAUNT

Roosevelt sat astride Little Texas and looked out over his sweating men. They had marched about a mile through the jungle from El Pozo and were now stopped in the trail, one of several frustrating halts that morning. At least the men were no longer carrying their heavy packs. They had placed them off to the side of the trail and would retrieve them later. The heavy Colt machine guns had also been left behind. This was a day for marching light.

Up ahead was the ford of the Aguadores River. The First Brigade, composed of the Third, Sixth, and Ninth U.S. Cavalries, had already splashed across. Gunfire from the Spanish trenches on the hills rising before them was picking up, and although the Spaniards could not see the ford through the jungle, they knew where it was and thus where to direct their fire.

The Rough Riders stood in formation, their nerves strained as shrapnel shells and bullets ripped the air above them. "The shriek of the shells is not pleasant music," Roger Fitch wrote later in his diary, "when they are coming toward one."

Roosevelt swung Little Texas around, looking to see if anyone was bringing him orders for his regiment. That's when he saw the Signal Corps's observation balloon—"huge, fat, yellow, quivering," is how Stephen Crane described it. Roosevelt's eyes followed the balloon's guide ropes down until he saw the eight men on the ground holding on to a long pole that held the ropes. The damn fools were dragging the balloon down the crowded trail in his direction, toward the ford. If the enemy didn't know where to shoot before, they sure as hell did now, and men were needlessly getting killed because of it. "It was one of the most ill-judged and idiotic acts I ever witnessed," Colonel Wood recalled.

Just then General Samuel Sumner rode up and told Roosevelt to take his men across the river and march about a half mile to the right and wait for orders. He said the lieutenant colonel should look to join flanks with General Lawton's infantry, as they should be arriving in that general area after taking El Caney. It was now 11:15 A.M.

With the balloon getting closer, Roosevelt led his men to the ford and across the stream on the double-quick. What he didn't know was that the troopers behind him were pausing in the river to fill their canteens, which they had already emptied this morning. General Sumner saw the resulting backup and ordered the Rough Riders' adjutant, Tom Hall, to put a stop to it. Hall, unquestionably the most disliked man in the regiment, now had the chore of denying the troopers water. The men had no way of knowing Hall was acting under orders. They only knew they were thirsty as hell, and Hall was exercising his usual meanness. It gave them even more reasons to curse him.

After most of the regiment had waded across at the ford, Sergeant David Hughes, Troop B, looked back over his shoulder at the balloon, which continued to draw all kinds of rifle and artillery fire from the Spaniards. "We could hear the bullets striking the silk bag," he wrote, "and the major [in the basket] yelling to the men to pull him down.

The last I saw of them they were fishing the major out of a tree that the balloon landed in."

The Rough Riders, about four hundred and ninety men, kept marching northeast through an area of scattered trees and tall grass, with Las Guamas Creek (a tributary of the Aguadores) on their immediate right. Heavy gunfire and the sound of booming artillery continued from the Heights as Roosevelt led the regiment behind the First Brigade, which was already deploying in a line of skirmishers. Suddenly, six men jumped up in front of the column with their hands raised, and the advance guard surrounded them. They looked like Spanish guerrillas but seemed to be claiming they were *insurrectos*. Roosevelt called up Captain Maximiliano Luna, who spoke fluent Spanish and was able to question the men. After a brief exchange, Roosevelt let the men go. There were some Cuban entrenchments nearby, so it was best to give them the benefit of the doubt. But an officer noticed that as soon as the men were released, they headed directly to the Spanish lines.

Roosevelt called the regiment to a stop after they reached a sunken road or lane that ran west across a valley for a few hundred yards to a hill just to the right and forward of San Juan Hill. A fortified ranch house stood on its summit, along with other structures fronted by rifle pits full of Mauser-toting Spaniards. Next to the buildings were three large cast-iron kettles used for refining sugar. The place would be dubbed Kettle Hill before the day was out. A heavy tree line at the hill's base revealed the course of the San Juan River.

Roosevelt ordered his men to face Kettle Hill and told them to lie down behind whatever cover they could find. They would be held in reserve until orders came for an advance. In characteristic Roosevelt fashion, he had already sent someone back to hurry those orders along.

The sunken road, lined on each side with a barbed-wire fence, dropped down about three feet. Many troopers flattened out in this depression. Others crouched behind the bank of Las Guamas Creek.

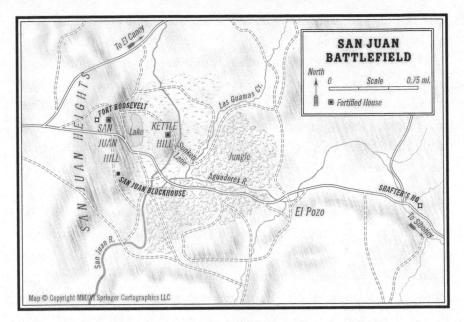

They got wet, but it was a lot better than getting shot. Roosevelt rode up and down his line on Little Texas to make sure the men were spaced far apart.

The battle was now fully on, and the Spaniards were engaging in heavy volley firing. "The Mauser bullets drove in sheets through the trees and the tall jungle grass," Roosevelt recalled, "making a peculiar whirring or rustling sound."

Even though the firing from the rifle pits was not directed at any particular trooper or groups of men, it was slowly taking a toll. And the Spanish snipers, hidden in the tops of tall palm trees where they were suspended on simple rope swings padded with grass, were finding the Americans to be easy targets. These snipers shot at everything that moved, including the wounded.

"There was no hiding from them," wrote Richard Harding Davis. "Their bullets came from every side. Their invisible smoke helped to keep their hiding-places secret, and in the incessant shriek of shrapnel and the spit of the Mausers, it was difficult to locate the reports of their rifles."

Roosevelt's position on horseback caused him to attract nearly as many bullets as the observation balloon. He had tied his blue polka-dot bandanna onto his Stetson so that it draped back over his neck like a havelock. He wore no uniform jacket, only the blue flannel shirt, open at the collar, the same as the men. A pair of white cotton suspenders ran down from his shoulders and buttoned onto his Brooks Brothers khakis, now wrinkled and muddied. His eyeglasses flashed in the sunlight, perspiration occasionally dripping from his forehead onto the lenses of his glasses and forcing him to stop and wipe them clean.

"Boys, this is the day we repeat what we have done before," Roosevelt shouted. "You know we are surrounded by the Regulars. They are around us thick and heavy."

With this, he wanted to reassure his men that they were not in this battle alone; they were part of a large force that included hardened veterans, both white and black. Between them and Kettle Hill, in positions that were even more exposed than the Rough Riders, were the skirmish lines of the First Brigade. On the left were the First and Tenth Regiments, although their lines were beginning to overlap with those of the Rough Riders. The Cavalry Division had brought 2,649 men into this fight.

"Don't forget where you belong," Roosevelt continued. "Don't forget what you are fighting for. Don't forget, boys, that your reward is not in the immediate present, but think of what will come in the future."

As Roosevelt rode along and saw men clutching a fresh wound in the arm or leg, he held up his bandaged wrist and said, "See here, boys, I've got it, too."

Captain Buckey O'Neill strode up and down the sunken road in front of his crouching and ducking men, calmly smoking a cigarette. He was, according to one of his troopers, "constitutionally opposed to getting under cover." Although many nineteenth-century commanders feigned disapproval of officers dangerously exposing themselves in combat, it was nevertheless expected and praised. And there was no better example than the Rough Riders' two colonels. General Young wrote in his Las Guásimas report, "Both Col. Wood and Lieut.-Col. Roosevelt disdained to take advantage of shelter or cover from the enemy's fire while any of their men remained exposed to it;—an error of judgment, but happily on the heroic side."

O'Neill could see the nervousness on his men's faces, and he thought that pretending to be indifferent to the hailstorm of bullets would bolster their courage. Instead, he made them scared he would be killed, and they practically worshipped him. Several called out to him—begged him—to get down.

"Captain," shouted a sergeant, "a bullet is sure to hit you."

O'Neill turned to the sergeant, exhaled a puff of smoke, and laughed. "Sergeant," he said, "the Spanish bullet isn't made that will kill me."

About three minutes later, Troop A's First Lieutenant Frank Frantz heard a sharp crack behind him, something like the snapping of a twig but different. He spun around just in time to see O'Neill, ten feet away, collapse backward to the ground. Frantz rushed to his captain, kneeled beside him, and looked into the open eyes staring into nothingness; a white film quickly spread over them.

A spot of blood and a cut on O'Neill's lower lip showed where a Mauser bullet had entered his mouth and traveled through the back of his head. The noise that caused Frantz to turn around was the sound of the steel-jacketed bullet breaking O'Neill's teeth. "He never knew what struck him," a trooper wrote home, "and he never even moaned."

News of O'Neill's death spread rapidly from man to man. First the men's hearts sank, but this feeling was swiftly replaced with rage. Those nearby when O'Neill fell suspected he had been killed by a sniper, and they gazed in the direction the captain faced when he was hit. Finally, about three hundred yards to the left, they spotted a Spaniard high in a coconut tree. James Raudebaugh, a Flagstaff boy of Troop A, and two unnamed black troopers of the Tenth plotted a route through the high grass that would take them closer to the suspected killer.

The three crawled along, their carbines cradled in front of them, until they were one hundred yards from the tree. From here the Spaniard was plainly visible in the palm leaves. The troopers raised their Krags and pulled the triggers simultaneously. "[H]e fell with two holes in his left side," Raudebaugh reported in a letter to his uncle, "and of course I missed him."

Casualties among the Rough Riders continued to mount, their time waiting as reserves approaching an hour. "If I had all the lead and steel [the Spaniards] sent over our heads," wrote an Arizona trooper, "I would have enough metal to dam the Grand Canyon. Those shells they sent us had a mournful sound."

Roosevelt, newly in command of the Rough Riders, seemed to be everywhere, which was a problem for the twenty-five-year-old orderly, William "Willie" Sanders, who was following along on foot. "Teddy is as brave as a lion," Sanders wrote his mother, "but in his rushing about on horseback he lost Willie, who was not speedy enough to keep up." Private Sanders, who had graduated from Harvard just a year before, wouldn't connect with his colonel until much later, after walking up and down the line nearly a dozen times.

Roosevelt was overheard saying, again and again, "I wish they'd let us start, I wish they'd let us start." And he regularly sent men back to find Wood or Sumner to try to get permission to advance. On one of the rare occasions when he wasn't sitting atop Little Texas, Roosevelt sat on the bank of the creek, giving orders to yet another messenger. He told him to go back and find whatever general he could and ask if the Rough Riders could advance, as they were taking too many casualties.

The messenger stood up, saluted, and then pitched forward across Roosevelt's knees, blood bubbling from his neck. A bullet had punctured the man's throat, cutting his carotid artery.

Not far away, under the bank of that same creek and unnoticed, Private Oscar Wager had his own problem. Wager, a twenty-year-old cowboy from Jerome, Arizona, was short, standing only five feet four and a half inches tall. But cowboys didn't have to be tall, and today,

being short had its advantages. Wager had helped carry a wounded sergeant to the field hospital and was returning to his troop, walking along
the creek to stay out of the line of fire, when a black trooper suddenly
flipped down the bank in front of him and splashed into the water.

Wager waded into the creek, grabbed the comatose trooper, and
pulled him to the bank. Blood was gushing from a wound in the man's
neck. Wager pressed his thumb over the wound and stopped the bleeding. He then yelled for help, but no one heard him, and whenever he
lifted his thumb, the blood spurted from the wound again. So Wager
sat there with his thumb on the Buffalo Soldier's neck, even after his
fellow Rough Riders had been called into action.

"I was tempted several times to leave him and rejoin my company,"
Wager admitted, "but he looked so pitiful and grateful that I stuck it
out until finally relieved by two of the Medical Detachment."

The black trooper, whose name Wager never learned, survived.
Later, in the hospital, the Buffalo Soldier spoke in awe of the Arizona
Rough Rider: "He done that to me, he did; stayed by me an hour and
a half, and me only a nigger!"

It was past noon, and the Rough Riders still did not know if they would
be called forward. The entire Cavalry Division had moved very little
since being deployed, and no one had seen General Lawton's infantry,
which was supposed to have taken El Caney by now.

"What in hell has become of the dinner bell?" a Troop G man yelled
to his buddies. "I can see where I'm goin' to miss my eats." They told
him to shut up; he was only making them hungry.

Roosevelt wasn't thinking about food. He had had far too much
of this waiting while his Rough Riders were being shot to pieces. He
remembered the old military aphorism, "go to the sound of the guns,"
and had nearly decided to advance on his own initiative when an officer galloped up with orders from General Sumner: "Move forward
and support the regulars in the assault on the hills in front." The ob-
jective was the red-tiled house visible on top of Kettle Hill.

This began what Roosevelt would fondly call "my 'crowded hour.'" He jumped on Little Texas and rode down the line, shouting to the captains and lieutenants to send their men forward. Advance in a column of troops, he told them, and in open skirmish order. Roosevelt came across one man who was lying on the ground while his comrades were all standing and ready to march. He ordered the trooper to jump up, but the young man, a worried look on his face, remained motionless.

"Are you afraid to stand up when I am on horseback?" Roosevelt shouted.

The man began to rise when he abruptly fell forward on his face. Roosevelt called to another trooper to roll the man over. A Mauser bullet had plowed through the length of his body, killing him instantly. "I suppose the bullet had been aimed at me," Roosevelt surmised later. "[A]t any rate, I, who was on horseback in the open was unhurt, and the man lying flat on the ground in the cover was killed."

After one troop deployed in its skirmish line, Roosevelt rode up and yelled, "Well, come on!"

No one moved, although every soldier had plainly heard the lieutenant colonel.

"What, are you cowards?" a flustered Roosevelt spit out.

A grinning trooper replied, "We're waiting for the command."

Roosevelt's face relaxed, and there was a slight hint of a smile. "Forward, March!" he yelled, and the men started forward.

Five troops were on the left of the sunken lane and three to the right, their advance a series of short, steady rushes. The Rough Riders sometimes walked, sometimes ran through the waist-high grass, brush, and cactus. They would advance several yards and then kneel or fall flat and then jump up and move forward again. In Troop D, Robert McMillen, a twenty-five-year-old clerk from Oklahoma Territory, started feeling sick and said so to his buddy, Cliff Scott. Scott figured it was only a case of nerves. "I . . . told him that it wouldn't do to get sick now," Scott recalled, "that I was just as bad scared as he was."

At this, McMillen began to cuss his friend, but he kept moving.

Then, after only a few more yards, McMillen started throwing up blood. Scott asked if he'd been hit and rushed over to his buddy's side. McMillen said he felt numb all over. They tore at McMillen's shirt and discovered a small hole oozing blood in his right breast. He turned around and started for the field hospital.

Roosevelt rode to the rear of his column, the place a commander of his rank was expected to be, but as he followed and encouraged the last line forward, it overtook the line immediately in front. Roosevelt rode ahead and urged this line forward to get some separation, but it, too, moved faster with Roosevelt behind it and overtook the line of skirmishers just ahead. Consequently, while trying to keep his column from bunching, Roosevelt rode Little Texas through line after line until he found himself at the head of his regiment.

Many of the officers in the cavalry regiments between the Rough Riders and Kettle Hill had not received General Sumner's orders to advance. These were the Regulars who were supposed to be leading the assault, yet their first indication an advance was being made was the surprise appearance of Roosevelt and his men fast approaching their ranks from behind.

Roosevelt came to several men of the Ninth and First Cavalries lying on the ground in his path, their officers pacing to and fro along the line. Spotting Captain Eugene Dimmick of the Ninth, Roosevelt rode up and said he'd been ordered to support the Regulars in an attack on the hill just ahead. He said there was no use remaining there and firing at the Spaniards in their rifle pits; they could do that all day with little effect. The hill must be rushed, and he intended to do it.

Dimmick said he'd been ordered to keep his men where they were, and he couldn't send them forward without approval from his colonel. Roosevelt promptly asked him where his colonel was, and when the captain couldn't point him out, Roosevelt said, "Then I am the ranking officer here, and I give the order to charge."

This put Dimmick in a tight spot. A fifty-seven-year-old Civil War vet, Dimmick knew all about following orders, but this one was coming from an officer of volunteers and was in direct violation of the one his commanding officer had given to him. Roosevelt abruptly ended the man's torment by saying, "Then let my men through, sir."

Around this same time, First Lieutenant Henry Anson Barber of the Ninth had seen Roosevelt and the Rough Riders moving up and immediately alerted the First Brigade's Colonel Henry Carroll. Carroll sent Barber to Roosevelt with a message cautioning him to be careful of his men; he didn't want the Rough Riders accidentally firing into them. Barber also told Roosevelt they were under orders not to advance and asked him what orders he had. Roosevelt said he was going to charge the hill.

The Spaniards continued to pour volleys from the hilltop as Barber raced back to Colonel Carroll with the news of Roosevelt's planned charge. That a decisive moment had been reached seemed to come to the men of the different regiments all at once. Word spread down the line that one troop of Regulars and then another was about to join the charge, orders or not. "The cheer was taken up and taken up again, on the left, and in the distance it rolled on and on," Barber remembered. "And so we started. Colonel Roosevelt, of the Rough Riders, started the whole movement on the left, which was the first advance of the assault."

Sergeant William E. Dame, a forty-year-old miner in Troop E, came up on several men of the Tenth Cavalry. One of these Buffalo Soldiers asked Dame who he was and where the hell he was going.

"Rough Riders going to take that hill," Dame answered. "Get out of the way or fall in with us."

"I will be damned if those Rough Riders will get ahead of me," a Buffalo Soldier snapped back.

Just then, one of the white officers of the Tenth, seeing the Rough Riders in his line of Regulars, shouted, "E Troop to the front!" His command was meant for the Tenth's Troop E, but his voice sounded similar to one of the Rough Riders' officers, and the men of the Rough Riders' Troop E sprang forward. The Buffalo Soldiers charged with them. Later one of the Rough Riders wrote: "I most positively assert that every face I looked into, both white and black, had a broad grin upon it."

Before starting up Kettle Hill, the San Juan River had to be crossed. The men jumped in and discovered that the water came up to their waists. George Hamner, Troop F, was about midstream when he saw the splash of a bullet in the water and said to the soldier next to him, "That one came close, didn't it?"

"Yes," the trooper replied, "but it went through me first."

The trooper (Hamner could not remember his name) struggled to the bank, where he collapsed on a small grassy spot. Aware that he was dying, he refused Hamner's attempts to help him. In "his last gasping words," Hamner recalled, he said "to go on up there [where] I was needed."

The climb up Kettle Hill was like the advance across the valley. The men ran a few feet and then fell flat, firing their Krags at the house, outbuildings, and trenches. "The top of the hill sputtered like a disturbed volcano," remembered Arthur Cosby, "and the hail of bullets spattered down on the troops moving upwards."

Cosby also noted that sometimes a man would drop to the ground and not get up again. A correspondent observed that men struck by a bullet "never failed to fall in little heaps with instantaneous flaccidity of muscles. There were no gradual droppings on one knee, no men who slowly fell while struggling to keep standing. There were no cries. The injured ones did not throw hands up and fall dramatically backward with strident cries and stiffened legs, as wounded heroes fall upon the stage. They fell like clods." And they made a strange sound, "a combination of the metallic jingle of canteens and guns, and the singular, thick thud of a falling human body."

About a quarter of the way up the hill, Cosby lay on the ground, pulling his campaign hat tight on his head, when he felt a sting in his right hand and a thud in his chest. He looked at his hand, which was spewing blood, and when he looked down at his chest, he saw a tear in his shirt.

Cosby was lucky he could still breathe—a single Mauser bullet had ripped through his hand, punctured the brim of his hat, grazed his temple, and entered his chest just below his right collarbone. The bullet was still somewhere inside him, although he felt no pain internally. But his hand wound was the most troubling because it prevented him from working the action of his Krag. Cosby reluctantly informed his sergeant he was wounded and started for the rear.

Twenty-seven-year-old Arizona gold miner Henry Peck Bardshar was a member of Buckey O'Neill's Troop A. A brawny man standing five feet eleven inches tall, he had latched on to Roosevelt after O'Neill fell, and Roosevelt, who had lost yet another orderly, was happy to give Bardshar the job.

On the slope of Kettle Hill, Bardshar was frustrated because he couldn't get a good bead on the enemy while lying down. So in spite of the flurry of Mauser bullets from the trenches, Bardshar stood up, and each time before he fired, he took careful aim with his Krag. A Regular Army lieutenant spotted Bardshar doing this, went up to him, and angrily shouted, "What do you mean by exposing yourself in that fashion? There have been enough men killed and wounded as it is. Don't you know enough to lie down when you fire?"

Bardshar's blood was already pumping from the stress of the firefight, and this dressing down by the lieutenant, who didn't even belong to his regiment, made him seethe. For a few seconds, he coldly stared at the officer, standing a short distance off, seriously considering whether or not to murder the man. Suddenly, the officer pitched forward on his face. Bardshar ran up to him and saw bright red blood oozing from a hole in the officer's forehead—he was stone dead.

Not far away, Roosevelt waved his hat from atop Little Texas, urging the men on—Rough Riders, Buffalo Soldiers, and white Regulars from the First Cavalry. As they neared the summit, an odd, metallic pinging could be heard over the gunfire. Several enemy soldiers were firing from behind the large cast-iron kettles, and when an American bullet hit one of the kettles, it rang like a bell.

About forty yards from the top, Roosevelt came to a wire fence put up by the Spaniards. He had already navigated one fence at the base of Kettle Hill. There, some troopers had pulled up a few posts and knocked the fence down so he could ride across. But with the Spaniards now running out of the buildings and fleeing their trenches, there was no time if Roosevelt wanted to be in on the capture. He leaped out of his saddle, jumped the fence, and ran toward the buildings—there would be no tripping over his saber today, as he had purposely left it with his belongings in camp. A short distance ahead, Roosevelt saw the arrow-straight Bardshar emptying his magazine at the retreating Spaniards. Two of his targets flopped into the dirt.

As Roosevelt rushed forward, two Spanish soldiers jumped out of a trench ten yards away and fired at him and Bardshar. When the shots went wide, the terrified Spaniards turned to run. Roosevelt, without slowing his pace, raised his revolver, the one recovered from the sunken battleship *Maine*, and fired once at each man. His first shot missed, but the second sent its target headfirst into the dirt. An exultant Roosevelt later wrote his friend Henry Cabot Lodge, "Did I tell you that I killed a Spaniard with my own hand . . . ?"

A disorganized throng of men and officers from various troops converged on the buildings at the summit. Guidon bearers raced to plant their staffs on the hill and claim for their units the honor of being the first. "[I] will say that myself, my Guidon, and most of E Troop with a few of the 10th Cav were the first on top of the hill," wrote New Mexico's Captain Frederick Muller. One of Muller's men also boasted of their triumph, writing in a letter home that "our guidon, which was carried by Sergeant Albert Jones, was the first on the hill, so was nearly all of Troop E."

Roosevelt admitted later that it was really impossible to say who was first. Legitimate claims, he said, could also be made by Troops G and F and two troops of the Ninth Cavalry, the latter arriving at the top from the opposite side of the hill. But these were things to be argued later; the fight was not nearly over. The swarming troopers on Kettle Hill almost immediately began drawing heavy rifle fire and shelling from the earthworks and buildings on the long, high ridge several hundred yards to their front—San Juan Hill.

The Rough Riders' Charge on Kettle Hill, oil painting by Frederic
Remington, 1898. (From a photo by the author.)

To the left, Roosevelt could see lines of dark, blue-clad figures—more than one thousand men—slowly climbing the hillside toward the San Juan blockhouse. They were part of General Jacob Kent's infantry division. "Obviously the proper thing to do was to help them," Roosevelt wrote later. He quickly gathered several men and, as an occasional shell burst over their heads, commenced sending volleys of Krag bullets at the blockhouse and surrounding trenches. Some Rough Riders fired from behind the iron kettles in the same way the Spaniards had used them as cover just moments before.

John W. Swetnam, a twenty-four-year-old Arizona cowboy in Troop B, had a reputation for being a good shot, and he advised his comrades to take their time and "be sure you have it on him when you pull!" Then Swetnam got down on one knee and, following his own counsel, took careful aim and slowly began to squeeze his carbine's trigger. In that instant, a split second before the trigger could release the carbine's spring-loaded firing pin, Swetnam's head popped back, and he collapsed to the ground. A Mauser bullet had pierced his skull.

"You couldn't place your finger more in the center of his forehead than that bullet that hit him was placed," wrote Sergeant Hughes. "He never even kicked."

Hughes, a blacksmith from Tucson, Arizona, was bleeding freely from his own head wound, which he had received during the assault on Kettle Hill. A friend had wrapped a bandage around his head, but the bandage had fallen off, and the blood running down Hughes's face looked fairly gruesome.

Roosevelt passed by, took one look at Hughes and another man with a head wound, Fred Bugbee of Troop A, and told them both to go to the rear, as their appearance could not have a good effect on the men. A minute later, Roosevelt saw the pair still on the firing line and said, "Didn't I order you men back?"

"You go to hell. We are not going back," Bugbee said.

Roosevelt turned and walked away, pretending he hadn't heard the young cowboy, whom he could've court-martialed for insubordination. Instead, he would later give Bugbee and Hughes official commendations for bravery.

For a good ten minutes, the Rough Riders and troopers from the other cavalry regiments on the hill fired round after round into the Spaniards on the far ridge. Theodore Miller lay next to his childhood friend, Second Lieutenant David Goodrich, the man who had promised Miller a spot in his Troop D just five weeks earlier. Goodrich looked over at "Thede," as he called him. "He seemed to be enjoying himself immensely," Goodrich wrote later.

Then someone shouted, "The Spanish machine-guns!" A rhythmic *boom-boom-boom-boom* cut through the gunfire, and it gave each trooper a feeling of dread. The men had faced the rapid-fire guns of the enemy at Las Guásimas, and no one wanted to go through that again. Roosevelt continued to listen—the sound was different, and it was coming from the flat ground to the left, below San Juan Hill. Suddenly, Roosevelt jumped up and slapped his thigh. "It's the Gatlings, men! It's our Gatlings!" he yelled gleefully. Hearty cheers erupted from the men's throats.

The Gatling was not a true self-acting machine gun. It consisted of ten long barrels around a central shaft that rotated and fired, one barrel at a time, with the turning of a hand crank. There were four of these guns with the Fifth Corps, in a special detachment under the command of First Lieutenant John H. Parker. Parker's Gatlings were the Model 1895, the most advanced version of a weapon first patented in 1862. They were manufactured by Colt and fired the same .30-caliber round as the Krag carbines.

Every so often, Roosevelt noticed, the drumming stopped, but it would start up again moments later, each time a little closer to San Juan Hill. When Roosevelt at last observed the American infantry-men rushing the rifle pits near the San Juan blockhouse and the Span-iards jumping out and running away, he quickly ordered a cease-fire so they wouldn't shoot into their own men.

Oblivious to the bullets buzzing past him, Roosevelt stepped in front of his line, raised his pistol high in the air, and shouted, "Now by God, men! Let's charge 'em, God damn 'em!" He jumped a wire fence and started running down Kettle Hill. A grassy valley with a small, shallow lake separated Kettle Hill from San Juan Hill, and on the crest above the lake was a frame house surrounded by an earthwork from which the Spaniards had been wreaking havoc on the men on Kettle Hill. Roosevelt intended to take that house and the trenches, but most of his men, caught up in the shooting, cheering, and dodging bullets, did not hear the order to charge, nor had they seen Roosevelt start.

Trooper Oliver B. Norton yelled, "For God's sake, follow the colo-nel." But as Norton rose to join Roosevelt, a bullet slammed into his head, killing him instantly.

After running a hundred yards, Roosevelt looked over his shoulder and saw only five of his men following him. He stopped in his tracks, and two of the men with him were hit by Mauser bullets. He couldn't take the Spanish position with three men any more than he could with five.

"Lie down, boys," he told the troopers, "and wait here till I return."

Then Roosevelt left to fetch the rest of the brigade. It was a rare poor decision from a leader who was famous for his clear thinking in times of stress.

"[T]here was really no possible point in letting them stay there

Lieutenant Parker's Gatling gun battery. (Author's Collection.)

while I went back," Roosevelt would afterward admit, "but at the moment it seemed perfectly natural to me, and apparently so to them, for they cheerfully nodded, and sat down in the grass, firing back at the line of trenches from which the Spaniards were shooting at them."

One of those men, when later asked about Roosevelt's order to stay put, said, "Well, it was a ticklish place, but we'd have lain on a gridiron of hell, if he'd given the order."

According to another, Herbert P. McGregor of Troop F, it might not have been hell, but it came damn close. "Every S.O.B. of us got shot while lying there waiting for the Colonel to come back," he recalled.

Roosevelt's orderly, Henry Bardshar, also didn't see his lieutenant colonel take off over the hill. He had been standing near the iron kettles when an artillery shell exploded overhead. Two men next to him were struck by shell fragments, their blood splattering Bardshar's face, clothing, and carbine. He saw the two troopers motionless on the ground and men running and firing their Krags—all the commotion of battle—but he heard no sounds. It was a weird, peaceful silence, and Bardshar began to think he was dead.

He started walking toward the lake, hoping to wash away all the blood, when he met Roosevelt running back up the hill alone. Bardshar thought it strange that Roosevelt was talking to him. Roosevelt's lips moved, but it was like one of Edison's silent moving pictures. Bardshar wrote later that his first thought was, "He doesn't know that I am dead." Then Roosevelt began to look angry, and he kept moving his lips. Finally Bardshar pointed to his ears. Roosevelt stepped closer, put his mouth to one of Bardshar's ears, and shouted, "Didn't you hear me call for a charge?"

That Bardshar could hear. He wasn't dead after all, just temporarily deaf from the concussion of the exploding shell. Bardshar shook his head no to Roosevelt's question and followed him back up the hill.

Roosevelt was livid when he encountered his Rough Riders, but he quickly realized they were not to blame for remaining behind. "[E]ven while I taunted them bitterly for not having followed me," he recalled, "it was all I could do not to smile at the look of injury and surprise that came over their faces." One trooper said it made him feel like "my mother had accused me of striking her." Several shouted for the colonel to lead them now—they would follow.

Roosevelt wanted the other regiments with him on that charge as well. He ran over to General Sumner, who had arrived on Kettle Hill behind the Tenth Cavalry, and asked permission to assault the trenches on the ridge opposite. Sumner gave him the desired order; he knew there was no denying this man. But the general wisely retained a portion of the cavalry, including some of the Rough Riders, on Kettle Hill as a reserve.

The staccato notes of a bugle cut the air, and all eyes were now on Roosevelt. When he again jumped the fence, hundreds of men— Buffalo Soldiers, Rough Riders, and white Regulars—followed. The Spaniards concentrated their fire on the charging mass. As Troop D ran out over the crest of Kettle Hill, five of its troopers dropped almost simultaneously. Theodore Miller was one of the five. Lieutenant Goodrich rushed to his prostrate friend as two men worked to push his shirt back. After a brief examination, they determined that a Mauser bullet had entered Miller's left shoulder and cut a vicious course across his upper body before exiting the right shoulder. There was obvious spinal cord damage, as he couldn't move anything below the shoulders.

Miller forced a smile and said he didn't think he was badly hurt, but a moment later he whispered to Goodrich that it was a little hard for him to breathe. Goodrich detailed a couple of men to look after Miller and sent for a first aid man. Then it was time for the lieutenant to rejoin his troop.

"I said goodbye to Thede and took a last look to see that he should be cared for," Goodrich wrote later. "He was pale but perfectly calm and collected."

One of the men who remained by Miller's side was his Troop D comrade Harrison Jewell Holt, a twenty-two-year-old fresh out of Harvard. Miller looked up at Holt with a troubled expression on his face.

"I'm going, Harry," Miller said, "but it's in a good cause, isn't it?"

The ragged line of troopers flooded down Kettle Hill, with several of the "long-legged men" passing the huffing Roosevelt. The charging horde swung around to the right of the lake, although some men chose to wade through it. Then they went straight up the steep, open hillside toward the rifle pits and the fortified house on the ridge. "It was the grandest sight I ever saw," wrote Second Lieutenant John Greenway to his mother. Another Rough Rider later described it as "just a mob that went up a hill. If the Spaniards had been able to shoot, we'd never have made it to the top."

Volleys rained down from the trenches while individual troopers stopped occasionally to return the fire, but always climbing. Roosevelt heard William Pollock, a Pawnee Indian in Troop D, let out an "ungodly war-whoop." Drunk on the glory of it all, Roosevelt turned to Henry Bardshar as they charged side by side and shouted, "Holy Godfrey, what fun!"

As the troopers closed to one hundred and fifty yards, the Spaniards began to pile out of their earthworks and scatter. The first Americans to reach the trenches were Greenway, Roger Fitch, and John Beissel (all Troop G men), and a captain of the Tenth Cavalry.

"There were a good many dead & wounded Spaniards in & about the trenches," Fitch wrote in his diary. "We also captured one 'playing possum' in the trench. He was nearly scared to death & piteously begged for mercy." The possum-playing Spaniard was a bugler. Greenway confiscated his bugle as a souvenir and sent the much relieved prisoner to the rear under guard.

The time was approximately 2:30 P.M. After the climb up San Juan in the stifling heat, the men desperately needed a halt to catch their breaths. Meanwhile, the trenches and house were thoroughly searched. Roosevelt gazed upon the enemy dead sprawled in the trenches, their crumpled forms not unlike the dead soldiers in old photographs of Civil War battlefields. He noted that most of the dead were oozing blood and brain matter from small holes in their heads. Their heads had been the only things visible to shoot at.

All the regiments were mixed up and some troops were now without officers, either killed or wounded. But Roosevelt was used to

San Juan Hill. The blockhouse Roosevelt and his men charged is out of view to the right, where the trooper is pointing. Visible is the south end of the shallow lake the Rough Riders circled around; some splashed through it. (Author's Collection.)

making order from chaos. He soon got the milling men organized and started on another advance west across the hilltop toward Santiago. "This last charge was the prettiest of all," J. Ogden Wells penned in his diary, "for the country being open, the men kept a good line, kneeling now and then to fire."

Roosevelt double-quicked his line—between three hundred and four hundred men—to a point directly overlooking the city, its houses visible only a thousand yards distant. Just in front of the town was another line of defenses, which now held the Spaniards who had retreated from the top of San Juan Hill. Roosevelt hastily began to reform his troops to charge these positions, but as he did so, one of General Sumner's aides rode up and told him to halt the advance where he was. Sumner wanted Roosevelt to "hold the hill at all hazards."

Lieutenant Greenway, one of the long-legged men, didn't want to stop. He and about thirty of his troopers advanced another hundred and fifty yards beyond Roosevelt, but they were soon called back. Greenway hardly liked the order—he was convinced he could have marched his little squad right into the city.

Silhouetted on the rise of the hill, Roosevelt's men made fine targets for the Spaniards below them. Lying next to J. Ogden Wells was Roy Cashion, a clerk from Oklahoma Territory. At nineteen years, the brown-eyed, dark-haired Cashion was the youngest man in the Rough Riders. Wells happened to look over and saw that the boy's face was resting on the ground. Crawling to get a closer look, he discovered that the trooper had taken a bullet between the eyes.

Corporal Henry Meagher, on the other side of Wells, suddenly jerked and grabbed his shoulder. They were taking too many casualties. Roosevelt pulled his troopers back fifty yards and ordered them to lie down. The men were now hidden behind the crest, but not by much. Mauser bullets buzzed three or four inches above their heads, snipping the tall, green blades of grass around them.

It was brought to Roosevelt's attention that his men's cartridge belts, which held one hundred rounds, were getting used up. Some were down to thirty cartridges; others, even less. He ordered a cease-fire to conserve the ammunition—and to prevent his men from drawing the enemy's fire.

Despite their orders, the men found it hard to resist peeking over the crest. After the shooting died down, J. Ogden Wells slowly raised his head until he could see the Spanish earthworks. His eyes widened when he spotted three Spanish officers on horseback, riding along the line just over a quarter mile away.

Wells asked his lieutenant for permission to crawl forward and take a shot at the officers. The lieutenant told him to go on. Wells slid on his belly out in front of the line until he had a good view of the officers. He flipped up his Krag's ladder sight and moved the crosspiece up to a range of five hundred yards. He fired several quick shots in succession, his gun blasts breaking the temporary calm. On the third shot, the officer in the middle tumbled off his horse. Wells hurried back behind the crest as Mauser bullets thudded into the hillside.

Roosevelt was always moving, looking to the men's spacing and urging them to keep alert. At one point, he noticed several black troopers leaving the line and heading to the rear. Some of these men simply wanted to find their own regiments; one or two claimed to be going for ammunition, and a few appeared to be helping wounded comrades to the rear. Roosevelt suspected some were taking advantage of the absence of their officers to shirk their duty. Whatever their reasons, legitimate or otherwise, Roosevelt could not allow them to go. He was the ranking officer present, and his orders were to hold his position. He needed every available man.

Drawing his Colt revolver, Roosevelt stepped in front of the Buffalo Soldiers and ordered them to halt. Holding his handgun up, but not pointing it at the men, Roosevelt calmly told them that while he appreciated their gallantry thus far, the first man he suspected of going to the rear would receive a .38-caliber bullet between his shoulders.

"Now, I shall be very sorry to hurt you," Roosevelt continued, "and you don't know whether or not I will keep my word, but my men can tell you that I always do."

Some Rough Riders chimed in, "He always does; he always does!"

But there were others who spoke up for the black troopers: "[Y]ou won't have to shoot those men, Colonel. We know those boys." And several black troopers shouted, "[W]e will stay with you, Colonel!"

A sergeant of the Tenth Cavalry recalled, "Everyone who saw the incident knew the Colonel was mistaken about our men trying to shirk duty, but we all knew that he could not admit of any heavy detail from his command, so no one thought ill of the matter."

Roosevelt afterward apologized to the soldiers of the Tenth, acknowledging that "he never expected to have, and could not ask to have, better men beside him in a hard fight." A year later, he would credit the Ninth and Tenth's white officers for the Buffalo Soldiers' exemplary conduct in the campaign.

The Spaniards were suddenly out of their trenches. At least four hundred, maybe more, rushed forward to retake the hill. Someone yelled the alarm, and Roosevelt's men sprang off the ground and ran forward to the crest. They shouted gleefully, Roosevelt recalled, because they now had a target out in the open to shoot at.

Worried that Roosevelt's thin line might not be able to withstand the attack, Colonel Wood dispatched an aide to Lieutenant Parker of the Gatling Gun Detachment, whose gleaming guns were now atop San Juan Hill, near the main blockhouse.

"Colonel Wood orders you to send one or two of your guns over to help Roosevelt," the aide shouted.

Parker ignored the orders; his guns were doing good work where they were. The aide became agitated and shook his arm, pointing to the right, trying to get Parker to look. When Parker did, he saw the large body of Spaniards at a distance of six hundred yards but only two hundred yards from Roosevelt's position. Parker shouted to the gun crew nearest him to turn their Gatling to the right and cut loose on the enemy advance. Within seconds, the gunner was cranking five hundred shots a minute.

The Spaniards retreated to their trenches, but they had no intention of letting their Mauser barrels cool, nor their artillery. Bullets and shrapnel flew over the crest while the Rough Riders and Buffalo Soldiers hugged the ground. One man asked, "[W]hy didn't God make a man like a mole so he could dig a hole and crawl in the ground?" His buddies broke out in laughter.

Roosevelt could never be a mole. This day he was more like a caged tiger. Robert Ferguson, Roosevelt's old ranch partner and a sergeant in Troop K, wrote that "Theodore moved about in the midst of the shrapnel explosions like Shadrach, Meschach & Sons in the midst of the fiery furnace. . . . Theodore preferred to stand up or walk about snuffing the fragrant air of combat. I really believe firmly now, that they cannot kill him."

The enemy fire died down toward evening, and the men's thoughts turned to food. Actually, they had been thinking about food for hours. It was nearly 6:00 P.M. and no one had eaten since early that morning, and because they had thrown off their packs and haversacks back on the Santiago road, there were no rations. The Rough Riders knew by now that, with all the supply problems since their arrival in Cuba, they had a better chance of dying of starvation than from a Spanish bullet. But they were old hands at "rustling," and they made a very fortunate discovery in the frame house just back of their line.

The house had apparently been used as Spanish officers' quarters, and when the troopers went inside, they found the officers' mess still cooking (the former occupants were obviously under the impression they wouldn't be leaving their defenses anytime soon). There were steaming hot kettles of fresh beef stew, boiled rice, and boiled peas, as well as loaves of rice bread, dried herring, and cans of preserves. They also found ten gallons of rum.

Several men hauled the steaming kettles and other grub to the front line, where it was carefully doled out to each trooper in equal portions. Ben Colbert gobbled up his small serving of pea soup and bread "like it was chocolate cake," he wrote later.

Roosevelt was about to sample a cupful of stew when George Hamner stopped him. The Spaniards might have poisoned the food, he warned. Wouldn't it be wise to allow himself and some others to taste it first?

"By George, sir!" Roosevelt blustered, "they didn't have time to poison it!" And he dug into his share as quickly as his men and was just as satisfied.

Chapter Eight

The Siege

*I had the desire to be in a big battle, but I'll never
have it again. Such a one as we had was an inferno
and I don't care to experience another.*

SAMUEL MCLEARY WELLER, TROOP F

Two captains from the Third Cavalry came to Roosevelt late in the afternoon of July 1 to lodge an "emphatic protest" against what they had heard was a withdrawal from San Juan Heights. Withdrawal? It was the first Roosevelt had heard of this, which could only be termed a retreat. This had to be false, he told them, but he agreed with the captains that "it would be far worse than a blunder to abandon our position."

About 9:00 P.M., the white-bearded General Wheeler approached Roosevelt from out of the darkness. Fever or not, there was no keeping Fightin' Joe off a battlefield. As soon as he heard about the attack that was planned for that morning, he jumped on his horse and rode to the front. He was wise enough not to take back the Cavalry Division from General Sumner—it would have been cruel to deny Sumner the honor of leading the division into battle after it had just been promised him. Wheeler waited until the Heights were captured to resume his command.

The news Wheeler brought Roosevelt was stunning: the talk of a withdrawal was true. Wheeler said that several officers had appealed to him to leave the Heights and establish a strong line farther back. He suspected that these officers had also appealed to General Shafter, and he had written the commanding general, strongly disapproving of such a move. It would "cost us much prestige," he wrote. Wheeler was confident, he told Roosevelt, they wouldn't be going anywhere.

Yet in the same dispatch to Shafter, Wheeler had made comments that tended to bolster the case for a retreat. The men were completely exhausted, he wrote, and so many wounded men had been helped to the rear that the front lines were very thin. In some places, the enemy was only three hundred yards away. If his men entrenched, "we ought to hold tomorrow, but I fear it will be a severe day."

By this time, Colonel Wood wished the Cavalry Division was being led by someone else. He subsequently wrote his wife that Wheeler spent most of his time talking to the war correspondents "and while a dear old man, is no more use here than a child."

Roosevelt thought that retreating was outrageous and shameful. Good, brave men had died to take this hill, and the prize, Santiago, was only a thousand yards off. And if they fell back, the Spaniards would surely reoccupy the trenches—it would take another battle to rout them, in which even more Americans would die.

"Well, General," Roosevelt said, "I really don't know whether we would obey an order to fall back. We can take the city by a rush, and if we have to move out of here at all I should be inclined to make the rush in the right direction."

Fortunately, Roosevelt didn't have to make that decision because shortly after their meeting, Wheeler sent word to entrench. In later years, Roosevelt remained uncertain as to what he would have done if Shafter had ordered the withdrawal. "Had I disobeyed the order," he confided to an aide in 1908, "it would have been regarded as an impetuous act, I presume, but it really would have been the result of careful thought after carefully weighing the pros and cons."

Earlier in the day, some troopers discovered a supply of picks and shovels in the outbuildings connected with the fortified house in the rear. Several men were now sent to retrieve the tools, including J. Ogden Wells. "As we went silently back to the block house," Wells wrote, "we passed four or five dead Spaniards and quite a number of Rough Riders, their upturned faces looking ghastly in the moonlight."

The men were more than just worn out. The excitement of the charge had long passed, and they hadn't gotten nearly enough to eat. Yet the trench digging began immediately, the men working in shifts. It helped that the reserves kept on Kettle Hill during the afternoon had been brought up to the front lines that evening; more men to take turns at the shovels.

Warren E. Crockett, a short trooper of slight build from Marietta, Georgia, didn't feel he would be any use to the regiment as a ditch digger. He had worked for the Internal Revenue Service in Georgia for the last seven years, and while he was very good at chasing moonshiners, he wasn't a particularly strong man. Crockett told Roosevelt that he'd found a quantity of Spanish coffee, and if the lieutenant colonel would let him make it, "it would be worth as much as three men digging trenches." Roosevelt, a coffee drinker himself, approved wholeheartedly, so for the next few hours, Crockett worked over the fire and trudged back and forth with steaming cups of the black liquid. "[H]e cooked some of the finest Spanish coffee I ever tasted," Roosevelt would say years later.

When it wasn't their turn to dig, the men tried to get some sleep, but their blankets were with the packs they had thrown off before the battle. They scrounged a few Spanish blankets—thin and made of cotton—enough for one in ten men. The rest suffered in the cool night air heavy with dew, their clothing still wet with sweat. Bardshar secured one of the Spanish blankets for Roosevelt, who slept on the ground with his orderly and Lieutenant Goodrich so they could share it.

Before turning in, Roosevelt pulled his diary from his shirt pocket and made a hurried entry in pencil under the date of July 1: *Rose at 4. Big battle. Commanded regiment. Held extreme front of firing line.*

About 3:00 A.M., the crack of a single carbine split the stillness, followed by the pitiful squealing of a dog, obviously in much pain. A barrage of gunfire suddenly erupted from the Spanish lines, which was vigorously answered by the Americans. Small bright flashes of light—the muzzle flashes of hundreds of Mausers and Krags—blinked at each other like so many fireflies in the inky blackness.

The shooting eventually died down, and everyone got back to either digging or shivering. It was later learned that one of the Rough Riders on lookout had seen what he believed were "two heads." He thought they were Spanish skirmishers, but he accidentally fired low and said he must have hit a dog belonging to one of the Spaniards. The more likely explanation: the young trooper saw something moving in the darkness and shot at it, only to discover that he'd simply seen a stray dog.

As soon as the morning brought enough light to see the iron sights on their rifles, the Spaniards began the fight again. "A perfect hail of bullets came over the hill and the batteries in the city, and the ships in the harbor opened on us with shrapnel," J. Ogden Wells wrote. One shell exploded just above where Roosevelt had established his headquarters, its spherical bullets killing or wounding five men just steps away.

The men in the newly dug trenches were fairly safe, but those on the hilltop weren't, so Roosevelt ordered the men to move halfway down the rear slope, making the hill serve as a natural breastwork. Here they tried to rest, as best they could in the midst of gunfire and shrieking artillery shells. A number of the men could be seen with crude bandages wrapped around their heads, arms, or legs from wounds received during the previous day's fighting.

Corporal Granville Roland Fortescue of Troop E didn't have a bandage, but Roosevelt had seen him limping the day before. The twenty-two-year-old New York–born Fortescue, known as "Roly" to family and friends, had left his studies at the University of Pennsylvania to join the Rough Riders. He was short, only five feet six inches tall, and he definitely wasn't a westerner, but, on the other hand, his stepfather was Robert Roosevelt, Theodore's uncle.

Lieutenant Colonel Roosevelt found Fortescue a sharp, dependable young man and had been using him as an extra orderly. He wondered about the limp but hadn't asked. But now it was obvious because the wincing Fortescue sat on the ground and pulled off his boot to reveal a blood-drenched sock. A bullet had passed through his foot.

Those nearby didn't give a second thought to Fortescue's wound; lots of men were bleeding that day. No one knew that locked within Fortescue's blood was the greatest secret on San Juan Hill—a secret known only to Roosevelt and Fortescue, who was the offspring of a long-running affair between Robert Roosevelt and his Irish maid. Fortescue's two siblings were fathered by Roosevelt as well. When Roosevelt's first wife died, he'd married his mistress, Marion "Minnie" O'Shea Fortescue (the surname being an alias), and adopted their children. The three children would retain the Fortescue surname and the façade of propriety, but Roly Fortescue was actually Theodore Roosevelt's first cousin by blood.

Not all the casualties were a result of bullets or shrapnel. When J. Ogden Wells moved down the back of the hill following Roosevelt's order, he stumbled upon Troop D's First Lieutenant Joseph Armistead Carr, lying on the ground unconscious. The thirty-year-old Carr, a resident of Washington, D.C., was faceup with no shirt, and his tongue was sticking out of his mouth.

Wells grabbed Carr's canteen to give him a drink; the man was clearly dehydrated. But Wells discovered that the canteen was filled with rum, some of the ten gallons discovered the day before—and Carr didn't need any more of that. Wells shook the lieutenant, but his rolling eyes indicated he was a long way from wearing off the alcohol's effects. Captain Frederick Muller, who was apparently oblivious to the fact the soldier was inebriated, ordered Wells and Private Peter Byrne to take him to the field hospital in the rear.

Bullets and shrapnel shells were still screaming across the flats between San Juan Heights and El Pozo, making this a dangerous assignment. Then Wells spotted a captured Spanish artillery mule and thought that would save time and effort. But Carr said there was no way he could stay in its saddle. So the three men continued their slow walk, Carr held up by Wells on one side and Byrne on the other.

They came up on a soldier with a head wound who was also making his way to the rear. "He presented a sickening sight with blood streaming down his face," Wells wrote, "but we were used to such sights by this time." Wells took a look at the wound and bandaged the soldier's head.

When they reached the area of their first skirmish line of the day before, near Las Guamas Creek, Carr suddenly stiffened and collapsed, shouting, "My God! I am shot!" Wells believed Carr was hallucinating. A bullet had thumped the ground very close, but that was all. Yet Carr was curled in a fetal position and seemed to be in real agony. Taking a closer look, they spotted a hole in Carr's trousers, and, after pulling down his pants, saw the ugly wound in his groin.

The odd thing, though, was that the bullet had struck Carr in the front as they were walking to the rear, meaning the bullet must have come from their own men. Wells jumped up and shouted that they were Americans, but no one answered. Carr was in too much pain to stand, and he would have to be carried. Byrne started off for more help.

Shortly after Byrne left, a surgeon happened by on his way to the front and stopped long enough to give Carr's wound a proper dressing. The surgeon also answered the mystery of the bullet's origin, telling Wells there were still Spanish snipers in the trees. This made Wells curious, and he foolishly stood up and walked around, gazing up into the trees for the sniper. Within seconds, a bullet buzzed by his head, convincing him that a sniper was nearby. Wells then came up with a plan that involved using himself as bait. He waited for the next shot, which soon came, again narrowly missing him, then fell to the ground as if he had been hit.

Playing dead, Wells carefully studied the treetops within view until he spotted the man in a tree about three hundred yards away. By this time, Byrne had come back with two more Rough Riders. Wells sat up, pointed out the sniper to his comrades, and took a shot. The Spaniard seemed to jerk as if hit, but he immediately shot back, and while the other Rough Riders reached for their Krags, Wells took three more shots. On his last try, the sniper's limp body tumbled out of the treetop.

The gunfire started a brief surge of shooting around them, so the men hunkered down and waited for it to calm before continuing. Carr's drunkenness had not only gotten him a painful bullet wound, but it was still a question whether or not his companions would get through this without being shot themselves. The gunfire finally subsided, and Wells and the others placed Carr on a litter made of two carbines and half of a shelter tent. In a short time, the litter bearers safely reached the temporary hospital at El Pozo, where they found Surgeon Church. Leaving Carr in Church's care, they said their goodbyes and turned back to San Juan.

In the midst of his unrelenting Atlanta Campaign, William T. Sherman had written, "To realize what war is one should follow our tracks." Along the road from El Pozo to San Juan Hill, the surreal chaos of war was frighteningly on display. Everywhere the men could see bloated bodies without heads, bodies with gaping holes from jagged fragments of shrapnel shells, and disemboweled horses and mules littering the landscape. Large black flies swarmed around the mutilated corpses while buzzards tore at eyes and lips. Even more repulsive were the large land crabs that slowly surrounded the fallen.

Strewn on each side of the road were haversacks, uniform jackets, bibles, hardtack, blanket rolls, and band instruments (the musicians were serving as litter bearers). A steady stream of wounded flowed through this detritus of battle. Correspondent John Fox Jr. encountered men "with arms in slings; men with trousers torn away at the knee and bandaged legs; men with brow, face, mouth, or throat swathed; men with no shirts, but a broad swathe around the chest or stomach." Almost all these wounded, he wrote, "were dazed and drunken in appearance, except at the brows, which were tightly drawn with pain."

The wounded arrived at the dressing stations and field hospitals on their own two feet, leaning on comrades, or carried on crude litters. The *insurrectos* were frequently seen on the San Juan battlefield carrying or helping the wounded to the rear, sometimes a distance of three or four miles. Very few wounded were moved by mule-drawn ambulance—only two were available for the entire army. Several ambulances were still stowed away on the transports and never unloaded.

The primary field hospital was about two miles behind (east) of El Pozo. The hospital's "tents" were large tarpaulins stretched over poles. Each tarpaulin sheltered two or three operating tables that were constantly in use, the surgeons dousing the tables with water after each patient to wash away the blood. As many as four hundred wounded sat and stretched out on the ground near the tents, waiting in the boiling heat for their turn with the surgeons.

Hearst photojournalist John C. Hemment set up his tripod and camera near one of the operating tables where a surgeon was sawing off a man's leg. Being a fastidious photographer, and also aware of the possibility that a glass plate could break before getting to the darkroom or even during developing, Hemment was intent on making several exposures. As he turned to ask his assistant for a third plate holder, he saw that the man was in tears and shaking uncontrollably. Hemment took hold of his helper and asked him what was wrong.

"Jack," said the assistant, "I can stand to see these men shot. I saw them fall in battle; but this is something beyond my endurance."

The man fell into Hemment's arms, sobbing. Hemment learned later that it wasn't the close-up view of the amputation that had overwhelmed his assistant but "the other scenes of the poor, helpless

Cubans helping a wounded Rough Rider to a field hospital.
Photo by John C. Hemment. (Author's Collection.)

wretches sitting around and biding their time for an opportunity to come under the edge of the knife or the grinding teeth of the surgical saw."

There were no cots or blankets, and rations were just as scarce at the hospital, where they were most needed, as they were at the front. The surgeons "worked like Trojans," wrote one correspondent, but there just weren't enough of them. The situation at the field hospitals was so dire that Colonel Wood ordered that only the most severe cases be sent to the rear.

Theodore Miller, still clinging to life after falling on the slope of Kettle Hill, had been carried by his comrades to the field hospital, but after examining the entry and exit holes on his body, the surgeons could do little more than clean them up and try to make the boy comfortable—amputations were easy, but even the best hospitals in the States couldn't help someone whose spinal cord had been shredded. He was soon transported in a cart to Siboney, to a hospital established by the American Red Cross.

Arthur Cosby, a bullet lodged in his chest, also ended up in Siboney. He wasn't transported; he walked alone after spending a night at the field hospital. Borrowing some stationery from a correspondent, Cosby wrote his mother on July 2, assuring her he wasn't seriously wounded. He did admit that his hand was so badly cut up that he likely wouldn't return to active duty anytime soon and would probably be put on a ship for Tampa.

John Fox Jr. recognized Cosby sitting on the sand at Siboney. He'd first noticed the handsome fellow the previous winter at sundry Washington social functions. He'd spotted him again in Tampa, standing in formation with other Rough Riders waiting to move

Arthur F. Cosby, photographed at Tampa, Florida, June 6, 1898, and Cosby after being wounded on July 1, 1898. (Arthur F. Cosby scrapbook, Theodore Roosevelt Collection, Houghton Library, Harvard University.)

out, looking so trim in his uniform, his rolled pack over his shoulder. Their next meeting was a shock. They'd run into each other on the rutted Siboney-Santiago road, Cosby with "his hand bandaged—weak, white, trembling, but walking alone, still gentle, considerate, uncomplaining, asserting that he was not hurt except in his hand, and not mentioning the bullet in his chest."

Cosby now patiently sat in the glaring sun on Siboney's beach, waiting to board a hospital ship, although he wasn't sure exactly when that would be. Fox asked if there was anything he could do for him, and Cosby said he would truly appreciate a canned peach if one could be procured from the commissary. Fox started off for the peach, but it was no simple matter. He was able to get it only after finding a surgeon and obtaining a doctor's order. Unfortunately, by the time Fox returned, Cosby was gone. He had been called to board the ship.

Fox felt horrible. "I hope he will pull through," the correspondent wrote later. "Such a man and such a spirit has not been hard to find in this fight."

General Lawton's infantry moved into position on the right of the Cavalry Division on the morning of July 2. Instead of the two hours Lawton had estimated it would take to capture El Caney, it had been ten hours of intense fighting, which accounted for his absence from the assault on San Juan Heights. And with 81 killed and 360 wounded, his victory had been hard earned.

Kent's First Division, infantry, held the Heights to the left, which included the San Juan blockhouse. The position of the Rough Riders, situated due east of Santiago and next to the Siboney-Santiago road, was closest to the enemy. Theirs was a natural salient, projecting from the ridge and overlooking the city. But the trenches they hurriedly dug during the night had no approaches that would allow for unexposed movement between the firing line and the Rough Rider camp over the brow of the hill. So the troopers in the trenches were

essentially stuck there during daylight hours. If they needed to uri-
nate, they did so in the trench.

By midafternoon, some troopers had been hunched over in those
cramped pits for ten hours. It wasn't just the stench and close quarters;
there was also no protection from the tropical sun. Roosevelt was determined to give the men a break, and he could think of only one
way to get that done: he waited for the Spanish gunfire to let up, then
quickly ordered his relief party forward—and they ran like hell. This,
of course, resulted in a storm of flying lead from the Spaniards, but
not before the Rough Riders dove into the trenches. The men being
relieved waited for this barrage to die down before they jumped out
and scrambled for the other side of the crest, the Mauser bullets again
tearing up the hillside.

That afternoon, the Rough Riders at last received a few boxes of
rations. Unfortunately, the men in the trenches had just begun their
several-hour stint. Roosevelt asked for a volunteer to take a box to
them. Bowlegged cowpuncher Bill McGinty stepped up. He hefted
the box and positioned it on his shoulder until it was well balanced,
but just as he was about to start, Roosevelt stopped him. "Wait, I'll go
with you," he said.

Woodbury Kane, now the acting captain of Troop K, didn't like
that idea. "No, no, Colonel Roosevelt. If anyone goes with him, I will
go. The whole regiment is depending on you."

Then McGinty jumped in, insisting he go alone. It didn't make sense
to risk two men, he told them. Roosevelt and Kane concluded he was
right and wished him luck, after which the cowpuncher turned and
broke into a run.

When he crested the hill, it seemed to McGinty as if the entire
enemy line started firing. He hunched over, trying to stay as close to
the ground as he could. The little trooper heard two or three bullets
strike the box, and he immediately felt something wet on his face and
back. But he continued to run, and he reached the trench after what
seemed like an eternity and jumped in. After putting the box down,
he felt his head and the wet liquid, and then looked at his hand. It

wasn't blood. He looked in the box. Mixed in with the hardtack were some canned tomatoes—they didn't make it.

McGinty was followed a short time later by another trooper swinging a pail of hot coffee. The man—and the coffee—didn't get a scratch.

A heavy rain soaked everyone during the afternoon, followed again by the blistering sun. The firing continued off and on, with an occasional shrapnel shell exploding nearby. "It looks real funny to see the men so unconcerned about bullets flying around," Ben Colbert wrote in his diary. "The troops that are not engaged are walking from place to place, begging cigarettes and chewing tobacco." He was amazed to see tobacco selling at the rate of $50 a pound.

It wasn't so funny when Colbert's buddies got hit, though, which seemed to happen often, because the Spanish snipers kept firing away, both in the tall palms to the front and in those scattered in the rear. The snipers behind the lines had been stranded in their perches when the Americans swept forward to capture San Juan Heights. And because these snipers had been told by their officers that the Americans would chop off their heads as quickly as the Cubans, they were afraid to surrender. They "kept up in their trees and showed not only courage," wrote Roosevelt, "but wanton cruelty and barbarity . . . they fired at the doctors who came to the front, and at the chaplains who started to hold burial service; the conspicuous Red Cross brassard worn by all of these noncombatants, instead of serving as a protection, seemed to make them the special objects of the guerilla fire."

Roosevelt hand-picked a detail of sharpshooters from the Rough Riders to hunt and kill the tree-dwelling Spaniards. This gave the troopers an opportunity to display those "special qualifications" as marksmen they had been enlisted for. Roosevelt later singled out two men as being particularly good at this deadly game of kill the sniper before the sniper kills you. They were rancher William B. Proffitt and miner Richard E. Goodwin, both of Arizona's Troop B.

The twenty-five-year-old Proffitt, a native of the Appalachian Mountains of western North Carolina, stood nearly six feet tall. His father had enlisted as a private in a North Carolina infantry regiment at the outbreak of the Civil War, rising to lieutenant before the war ended. Roosevelt described his son as a "tall, sinewy, handsome man of re- markable strength." He had distinguished himself at Las Guásimas when he braved the enemy's bullets to drag the wounded Captain McClintock away from the firing line. McClintock had handed his Colt revolver to Proffitt, and Proffitt still carried it.

Goodwin, also nearly six feet tall but two years older, was born in California. He served as Troop B's saddler. Goodwin teamed up with a Buffalo Soldier to hunt the snipers, and after crawling through the high grass and brush for some time, they eventually located two trees near each other where they heard shots. Goodwin and the black trooper easily spotted one of the snipers, but they couldn't see the shooter in the second tree. The Buffalo Soldier suggested they go ahead and shoot their bird in the hand, after which they could change

Hunting Spanish snipers in the palm trees. Photo by
John C. Hemment. (Author's Collection.)

position and maybe get a bead on the other Spaniard. But Goodwin wanted to wait until they had spotted both snipers so they would each have their own target.

Try as they might, they couldn't see the second sniper hidden in the palm leaves, and the more they delayed, the more time they were giving the Spaniards to kill Americans. So the troopers sighted down their Krags' barrels at the first sniper and simultaneously squeezed off a round. The Spaniard fell lifeless to the ground. A second later, a rifle dropped out of the other tree, followed by a man with a machete shinnying down the tree's trunk. Goodwin and the black trooper ran over to the tall palm and held their carbines on the Spaniard as he reached the ground. In broken English, he pleaded with them not to shoot.

Later, back at camp, Goodwin and the Buffalo Soldier approached headquarters with two Spanish rifles and two straw hats. The pair proudly recounted how they had snuck up on the snipers, killing one outright and scaring the other into surrendering. But Roosevelt saw no Spaniard and asked what had become of him.

"Sir," Goodwin replied, "you said not to take any prisoners, so the nigger cut his throat."

Roosevelt's sharpshooters killed a total of eleven snipers that day and the next morning—without receiving a single wound.

General Shafter had been ill for the last four days. Most of the time he was flat on his back, unable to bear the thought of moving about in the horrid heat. He claimed that during the battle of July 1, he'd had a "general view of the battlefield" from a high hill near his headquarters and that he'd relayed his orders through orderlies and a recently laid telephone line. But a journalist later revealed there was no such hill near Shafter's headquarters, which was at least four miles from San Juan. In reality, Shafter's staff had often made decisions and issued orders at the front on their own initiative because there was no time to consult the general.

Shafter, then, was a nonfactor in the battle's outcome, but so, too, were most of his generals on the field that day. As one admitted later, "San Juan was won by the regimental officers and men. We had as little to do as the referee at a prize-fight who calls 'time.' We called 'time' and they did the fighting." Roosevelt couldn't have agreed more, writing that "it was essentially a troop commanders', indeed, almost a squad leaders', fight."

But again Shafter was considering withdrawing closer to his supply base. He called an early evening meeting of his division commanders at El Pozo. Shafter was worried about reports from his Cuban allies of several thousand Spanish reinforcements on their way to Santiago. His army was stretched over the hilltops for more than five miles, and the rains were threatening to make the road from Siboney impassable, which would shut down what was a meager supply line at best.

As he had the evening before, General Wheeler argued that not one inch should be yielded, but not all his fellow officers agreed, and the group discussed in detail how they would go about a withdrawal if ordered. Shafter instead opted to put off a decision for another twenty-four hours. The meeting over, the commanders returned to the front, and Shafter rode in the darkness to his headquarters farther to the rear. It was about 10:00 P.M. when the weary commander of the Fifth Corps dismounted at his tent. As he did so, he thought he heard distant gunfire over the creaking of his leather saddle. He perked his head. There was no mistaking it now. It sounded like a hell of a fight had broken out on San Juan Heights.

Warren Crockett, now the Rough Riders' coffee brewer of choice, had been on picket duty when the first bullets zipped out of nowhere. He went down, blood pumping with every heartbeat from a hole in his left leg. Several comrades yanked him up and carried him to the rear. Roosevelt ran past Crockett and his companions and over the hill's crest. What had started out as a smattering of gunfire had quickly turned into intense volleys, accompanied by artillery shells exploding overhead. His troopers in the pits were answering with a crackling fire of their own.

Reaching the trenches, Roosevelt squinted and peered down the slope toward the Spanish positions, looking for any sign the enemy was bringing a major assault. He had given orders for the men in camp to come to the trenches and lie down in a skirmish line. Excited and edgy, they also began blazing away with their Krags. Roosevelt calmly reminded them to fire low. To his right, the Buffalo Soldiers of the Tenth were burning through an equal amount of gunpowder. "[I] tell you the black boys set a pace that is damn hard to keep up with," a Rough Rider wrote home, "for they fight like demons and never know when to stop."

The hillside melted into darkness just a few yards ahead of the line, but Roosevelt could see the spurts of flame coming from the Spanish Mausers. Some of the enemy were indeed firing in advance of the Spanish position, likely scouts or pickets. But most of the gunfire was clearly coming from the Spanish trenches, and it soon became obvious to Roosevelt that those gunshots weren't getting any closer. This was not an assault after all—it was a waste of ammunition.

What happened next was a display of pluck that Lieutenant Parker of the Gatlings never forgot. Over the deafening gunfire, he suddenly heard the shouts of both Roosevelt and the Tenth's Captain Charles Ayers. The two officers were "tramping up and down the trench in front of their men, haranguing, commanding, ridiculing their men for shooting in the dark," Parker later wrote. "Ayers told his men that they were no better than the Cubans, upon which the burly black troopers burst into a loud guffaw, and then stopped firing altogether. Roosevelt told his men that he was ashamed of them. He was ashamed to see them firing valuable ammunition into the darkness of the night, aiming at nothing; that he thought cowboys were men who shot only when they could see the 'whites of the other fellow's eyes.' They also stopped firing."

As the American lines fell silent, so did the Spanish. Most of their shots had been far too high, anyway, which helped explain how Roosevelt and Ayers had escaped injury while so exposed to the enemy fire.

With the excitement over, Ben Colbert tried to get back to sleep, but the Rough Riders still had none of their blankets or ponchos. He made a fortunate acquaintance on the skirmish line, writing in his diary: "I chanced to get half of a blanket with a negro soldier and slept with him."

Colbert's experience was not unusual. Henry Bardshar warmly recalled the Buffalo Soldiers he fought side by side with. "In one way or the other they were always helping the white troopers out," he remembered. " 'What's the matter, yo' white man?' they would say. 'Ain't yo' got no blanket?' Then they would split their own blankets end to end and give the white man half."

The shooting between the trenches commenced again at daybreak on July 3, even as the morning's usual heavy mist obscured the view. All up and down the American line, the soldiers were exhausted, wet, sunburned, and famished. They had been fighting now for more than forty-eight hours, mostly on empty stomachs, and there were no reserves to come to their relief. "They were hanging to the crest of the San Juan hills by their teeth and finger-nails," wrote Richard Harding Davis, "and it seemed as though at any moment their hold would relax and they would fall."

To his men, Roosevelt appeared to be the same bulletproof force of nature. With his typical fervor, he told them how proud he was of them. If they kept up their good fighting record, he would send the entire regiment, at his own expense, to the Paris Exposition Universelle in 1900. But deep down, Roosevelt was worried, too. That morning, he dashed off a frantic letter to his friend Henry Cabot Lodge:

> *Dear Cabot: Tell the President for Heaven's sake to send us every*
> *regiment and above all every battery possible. We have won so far*
> *at a heavy cost; but the Spaniards fight very hard and charging*

those intrenchments against modern rifles is terrible. We are within measurable distance of a terrible military disaster; we must have help—thousands of men, batteries, and food and ammunition. . . . Our General is poor; he is too unwieldy to get to the front. I commanded my regiment, I think I may say, with honor. We lost a quarter of our men. For three days I have been at the extreme front of the firing line; how I have escaped I know not; I have not blanket or coat; I have not taken off my shoes even; I sleep in the drenching rain, and drink putrid water.

When Washington learned that Shafter was contemplating a withdrawal (he'd sent Secretary of War Alger a telegram that same morning), those in the War Department were just as rattled as the officers at the front. They knew that such a move would encourage Spain to keep fighting the war. Alger replied immediately with his own telegram, and although he deferred to Shafter's judgment, he stressed that if "you can hold your present position, especially San Juan Heights, the effect upon the country would be much better than falling back." The secretary also said he was sending reinforcements at once.

Back on the ridge overlooking Santiago, some of the boys were already referring to their commander as "Fall Back Shafter."

The booming of big guns suddenly sounded over the sporadic rifle fire from the enemy's trenches. It was 9:35 A.M. Several Rough Riders speculated that the American fleet was bombarding Santiago, or perhaps the batteries at the harbor's mouth. The men's curiosity was nearly more than they could bear, because the thunder of the guns lasted a good hour before drifting away. But it was far too risky to raise their heads above the trenches for more than a second or two, and they couldn't view the sea from their position anyway.

They were correct that the shelling was coming from the fleet. Admiral Cervera was making a run for the open sea. He had declared that "it was better to die fighting than to sink his ships" in the harbor.

Cervera didn't die that day, but after a desperate fight lasting four hours and covering several miles, Spain's Atlantic battle squadron was destroyed. The news of the American victory would not reach San Juan Heights for a few more hours.

About noon, shouts of "Cease fire!" echoed all along the trenches. A flag of truce had been hoisted so that a letter from Shafter to the commander of the Spanish forces, Brigadier General José Toral y Vázquez, could cross between the lines. The letter contained Shafter's demand for the surrender of Santiago, or else he would shell the city. The demand was a ploy devised by Shafter's adjutant general, Lieutenant Colonel Edward J. McClernand, who, like Wheeler and Roosevelt, strongly opposed any kind of withdrawal. Shafter had no artillery in place to shell Santiago, but McClernand believed that if the American army could simply get a little rest while the two sides negotiated—allow their nerves to unwind—there would be no more talk of pulling back.

The truce had exactly the effect McClernand intended, and that afternoon there was a tremendous morale boost when the troops learned that the Spanish fleet had been destroyed. One of the regimental bands had lugged their instruments to the top of San Juan Hill and now began playing "The Star-Spangled Banner," followed by the Rough Riders' unofficial anthem, "A Hot Time in the Old Town." All up and down the line, the men climbed out of their trenches and cheered and whooped.

Toral declined to surrender, but Shafter later extended the truce until 10:00 A.M. on July 5 so that noncombatants could evacuate the city. For the rest of the day on the third and all through the night, the fatigued Rough Riders feverishly worked to improve their earthworks, adding entrances, traverses, sandbags, and bombproofs. The two Colt machine guns and the pneumatic dynamite gun had been brought up the day before, and now zigzag trenches were dug to a commanding knoll slightly in advance of the main line and the Colts installed. Approximately ten thousand rounds of Mauser ammunition had been found in the Spanish trenches, and it fit the Colts perfectly.

*Roosevelt and his Rough Riders, flanked by members of the Third and Tenth
U.S. Cavalries, who shared the American line with them on San Juan Hill.
Probably photographed on July 3, 1898, following the truce. (R560.3.Scr7-037,
Theodore Roosevelt Collection, Houghton Library, Harvard University.)*

Three of Parker's Gatlings were also placed here, their large wheels
removed and sandbag revetments constructed in front, while the remaining Gatling was kept just behind as a reserve.

Including the dynamite gun, which was positioned to the right of
the Colts and Gatlings at a point where the knoll ran back to the main
ridge, there were a total of seven guns in the semicircular fortification, all under the command of Lieutenant Parker. "It was the most
powerful and unique battery ever used in battle," he boasted later.
The men dubbed it Fort Roosevelt.

On July 4, the troopers witnessed the long column of thousands
of noncombatants, mostly women and children, fleeing Santiago in
advance of the threatened bombardment. Because of the naval blockade in place since May, there was no food to be had in Santiago, and
there hadn't been any for days. Many of the refugees, then, were little
more than walking skeletons. "The sight is truly pitiful," wrote one

trooper. "They are nice looking women, but I think the most of them will die."

Roosevelt slowed down just long enough on July 4 to write his official report of the San Juan engagement for Colonel Wood. Out of the approximately 490 men he entered the fight with, his casualties were 86 killed and wounded, and there were still half a dozen missing. "The great heat prostrated nearly forty men," he wrote, "some of them among the best in the regiment." As it turned out, the Rough Riders suffered the highest casualties of all the cavalry regiments at San Juan, which in subsequent years Roosevelt proudly brought up from time to time.

The enemy's numbers were not mentioned in Roosevelt's report (it was something he had no way of knowing at the time), but in later discussions with various Spanish officers he concluded that Shafter's army had faced 4,500 Spaniards at San Juan. The actual figure, however, was 1,197, and of these, the enemy's first line, 521 officers and men, had inflicted most of the damage as the Rough Riders and other

Santiago refugees. Photo by John C. Hemment. (Author's Collection.)

regiments advanced. Spain's total force amounted to more than 10,000 men, including sailors borrowed from the Spanish fleet, but they were spread among several points on both sides of the harbor and around Santiago itself.

The incredibly small number of Spanish defenders on San Juan Heights was yet another testament to the superiority of the Mauser rifle with its fast-loading stripper clips, as well as the lack of effective artillery on the American side. And there was more: "The Spaniards have been underestimated in almost everything," a Rough Rider observed in a letter home. "They have more and larger guns and artillery with the range all surveyed off. They can shoot well and have better rifles and longer range, have fine positions and are courageous." But the Rough Rider also noted a fatal flaw with the Spaniards. They "can't stand a charge," he wrote.

Like any good commanding officer, Roosevelt singled out in his report several Rough Riders for commendation, naming in all forty officers and men. Of these, however, Roosevelt considered Private George Roland to have demonstrated "the most conspicuous gallantry." The twenty-seven-year-old cowboy, who days before had slipped out of the hospital window at Siboney to return to the regiment, fought "with such indifference to danger that I was forced again and again to berate and threaten him for running needless risk."

There was no mention of Adjutant Tom Hall, nor would Roosevelt ever write of him. Hall had again displayed his cowardice during the San Juan fight, disappearing to the rear and spending the evening comfortably at the field hospital while the rest of the regiment had a sleepless night digging trenches. When he did return to the front, he disgusted the men by constantly seeking shelter from the bullets and shrapnel. It all came to a head one day when some troopers sitting in the grass near Roosevelt's tent looked the other way as Hall walked in front of them.

"Salute! Why don't you men salute?" he shouted.

The men didn't budge. Finally one of them said, "We ain't salutin' a yellow dog."

Roosevelt heard the commotion and came out of his tent, his jaw set like a steel trap. He said to the adjutant, "For the good of the regiment, Hall, and for your own good, the sooner you get out, the better."

Hall bowed his head, turned, and walked away. He later went to see Surgeon Church and, with tears rolling down his face, begged Church to use his influence to persuade Roosevelt to reconsider. "Hall went completely to pieces," remembered one of the hospital stewards. But Church refused, and Hall had no other choice but to resign. He left immediately for the States.

As for Roosevelt, there was already talk of a Medal of Honor—contingent on whether or not he lived. "If there is another battle as hot as the last," Trooper Sam Weller wrote his parents, "and he exposes himself again as he did then, I look for him to fall."

For the next six days, there were more letters between Shafter and Toral, more demands for surrender followed by counterproposals on the surrender terms, and more telegrams between Shafter and Washington. The Rough Riders referred to these negotiations as "making medicine."

With the truce extended, there was time to tend to the dead on both sides. In a ravine between the lines, Spanish soldiers stacked bodies that were "past burial" and set them on fire. "We covered up lots of Spaniards to keep them from stinking, and I don't think they will try to charge us anymore," wrote one Arizona trooper.

News, rumors, and gossip constantly traveled between the front lines and headquarters. Shafter seldom came off well, and then the news spread that the commanding general was weakening on his demand for an unconditional surrender. "We on the firing line are crazy just at present because Gen. Shafter is tacking and veering as to whether or not he will close with the Spaniards' request to allow them to walk out unmolested," Roosevelt wrote Lodge.

"An unconditional surrender is all that will go with us now," wrote one Rough Rider, "for we have lost too many men in the fight."

Shafter had indeed recommended to Secretary of War Alger that they allow Toral to march out of the city, and it disturbed Alger and President McKinley as much as it did Roosevelt and his men on San Juan Heights. Alger promptly ordered a telegram sent to Shafter. In no uncertain terms, the recommendation to accept Toral's proposition was not approved.

The truce ended at 4:00 P.M. on July 10, and the Spaniards opened up the festivities with heavy rifle and artillery fire from their trenches and batteries. An especially annoying battery sounded like it was only a few hundred yards in front of Fort Roosevelt, but that was where a brick hospital building flying several Red Cross flags was located. And the smokeless powder of the Spaniards made it all the harder to locate the battery's position. Finally, after carefully glassing the area around the hospital, the hostile guns were spotted under a clump of trees and next to one of the flagpoles flying the Red Cross banner. Lieutenant Parker ordered the dynamite gun crew to send a shell directly at it.

So far, the dynamite gun had been a disappointment. It had been plagued by several problems due to flaws in the weapon's construction and the materials used in its manufacture—the gun had only gotten off four shots during the San Juan battle. But the sergeant in charge of the piece had been able to work around some of the defects and was ready for another test. He meticulously sighted the gun's long barrel and then stood to the side as a gunner yanked the firing lanyard, sending a long torpedo-like projectile speeding through the air.

Each of the dynamite gun's shells, which cost $35, carried four and a half pounds of a nitroglycerin-based gelatin equaling nine pounds of dynamite. Of this, the Spaniards got full value, for the sergeant's aim could not have been more perfect. A tremendous explosion shook the ground as a plume of dirt, men, tree limbs, and gun parts sprayed upward, almost as if in slow motion. The Rough Riders watching in the trenches instantly jumped up on top and cheered.

Next the dynamite gun was trained on one of the enemy trenches. Another awful explosion followed, causing several terrified Spanish soldiers to leap out of their pit. Within seconds, these men were cut down by the spitting lead from the Colt machine guns and Gatlings.

The pneumatic dynamite gun and crew at Fort Roosevelt. (R560.3.Em3-066,
Theodore Roosevelt Collection, Houghton Library, Harvard University.)

The dynamite gun continued to achieve spectacular results during the rest of the day and the next morning, but it was very slow to operate and required constant tinkering. It would successfully fire only twenty shells during the campaign.

The rest of the artillery didn't do much better. Most of the siege guns were still in the holds of the transports, and the two that were brought ashore sat on the beach at Daiquirí. "A siege without siege guns," wrote one officer, "was the logical climax of a battle without tactics and a campaign without strategy."

On that same Sunday, July 10, a world away from the gunfire, mud, and stench of dead animals and men, Mrs. Mina Miller Edison was in labor in her Llewellyn Park, New Jersey, home. It would be her third child with famed inventor Thomas Edison. Tom Edison had been through these waits before, but that made it no less nerve-racking. There was so much that could go wrong in childbirth.

As Edison paced the floor of his study that morning, listening to the sounds of his servants rustling through the different rooms on various errands of the doctor, a knock came at the front door. A servant swung open the door and was greeted by a telegraph boy. The servant took the envelope from the boy's outstretched hand and quickly carried it to the study and Edison, who opened it immediately. The message was brief. Theodore Miller, his wife's beloved younger brother, had died at Siboney on July 8.

Edison folded the telegram and put it in his pocket, worried that this horrible news on this momentous day might somehow be tidings of something dark still to come. But these thoughts were suddenly interrupted by the cries of a baby. Edison stepped out of his study just as a maid hurried past. It was a boy, she told him, "and a beauty."

After a few hours had passed and the household had settled back down from the morning's excitement, Edison went into the bedroom and sat down next to his wife, who was cuddling their child. He tenderly took Mina's hand in his and told her the news of Theodore's death. Mina broke into sobs and clutched her little baby even tighter, her thoughts racing back to the handsome brother she had last seen at

Theodore Westwood Miller, Troop D. (Author's Collection.)

breakfast in that very house just a little more than six weeks before. Her darling child would never know his Rough Rider uncle, but he would forever bear his name: Theodore Miller Edison.

Two days later, another Rough Rider family, this one living on a farm near Guthrie, Oklahoma Territory, received a large, stained yellow package from Siboney, Cuba. It was addressed to Al Norris, the father of Edmund Norris, a private in Troop K, and had been shipped express by Captain Robert B. Huston. To the senior Norris, this could only mean one thing: his son was dead and the parcel contained his personal effects.

Opening the package, Al Norris found a revolver, Spanish money, three pieces of silverware, gauntlets, a Cuban machete, and other small items. There was no note of condolence. There was no note of any kind, leaving Al Norris to wonder what all this meant. The mystery was finally solved when a letter arrived—from Ed. Written on July 2, Ed explained that the revolver had belonged to journalist Edward Marshall. Sometime after Marshall was wounded at Las Guásimas, Ed had found the journalist's pocketbook containing $700. Ed was on detached service with the Hospital Corps and returned the pocketbook to Marshall, who was one of his patients. In gratitude, Marshall presented Ed with the revolver, along with several of the other souvenirs in the package.

Ed's letter was brief, but it contained cash—not Spanish, but U.S. currency—along with specific instructions for his father: "Enclosed find $50, my army pay. Buy calves with it for me."

Chapter Nine

The Real Foe

*To keep us here, in the opinion of every officer
commanding a division or brigade, will simply
involve the destruction of thousands.*

THEODORE ROOSEVELT

Monday morning, July 11, 1898
Fort Roosevelt

Fred Herrig stood in the trench behind one of the two Colt machine guns, his hand on the weapon's grip. The booming of American artillery had begun at daybreak. From behind the San Juan ridge, rifled field mortars lobbed twenty-pound shells at the Spanish trenches on the other side of the hill, although few were hitting their targets. Herrig could also hear the big guns of the U.S. Navy warships just outside Santiago's harbor. Sometimes their large rounds could be seen against the blue sky as they fell into the city.

The soldiers at Fort Roosevelt had seen little action, with only occasional rifle fire, but then suddenly a flurry of Mauser bullets buzzed by Herrig's head. One slammed into the machine gun's tripod. Another put a hole in the crown of Herrig's hat, barely missing his head. He ducked down behind the gun, wondering what he had done to draw

Colt machine gun in trench at Fort Roosevelt. (R560.3.Em3-065, Theodore Roosevelt Collection, Houghton Library, Harvard University.)

the enemy's fire. Then he looked behind him and saw George Smith, a fellow member of the Colt detail, swinging his hat high in the air from the barrel of his Krag. Herrig asked Smith what the hell he was doing.

"I thought I'd let the Spaniards shoot at my hat for a while," Smith calmly replied.

"Step about ten feet to one side and let them shoot at you," Herrig said testily. "I would just as soon not be shot at."

Smith suddenly looked sheepish. He hadn't thought about a stray bullet possibly striking one of his buddies. Smith lowered his gun and put his hat back on his head where it belonged.

About noon, a flag of truce was raised, hanging limp in the stifling heat. General Shafter had forwarded yet another formal demand for the surrender of the Spanish forces, setting off a new round of back-and-forths with General Toral. That afternoon, the regiment was ordered to a new position approximately a quarter mile to the north, where they would guard the road from El Caney. They left behind their old comrades, the Buffalo Soldiers of the Tenth, and were now between the First Cavalry and the First Illinois Volunteers, the latter reinforcements who had arrived in Cuba two days before. Their crisp new uniforms and clean flags were a marvel.

During the past few days, the Rough Riders had been able to bring up some of their bedding and tentage. Roosevelt now had a proper tent, inside of which he had strung up his hammock. He was without his valet Marshall and had been for most of the campaign. Marshall had taken ill shortly after the landing at Daiquirí.

With a truce in effect, and quite satisfied with his tent and sleeping arrangements, Roosevelt decided to remove all his sweaty, mud-stained clothes and underwear—for the first time in two weeks—and try for a comfortable night's sleep. But the heavens must have been unhappy with the calm that had settled over the battlefield, because there was a tremendous storm that evening. Horses shrieked and jerked at their tethers as lightning zigzagged across the sky, followed by deafening claps of thunder that rolled over the hills. The rain came down in torrents.

Ben Colbert went on guard at midnight as the storm raged. "Oh! how disagreeable," he wrote in his diary. "I wish there was no fighting. I wish there was no war. I wouldn't take $1000 for my experience, but I don't want 5¢ more."

The storm rattled the men standing watch on both sides, and they began firing their weapons at ghost soldiers flickering in the lightning flashes. The Rough Riders were called out from their tents and ordered to the line, but all they got for their trouble was another good soaking.

Roosevelt was in awe as he listened to the wind and rain pounding down upon his tent. The rain seemed as if it was being poured from a bucket. Without warning, he felt himself falling, the tent upending and flapping in the wind. He floundered around in the dark and the mud until he found his clothes and a pair of spectacles and then, naked and cold, went in search of shelter.

"The water was running over the ground in a sheet," he wrote his daughter Ethel, "and the mud was knee-deep; so I was a drenched and muddy object when I got to a neighboring tent."

About 2:00 A.M., Roosevelt stumbled into the kitchen tent, where cook Bert Holderman, a Cherokee from Vinita, Indian Territory, wrapped him in dry blankets. Holderman had just scavenged a table from an empty Spanish house, and he helped his lieutenant colonel up on it. Roosevelt curled up and slept for the rest of the night.

Just hours earlier, in Washington, President McKinley and Secretary of War Alger had signed the commission making Roosevelt colonel of the Rough Riders.

No matter how hot, wet, and filthy it was on San Juan Heights, the dapper Woodbury Kane always looked as if he had just stepped out for a Sunday stroll along Fifth Avenue—infuriatingly so. Lieutenant Parker never ceased to be amazed:

> Kane turned up every morning clean-shaved and neatly groomed, shoes
> duly polished, neat khaki, fitting like a glove and brushed to perfection,
> nails polished, and hair parted as nicely as if he were dressed by his
> valet in his New York apartments. How did he do it? We never knew. He
> kept no servant; he took his regular in the ditches, in the mud, or torrid
> sun, or smothering rain. No night alarm came that did not find Kane
> first to spring to the trench—and yet he did it, somehow.

The mustachioed Kane seemed to thrive, much like Roosevelt, under hostile conditions. The two were practically the same age, Roosevelt being older by less than four months. As far as anyone could tell, neither got ill or seemed to suffer from fatigue. Roosevelt was perhaps the more remarkable of the two in this regard because of his history as an asthma-suffering sickly youth. In his letters to family and friends, Roosevelt seldom failed to mention his good health. He wrote to Henry Cabot Lodge: "I am as strong as a bull moose, although I sleep out on the firing line, on the ground, often wet through."

The same could not be said for the majority of his troopers. Straining their bodies daily in the tropical heat with endless trench digging, short rest, and little nourishment caused everyone to experience dramatic weight loss, most in the double digits. Sickness ravaged their bodies, too. Writing to the *Philadelphia Medical Journal* on July 12, Dr. Frank Donaldson, who had recently joined the Rough Riders' surgical staff, estimated that "fully 60 percent of the men in this regiment have one form or another of malarial fever or diarrhea or a general gastroenteritis. Their stomachs have revolted against the food, but not before this ruined their digestions for many a day."

And it didn't help matters that, in attempting to prevent and treat the fevers, the men were consuming quinine like it was candy—thirty to sixty grains daily—either from personal supplies they had brought with them or doses administered by the surgeons. "All of us took a tablespoon of quinine once or twice a day," recalled Royal A. Prentice, "we having become so used to quinine that normal doses had no effect." Quinine, of course, was only beneficial in treating malaria. If a soldier had yellow fever, the drug would do nothing for him. Either one was bad enough, but now the men were suffering from classic symptoms of quinine overdose: nausea, vomiting, deafness, and blurred vision. But they kept taking the quinine, mostly, as one trooper pointed out, because "there was nothing else to take."

James Robb Church, who had become the de facto regimental surgeon due to the frequent absence (some said cowardice) of Chief Surgeon La Motte, was also suffering from malaria, although he continued to administer to the sick troopers even while ill. Because no cots had been delivered to the front, the patients lay on the ground on top of their ponchos. Church's single hospital shelter (two tarpaulins) did little to protect his patients from the weather, which alternated between pouring rain and burning sunlight.

Drinking water remained as grave a problem as the rations. "It is simply astounding," Donaldson continued, "that every one of our men is not down with typhoid or worse. They have been compelled to drink the most disgusting water: for several days, for instance, we drank water from a well out of which finally two dead Spaniards were fished."

Donaldson further warned that unless Santiago was soon taken, far worse was likely to occur. To "witness the awful suffering of our men and to see them falling sick by the hundreds," he wrote, "is sufficient to make one pause and seriously doubt whether the whole lot of miserable Cubans are worth the sacrifice."

Roosevelt spent much of the truce scrounging rations for the men. There was food at Siboney, but it seldom came to them; they had to go to it. And they had to provide their own transportation. Fortunately, several of the Rough Riders just happened to have a talent for rustling livestock.

The former cowboys gathered up captured Spanish cavalry horses, wounded or lame mules that they doctored, and stray Cuban ponies, using barbed wire for a picket rope. When the owners of the ponies came to claim their stock, the Rough Riders were forced to turn them over, but they rounded up more ponies after a day or two, making sure this time to stake them a long way from camp.

The best rustler in the regiment was not one of the cowboys, however; it was the chaplain. Thirty-four-year-old Henry Alfred Brown had been serving as the rector of the Church of the Advent in Prescott, Arizona Territory, when Roosevelt telegraphed him to come to San Antonio. He had a bit of the "fighting parson" in him and carried a revolver his first couple of days in Cuba, saying he "could settle a Spaniard at fifty paces." Brown nearly cried when Colonel Wood told him he would have to put his pistol away, it being quite against the Articles of War for a regimental chaplain to shoot people.

One day at General Wheeler's headquarters, a visiting clergyman announced his plans to go to the Rough Rider camp and visit Colonel Roosevelt, whom he knew. A staff officer overheard this and asked the clergyman, "But do you know Colonel Roosevelt's regiment?"

"No," he replied.

"Very well, then, let me give you a piece of advice," said the officer.

"When you go down to see the colonel, don't let your horse out of your sight; and if the chaplain is there, don't get off the horse!"

Roosevelt frequently gave Brown money donated by himself, Woodbury Kane, and other New Yorkers in the regiment and sent him to Siboney to purchase whatever food he could get. On one of these trips, Brown returned with a wagon chock-full of commissary stores. Roosevelt couldn't believe his eyes and asked the chaplain how he got it.

"God put it down there and kept it for me," answered the chaplain. "When I reached Siboney I found a great body of men packing supplies into a number of wagons. One wagon which was entirely loaded was without a driver. I supplied the deficiency and drove away. That was all."

When a shipment of tobacco finally made it to the front, there was nearly as much excitement in the ranks as when they had charged the San Juan trenches. But this tobacco was not a ration; it was offered for sale by the Commissary Department. Consequently, it looked like many of the Rough Riders would have to go without, until Woodbury Kane stepped up, took $85 out of his pocket, and paid for the tobacco. Later, Kane received a package from his sister containing six hundred tins of premium Golden Sceptre tobacco and several cases of canned peaches for the boys. One trooper said the New Yorker instantly became "the most popular man in camp."

Even with the efforts by Roosevelt and his officers, the regiment was just able to get by. Fresh meat could not be had at any price, and the canned roast beef, when they had it, was even worse than what they remembered from the *Yucatan*. In the tropical heat, it spoiled in minutes after opening. The rations were so meager and infrequent, wrote one trooper to his family, that "I think a square meal would kill any of us now."

"Colonel, this man is insubordinate."

Roosevelt sat on the stump of a coconut tree, carefully shaving in front of a small mirror. The man who interrupted him was the sergeant in charge of the dynamite gun. Standing at attention next to the sergeant was one of his gun crew. Roosevelt put down his shaving brush and gave the man a hard look.

"Have you any excuse to make?" Roosevelt asked the trooper.

The accused man, who appeared as if he would prefer to be anywhere just then but in front of his colonel, dropped his eyes to the ground.

"Now look here, my man," Roosevelt admonished, "do you understand what you are doing? Do you fully realize that you are in front of the enemy? We have a truce, but it may end any moment. I will maintain discipline as strictly under the truce as if actual hostilities were on. I shall punish you and every man in the regiment who shows the slightest insubordination in the face of the enemy. It is the same as treason, and we will have none of it. Order this man to the guardhouse."

Not long after this episode, Roosevelt left one of his lieutenants quaking with a similar rant. The lieutenant had made the mistake of relaxing the watch because of the truce.

"[O]ur men must have absolute discipline at all times," Roosevelt told the lieutenant. "There must be no relaxation. I want as many men on guard as before. Our enemy is insidious. No life in the command is safe while one Spaniard remains in yonder trenches."

If any regiment was to be taken by surprise by the Spaniards, it wouldn't be the Rough Riders. Roosevelt made sure of that. Another commanding officer might have fallen out of favor for demanding vigilance and discipline while, from all appearances, the enemy was ready to capitulate. Not Roosevelt. His men were devoted to him. "He would lead us through hell and back," an Arizona trooper told a correspondent, "and you bet we'd go."

Fortunately, there would be no marches to hell, at least not anytime soon. On July 14, about noon, the sound of cheering rose in the distance, growing closer and louder. News of a surrender raced from man to man, troop to troop, and regiment to regiment. Roosevelt instructed his men not to cheer, as he had received no official confirmation. But General Toral had finally agreed to surrender the city and his forces on the condition that his men would be returned to Spain. All that remained was to draw up a document with the terms of the surrender, although, like all the negotiations thus far, this was not as easy as it sounded. It would be two more days before the final agreement was signed.

Following on the heels of the surrender came a sudden and unexpected improvement in the Rough Riders' rations. Roosevelt had gone to Siboney and, with private funds and donations from the American Red Cross (under its founder, Miss Clara Barton, age seventy-six), was able to make a pretty good haul. He returned to camp leading a string of horses and mules carrying 500 pounds of rice, 800 pounds of cornmeal, 200 pounds of sugar, 100 pounds of tea, 100 pounds of oatmeal, five barrels of potatoes, two of onions, and cases of canned soup and condensed milk.

"This is a red letter day in my army experience," J. Ogden Wells wrote on July 16, "for we had oatmeal for breakfast this morning. To say it tasted fine would be expressing it mildly; it seemed as if I couldn't eat enough."

In an unsettling coincidence, just as the troopers were being decently fed for the first time, the noncombatants who had fled Santiago a few days previous were streaming past the Rough Rider camp on their way back to their homes.

"The horrors of war!" wrote Sherrard Coleman, the regiment's acting commissary:

> You can form no idea of what it means to these poor Spanish and Cuban women. Such a sight would melt a heart of stone. . . . These poor people are in our lines in the pouring rain without shelter and nothing to eat. Hundreds of little, helpless babes, clinging to their mothers, crying for something to eat. About 50 died last night from starvation. Rich women in their silks and satins, offering all their jewels for a few hardtacks to keep their little ones from starving— how sad they look as they beg the Americans for mercy, drenched to

the skin and covered with mud to their necks, begging and weeping for
their children who are starving—and we have nothing to give them.

Some men did share their rations with the refugees, and there were
coldly opportunistic individuals who made very one-sided trades. But
Roosevelt soon forbid all of it. There was no guarantee when they
would get their next rations, and with a good possibility that the regiment would be shipped to Puerto Rico for another campaign against
the Spanish, his men must be kept in fighting shape.

Still, a few of the Rough Riders couldn't keep from helping in some
way. They went out into the El Caney road and carried the elderly
women's bundles and even picked up small children and packed them
for a good quarter mile. Eventually Roosevelt had to put a stop to this
as well. The surgeons warned that the children, and even the baggage, might carry yellow fever germs.

One trooper, Charles "Happy Jack" Hodgdon, had been assisting the
refugees all day and became very upset when he heard of Roosevelt's
order. The twenty-nine-year-old miner from Prescott couldn't understand the reasoning behind it, explaining, "The Almighty would
never let a man catch a disease while he was doing a good action."

At 11:45 on July 17, officers assembled their men on top of the long
line of trenches for the formal surrender ceremony. Fifteen minutes later, the American flag was slowly raised over the Governor's
Palace in the city. The artillery battery of Captain Allyn Capron fired
a twenty-one-gun salute, followed by the regimental bands playing
"The Star-Spangled Banner" and "My Country, 'Tis of Thee." The
Rough Riders cheered so loudly that many of them were hoarse later.
When they finally quieted, someone down the line yelled, "What's
the matter with the Rough Riders?," and the ruckus started back up
again.

For J. Ogden Wells, though, the victory was bittersweet: "As I
glance down the line and see the many vacant places, I think of the
comrades who are not present to exult in the reward of their bravery
and my happiness gives way to sorrow."

Troopers celebrating the surrender of Santiago. (R560.3.Em3-077, Theodore Roosevelt Collection, Houghton Library, Harvard University.)

There were no melancholy reflections for Roosevelt. He was brimming with satisfaction and pride. For the artillery salute, he had given the command "Present arms!" and his men had flawlessly swung their Krags forward, holding the carbines vertically in front of their chests, standing motionless like so many statues. After the salute, Roosevelt had gone down the line congratulating his troopers.

"By George, men, you did that well!" he said, his teeth flashing. "This is a great day in American history—a much greater day than any of us can at the present moment realize."

Although the Spaniards had been defeated, the other, more worrisome, enemy stepped up its assault on the Fifth Corps. It was the real foe of any army: disease. Hoping to slow down the rampant spread of fever and other illnesses, Shafter ordered the Cavalry Division to a new camp in the hills near El Caney. Word of the impending move came to the Rough Riders just after they had completed digging a deep well. "The boys certainly made a howl," Ben Colbert wrote in his diary.

The Rough Riders broke camp at 9:00 A.M. on July 18. It was a march of about five miles, and the heat was brutal. Fully aware of the weakened condition of the troopers, the Cavalry Division officers made sure to keep the march to a slow pace. It was still too much; nearly half the men in the division fell out from exhaustion along the way. The next morning, 123 Rough Riders reported sick. Of the nearly 600 who had landed in Cuba less than four weeks earlier, only 275 were on the active list.

Their new camp was next to a clear stream in a lush green valley. But with the daily downpours, the camp soon became a muddy mess—or, as one soldier remembered it, a lake. Roosevelt ordered the men to build up bunks in their tents to get them off the sopping ground. In no time, crude platforms made of bamboo stalks and wooden boards from a blockhouse sprang up throughout the camp. It "made us look like tree-dwellers," recalled one trooper. The men were generally much longer than the tents, however, so their feet stuck out the ends. But that "made little difference," wrote Royal A. Prentice, "as our clothing was wringing wet for twenty-four hours a day."

There wasn't much now for the men to do other than answer the morning roll call and draw rations. Roosevelt learned of a ship that had steamed into Santiago's harbor loaded with cattle from South America. "Do you think they would sell them?" he anxiously asked one of his lieutenants. They would. Ben Colbert was appointed "regimental butcher" with orders to cut up one beef each day. "Had fried tenderloin steaks for dinner, & soup & stew for supper—'out-of-sight,'" Roger Fitch jotted in his diary on July 22.

Those men who were healthy used their free time to explore the nearby hills, hunt mangoes, visit the other regiments, and trade with the Cubans for souvenirs. J. Ogden Wells tried to buy a machete for $5, but the Cuban owner refused. Wells put his cash away and offered three hardtack, and the deal was sealed.

A large delivery of back mail arrived, many of the troopers receiving multiple letters from family. Captain Robert B. Huston's wife, Vianna, had written him from Guthrie, on July 2. That evening's front page of the *Guthrie Daily Leader* had been filled with news of the fight before Santiago. For a mother with a young child and a husband off with the Rough Riders, headlines such as "Loss Is Heavy" were terrifying:

> *Where are you today, and what are you doing? I know the dreaded battle is on and that you are in it if you are among the living. It is almost impossible for me to write and you in such danger. Is it right for you to take your life in your own hands. It seems as if I must rebel against it all, but here I am powerless to do anything but wait the result.*

It seems Vianna Huston and Edith Roosevelt shared much in common.

Very few of the Rough Riders were allowed to enter Santiago or El Caney unless sent on some errand. This was thought best because the city was considered unsanitary and the men might be exposed to fever and other diseases. Sergeant Prentice got to go into town with his troop captain, where he witnessed the hubbub of Spanish, Cuban, and American soldiers crowding the narrow streets. Most memorable to him, though, was the local fare: "We had coffee served in little cups that was as strong as lye and round, hard bread and rice with guava jelly."

A bright spot during these muggy days of rain and more rain was General Wheeler's thirty-year-old daughter, Annie, who was in Cuba volunteering for the Red Cross. She was often at General Wheeler's headquarters, but once she rode through the Rough Rider camp, and as Ben Colbert recorded in his diary, "She being the first American lady seen for some time, the boys almost stampeded trying to get a glimpse of her."

Bathing was allowed in the creek each night, and many troopers took advantage of a water hole just downstream to swim. Roosevelt, however, went swimming in a much larger hole: Santiago Bay. He had gone down to the bay with Wood and other officers to visit the Castillo del Morro, where there was a good view of the wreck of the

USS *Merrimac,* scuttled by American sailors more than a month earlier in a daring attempt to trap the Spanish fleet in the harbor. The
wreck was only three hundred yards from shore, and Roosevelt decided to swim out to it—he had been taking much longer swims in
Oyster Bay for years.

But Oyster Bay didn't have sharks. As Roosevelt and one of his
young officers swam toward the wreck, the classic silhouette of a
dorsal fin appeared above the shimmering water, and then others. The
officers watching from the castle shouted and waved, and Roosevelt
asked his swimming companion what they were saying. "Sharks," he
gasped. The young man never forgot what Roosevelt said next:

> *"Sharks," says the colonel, blowing out a mouthful of water, "they"*
> *stroke "won't" stroke "bite." Stroke. "I've been" stroke "studying*
> *them" stroke "all my life" stroke "and I never" stroke "heard of one"*
> *stroke "bothering a swimmer." Stroke. "It's all" stroke "poppy cock."*

The two safely reached the *Merrimac,* and, after exploring for a
while, swam back to shore, escorted again by the sharks.

No one knew exactly what was next for the Rough Riders, or the Fifth
Corps, for that matter. Shortly before the surrender, Roosevelt told his
men they would probably go to Puerto Rico within five days. There
were rumors, though, that the regiment would garrison Santiago;
others said they would be returning to the United States. Roosevelt
wanted to be where the action was. He was never one to sit and let
fate take its course. On July 23, he wrote to Secretary of War Alger:

> *My Dear Mr. Secretary:*
>
> *I am writing with the knowledge and approval of Gen. Wheeler. We*
> *earnestly hope that you will send most of the regulars, and at any*
> *rate, the cavalry division, including the Rough Riders, who are as*
> *good as any regulars, and three times as good as any State troops, to*
> *Porto Rico.*

There are 1,800 effective men in this division; if those who were left behind were joined to them we could land at Porto Rico in this cavalry division, close to 4,000 men, who would be worth easily any 10,000 National Guards armed with black powder Springfields or other archaic weapons.

Very respectfully,
Theodore Roosevelt

It was pure Roosevelt boyish enthusiasm. It was also wishful thinking. The cases of fever in Cuba were increasing daily. Because the field hospitals were full, the surgeons stopped admitting anyone with a temperature of less than 104 degrees. Feeling "as bad as ever" one morning, J. Ogden Wells went to see the surgeon, but his fever was only 102.5, so the surgeon reported him for duty. It "gave me some hopes," Wells wrote in his diary, "although I could hardly stand."

On July 31, there were just 175 Rough Riders on the active list. One officer wrote home that "the hospitals and ground under the shade trees is covered with sick unable to raise a hand." By this time, the War Department had decided that the Fifth Corps would be sent to Long Island, New York, to recuperate, but only once the fever cases had subsided. This last caveat enraged Roosevelt and his fellow officers. "Of course, the malarial fever won't lessen," he wrote Lodge, "it will increase, and if [Secretary of War Alger] does as he says, he will simply keep us here, growing weaker and weaker, until Yellow Jack does come in and we die like rotten sheep."

Roosevelt wasn't worried about himself, he told Lodge, as he didn't believe yellow fever would kill him if he did catch it, but "if I do go," he continued, "I do wish you would get that medal of honor for me anyhow, as I should awfully like the children to have it, and I think I earned it."

Because of illness among the officers, Roosevelt had the temporary command of the Cavalry Division's Second Brigade (his colonel's commission had just arrived). He now had a secretary and a typewriter, although much of his considerable correspondence was devoted to answering the anxious letters from the families of the dead and wounded. Like the one he wrote the father of Tilden Dawson:

> *I wish I could give you more definite assurances about the body of your gallant son, who was killed in our first fight, but I do not know whether the Government will send him back or not. I have no power to do it myself, glad though I would be to send back every one of the gallant men who now lie dead on the Cuban battlefields. . . . Pray accept my deepest sympathy, and yet though I sympathize with you, I must congratulate you upon having a boy who did so well and who died a hero's death.*

Meanwhile, Shafter was receiving contradictory instructions from the War Department about when the troops would be shipped north and, in fact, on August 2, Alger proposed that Shafter move the camps yet again, farther inland and higher up in the mountains. Once this was accomplished, the troops would be sent to New York "as rapidly as possible." But, Alger warned, it "is going to be a long job at best to get so many troops away."

Obviously, Alger did not comprehend the seriousness of their situation. August was well known as the height of the sickly season, and Shafter had been advised that a yellow fever epidemic could break out at any time. The following day, then, Shafter called a conference of his division and brigade commanders.

Roosevelt and Leonard Wood, promoted to brigadier general and now in command of the city of Santiago, were present, as were seven general officers and the chief medical officers. Shafter explained his trouble with the War Department and suggested that something be done to get their predicament before the public. This would anger Secretary Alger, of course, which is why they turned to Roosevelt. Roosevelt was a volunteer and would return to civilian life after the war. The other officers had careers to consider. Besides, if anyone knew how to work the press, it was Roosevelt.

The original plan was for Roosevelt to make a statement to an Associated Press correspondent, but Wood advised his friend to put his thoughts in a letter addressed to General Shafter. After Roosevelt did so, both he and the correspondent went to Shafter's tent. Roosevelt held the letter out to the general, but Shafter waved it off. "I don't want to take it," he said, "do whatever you wish with it." Roosevelt did not withdraw his hand, and finally Shafter pushed the letter toward the correspondent. The AP man was quite happy to take possession.

While this was going on, Shafter's generals surprisingly decided that a written statement of their own would be a good idea. Wood dictated it, and it was signed by all present, including Roosevelt. This became known as the "round robin." That evening, Shafter overworked his telegraph operator with several lengthy messages to the War Department: his own detailed report arguing for an immediate move to the United States, a statement from his medical officers attesting to the critical condition of his army, and finally the round robin.

The AP correspondent was busy, too, and the next day, August 4, newspapers across the country carried the complete texts of Roosevelt's letter and the round robin. Roosevelt's was the more strident (and alarming) of the two:

> *If we are kept here it will in all human possibility mean an appalling disaster, for the surgeons here estimate that over half the army, if kept here during the sickly season, will die. This is not only terrible from the standpoint of the individual lives lost, but it means ruin from the standpoint of the military efficiency of the flower of the American army, for the great bulk of the regulars are here with you.*

Secretary Alger wasn't just angry—he was livid, especially as he had replied to Shafter's recommendation early that morning with orders to begin removing the troops north, hours before the newspapers hit the streets. Roosevelt's information about the Fifth Corps's dire straits, and the round robin, naturally caused a public outcry and considerable embarrassment for the War Department. But more than that, this information had the potential to disrupt the peace talks then going on between the United States and Spain.

Alger telegraphed Shafter an immediate rebuke for letting the press have the round robin, but he singled out Roosevelt for special retribution—how dare Roosevelt humiliate him when he had effectively given the man a regiment? The same afternoon Roosevelt's letter appeared in the papers, Alger gave the press the private letter Roosevelt had sent him on July 23, along with a freshly penned reply:

> *War Department.*
>
> *Your letter is received. The regular army, the volunteer army, and the Rough Riders have done well, but I suggest that, unless you want to spoil the effects and glory of your victory, you make no invidious comparisons.*
>
> *The Rough Riders are no better than other volunteers. They had an advantage in their arms, for which they ought to be very grateful.*
>
> *R. A. Alger*
> *Secretary of War*

One paper that ran the exchange commented, "Everywhere they are the talk of the Capital. The letters are taken as having slaughtered Col. Roosevelt as a political factor for years to come." (This would turn out to be hardly the case.) More than one editorial noted that Roosevelt's July 23 letter was a private one, and for Alger to make it public eleven days later, along with his own stinging dressing-down, was "as gross a violation of the decencies of life as can be imagined." And its timing, when Roosevelt was just now being discussed as a Republican candidate for governor of New York, was clearly calculated to do damage. It "is just about the level of Algerine imagination," observed the *New York Times*, "to suppose that the publication of it would injure the author's prospects."

The public was unmistakably on the side of Roosevelt. One woman wrote the editor of the *New York Herald* praising Roosevelt's letter as a courageous act: "Every mother of us, every mother's son of us, and every soldier of us will stand by this heroic deed, and, 'if you don't look out' the battle cry of the next Presidential election will be 'Roosevelt and humanity.'"

Roosevelt was fully aware of all the talk of political office now that he was a bona fide war hero, but politics was not his priority for the time being. As long as there was a war, he wrote Lodge, "the only thing I want to do is command this regiment and get it into all the fighting I can."

Chapter Ten

Crackerjacks in New York

I wouldn't have missed my little share in this affair for worlds.

CAPTAIN WOODBURY KANE

The Rough Riders got their "canary coats" on the morning of August 3. That's what they nicknamed the new uniform coats. The men had been in Cuba just six weeks, but their old brown canvas fatigues were in tatters. The replacement uniforms issued that day were the Model 1898, or "warm-climate uniforms." Made of khaki, they were much like the officers' uniforms that Wood and Roosevelt wore. The coats sported canary yellow facing on the pocket flaps, cuffs, shoulder tabs, and standing collar (yellow designated the cavalry branch).

Most of the men thought the new uniforms were very handsome. But several got a shock when they tried on the khakis for the first time. "I am so thin that a Number 2 suit is too large for me," wrote J. Ogden Wells, "whereas when I enlisted, I required a Number 3 suit." Those lost pounds wouldn't be coming back anytime soon.

The next morning, news came that the Fifth Corps would be leaving Cuba for the United States as soon as possible. The soldiers and most Americans credited Roosevelt's letter for this sudden development, and though Alger would always point to the orders he issued to Shafter shortly before the letter was published, Roosevelt's sensational missive did force the War Department to treat the removal with a new sense of urgency.

"All the boys are delighted," wrote Roger Fitch upon hearing the news, "as we are all 'dead tired' of lying around here, feeling sick & weak as most of us are."

Ideally, the regiment would reunite on Long Island with the troops and horses left behind at Tampa, get healthy again, and be ready for the operation against Havana, which was still under a blockade by the navy. A campaign against the fortified city, which held approximately sixty thousand Spanish soldiers, would probably take place in the fall. The invasion of the Spanish-held island of Puerto Rico had already begun.

Columns of sooty smoke rose above the Rough Rider camp on the morning of August 7, a Sunday. The men stood around large fires in their new uniforms, tossing the old ones onto the flames. At noon, the regiment marched out of camp, leaving their sagging dog tents in place. Their ponchos and blankets were transported by wagons, so the men carried only their carbines, ammunition belts, canteens, and any souvenirs they had picked up.

After going about two miles west, they reached a railroad siding and climbed into dilapidated boxcars that looked to Sergeant Royal Prentice like they had been "made in the year one hundred, but they beat walking all to pieces." In twenty minutes, the train pulled into the Santiago depot. The regiment fell into line near the tracks and marched to the pier, Roosevelt riding at the head on Little Texas and each troop preceded by its red-and-white guidon. The regiment marched up the gangplank of the transport *Miami,* which they would share with men of the First and Third Cavalries.

The paymaster soon appeared and paid off the troopers, and Roosevelt allowed the men to go into the city and buy provisions for the voyage. Being a Sunday, not many shops were open, and in those that were, what little was available was expensive. The men came back with canned fruit, cheese, and guava jelly.

The next morning, at about 7:30, the transport pulled away from the quay amid cheering from the shore and the soldiers on board. As the *Miami* steamed out into the harbor, its upper decks crowded with troopers and men clinging to the rigging, the Third Cavalry's band played a rousing set of tunes: "Dixie," "Old Folks at Home," "Home, Sweet Home," and "Yankee Doodle." When the band played "The Star-Spangled Banner," the men took off their campaign hats and shouted and whooped.

Five sick Rough Riders remained behind to follow on a hospital ship in a few days. Another Rough Rider left behind was Leonard Wood, now on course for a distinguished career as a general officer. The regiment was no longer his, anyway—and most folks didn't know it ever had been.

Rough Riders on the transport Miami, *about to depart Cuba. (R560.3.Em3-087, Theodore Roosevelt Collection, Houghton Library, Harvard University.)*

Roosevelt left no record in his pocket diary of his thoughts on leaving Cuba. His diary pages were now devoted to short notes to himself about the regiment's various personalities and colorful episodes of the last few weeks. Back in May, he had made arrangements with Charles Scribner's Sons to write a history of the Rough Riders. A good chunk of Roosevelt's income came from his writings, and this had all the makings of a bully book.

One item the soldiers had no trouble acquiring before departing Santiago was Cuban rum, and they were happy to share it with the *Miami's* stokers and engineers, who immediately got drunk. As soon as the captain let Roosevelt know about the problem, he began a thorough search of the ship, telling his men that if they handed over the liquor now, he would give it back once they got to Long Island. Those soldiers who were sick and needed it would be allowed to have some during the voyage. Any liquor they tried to hide would be thrown overboard. In short order, seventy flasks and bottles were handed over. Twenty more were discovered during the search and dumped into the sea.

Finding their supply suddenly cut off, the ship's stokers and engineers became belligerent. Roosevelt posted an armed detail in the engine room to ensure they did their work, and the "near-mutiny" soon passed.

The Rough Riders experienced many of the same problems on the *Miami* that they had had on the *Yucatan*: bad drinking water, no ice, revolting canned beef, and a shortage of vegetables. But there was great comfort in knowing they were headed back to the United States. As Ben Colbert commented in his diary, "I would like to bid farewell to Santiago forever."

The decks were too crowded for any exercise, so the men passed the time sitting in circles playing poker, several games going at once. "On shore this was not allowed," Roosevelt explained later, "but in the particular emergency which we were meeting, the loss of a month's salary was as nothing compared to keeping the men thoroughly interested and diverted."

On the morning of August 12, the troopers gathered for the funeral of George Walsh, who had died the night before. Walsh, one of the older troopers in the regiment, was a forty-three-year-old painter from San Francisco. His official cause of death was listed as "chronic dysentery." According to Roosevelt, the man had brought his illness on himself by getting drunk the first night ashore and then undertaking the grueling march to Siboney before getting sober. "He never recovered and was useless from that time on," he wrote.

Chaplain Brown performed the funeral service while the bareheaded Rough Riders looked on. The band softly played a hymn, and Walsh's body, sewn up in a canvas hammock with metal weights, was released. It splashed into the water and instantly disappeared beneath the rolling surface. During the service, Ben Colbert gazed out to the horizon and saw two schooners under full sail: "Twas quite a sad but pretty view."

Two days later, in the afternoon, someone shouted they could see land, causing the men from the decks on the starboard side to push into the throngs at the bow and port side to get a look. Long Island's sandy bluffs were visible plain as day. Soon they saw houses and boats and steamships large and small. The *Miami* set a northeasterly course, following the coast to the island's tip at Montauk Point, its ancient lighthouse protruding up from a windswept knoll.

Swinging around the point and into Long Island Sound, the transport was met by a dispatch boat. The boat came alongside the *Miami*, its captain and crew saluting the Rough Riders with cheers. "I am happy to take my hat off to you and your regiment," the captain gushed to Roosevelt. Then the Rough Riders gave a cheer for the navy. The Regulars looking on were visibly irritated.

The captain told Roosevelt that a preliminary peace agreement with Spain had been signed in Washington on August 12, the news racing among the men crowded on the different decks. There would be no Havana campaign after all—and apparently no more fighting for the Rough Riders. Roosevelt had been right about getting the regiment to Cuba with the first invasion force. The other two volunteer "cowboy regiments," composed of men from nine western states, got only as far as military camps in Georgia and Florida before the war ended.

The *Miami* anchored about four miles off Montauk so that quarantine officers could come out and inspect the ship for yellow fever. A doctor arrived on a tug that evening, and the men immediately peppered him with questions about when they could go ashore. Roosevelt rescued the quarantine physician from the troopers and escorted him around the ship.

"Nearly all my men are well," he told him. "There is not a bad case among them and nearly all those who left Santiago in bad shape are now well on the road to health."

Roosevelt was stretching the truth considerably, but he was convinced none of his men had yellow fever, and he knew the best thing for them now was to get them off that damn ship. They got their wish the next morning when the *Miami* docked at the pier at 11:55, with a large crowd waiting to greet them. While the gangplank was secured, the air was filled with incessant cheering and banter between the soldiers on the ship and those on the shore.

General Wheeler and Roosevelt were the first ones off, Roosevelt a good twenty pounds lighter than when he left Tampa for Cuba. A throng of excited friends, soldiers, and reporters swarmed the colonel, who shook the numerous hands thrust at him as fast as he could, all the while flashing his famous teeth. Several men shouted in unison, "Will you be our next governor?"

"None of that," Roosevelt said firmly, throwing up his hands. "I won't say a word about myself. All I'll talk about is the regiment. It's the finest regiment that ever was, and I'm proud to command it."

The Third Cavalry band struck up "Battle Cry of Freedom," and the different troops began to come down the gangplank in double file, first the Third Cavalry, then the Rough Riders. The sight of them brought audible gasps from the crowd, for they weren't expecting to see men so pale and thin, some barely able to walk, some with scraggly beards. At the end came about fifteen troopers propped up by their comrades, too weak to carry their carbines and blanket packs or keep pace in the ranks. Still others remained on the ship bedridden and would have to be transported to the military hospital by ambulance.

The Rough Riders formed on the beach, a bugle call snapping them to attention. The crowd roared again as the regiment began the mile and a half march to the detention camp, where they would go through a quarantine of four days.

Shortly after getting settled in their tents, the troopers were brought their first meal: tainted beef and moldy hardtack from the *Miami*. Disgusted, the men refused to eat it and demanded that as "they were on American ground they wanted something fit to eat." Fortunately, the Red Cross was able to fix them up with soups, canned meats, and fruit.

The next day, Roosevelt ordered from New York fresh fruit, eggs, and milk for the entire regiment—and paid for it himself. In addition, two large packing cases filled with roasted turkeys, hams, beef tongues, sardines, lemons, gingersnaps, and cigars arrived express courtesy of members of the New York Stock Exchange. The cases were addressed to Charles Knoblauch and John Lorimer Worden, Rough Riders who both had seats on the Exchange.

Named Camp Wikoff in honor of Colonel Charles Wikoff, killed during the San Juan battle, the Montauk camp covered more than four thousand acres of rolling grassland and would eventually receive more than twenty thousand soldiers, not to mention thousands of cavalry mounts. Most of the four Rough Rider troops left behind in Florida had already arrived by train, together with the regiment's horses. These men had suffered just as much from disease at Tampa, particularly typhoid and malaria, as their comrades in Cuba. Much worse than this, at least in their minds, was that they had missed the "bully fight." They had won no glory and had no tales to tell. At one station stop, the crowd that greeted them thought they were the Rough Riders returning from Santiago.

"We want to see Teddy!" they shouted, and, "Three cheers for Roosevelt!"

When the quarantine expired on August 19, the Rough Riders packed up their gear and marched to the regular camp. About halfway, they were met by the Tampa contingent, who were leading the horses of their fresh-out-of-quarantine comrades. Whooping and hollering, the Tampa men jumped down from their mounts and ran up to their mates, the next several minutes filled with handshakes and backslaps, friendly ribbing, and loud guffaws.

Furloughs were now readily granted to the troopers, and about one hundred Rough Riders obtained five- to ten-day furloughs that afternoon. With few exceptions, the men headed straight for the train station and bought tickets for New York City. The McCurdy brothers, Kirk and Allen, of Troop D, had been sent new tailor-made uniforms, the best that money could buy, from their father. While on the train, an old man looked the brothers up and down and said, "What a pity you boys had no chance to see any service in this late war."

The Rough Riders' distinctive uniforms made them instantly recognizable to the New Yorkers as Teddy's boys. Everywhere they went, men and youths bombarded them with shouts of "Hurrah! for the Rough Riders!" Women followed them and begged for buttons, photographs, and autographs.

"We could not spend a cent for anything," Ben Colbert wrote in his diary. "If we tried, they would take the money away from us and after paying for things they would give it back—we were simply treated royally."

Woodbury Kane and the other New York Rough Riders went to their homes, but most of the rest spent their furloughs taking in the city: Grant's tomb, Coney Island, the Statue of Liberty, the Casino

Theatre (its current production, *Yankee Doodle Dandy,* included actors as Rough Riders), and the Waldorf Astoria Hotel, which Royal Prentice found "simply immense, the finest thing I ever saw." Several troopers witnessed a grand naval parade of Rear Admiral Sampson's North Atlantic Squadron up the Hudson River. And there were even a few Rough Riders spotted in the crowd of ten thousand that watched the Futurity horse race at the Sheepshead Bay Race Track.

Roosevelt also left Camp Wikoff for a few days of rest with his family at Sagamore Hill. He was met at the Oyster Bay train station the night of the nineteenth by a raucous crowd of fifteen hundred people, a hastily organized brass band, and a massive bonfire in the street. The whistle on his train was held wide open and muskets and pistols were fired into the air. Roosevelt had a difficult time making his way through the jubilant throng to get to the wagon that would take him home.

There was actually little free time for him at Sagamore Hill. He had piles of letters and telegrams to go through and a steady stream of guests and newspaper reporters. One of those guests was an assistant editor from Charles Scribner's Sons. Their topic of conversation was Roosevelt's planned book on the Rough Riders.

"It was all perfectly clear in the colonel's mind," remembered the editor. "He knew the grand divisions of his story, although he had not written a line." The book would first be published serially in *Scribner's Magazine,* six articles at $1,000 each. The first installment was scheduled for the January 1899 number, just four months away.

Although Roosevelt had refused to speak publicly about running for governor, it was assumed he would be mulling it over while at home, and he indeed received visitors who came to discuss just that. According to one of the Rough Rider officers, it was already a done deal. This anonymous officer told a reporter for the *Sun* that "Col. Roosevelt will accept the nomination for Governor if it is offered him by the Republican party. He would appreciate the honor very much, and while he has not sought and will not seek a nomination, you can say that he will accept if it is offered to him."

The Rough Rider said that a prominent Republican Party member had visited Roosevelt at Camp Wikoff before he left for Oyster Bay, and "the subject of their conversation was politics." The boys in camp were excited about the possibility, too, and were itching to start campaigning for their colonel.

Roosevelt returned to Camp Wikoff on August 25, the same day disturbing news came of the death of Second Lieutenant William Tiffany at the age of twenty-nine. Tiffany, who had become one of the best-liked men in the regiment, was one of the convalescents brought to the States on the hospital ship *Olivette*. His brother described Tiffany as "skin and bones" when he arrived for treatment in Boston, and he was still suffering from a high fever. The best doctors were called, but Tiffany's emaciated body was too far gone. He was so weak he could hardly speak. Tiffany died surrounded by his mother, sister, brother, and fiancée.

What was most startling about Tiffany's death was the cause listed by his physician: "prostration, starvation, and exhaustion following fevers." That word *starvation* was shocking to those reading about Tiffany in the nation's press. His doctor hastened to add that he wasn't implying that Tiffany didn't get fed on the *Olivette;* it was just that he didn't get the proper nourishment for his condition. The family had serious doubts, and Roosevelt remained convinced that if Tiffany had been allowed to come with the regiment on the *Miami,* he would have lived.

There had been two additional Rough Rider deaths related to fever since the regiment arrived at Camp Wikoff, and several of the men who had gone to New York City on furloughs experienced bouts of fever, the waxing and waning being a common symptom of malaria. Ben Colbert became so ill that he checked himself into a hospital. Sergeant Thomas Fennessy of Troop F fainted while visiting Warren Crockett in Bellevue Hospital (Crockett was being treated for the leg wound he received on San Juan Hill). A doctor rushed into the room and determined that Fennessy was "in a well-developed state of malarial fever" and that he was lucky he was in Bellevue when he collapsed.

Several ill Rough Riders had been sent to their homes on thirty-day furloughs or, as in the case of J. Ogden Wells, with early discharges, the thinking being that they would have a better chance of recovering in the care of loved ones. Many suffered with periodic fever symptoms for months, while others returned home, seemingly in good health, only to fall ill a short time later. Because their bodies had been overworked and malnourished, and their immune systems wracked by malaria, a later infection or virus could kill them.

The military hospitals at Camp Wikoff were to be avoided, at least in the beginning, much the same way soldiers avoided the dreaded hospitals in Cuba. Sergeant Paul Hunter of Troop D wrote about the shortage of food and adequate care in a blistering letter to the *Guthrie Daily Leader* dated August 26: "No condemnation of the United States hospital service can be too great or need cause any sympathy for these men who have robbed the government and starved the sick and dying soldiers." It was the Red Cross, he wrote, that was the one bright spot. "Where there are no women there is needless suffering. Every soldier blesses the Red Cross."

Hunter finally fled the hospital, eluded the guard, and returned to camp. At least they got milk there every day. Assistant Surgeon Frank Donaldson and his wife had established a kitchen to prepare special foods for those who couldn't eat the ordinary camp fare. And unlike in the hospitals, the men were able to buy any little extras they desired. If they didn't have money, Roosevelt made sure they did, giving any needy man five to ten dollars, sometimes more. He frequently handed out the cash personally, placing the rolled bills in their hands. This caused tears to well up in the eyes of a number of men.

Roosevelt also distributed funds to the families of the killed and badly wounded. He had received several checks from his wealthy friends for the benefit of the regiment and decided to use this money in the name of William Tiffany to help these grieving families. Roosevelt would carefully query his captains as to whether or not a deceased trooper had a wife or children. If he learned there was a baby at home, he said, "Well, we will make it a trifle more for the baby's sake." His only instructions were to make sure the mother "gets it in memory of poor 'Willie' Tiffany; you need not mention me."

George Hamner, now detailed as Roosevelt's personal secretary, saw the little girl outside the headquarters tent, standing between the regimental flags. She looked to be about eight, and her nice clothes were lightly covered with road dust; one stocking had slipped down on her shoe. She confidently stepped up to the open flap, and the secretary motioned her in. Hamner had been taking dictation for Roosevelt, but the colonel had stopped to think, and Hamner was intrigued about this cute young lady.

He leaned down and whispered, "What do you want?"

"I want to see Col. Roosevelt."

Hamner stood up, and with much formality, said, "Colonel, here's a young lady come to pay her respects to you. Miss, this is Colonel Roosevelt."

Roosevelt turned and began to bow when his eyes suddenly focused on the smiling eight-year-old in front of him.

"Well, well," he said. "Who are you? What is your name?"

"Jennie."

"So, Jennie . . . where do you live?"

"Am'gansett." (Amagansett was fourteen miles from Camp Wikoff.)

"That's a long way from here. What did you come so far for?"

"I came to see Colonel Roosevelt."

"That's bully. But how did you come so far?"

"I kept saying what I wanted and everybody helped me. The conductor was real nice."

"He was, eh! The conductor was a nice man. Well, who helped you from the station?"

"A colored man."

"A colored man. How?"

"In his sojer [soldier] wagon. Then he gave me to another colored sojer on a horse and he carried me on his horse."

"What did he say?"

"He didn't say nothing to me. He just kept laughing to himself; not out loud."

"So, does your mother know that you came to call on Colonel Roosevelt?"

"No; but it is all right. She said she wanted to see him, too."

"Um. Well, I'm Colonel Roosevelt." And with that, Roosevelt picked up the delighted child and kissed her on the cheek. "Now, how am I going to get you home? Let me see. How would you like to ride home on horseback with a Rough Rider?"

The girl nodded eagerly.

"Here, McGinty!" Roosevelt shouted, and Bill McGinty quickly rode up and dismounted.

"Do you think, McGinty, that you can take this young lady to Amagansett and deliver her safe and sound to her mother?"

"Yes, sir."

"Now, careful, McGinty. She's a friend of mine, a particular friend of mine, and I want her to get home before dark, and happy, too. You understand?"

"Yes, sir."

Roosevelt returned to his tent, but as McGinty started to ride away with the girl seated in front of him, Roosevelt suddenly rushed out and called to the trooper.

"Hey, McGinty. You tell her mother it's all right. Say that Colonel Roosevelt said it was all right."

That last week of August, Roosevelt was told that his regiment would soon be mustered out of the service, possibly in as little as ten days. There was little for the men to do at this point. They filled their days with swims in the surf (a favorite Roosevelt pastime), crap shooting, and bucking contests—some of the horses had grown quite wild in the intervening weeks. A favorite bit of mischief of the western boys was to offer some innocent visitor a pleasant horseback ride around the camp, then providing him with one of the more vicious animals on the picket line. If the victim questioned the horse's gentleness, the Rough Rider would say, "I'd let my sisters ride that brute of mine, standing over there, any old time, without a bit of hesitation. Wouldn't you, fellows?" Fortunately, no one was seriously injured.

One day, a few of the Rough Riders witnessed a trooper of the Third Cavalry get bucked off a big muscular sorrel. When the man remounted, he was thrown a second time. The trooper refused to try again, and none of his comrades were willing to get up on the outlaw bronc, either. The Rough Riders, who often boasted they could ride anything with hair, mocked and laughed at the Regulars, who immediately dared the Rough Riders to take a turn on the animal. The Third had recently gotten paid, so they had plenty of money to wager. The Rough Riders accepted the challenge, but in fairness, it was decided to give the horse a day's rest so it could do its best bucking.

The contest took place in a large flat area in front of Roosevelt's tent. A crowd of men from both regiments gathered to watch the rodeo. The Rough Riders sent their top broncobuster: Sergeant Tom Darnell, a five-foot-ten-inch, red-haired cowboy from New Mexico. It was rumored, wrote a newspaperman, that Darnell "once mounted

Rough Riders "surf riding" off Montauk Point. (R560.3.Em3-097, Theodore Roosevelt Collection, Houghton Library, Harvard University.)

Tom Darnell, Troop H, giving a bronc-riding demonstration. (R560.3.EL61-059, Theodore Roosevelt Collection, Houghton Library, Harvard University.)

a tornado that was threatening his native town, diverted its funnel upward, and nearly put the orb of day out of business."

The twenty-four hours' rest appeared to have only made the horse meaner. As soon as Darnell swung into the saddle, the animal went wild. The troopers cheered as the horse pitched, spun, and crow-hopped, kicking up clouds of dust. Roosevelt couldn't decide "whether most to wonder at the extraordinary viciousness and agile strength of the horse or at the horsemanship and courage of the rider."

Unable to buck Darnell off its back, the horse lit into a gallop, breaking through the crowd and disappearing from the spectators' view, the cowboy still glued to the saddle. A few moments later, however, Darnell came riding slowly back, gently patting the horse's neck. "Nice little horse for a lady," he said, "kind and gentle; no bad tricks; easy gait. Like to take him home to my wife."

On September 3, President McKinley visited Camp Wikoff, followed by hordes of journalists, photographers, and a moving picture camera operated by the American Mutoscope Company. He rode in an open carriage with Vice President Garret Hobart and Secretary of War

Alger. When McKinley spotted Roosevelt on horseback, he called out, "Colonel! I'm glad to see you."

Roosevelt spurred his horse and rode toward the president's carriage, making an impressive dismount while the horse was still moving forward. McKinley climbed out of the carriage and started walking toward the colonel. As they met, the president held out his hand while Roosevelt struggled to remove the gauntlet from his right hand. Finally, Roosevelt grabbed the fingers of the gauntlet with his teeth and jerked his hand free.

"Colonel Roosevelt," McKinley said, "I'm glad to see you looking so well."

"Thank you, Mr. President, there isn't a healthier man in the camp than I am. I am delighted to see you down here, sir, and hope you will enjoy the trip. I do want you to see my boys while you're here."

"Oh, I will, Colonel, I will."

A short time later, McKinley arrived at the Cavalry Division camp, his carriage passing between two long lines of mounted troopers. When he got to the Rough Riders, one of the men shouted, "Three cheers for the President of the United States!" Instead of the expected "huzzahs," the troopers whooped and hollered like a bunch of rowdies. McKinley had a surprised look on his face until General Wheeler told him those men were the Rough Riders. The president stood up in the carriage and gracefully bowed to the regiment, which brought forth even more whoops.

There had been much talk of a Rough Rider parade along Broadway in New York City, and Roosevelt was all for it. "I'm proud of these boys, and I want to show them to New York," he told a reporter for the *Sun*. He could furnish between 450 and 500 troopers, unless his regiment was mustered out before the parade, in which case some of his men would likely head for home. But Roosevelt offered to pay for his men's expenses to New York City as well as the expenses of the parade. He later decided it was only right that the entire Cavalry Division be in the parade, but the invitation would have to go through Secretary Alger.

While Alger was at Montauk with the president, a reporter asked him about the prospects for a parade, and he said it was not possible. Here was an opportunity for Alger, stinging over the criticism he was receiving for the lack of food and medical care for the Fifth Corps, to demonstrate his awareness of the situation at Camp Wikoff. The men were exhausted from hardship and disease, he told the reporter, and to force them to take part in a parade in their condition would be "cruel." As for the Rough Riders, they were going to be mustered out—"What they will do after that is entirely their affair, to be decided by themselves."

This last statement by Alger came off as sarcastic. He knew full well that the men would no longer have their arms or horses after they were mustered out. There would be no glints of steel from the carbine barrels, or neighing steeds. "It would be a rather ridiculous parade, I think," commented one officer. Disappointed, Roosevelt gave up on the idea.

Edith Roosevelt brought the children to see their father on September 7. Ten-year-old Ted and eight-year-old Kermit wanted to ride horses. Being Roosevelt children, they had been riding horses for most of their young lives. Roosevelt asked McGinty to pick out a couple of mounts and take the boys around Montauk. They were thrilled when McGinty asked them to help him catch a dun-colored horse he had recently seen running loose. The trio was soon galloping down the beach after the dun, McGinty swinging his lariat above his head. They crowded the horse into the water and mud, and the boys watched in amazement as McGinty lassoed the animal and dragged it onto the beach.

When they arrived back at camp with the dun, there was a large crowd around Roosevelt's tent. One of the boys said to McGinty, "I hope to be as great a man as my father someday."

Fourteen-year-old Alice Lee asked Frank Brito to escort her around the Rough Riders' camp. She was fascinated that he spoke Spanish and would ask him the Spanish word for nearly every object they came across. Her mother visited the sick Rough Riders in the hospital.

Other attractions for the Roosevelt children were the regiment's mascots, which had all arrived safely at Camp Wikoff. There was the dog Cuba, the mountain lion Josephine, and also Teddy, the golden eagle from New Mexico that was allowed to walk—and fly—up and down the company streets. Cuba was the only one of the mascots to accompany the regiment to Cuba, but his adventures, and there were surely some, went unrecorded.

The family twice lunched at headquarters. Oranges and tea were among the many items on the menu, as Roosevelt had used donated funds to purchase three thousand oranges and two hundred pounds of tea, per the wishes of the men. Ted and Kermit spent the night in their father's tent, one boy on Roosevelt's cot and the other on his air mattress. Roosevelt slept on a table. The girls and their mother lodged in a nearby house. The family left for Sagamore Hill after lunch on the second day. Edith deemed their trip a "great success." To her sister Emily Carow, she gushed about the regiment's officers: "such attractive, handsome young fellows some of them were, & just about twenty-one years old, so I felt about a hundred."

Only a few days remained before Roosevelt's Rough Riders would be disbanded. Muster-out rolls were prepared and troop pay arranged. The men gathered up their saddles and bridles and turned them over to clerks with the Ordnance Department. They also had to surrender their trusty Krags. Most of the men would have purchased their carbines if allowed, but the weapons were government property. There was at least one exception, though. Bob Wrenn, the champion tennis player, was able to keep his weapon, the presentation Winchester Model 1895 lever-action Roosevelt had given him in Florida. It was personal property.

Knowing that the Rough Riders were soon to go home, souvenir peddlers invaded the camp selling dollar gold watches and chains for five and ten dollars apiece, and fake jewelry intended for mothers and lady friends. The Rough Riders decided it was time to teach the

"Jewelry Fakers" a lesson. Private Anthony Gavin of Troop C walked over to where a peddler was doing a good business and announced, "Boys, you all have bought watches, and got fooled badly. Now to prove it. He is under arrest and in my charge. We will proceed to give him a general camp court-martial, under the rules of Roosevelt's Rough Riders, at the present day and hour."

The troopers in camp quickly gathered to see the fun. The trembling peddler was placed up on a soapbox and charged with "defrauding the Rough Riders, and separating them from their hard-earned U.S. dollars." He was swiftly found guilty and sentenced to be "tossed skyward in a real horse blanket by those basely defrauded boys of the West." The poor man got down on his knees and begged as a blanket was brought forth. He got no sympathy from the men, however, who grabbed the peddler by the collar and threw him on the blanket.

"He went up in the air like a rocket, time and again," remembered Gavin, "and you can imagine every time he went up, out came things from his clothing, such as phoney watches, rings, and the cheapest kind of jewelry, and the boys' hard-earned money."

Roosevelt heard the yelling and, imagining a fight had broken out, hurried over to see what the trouble was. The troopers saw Roosevelt approaching but Gavin told them to keep at it; he would explain to the colonel. So up the peddler flew into the sky again.

"Attention!" Gavin called out, and the men stopped for the moment, laughing and smiling as they held the edge of the blanket and looked at Roosevelt.

"Who tried him?" Roosevelt asked.

"Tony Gavin," said several men.

"And was he tried fair?"

"Yes, sir."

"That's fine. Bully for you, Tony!"

Roosevelt walked away, a smile on his face.

On September 12, the cowpunchers held a final bucking contest, and that night they noisily celebrated into the early morning hours.

Roosevelt let them have their fun, whooping, dancing, and singing. The Indians took the lead in the dances, he wrote, "pure bloods and half-breeds alike, the cowboys and miners cheerfully joining in and forming part of the howling, grunting rings, that went bounding around the great fires they had kindled."

The following afternoon, a group of Roosevelt's officers asked him to step out of his tent. As he did so, Roosevelt saw facing him a hollow square of troopers three men deep: five hundred Rough Riders, two hundred Buffalo Soldiers from the Ninth and Tenth Cavalries, and dozens of visitors, including many women. In the center of the square was a small table on which some unknown object was covered by a horse blanket.

A curious Roosevelt was led to the table, after which Private Will Murphy of Oklahoma stepped from the ranks and made a short, heartfelt speech. The Rough Riders, he explained, wished to present the colonel with "a very slight token of the admiration, love and esteem in which you are held by the officers and men of your regiment." Once finished, Murphy reached for the blanket and lifted it away. Underneath was a marvelous bronze sculpture of a cowboy on a rearing horse, the animal's head arched down, its ears pinned back. The bronze was *The Bronco Buster* by Frederic Remington, the first sculpture the artist had ever created. The men had all chipped in to purchase it.

Roosevelt was deeply touched. He claimed he didn't know what to say, but, rapidly gathering his thoughts, he spoke at length. Roosevelt expressed his love and pride for the men, not forgetting those who were no longer in the ranks:

> *We parted with many in the fight who could ill be spared, and I think that the most vivid memories that we will take away with us will be of those whom we left under Cuban sod, and those who died in the hospitals here in the United States; the men who died from wounds and the men who, with the same devotion of country, died from*

disease. I cannot mention all the names now, but those of Capron, O'Neill, and Fish will serve. They were men who died in the pride of their youthful strength.

And neither did he forget those regiments with which the Rough Riders had fought side by side. Long applause broke out when he acknowledged the Ninth and Tenth Cavalries. "The Spaniards called them 'Smoked Yankees,' but we found them to be an excellent breed of Yankee. I am sure that I speak the sentiments of men and officers in the assemblage when I say that between you and the other cavalry regiments, there is a tie which we trust will never be broken." The crowd erupted in cheers.

Roosevelt closed by saying, "To have such a gift come from this peculiarly American regiment touches me more than I can say. This is something I shall hand down to my children, and I shall value it even more than I do the weapons I carried through the campaign."

Someone shouted, "Three cheers for Colonel Roosevelt!" and as soon as the whoops and yelps died down, there was a call for "Three cheers for the next governor of New York!" Another roar went up.

Roosevelt asked the men to line up and file by him so he could shake each of their hands. He spoke briefly to each trooper, calling most of them by their first names. After the last man filed past, Roosevelt turned to a friend and said, "I made Pollock, the Pawnee, smile today, and I do not believe anyone ever saw him smile before."

Four troops were mustered out after the presentation. The enlisted men received, on average, $120 in pay; the noncommissioned officers about $160. Some 350 rowdy Rough Riders left immediately for New York City, their money burning holes in their pockets.

The rest of the regiment was mustered out the next day. Roosevelt was busy signing muster-out papers when all the men of Troop I came to his tent. They had with them Teddy, the golden eagle. A trooper spoke up and said, "Colonel, we men present that eagle to you, and we want you to have it, and if anyone knocks you, send him to us and we'll fix him."

Roosevelt's farewell to his men at Camp Wikoff. Note the Remington bronze
The Bronco Buster *on a table to the left of Roosevelt. (R560.3.EL61-098a,*
Theodore Roosevelt Collection, Houghton Library, Harvard University.)

Later, after all the men had been discharged, the mustering officer, a member of the Regulars, went to Roosevelt's tent and asked about "the prisoner." Roosevelt looked puzzled, and then it suddenly came to him. A New Mexico trooper by the name of William Shields had caused a problem on the *Yucatan*. Shields understood he needed to obey the orders of his officers, but no one had told him that applied to the officers of other regiments as well. One such officer had given Shields an order and he'd refused it. When the officer told Shields to consider himself under arrest, Shields challenged him to a bout of fisticuffs.

Poor Shields was court-martialed and sentenced to a year of hard labor and a dishonorable discharge; General Wheeler signed off on it. When the *Yucatan* got to Cuba, Shields, fearing he was to be left behind, begged Roosevelt to let him fight with his troop, promising he would obey any man the colonel wished. Roosevelt gave him a stern look and said, "Shields, there is no one in this regiment more entitled to be shot than you are, and you shall go to the front."

The grateful Shields did exactly as promised, and he distinguished himself in the fighting at both Kettle Hill and San Juan. Consequently, Roosevelt called the trooper to headquarters one day and remitted his sentence.

There was no prisoner, Roosevelt now told the mustering officer: "I pardoned him."

"I beg your pardon; you did what?" the officer gasped.

"Well, I did pardon him, anyhow, and he has gone with the rest."

"He was sentenced by a court-martial, and the sentence was approved by the major general commanding the division. You were a lieutenant colonel, and you pardoned him. Well, it was nervy, that's all I'll say."

The Rough Riders were again the toast of New York City, where the latest fashion in ladies' headwear was a felt walking hat called the "Rough Rider," available in black, pearl, and nutria at the John Wanamaker store on Broadway.

On September 16, twenty-five Rough Riders showed up unannounced at the office of the Central Park Zoo superintendent. Trooper Stephen Kennedy of Troop F held Teddy under his arm. Kennedy saluted the superintendent and handed him a note:

> *This is the golden eagle (the Indians call it a war eagle) which the Rough Riders had as their mascot. Just at the moment I have no place to keep it. Will you keep it for me? I will arrange terms later.*
>
> *Theodore Roosevelt*

The superintendent called a zookeeper and asked him to take Teddy to the eagle cage. All twenty-five troopers followed. After Teddy was placed in the large enclosure, Kennedy asked to go in and say good-bye. He stroked the bird's muscular body and kissed it. There were tears in his eyes as he turned away. Next the troopers

A trooper holding Teddy, the regiment's golden eagle mascot. (R560.3.EL61-089, Theodore Roosevelt Collection, Houghton Library, Harvard University.)

lined up outside the cage and gave Teddy three cheers, startling more than a few park visitors.

Many Rough Riders stuck around for the auction of the regiment's horses on September 20, which had been ordered by the War Department. More than one thousand animals went on the block at Fiss, Doerr & Carroll Horse Company on East Twenty-Fourth Street. Some of the Rough Riders were determined to buy the horses originally assigned to them, no matter the cost. The trick was finding them. Captain Day of Troop L spent all afternoon looking for his mount only to come up empty-handed. Perry Tiffany, Lieutenant Tiffany's brother, desperately wanted to purchase the horse ridden by his deceased brother, but it couldn't be identified either.

A few Rough Riders were successful bidders, although the horses didn't come cheap. When a trooper's arm shot up to bid, it was assumed by the crowd that the animal was a particularly good one, and the bidding climbed higher. At any other sale, the horses would have gone for about $5, but they were selling this day for from $25 to $30. Their association with the celebrated Rough Riders had a lot to do with the lively bidding, but the animals were still a bargain considering that, back in May, the army had paid $65 each for them.

Five days later, two mounted Rough Riders were spotted loping along Third Avenue. They stopped several times to stage impromptu equestrian exhibitions. Near Lexington and Fifty-First, a crowd of almost five hundred people cheered them on, the women waving their scarves and handkerchiefs. They watched with delight as the troopers put their horses through "all sorts of funny tricks, one standing on its hind legs while the other danced in the air."

Sixteen Rough Riders on their way home to New Mexico Territory made a brief stop in Washington, D.C., to visit the White House and shake President McKinley's hand. They were not on the president's schedule, and it was after visiting hours, but he graciously took time to greet each trooper personally in the East Room and then speak to them as a group, expressing genuine enthusiasm for their regiment's accomplishments. The troopers left extremely satisfied with their visit.

That evening, at about 9:15, a sharp explosion, very much like a gunshot, was heard outside the White House, followed by bloodcurdling yells. McKinley, who had already retired, jumped out of bed and called an aide to ask what had happened. Out on Pennsylvania Avenue, people came running from different directions, imagining something awful had just occurred. What they saw was a group of Rough Riders, one of whom was holstering his Colt. Seeing their startled expressions, the Rough Rider explained, "We are going home, and I could not help giving the President a parting salute. After I fired off my gun, the boys just naturally gave the Rough Rider yell. That was all."

When McKinley was told about the cause of the commotion and that it was meant as a salute in his honor, he laughed it off. He had no way of knowing, and neither did anyone else, that it wouldn't be the last time a Rough Rider caused a commotion at the White House.

Chapter Eleven

Children of the Dragon's Blood

*Those of us who come out safe will be bound
together all our lives by a very strong tie.*

THEODORE ROOSEVELT, JUNE 14, 1898

Roosevelt was in a foul mood as he dashed off a letter to Senator
Henry Cabot Lodge in early December 1898. He was less than four
weeks away from taking up residence in Albany, New York, having
won the governorship in November. But what was foremost on his
mind was not his recent political triumph; it was the Medal of Honor.
It was becoming increasingly clear that the War Department wasn't
going to give it to him.

A big part of the problem was the trouble Roosevelt had caused
Secretary Alger. First there was his sensational letter describing the
desperate condition of the Fifth Corps in Cuba, and the equally damning round robin. Then, in November, Roosevelt had testified before a
commission appointed by President McKinley to investigate the War
Department's blunders. Although Roosevelt hadn't named names,
he did speak frankly and honestly about the crippling deficiencies he

witnessed. And, of course, when Roosevelt spoke, it invariably ended up in the newspapers.

Also going against Roosevelt was the enormous media attention that had been showered upon him and his volunteer regiment, far out of proportion to the other military organizations in Cuba. More than eight thousand officers and men of the Fifth Corps had participated in the attack on San Juan Heights, but all the newspaper and magazine stories devoted to the Rough Riders made it seem like they had fought the Cubans single-handedly. Many officers in the Regular Army resented the attention the Rough Riders—especially Roosevelt—received.

Roosevelt was well aware that he had made enemies in the War Department, but he expected the department to act justly when it came to such a serious matter as the Medal of Honor.

"I don't ask this as a favor," he wrote Lodge, "I ask it as a right. . . . I am entitled to the Medal of Honor, and I want it." He ended his letter with, "If they want fighting, they shall have it."

It wasn't going to be a fair fight. The skirmish got into the newspapers after it was announced on January 4, 1899, that Roosevelt was to be recommended for the brevet rank of brigadier general for "gallant and meritorious service during the battle of San Juan"—and not the Medal of Honor. This infuriated unnamed friends of Roosevelt, who told the press their man was entitled to the Medal of Honor, the brevet promotion being a rather empty honor considering that other volunteer colonels slated to receive it had never been under fire. Besides, Roosevelt was no longer in the service. He would surely decline the brevet if offered, they said.

Alger chose to talk to the press as well, seemingly unaware that it was inappropriate for him, as secretary of war, to speak publicly about any soldier then under consideration for the medal. Despite having recommendations on Roosevelt's behalf from Wood, General Wheeler, and General Shafter, Alger stated that Roosevelt would have to file additional evidence with the department "showing he performed an extraordinary act of heroism."

Fight Between the U. S. Cruiser Brooklyn and the Spanish Cruiser Cristobal Colon—Pages 10-11.

THE
NEW YORK LEDGER

A JOURNAL OF CHOICE LITERATURE ROMANCE AND USEFUL INFORMATION

NEW YORK, SATURDAY, AUGUST 13, 1898.

ROOSEVELT'S CHARGE.

LEADING THE ROUGH RIDERS AT SANTIAGO.

A good example of the highly romanticized depictions of Roosevelt that followed the American victory at San Juan and rankled many in the Regular Army. This illustration, which inaccurately shows Little Texas being shot out from underneath Roosevelt, appeared on the front page of the New York Ledger of August 13, 1898. (Author's Collection.)

"In charging up San Juan Hill," Alger opined, "Colonel Roosevelt was carrying out the orders of his superior officers. If we were to award him a medal it would be necessary to reward in like manner every officer and man who participated in that charge, and, carrying out the same principle, it would only be just to award a medal to every officer and man who did his duty in the campaign before Santiago de Cuba."

In addition to displaying his apparent ignorance of Roosevelt's heroics before San Juan Heights, Alger followed up his wrongheaded thinking about the medal requirements by giving as an example one of his own heroic missions during the Civil War, one in which he had not received the Medal of Honor because, he claimed, he was only following orders from a superior officer.

Alger's ill-advised interview brought forth another round of criticism from the press. "We gather from Mr. Alger's latest statement in the matter," commented Washington's *Times*, "that Colonel Roosevelt will have to prove that he behaved better at Santiago than Alger did at Chancellorsville before the Secretary will give him a Medal of Honor."

Roosevelt hurriedly went about gathering the additional evidence, but what he heard from Washington was anything but encouraging. The War Department, he informed Lodge, "is indignant at what it is pleased to call my 'efforts to coerce the Board into giving me the medal,' saying that I had gotten you to bring pressure to bear upon them through the President." At this point, Roosevelt fumed, if he did get "that infernal medal of honor," it would look like it was obtained through political influence.

Roosevelt already had critics who viewed him purely as a political animal. In a Washington lecture that spring, writer Burr McIntosh made it clear he was no fan of the New York governor, saying that "every act of the officer [in Cuba] was due to politics or the effect it would have upon his political future." One of Roosevelt's men had the perfect response to such attacks: "If the Colonel was looking out for a prospective governorship, it must have been in Hades, for no one courted death more."

The War Department's three-member awards panel eventually received no less than nine eyewitness certificates regarding Roosevelt's actions at San Juan. When the final names of the Spanish-American War's twenty-five Medal of Honor recipients were announced in June 1899, however, Roosevelt's was not among them. The panel concluded he hadn't performed any actions under the law that would entitle him to it. Much closer to the truth was a stinging editorial in the *Times* from earlier in the year. The "Algerian point of view," it claimed (tongue-in-cheek), was that "the Constitution expressly forbids the granting of a medal of honor to any man who has had a hand in exposing the rottenness in the War Department."

Later that same June, Roosevelt boarded a train for Las Vegas, New Mexico Territory. He was going to be with his boys again. At Camp Wikoff, the Rough Riders had formed a veterans association, and their first reunion was being held in Las Vegas on the one-year anniversary of Las Guásimas, their baptism by fire.

Only about one hundred Rough Riders attended, but some ten thousand people came to witness the festivities and get a look at Governor Roosevelt, who donned his Rough Rider uniform for the weekend (one reporter described the tailored uniform as "lovely fitting"). There were eloquent speeches, several brass bands (with multiple performances of "A Hot Time in the Old Town"), spectacular fireworks displays (one portrayed the charge up San Juan Hill), and a mile-long parade through the town.

And there were plenty of medals and medal ceremonies. The Rough Riders wore the bronze medal designed for the regiment's veterans by Lieutenant Fred Wientge, a Santa Fe jeweler who had died from fever complications in October. New Mexico's governor Miguel A. Otero was presented one in Las Vegas and made an honorary member of the

Many Rough Riders returned home to marry their
sweethearts. This is Troop I trumpeter Clarence H.
Underwood and his fiancée, Mary M. Warner. They
wed on Christmas Day, 1898. (Author's Collection.)

Rough Riders. Otero joined other honorary members Richard Harding Davis, Edward Marshall, Lieutenant John H. Parker of the Gatling Gun Detachment, and Captain Lloyd Stone McCormick of the Seventh U.S. Cavalry.

Roosevelt got a medal for his lapel that weekend, too, except his was made of solid gold. The elaborate medal featured the New Mexico "coat of arms," crossed sabers, and, raised in relief, a highly detailed eagle with outstretched wings. Mounted on the eagle's chest was a brilliant diamond. In addition to Roosevelt's name, the medal contained the words *Las Guásimas, San Juan,* and *Santiago.* The beautifully crafted medal was a gift from the citizens of New Mexico, and Roosevelt was both surprised and stunned.

Among the thousands who came to Las Vegas to see Roosevelt was the Green family of Cerrillos, New Mexico: Richard and Mary, and their children Nancy, Effie, George, and Dick. Another child, Henry Clay Green, had died in Cuba next to Roosevelt. Clay, as he was called, was one of the five men who followed the colonel on his first attempt to charge San Juan Hill, and he had been mortally wounded when Roosevelt halted after realizing the rest of the regiment wasn't behind him.

Someone pointed the Green family out to Roosevelt and explained who they were, and he spent a moment talking to them. Before they parted, he put his hand on eleven-year-old Dick's head and said, "Dick, I sincerely hope you will grow up to be as fine a man as your brother Clay was." The family would remember those words for the rest of their lives.

Roosevelt's book, *The Rough Riders,* hit bookstore shelves on May 20. Priced at $2, it was an immediate bestseller and well into its third printing by the end of the month. And it received glowing reviews, both in the United States and abroad. Humorist Finley Peter Dunne had his popular alter ego, Mr. Dooley, review the book in *Harper's Weekly.* At the end of the review, in which Roosevelt is portrayed as charging San Juan Hill by himself, Mr. Dooley said, "[I]f I was him I'd call the book 'Alone in Cubia.'"

Dunne really should have aimed his satire at the national press. Nevertheless, Roosevelt seemed to enjoy being the subject of Dunne's humor. "I regret to state that my family and intimate friends are delighted with your review of my book," he good-naturedly wrote Dunne. "Now I think you owe me one; and I shall exact that when you next come east you pay me a visit."

Roosevelt's book was nothing like what Dunne's Mr. Dooley described, of course. The *New York Times* proclaimed it "one of the most thrilling pieces of military history produced in recent years" and noted that its author had been "very particular about giving credit to every one who did gallant work, and is hearty in his praise of Edward

Marshall and Richard Harding Davis. . . . He is also careful to praise heartily the splendid conduct of the regulars, and he expresses his belief that the newspapers failed to do them justice."

Those who truly shine in Roosevelt's book, though, are his own men, whether it was Buckey O'Neill, Pawnee Pollock, Woodbury Kane, or several others. The affection he had for them is evident on nearly every page. They were, he wrote at book's end, "children of the dragon's blood"—not unlike Roosevelt himself.

That bond only grew stronger as the years passed. Naturally, his men reveled in Roosevelt's political rise, from New York governor to vice president under McKinley in 1900 to president of the United States upon McKinley's assassination in 1901. And at each milestone in their old colonel's phenomenal career, a few Rough Riders were always close at hand. During the campaign for the New York governorship, Emilio Cassi blew his trumpet to announce the arrival of Roosevelt's train at whistle-stops across the state. In March 1905, for Roosevelt's triumphal inaugural parade after winning a second term as president, a mounted honor guard of twenty-eight Rough Riders escorted Roosevelt's carriage from the White House to the Capitol. When Roosevelt returned from his legendary African safari in 1910, a large contingent of Rough Riders was there to greet him and ride alongside his carriage for the enormous welcoming parade in New York City. "I certainly love all my boys," he had shouted to them as they began the procession.

Two years later, while running for president on the new Progressive Party ticket (a party Roosevelt had formed after a break with his protégé, President William Howard Taft), Roosevelt made a speech in Albuquerque, New Mexico, to a large crowd of mostly Hispanos. Standing next to him and translating every word into Spanish was George Washington Armijo, who had been a sergeant in Troop F. Armijo had named his firstborn Theodore Roosevelt Manderfield Armijo. More than a few Rough Riders gave the colonel's name to their baby boys, but unlike the others, President Roosevelt had actually stood as sponsor at the Armijo boy's baptism in Santa Fe in 1903.

Whether he was governor, vice president, or president, Roosevelt always made time for his boys. At the White House one day, Congressman Charles Grosvenor of Ohio stopped to see Roosevelt on some pressing matter. "The President is engaged," said the page, at the same time blocking the door.

"Who is in there?" Grosvenor demanded.

"Oh, one of his old Rough Riders, I think."

Grosvenor threw up his hands. "Then there's no hope for me," he said. "A mere Congressman doesn't stand a chance at all against a Rough Rider."

Some Rough Riders apparently thought the law didn't stand a chance, either, and when they got on the wrong side of it, they seldom failed to call on their influential colonel. An exasperated Edith Roosevelt felt "as if we were the parents of a thousand very large and very bad children."

Sometime in the fall of 1900, Roosevelt received a letter from Frank Brito, postmarked New Mexico. It read:

> *Dear Colonel: I write you because I am in trouble. I have shot a lady in the eye. But Colonel I did not mean to shoot the lady. It was all an accident, for I was shooting at my wife.*

The "lady" was Brito's twenty-one-year-old sister-in-law, Delfina Calles, and according to newspaper reports, the shooting was rooted in Brito's suspicion that his wife was having an affair. These reports differed from what Brito wrote Roosevelt. They stated that Brito had snuck up to his house in the dark and saw his wife through the window with another man. He decided to shoot the man when he came out the front door, but the person who walked out was his sister-in-law. It made no difference to Roosevelt: "I draw the line at shooting at women, I do not care what the provocation is."

Brito was prosecuted by local district attorney William H. H. Llewellyn, former captain of Troop G. Brito's defense had about the same effect on the jury as it did on Roosevelt, and he was sentenced to ten years in the New Mexico Territorial Penitentiary. "For the sake of the regiment I am very glad that you prosecuted Brito," Roosevelt wrote Llewellyn, "as we cannot afford to let it be thought that we either shield bad men because they are Rough Riders, or press second-rate men forward for the same reason."

Llewellyn, who remained friendly with Brito, visited him in the penitentiary two years later and reported to Roosevelt that Brito's wife had run off to Mexico with another former Rough Rider from Troop H. "This incident," wrote Llewellyn, "has tended to turn popular sentiment strongly in Brito's favor." Indeed, Governor Otero pardoned Brito in the summer of 1905, and Brito eventually went on to a long career in, of all things, law enforcement, serving as a deputy sheriff and jailer for Doña Ana County. He died in 1973—only one Rough Rider outlived him.

Edward Collier was another trooper who broke the law—repeatedly—and needed the help of his colonel. After a long crime spree in 1899 involving two cracked safes in Trinidad, Colorado; the

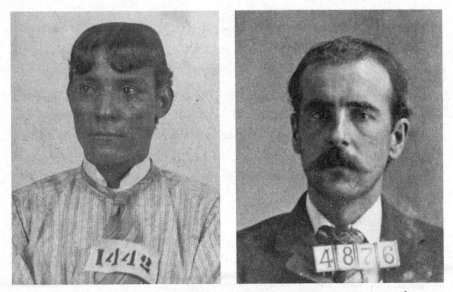

Two Rough Riders who went bad: Frank Brito, New Mexico Territorial Prison Inmate No. 1442, 1901; and Edward G. Collier, Colorado State Penitentiary Inmate No. 4876, 1900. (Courtesy of the State Archives of New Mexico, Santa Fe, and Colorado State Archives, Denver.)

burglary of the Las Vegas, New Mexico, post office; an Albuquerque jewelry store heist; and a jailbreak, Collier was finally brought
to trial, receiving eight years in the Colorado State Penitentiary in
Cañon City. In December 1902, he reached out to Roosevelt and asked
if he would write a letter to the Board of Pardons recommending his
parole. Roosevelt didn't remember Collier, so he contacted his captain, Troop B's James McClintock.

McClintock forwarded Roosevelt a copy of his own letter recommending Collier's parole. The convict had been a good soldier, he
told Roosevelt, ending with, "Assuredly he is no angel, but he ap-
pears to have had 'enough.'" That was all Roosevelt needed to know.
Soon the Board of Pardons received a letter from the president of the
United States asking that a parole be granted for one Edward Collier.
Roosevelt wrote McClintock again a few months later, saying he
would send money for Collier if he was released. Moreover, he promised to look into finding a job for the parolee in Colorado. It took a
year, but on December 10, 1903, Collier walked out of the penitentiary
a free man. He disappeared into civilian life, and Roosevelt never
heard from him again.

Tom Darnell, the bronco-busting hero of Camp Wikoff, didn't ask
for help, but he should have. Nothing was quite right for the cowboy
after he returned to New Mexico. He'd changed into a man easily
angered, especially when drinking, which he did a lot now. It was
common knowledge that he was still dealing with the humiliation of
being left behind in Tampa while his comrades found glory in Cuba.
In February 1899, Darnell's boss fired him from the Diamond A outfit
after he got into a gunfight on a cattle drive in Mexico. Darnell shot
twice at a man who was his good friend, fortunately missing.

Later that same month, Darnell rode into the town of Central, Arizona, and immediately started another spree. In one saloon, he wasn't
happy that the bartender was a black man and began to rant and rave
at both the bartender and the saloon's owner, A. J. Fowler. Darnell
finally left, but his parting words were a menacing "See you again, old
man." Darnell walked over to the livery stable and retrieved his horse

and gun, saying he had to kill a damned black man and a tall white man. The livery owner tried to calm Darnell down and told him to go to bed, but the drunken cowboy stormed off toward the saloon.

In the meantime, someone who overheard Darnell's angry threats ran to the saloon and cautioned Fowler to be ready. When Darnell entered the saloon, Fowler stood at the end of the bar and told the cowboy to stay back. Darnell kept coming. Fowler retreated behind a partition in the rear of the room and drew his revolver. Darnell rushed forward and grabbed for Fowler's gun with his left hand, at the same time drawing his own revolver with his right. "Damn you, I will get you anyway," Darnell shouted.

But Darnell's swipe for Fowler's gun missed, and his own revolver got tangled in his sweater. Fowler didn't give the cowboy a chance to untangle it and fired a bullet straight into the Rough Rider's heart.

Rough Rider George Roland, who had worked with Darnell on the Diamond A, wrote Roger Fitch with the news of their comrade's death: "Tom was dead when he hit the floor, or he would [have] made it interesting to the other fellow. . . . I was sure sorry to hear of him going, and he had plenty of grit too. No man ever called on him for a fight that he didn't get it."

William Pollock, the Oklahoma Pawnee who had smiled at Roosevelt that last day at Camp Wikoff, was entitled to wear two eagle feathers in his hair. The custom of his people allowed for a feather for each battle. Now a warrior, Pollock was also entitled to a new name and feasts and presents. But Pollock had spent ten years at the Haskell Institute in Lawrence, Kansas, starting at the age of thirteen. After graduating Haskell with high honors, he had attended the University of Kansas, where he studied in the Fine Arts Department. A gifted artist and musician, Pollock had been raised a Christian. He loved his people and attended their feasts in his honor, but he told a reporter he had no plans to wear any feathers. As a "Christian gentleman," he said, he had "outgrown their old-time superstitions and customs."

Pollock was also ready to see more of the world. In February 1899, he signed a contract to appear in Buffalo Bill Cody's Wild West. Cody had put out a call for a dozen men who were good cowboys and, more important, had served in the Rough Riders. A new feature of his show for the coming season was a reenactment of the charge up San Juan Hill. It would be advertised as a "vivid, truthful, thrilling, heart-stirring dioramic reproduction of which will be presented by some of the GENUINE PARTICIPANTS IN THE FAMOUS BATTLE." The job paid $50 a month, with all expenses covered.

But "Pawnee Pollock" was fated never to leave Oklahoma. He had been sick with fever in Cuba and also at Camp Wikoff and arrived home from the war thin and exhausted. He soon felt he was getting his strength back, and he made big plans to write the story of the Rough Riders and illustrate it with his own drawings. But shortly after signing the Buffalo Bill contract, he came down with pneumonia. As one newspaper put it, "the fever was in his veins and he went down to death with it." Pollock died on March 2 at the age of twenty-eight.

Bill Cody's manager eventually signed up sixteen Rough Riders. Most came from Oklahoma, including the part-Cherokee Tom Isbell and Bill McGinty. Governor Roosevelt went to see his boys when the popular show played at Madison Square Garden that April. He watched with delight as they battled up a replica San Juan Hill alongside Buffalo Soldiers and infantrymen, fake artillery shells exploding above their heads. Rough Riders portraying General Wheeler, Wood, and, of course, Roosevelt, encouraged the men forward. Upon driving the Spaniards from the blockhouse at the summit, the Rough Riders pulled down the enemy flag and raised the Stars and Stripes, which was the cue for the band to strike up "The Star-Spangled Banner." The performance ended with a snappy rendition of "A Hot Time in the Old Town."

That 1899 season, Isbell, McGinty, and their fellow Rough Riders charged up San Juan Hill 341 times in 132 towns in twenty-four states. The San Juan Hill act always drew the biggest applause. Roosevelt applauded, too ("excellent in every respect," he said), as did journalist Edward Marshall.

Rough Riders who appeared in Buffalo Bill's Wild West for the 1899 season, posing in front of a painted backdrop for the show. (Courtesy of the City of Las Vegas Museum and Rough Rider Memorial Collection.)

Marshall came to the Madison Square Garden show on crutches. Army surgeons claimed he was the only man in the war to survive having a vertebrae destroyed by a bullet. Although both of his legs had been paralyzed, he'd regained the use of the right leg and part of the left after undergoing surgery and massage therapy. That summer, his left leg would be amputated eight inches below his knee.

During his long recovery, Marshall had written a book, *The Story of the Rough Riders,* which beat Roosevelt's to publication by a month. The volumes were part of a flood of war books then flowing from the nation's publishers: cheap picture books, hasty cut-and-paste histories made from newspaper reports, firsthand accounts from several of the war correspondents, and volumes by some of the fighting men themselves.

Besides Roosevelt, only a few Rough Riders came out with books. One volume that hardly any in the regiment saw coming was written by Lieutenant Tom Hall. After his disgraceful exit from Cuba, Hall had entered the sanitarium of Dr. Amos Givens in Stamford, Connecticut. Givens specialized in "the treatment of Nervous and Mental Diseases, Opium and Alcoholic Habitues." Hall's physician later said that the lieutenant had been admitted for sunstroke, not alcoholism, but Hall's wife, Jennie, had filed for divorce in April, citing her husband's frequent drunkenness, which caused Hall to become "a perfect devil."

During the winter of 1898, Hall worked on his Rough Rider book with the help of Frank Hayes, a lieutenant in Troop L. Publishing magnate Frank A. Munsey provided the pair quarters at his recently opened Mohican Hotel in New London, Connecticut. In January 1899, as the two struggled to complete the book, Jennie got her divorce. The story was picked up by several newspapers due to Hall's reputation as a published writer and poet.

The Fun and Fighting of the Rough Riders by Tom Hall was released that October (price, fifty cents). Hall's book was not well received by his fellow Rough Riders, and they found its title especially grating. Arthur Cosby and Colton Reed fired off scathing letters to the *New York Times* denouncing the volume. At no time was Hall "in a position to partake of any fun and certainly none of the fighting that would justify any account being placed before the public by him," wrote Reed. After Hall disappeared to the rear at San Juan, his "name became a by-word for all that a Rough Rider held in abhorrence and contempt."

Hall does not seem to have made an effort to refute these damning charges. He died ten months later of "sunstroke." Hall was thirty-seven.

Unlike Hall's book, which had a New York publisher, J. Ogden Wells had his *Diary of a Rough Rider* printed by a small press in a limited run. It appeared a year or two after Roosevelt's *The Rough Riders,* for Wells plagiarized quite freely from his colonel's book to fill out his own slim volume. After the war, Wells had returned to his native home of St. Joseph, Michigan, and entered his father's hosiery manufacturing business. He eventually built the company up to one of the leading manufacturers in the country and became a wealthy and respected citizen.

One morning in December 1928, his chauffer discovered the "business genius," as Wells was often called, dead in his garage. The fifty-two-year-old Wells died of carbon monoxide poisoning, and the theory put forth at the time was that he'd been tinkering on his car when he was overcome by the fumes. More telling, perhaps: the newspapers also reported that Wells had suffered a nervous breakdown during the summer and had entered a sanitarium for treatment that fall.

Wells was the first to die of a trio of close Michigan friends who had been Rough Riders. The last was Wells's old bunkie, Frank Knox, with whom he'd spent many a night in Cuba on the wet grass under a too-small tent. Knox died in 1944 while serving as secretary of the navy under President Franklin Roosevelt.

The most poignant book to come from a Rough Rider was a privately printed keepsake published by the family of Theodore Westwood Miller in 1899. A year earlier, on July 11, Miller's mother had received a package from her dead son. It contained his worn and soiled diary and a letter written by Miller in the Siboney hospital the day before he died. This diary, along with a narrative of his short life and memories of Miller by his comrades, was published in an elegant small volume with the title *Theodore W. Miller, Rough Rider.*

This was not all that the grieving family and friends did to honor Miller's memory. At Yale, his alma mater, $1,000 was raised to build a memorial gateway. Erected between Battell Chapel and Durfee Hall, the stately stone arch with heavy iron gates has two large panels at the top, one on each side. The panel facing the street informs passersby that the gate is in memory of Miller, class of 1897, who fell mortally wounded in the charge on San Juan Hill.

The gateway "stands in the midst of the Yale life which he loved," reads the 1899 keepsake, and it still stands today. But the students who walk through it now rarely glance up, never imagining the sorrow that created the gateway more than a century ago.

Sometime in the 1950s, Arthur Cosby prepared a manuscript about his life, most of it devoted to his Rough Rider experiences. For whatever reason, his "A Rough Rider Looks Back" was never published, and the manuscript now rests in a box at Harvard's Houghton Library as part of the Theodore Roosevelt Collection. After recovering from the wounds he received in the San Juan fight, Cosby had not rejoined the Rough Riders. Thanks in part to an impressive recommendation from Roosevelt, he'd been promoted to a staff position as assistant adjutant general of volunteers with the rank of captain. Cosby received an honorable discharge in 1899, but he would eventually achieve the rank of lieutenant colonel in the U.S. Army Reserves.

In the decades following the war, Cosby was quite active in the Rough Riders Association and attended several reunions, including the first in Las Vegas. But it was in preparation for that Las Vegas reunion that some of the Rough Riders perceived a slight attitude coming from Cosby. He had objected to having the reunion in New Mexico because it was too far away. Another Rough Rider asked him, "Too far from where and from whom?" Cosby lived in New York City.

That friction only got worse over time. "Long ago," wrote one old trooper in 1948, "I found Cosby's supercilious airs toward our western comrades insufferably snobbish. . . . In my opinion all that Cosby really has to be proud of is his membership in our regiment and that he was wounded while following its colors."

Cosby died in 1957 at age eighty-four, missing by one year the sixtieth anniversary of the Spanish-American War and another reunion of the Rough Riders—held in Las Vegas. Still lodged in his chest was the Mauser bullet fired by a Spaniard from the top of Kettle Hill.

In the summer of 1901, while Roosevelt was serving as vice president, he was bombarded with requests from numerous Rough Riders hoping to obtain a government position. He grumbled about it in a letter to Llewellyn: "I have asked for so many favors for men of the regiment that I am positively ashamed to go to a single department in Washington, and above all, the War Department. Yet each trooper not unnaturally when he writes me thinks his own is the only case, and that if I chose to, I can surely do anything he wants."

Things changed dramatically later that year when Roosevelt became president of the United States after the death of McKinley from an anarchist's bullet on September 14. Many federal positions were presidential appointments, from territorial governor to post-master. During Roosevelt's nearly eight years as president, more than forty Rough Riders ended up in plum positions. He made Alexander Brodie, who had risen to lieutenant colonel in the regiment, governor of Arizona Territory. He appointed George Curry, captain of Troop H, governor of New Mexico Territory. And a particular favorite, Frank Frantz, who had succeeded Buckey O'Neill as Troop A's captain, received three appointments in succession: postmaster, Indian agent, and finally governor of Oklahoma Territory.

One article published in newspapers nationwide in 1906 revealed "how it paid to belong to the Rough Riders" and provided the salaries of several men Roosevelt had either appointed or helped to get jobs. It was even said that the local politics in Arizona, New Mexico, and Oklahoma were not so much Republican versus Democrat as they were Rough Rider versus anti–Rough Rider.

Some of these appointments proved to be temporary embarrass-ments. Roosevelt was enamored of westerner Ben Daniels, a private in Troop K, who had shown real bravery on the battlefield. Daniels's colorful history, including once serving as a Dodge City lawman, only made Roosevelt like him that much more.

Daniels pressed Roosevelt to appoint him U.S. marshal for Arizona Territory, and the president was more than happy to oblige, sending Daniels's name to the Senate for confirmation. Even though Daniels was a lifelong Democrat, the Senate bowed to Roosevelt's wishes and confirmed Daniels in January 1902. Just days later, however, reports surfaced that the new U.S. marshal had previously served more than three years in the Wyoming Territorial Penitentiary for stealing gov-ernment mules. Of the many Wild West tales Daniels had told his old colonel, he left out the one about being an ex-con.

Roosevelt forced Daniels to resign, but he remained a staunch friend and was determined to help him. In 1904, he persuaded Governor Brodie to make Daniels prison superintendent for the Arizona Territorial Penitentiary at Yuma. Then, less than a year later, Roosevelt reappointed Daniels to the Arizona marshal's post. Once more, the details of Daniels's unsavory past were dredged up. "Perhaps [Roosevelt] . . . thinks that to have been a Rough Rider is glory enough to atone for all previous sins," went one newspaper editorial. Nevertheless, Roosevelt pushed for Daniels's confirmation, and the Senate, after stalling for months, complied. Daniels ably served as U.S. marshal for the remainder of the Roosevelt administration.

Ben Colbert, the Chickasaw Indian, also caused Roosevelt difficulty. After the San Juan battle, Roosevelt learned that Colbert could take shorthand, as well as type. He promoted Colbert from regimental butcher to stenographer. "I have learned from sad experience," Colbert wrote in his diary following the promotion, "that it's not well to know how to do too many things. . . . the more I did, all the more was put on me." He performed his work well and gained Roosevelt's trust and admiration. In 1902, Roosevelt appointed Colbert U.S. marshal for the Southern Judicial District of Indian Territory.

Colbert's tenure was plagued by controversy. He was investigated for frequent absences from his district and for using his office to influence tribal elections. And he became a central figure in a scandal involving Chickasaw tribal payment warrants. In June 1905, he and several federal and tribal officials were indicted for fraud and conspiracy. His marshal's term would expire early the next year, but despite how much Roosevelt liked Colbert, there was no way he could reappoint a man facing such serious charges.

Like the case with Daniels, the friendship between Colbert and Roosevelt seems to have remained strong. In 1908, Colbert was acquitted in federal court, and four years later, he left the Republican Party to campaign for Roosevelt and his Progressives. Just as martially spirited as Roosevelt, he volunteered in World War I and worked in a U.S. defense plant in World War II. In 1960, Colbert, age eighty-seven, died in an Oklahoma veterans' home, leaving little behind except what appeared to be an old journal. One of his caretakers opened it and read the first line: "The experiences of a Red man with Roosevelt and his Rough Riders." Colbert's unpublished diary is now part of the collections of the Oklahoma Historical Society.

Roosevelt's political enemies carped about his nepotism with the Rough Riders, but they relished even more attacking the regiment's heroics, especially at election time. In 1904, multiple newspaper columns were devoted to whether or not Roosevelt and the Rough Riders had charged up San Juan Hill. Particularly vicious were the attacks from Alexander S. Bacon, a New York City lawyer and officer in the New York National Guard.

Just days before the 1904 presidential election, Democratic newspapers across the country printed a full page with Bacon's claims under the bold headline "President Roosevelt's War Record." Bacon asserted that Roosevelt "did not see a Spaniard on July 1st and was not in a position where he could see one," and he had the sworn testimony of one hundred participants to prove it. Kettle Hill was not occupied by Spanish soldiers, he wrote, nor did it have Spanish entrenchments. And Roosevelt had lied about charging up San Juan Hill on horseback.

In a closing sentence befitting the hyperbole of a trial lawyer, which Bacon was, he wrote, "Colonel Roosevelt has obtained promotions by a false report in his 'Rough Riders' of his own heroic deeds in an imaginary charge on an imaginary horse up an imaginary hill against imaginary Spaniards."

Little Texas was no imaginary horse. Roosevelt had ridden him most of the day on July 1, finally leaving him behind at a barbed-wire fence partway up Kettle Hill, forcing Roosevelt to make the later San Juan charge on foot. All of this Roosevelt recounted in his book. But numerous illustrators depicted the San Juan charge with Roosevelt on horseback; it was the way artists—and Americans—imagined him (often with a saber, too). Ironically, Frederic Remington's illustration depicting charging Rough Riders for Roosevelt's own book added greatly to the confusion.

Remington had accurately painted the Rough Riders' assault on Kettle Hill with Roosevelt at the front, riding Little Texas, but the full-page illustration as it appeared in both *Scribner's Magazine* and *The Rough Riders* carried the title "Charge of the Rough Riders at San Juan Hill." Making matters worse, Remington's illustration was published in other histories with that or a similar title. A decade later, one New York City newspaper blamed Remington for misleading the public, when he'd had nothing to do with the title used by Scribner's. Roosevelt apparently had no control over it, either.

Bacon and individuals like him didn't seem to be looking for explanations or the truth. Their aim was to damage Roosevelt by whatever means possible, and they succeeded in casting doubt on whether or not the Rough Riders had made their legendary charge. Much of the ensuing controversy, though, was a direct result of the San Juan battlefield's changing nomenclature.

San Juan Hill was a long rolling ridge with more than one blockhouse, and it was identified as such on the official maps prepared by the War Department. The larger blockhouse, which became known as the San Juan blockhouse, was assaulted by the white and black infantrymen of Brigadier General Jacob Kent's First Division at great loss of life. No more than six hundred yards to the north, on the same ridge, was another fortified house. This blockhouse was taken by different elements of the Cavalry Division in the charge led by Roosevelt. Over time, San Juan Hill came to be identified only as that part of the ridge where the San Juan blockhouse rested. Many in Kent's infantry, then, greatly resented the stories of the Rough Riders charging San Juan Hill and capturing "their" blockhouse.

Roosevelt did his best to clarify his regiment's actions at San Juan several times over the years, which he always found annoying. "The San Juan Block House was simply one of the points of attack," he wrote in 1909. "[T]he rest of San Juan Ridge, and the hills nearby, like Kettle Hill, form other points of attack. The cavalry charged at

'San Juan Hill' just as much as the infantry; to deny this is merely to quibble—and to quibble untruthfully at that."

Some of the Rough Riders weren't as restrained as their old colonel in setting the record straight. In 1952, *Life* magazine ran a photo essay on that year's Rough Rider reunion (attended by twenty-eight veterans), commenting in the accompanying text that the Rough Riders' charge up San Juan Hill "remains a high point in American exuberance, even though the hill had already been captured." The editors shortly received a letter from George P. Hamner, who had given up telegraphy after the war to become a medical doctor: "That's the grossest misstatement I have ever seen in print, and I'm wondering where in <u>hell</u> you acquired such defamatory misinformation?" The magazine didn't print Hamner's letter.

Unfortunately, the myth that Roosevelt and his Rough Riders did not charge up San Juan Hill survives to this day, mostly perpetuated by historians who, quite frankly, either have some bias against Roosevelt or have not done their research, or both.

Another aspect of Roosevelt's "war record" that came under fire during the 1904 election wasn't about what he did or didn't do at San Juan; it was about his perceived attitude toward the Buffalo Soldiers. Despite his praise for the "Smoked Yankees" in his farewell speech at Montauk, he had written in *The Rough Riders* that the black troopers were "peculiarly dependent upon their white officers." Their ranks might produce a noncommissioned officer as good as one who was white, he admitted, but "this cannot be expected normally, nor is it fair to expect."

The Broad Ax, an African American newspaper published in Chicago, ran a front-page story in the summer of 1904 titled "Col. Roosevelt and the Negro Soldier," highlighting Roosevelt's comments and railing against his failure to advance black soldiers during his presidency. "Has Col. Roosevelt as Commander-in-Chief of the Army and Navy, recommended for promotion in the regular army, any of the non-commissioned colored officers who were forced to kick the rough riders out of their way so that they could lead the memorable charge on San Juan Hill? He has not!"

No units kicked the Rough Riders out of the way at San Juan, but *The Broad Ax* had a solid point about the lack of black commissioned officers. "No officers, no soldiers," was the motto taken up by African Americans, although it did little good. Then, just two years later, came the most controversial episode in Roosevelt's relationship with the army's black fighting men. On a warm summer night in Brownsville, Texas, a small band of men had gone on a shooting spree, killing a white bartender and wounding a police officer. The townspeople blamed the violence on the Buffalo Soldiers of nearby Fort Brown, a group they already disliked. The post's officers reported that their men had been in the barracks all night.

After an investigation in which the black soldiers claimed no knowledge of the perpetrators, Roosevelt ordered dishonorable discharges for 167 men of the Twenty-Fifth U.S. Infantry, a regiment that had fought bravely under General Lawton at the Battle of El Caney. The men were barred from reenlisting, nor would they be allowed to take any job with the government. They would receive no military pensions.

Convinced that some of these black infantrymen were guilty, Roosevelt later argued that "these comrades of the murderers, by their own action, have rendered it necessary either to leave all the men, including the murderers, in the army or to turn them all out."

During his presidency, Roosevelt made many appointments of black citizens to federal offices. And he was the first president to invite a black man, Booker T. Washington, to dine at the White House. He did this at great political risk (southern whites were outraged at the Roosevelt-Washington dinner). But Roosevelt is now most remembered for the cruel injustice of the Brownsville Affair. And it is not too much of a stretch to draw a line from Brownsville back to San Juan, in that moment when Roosevelt believed the Buffalo Soldiers of the Tenth were shirking their duty, when he threatened to put a bullet in the back of the first man he saw going to the rear.

Roosevelt "was a man of many and strong emotions," remembered a friend. "And these, many times in his life, impaired his judgment."

Those strong emotions welled up again in the summer of 1915. A German U-boat had torpedoed the British passenger liner RMS *Lusitania* in May, killing nearly twelve hundred people, including 128 Americans. It looked as if the United States might enter the European conflict that had begun the previous year. And if the United States was going to war, Roosevelt desperately wanted to face the enemy on a battlefield. At that time, he had been an "ex-president" for six years. Here was something again worth doing.

He was eager to organize a fighting force of volunteers like the Rough Riders, but on a much larger scale. Roosevelt didn't have just a regiment in mind—he wanted an entire cavalry division: four brigades, each composed of two regiments; a horse artillery brigade of two regiments; a field battalion of signal troops; two "pioneer" battalions; and a battalion of machine gunners. He busily wrote letters with his plans to former Rough Riders and officer friends in the U.S. Army, offering them different positions in the division.

But President Woodrow Wilson kept the United States out of the war for the time being, much to Roosevelt's dismay. When the country did enter the conflict two years later, Roosevelt again devoted all his energies to getting approval to raise a division, pleading with both Wilson and his secretary of war to allow him to serve his country. France's most prominent leader, Georges Clemenceau, published an open letter to Wilson urging him to send Roosevelt. It was the one name in France, he wrote, "which sums up the beauty of American intervention."

But Wilson, a Democrat, was not about to let his political rival back on the front pages of the nation's press and definitely not anywhere

IT WOULD BE JUST HIS LUCK!

President Woodrow Wilson's worst nightmare. This cartoon, titled "It would be just his luck!" imagines an aged Roosevelt single-handedly bringing in the German emperor, Wilhelm II, whom he has lassoed. The cartoon appeared in the June 7, 1917, issue of Life. *(Author's Collection.)*

near a battlefield. It was a crushing disappointment for Roosevelt, as well as for his old comrades who had agreed to serve under him. James E. Amos, Roosevelt's black valet in later years, had never seen Roosevelt in a darker mood as when he learned that his final appeal had been rejected: "The thought that his country was at war and that he would not be permitted to draw his sword in its defense was intolerable to him. It wounded him to the quick."

Leonard Wood also craved combat. After the formal independence of Cuba in 1902, Wood's next station had been the Philippines, where he eventually commanded the entire military department. In 1903, he'd been promoted to a major general in the Regular Army, a promotion many believed was a result of Wood's friendship with the

president. At the outbreak of World War I, he was the senior serving
officer in the army, but Wood could not get a command at the front.
He was done in by snobbishness and jealousy on the part of West
Pointer General John J. Pershing and also his well-known association
with Roosevelt.

As bitter as Roosevelt was toward President Wilson's administration, though, his advice to Wood was that of a true leader. "This is
no time for differences," he told the old colonel of the Rough Riders.
"The war has got to be won, and we will have to put aside our personal grievances and fight on wherever they put us. We must be good
soldiers."

All four of Roosevelt's sons would fight in World War I. His youngest, Quentin, would not return.

Theodore Roosevelt died in his sleep at his Oyster Bay home on January 6, 1919, a Monday. Doctors concluded that a blood clot had detached
from a vein and entered his lungs. He was just sixty years old. Prior to
the public funeral at Christ Church, a private service for family members took place at Sagamore Hill. His coffin lay in the large trophy
room, the colors of the First U.S. Volunteer Cavalry draped over its
top. Just steps away was one of his most treasured possessions: the
Remington bronze given him by the men of his regiment. With other
reminders at Sagamore, such as his old Stetson and his Colt revolver,
he had never been far, it seems, from San Juan Hill.

Some credited luck for Roosevelt's meteoric rise. He had been lucky
to get his cowboy regiment and lucky to survive the Spanish Mausers,
not to mention the tropical fevers. And it was a turn of fortune that
had placed him a heartbeat away from the presidency.

Roosevelt's hunting partner and close friend Jack Willis scoffed at
such talk. "To my way of thinking," he wrote, "it was simply the natural reward of a dauntless courage. If it is true, as it ought to be, that
'God hates a coward,' by the same token it must be true that He loves
a brave man."

Brave as he was, though, Roosevelt was not opposed to having a little luck on his side. A year after Roosevelt's death, noted American sculptor Alexander Phimister Proctor received a commission to create a monumental equestrian statue of Roosevelt as colonel of the Rough Riders. Edith Roosevelt loaned Proctor two of her husband's khaki uniforms to help the artist accurately portray his famous subject. One day, while working on the sculpture in his New York City studio, Proctor picked up a uniform coat and noticed a small bulge in one of the pockets. Curious, he reached his hand in and retrieved the object.

It was a silver-mounted rabbit's foot.

EPILOGUE

Wednesday, January 16, 2001
The White House

A small, select audience waits in the Roosevelt Room. The intimate chamber, twenty-five by thirty-five feet, served as the office of President Theodore Roosevelt upon the completion of the West Wing in 1902. It is now a meeting room, and at its east end, above a fireplace, hangs an impressive portrait of Colonel Roosevelt in his Rough Rider uniform astride Little Texas.

On this day, a short distance in front of the fireplace, stands a podium bearing the seal of the president of the United States. A large door to the right of the fireplace opens and in walks President Bill Clinton, followed by several guests. The audience rises to its feet. After a brief prayer by Chaplain General David Hicks, Clinton steps to the podium and asks the audience to be seated. He explains that they are here today to honor two American heroes with "our highest military decoration": the Medal of Honor. The first of the two men to be honored is Corporal Andrew Jackson Smith, a black Civil War infantryman who risked his life to protect his regiment's state and federal flags after the color bearer had been killed. The second man to be honored is Theodore Roosevelt.

In 1996, Congress passed legislation that effectively waived the time restriction for the awarding of the Medal of Honor, thus allowing older cases to be considered or reconsidered. In July 1997, Pennsylvania congressman Paul McHale introduced legislation to award Roosevelt the coveted medal. Two months later, Congressman Rick Lazio of New York submitted a formal request to the Department of the Army to reconsider Roosevelt's case.

In a surprise to Lazio and many others at the time, the Senior Army Decorations Board determined that Roosevelt's actions did not rise above what was expected of him as an officer. It was as if the ghost of Secretary of War Alger had come back to slap Roosevelt in the face once again—history repeating itself. But Paul McHale's bill, cosponsored by Lazio and 161 additional representatives, passed the House and Senate and was signed into law by President Clinton on November 12, 1998.

Though the law authorized and requested Clinton to award the medal to Roosevelt, several House members expressed in a letter to the president that they expected him to consult the secretary of the Army in the matter, and to base Roosevelt's eligibility on "the same standard of merit that was applied to other members of the armed forces who received this medal during the Spanish American War."

During the course of the next year, then, the army solicited the public for information on Roosevelt's actions at San Juan Heights and formed an independent panel of historians to produce a report on Roosevelt's valor. On February 22, 2000, Secretary of Defense William Cohen forwarded to Clinton a recommendation that Roosevelt be awarded the Medal of Honor. Now, after nearly twelve more months of anxious waiting, the descendants of Theodore Roosevelt are about to see the leader of the Rough Riders receive the medal he deserved.

"TR was a larger-than-life figure who gave our nation a larger-than-life vision of our place in the world," Clinton tells the audience. "Part of that vision was formed on San Juan Hill."

Major William Mullen, Marine Corps aide to the president, reads aloud Roosevelt's Medal of Honor citation as President Clinton cradles the framed decoration in his arm. Once Mullen is finished, President Clinton turns to Tweed Roosevelt, Theodore's great-grandson, shakes his hand warmly, and presents him with the medal. A smiling Tweed Roosevelt takes his seat next to the family of black soldier Andrew Jackson Smith. It is fitting that Roosevelt shares this White House ceremony with a gallant African American.

Theodore Roosevelt joins James Robb Church as one of the only two members of the Rough Riders to receive the Medal of Honor, and he is the only United States president to receive the decoration.

Although Roosevelt was not awarded the cherished medal while he was alive, he acquired a variety of honors during his full life, from the Nobel Peace Prize (for his role in ending the Russo-Japanese War in 1905) to the naming of a massive dam for him on Arizona's Salt River. The honor he cherished most, though, was that of commanding the Rough Riders. "I regard the fact that I was one of them," he once wrote, "as well-nigh the most precious heritage I can leave my children."

But Roosevelt did much more than leave a legacy to his children. He and his men authored one of the iconic moments in American history. The Rough Riders forever charge up San Juan Hill, and Roosevelt forever leads them. In that way they are immortal. And it is all because Theodore Roosevelt craved something "worth doing."

ACKNOWLEDGMENTS

Pursuing the story of Theodore Roosevelt and his Rough Riders took me farther from home than any of my previous books. From Colorado, I traveled by rail (very appropriate, I thought, for a work rooted in 1898) to Boston, New York City, and Washington, D.C. My research also required lengthy trips to New Mexico, Arizona, and Texas. At several points in my journeys, friends provided me with excellent companionship and a comfy couch or bed, and knowledgeable archivists guided me to untold treasures in their collections.

While researching for several days in Washington, D.C., my old friends Laura and Patrick Anderson, and their children, Ellen, Wynne, and Cody, welcomed me into their Cabin John home. Laura drove me back and forth to Washington on her daily commute, and Wynne gave me a most useful tutorial on how to operate my new iPhone. And I'll always remember the evenings when we sat around their kitchen table, Pat and I playing guitar and banjo and singing timeless songs, from Dan Emmett to Johnny Cash.

In New Mexico, my compadre Ron Kil once again shared his casa with me (Ron also put me up when I was trailing Billy the Kid and Pat Garrett). Ron is a fine western artist, and it's always a huge treat to stay at his home, which is his studio as well. It's like spending the night in an art museum.

Marc Simmons, another New Mexico friend of many decades,

provided timely advice as I researched and wrote this book. One beautiful afternoon, he helped me locate a small, picturesque cemetery on a hill above Cerrillos, New Mexico, that contains the grave of Rough Rider Henry Clay Green. Green was killed on Kettle Hill while standing close to Roosevelt.

My literary agent and good friend James Donovan and his family were fine hosts for my Texas sojourn. I couldn't ask for a better literary agent than Jim. He read every page of my manuscript and provided a detailed critique. More impressive still, he never said no to any of my frequent pleas for help. I also wish to thank Jim's in-house editor and right-hand woman, Melissa Shultz, for valuable input on both the initial book proposal as well as the finished manuscript.

I should mention that Jim is the author of critically acclaimed works on the Battle of the Little Big Horn and the Alamo, and while I was conducting research in San Antonio, he took time to walk me through the storied mission. Getting a guided tour of the Alamo by the author of the definitive work on the 1836 siege and battle was pretty cool, to say the least.

Jim also introduced me to his San Antonio friends Pat Ryan and wife, Julie Lebrun, and they graciously put us up in their home during my time there.

My good friend (and preeminent Sam Peckinpah scholar) Paul Seydor gave me much food for thought as I wrote this story, and he and his family—wife, Danielle, and daughter, Samantha Rose— entertained me and my family at their home in Los Angeles for two very enjoyable days during yet another research trip.

I can't thank enough all the archivists and museum employees who assisted me over the last two and a half years. At the top of my list are Heather Cole and Kristin Hsueh. Heather is the curator of the incredible Theodore Roosevelt Collection at Harvard's Houghton Library. She alerted me to several unusual and obscure items in the collection that contained important Rough Rider materials. And not only was she of tremendous help during the week I spent at her institution, but she continued to provide prompt and cheerful assistance long after I had returned home.

Kristin Hsueh is the director of the Las Vegas Museum and Rough Rider Memorial Collection in Las Vegas, New Mexico. Kristin showed me the shelves with their important and very well organized Rough Rider manuscripts and photos and then left me to quietly work away. As the director of a modest city museum, Kristin faces a continuing challenge with her limited budget and staff, but from what I've seen, the museum could not be in better hands.

Other archivists and librarians who have my sincere thanks include Robert Mangum, National Archives and Records Administration; Sibel Melik, New Mexico State Archives and Records Center; Steve Friesen, Buffalo Bill Museum and Grave; Sam Fore, Harlan Crow Library; Michael Amato and Katherine Hansen, Theodore Roosevelt Birthplace National Historic Site; Elizabeth DeMaria, Sagamore Hill National Historic Site; Tomas Jaehn and Daniel Kosharek at the Fray Angélico Chávez History Library and Photo Archives; and the staffs of the Pikes Peak Library District's Regional History Department and Interlibrary Loan Office, the Denver Public Library's Western History/ Genealogy Department, the Colorado State Archives, the DeGolyer Library, and the Sharlot Hall Museum Library and Archives.

My doctor, Anthony J. Christoff, educated me about the immediate and long-term effects of malaria and yellow fever. He even consulted with specialists on the subject on my behalf. Forensics scientist Dr. James Bailey, who shares my interest in Old West history, graciously prepared a detailed report on the bullet injury of Rough Rider Arthur F. Cosby.

Michelle Cooke, Department of Culture & Humanities, Chickasaw Nation, Ada, Oklahoma, kindly provided me with a transcript of Ben Colbert's Rough Rider diary. Michelle is writing a biography of Colbert, which I am eagerly awaiting.

For various kind favors, I am indebted to Nancy Samuelson, Kip Stratton, John Oller, Margaret Bailey, Verna Stonecipher Fuller, Doug

Clausen, Dan Gagliasso, Tanya Kil, Andy Morris, Rex Rideout, and my in-laws, Jack and Mary Ann Davis. My friends Andy and Rex, especially, have endured my many Rough Rider stories—and my periodic exasperation—as I wrote this book.

Back in my old Missouri stomping grounds, numerous friends and family members continue to make my annual visits home fun and memorable. David Wayne Gardner, Tim and Teri Gardner, David Greenwood, Ivan Greenwood, Montie Maddux, and Stephen Reed all make it so that I and my boy, Vance, can chase wild turkeys in the spring. And my uncle Curly Gardner always has a spare shotgun or two for the Saturday night trapshoots.

As always, my parents, Claude and Venita Gardner, Breckenridge, Missouri, kept a light on and a door open—even when I didn't have their grandkids with me.

In the midst of writing these acknowledgments, my sister Terri Gardner told me that I had never mentioned her or my other sister, Robin Decker, in any of my books' acknowledgments. All I can say to this is that she either has never read my books, or if she has, she's not a very careful reader. Nevertheless, because they are my sisters, and because I was often an ornery big brother when we were growing up, Robin and Terri are certainly deserving of another mention and my gratitude here. (Happy now?)

This is the third book in which I have acknowledged my editor at William Morrow, Henry Ferris. In addition to the fact that I just plain like Henry, his sense of narrative is superb, and he has this uncanny ability to get the most out of me. Like any author-editor relationship, we have our occasional disagreements. Usually when that happens, his advice or suggestion for the manuscript will gnaw at me until, hours later, I'll end up concluding he was right. Thank goodness he's relatively patient with my hardheadedness.

I also want to thank Henry's assistant, Nick Amphlett. Nick has been my go-to man with technical questions about illustrations, manuscript preparation, and—well, just about everything having to do with the book. Henry's former assistant, Cole Hager, deserves my thanks as well. If it hadn't been for his clear instructions, I'm certain I would still be trying to find my way out of New York City's complex (at least to a first-time visitor) subway system.

Others at HarperCollins who have provided immeasurable assistance on this book include senior production editor David Palmer; designer Michael Accordino; marketing director, Amelia Wood; publicists Heidi Richter and Kaitlyn Kennedy; and William Morrow publisher, Liate Stehlik. My all-time favorite copyeditor, Laurie McGee, did another super job on my manuscript. I can't imagine publishing a book without the benefit of her meticulous attention to detail.

Last, but by no means least, my books would hardly see the light of day without the love and support of my family: Katie, Christiana, and Vance.

Mark Lee Gardner
Thanksgiving Day, 2015

A NOTE ON SOURCES

For his 1971 history of the Rough Riders, Virgil Carrington Jones struggled to find firsthand accounts written by Roosevelt's men. He assumed that "because of the brevity of the Cuban campaign, few [Rough Rider] diaries were kept and few letters were written by the men who took part."

What a difference forty-four years can make. Many of the Rough Riders were prolific letter writers, and several kept diaries. Dozens of Rough Rider letters appear in the back issues of newspapers in Oklahoma, New Mexico, Arizona, Texas, and elsewhere. Some of the men acted as official correspondents for their hometown newspapers. In other cases, proud parents and relatives would bring to the local newspaper office a just-received letter from a loved one, and it would shortly appear in print.

Jones had no way of knowing of these letters' existence because there was no Internet when he was doing his research so long ago. Today, millions of historic newspaper pages have been digitally scanned and made available online. The important letters of the Rough Riders are now easily accessed through a simple search. My book is the first to make use of this previously unknown and significant body of firsthand accounts.

I also located unpublished diaries and letters in several institutions across the country, from Prescott, Arizona, to Cambridge, Massachusetts. One collection that has been known to scholars but little consulted for writings on Roosevelt's regiment is Hermann Hagedorn's "Research Materials for the Rough Riders," part of the massive Theodore Roosevelt Collection at Harvard's Houghton Library.

In the 1920s, Hagedorn interviewed and corresponded with more than seventy members of the regiment and obtained from some of them lengthy written accounts of their wartime experiences. Hagedorn used this material for his 1927 book titled *The Rough Riders*. Unfortunately, that book is a novel, and a mediocre one at that. Thankfully, his valuable collection of Rough Rider reminiscences has been preserved, and I have made extensive use of it.

Another important collection that deserves to be better known resides in New Mexico at the City of Las Vegas Museum and Rough Rider Memorial Collection. In 1961, Roosevelt's Rough Riders Association (the regiment's veterans organization) turned over to the city its collection of materials gathered from members. The collection has been added to over the years and now consists of seven document boxes of letters, diaries, news clippings, and photographs, as well as original objects such as uniforms, bugles, and medals.

A very helpful source for the topography of the Cuban campaign is the website *Cuban Battlefields of the Spanish-Cuban-American War*. Hosted by the University of Nebraska-Lincoln, it provides interactive satellite imagery—from photographs made in 1968 and 2000—of the sites associated with the American advance on Santiago, along with an overlay of an 1898 War Department map of the San Juan battlefield. The website address is http://cubanbattlefields.unl.edu/.

Everything within quotation marks in this book comes from the primary sources cited below. Nothing has been altered or made up. It is their words, from their time.

Abbreviations Used in the Notes

Institutions

CNCH: Department of Culture and Humanities, Chickasaw Nation, Ada, OK

DL: DeGolyer Library, Southern Methodist University, Dallas, TX
FACL: Fray Angélico Chávez History Library, Santa Fe, NM
LOC: Library of Congress, Washington, D.C.
NARA: National Archives and Records Administration, Washington, D.C.
NMSR: New Mexico State Records Center and Archives, Santa Fe, NM
RRM: City of Las Vegas Museum and Rough Rider Memorial Collection, Las Vegas, NM
SHM: Sharlot Hall Museum Library and Archives, Prescott, AZ

Collections

TANM: Territorial Archives of New Mexico (microfilm), NMSR
TRC-H: Theodore Roosevelt Collection, Houghton Library, Harvard University
TRC-W: Theodore Roosevelt Collection, Widener Library, Harvard University

Publications

MOR: Morison, Elting E., John N. Blum, and John J. Buckley, eds. *The Letters of Theodore Roosevelt.* 8 vols. Cambridge, MA: Harvard University Press, 1951–54.

Names

HCL: Henry Cabot Lodge
LW: Leonard Wood
TR: Theodore Roosevelt

NOTES

Prologue

2   **"with formal and impressive ceremonies"** . . . **"the Victoria Cross":** *The Evening Star*, Washington, D.C., Jan. 9, 1906.

2   **"There is no distinction . . . in the trenches together":** *The Evening Star*, Jan. 10, 1906.

Chapter One: Some Turn of Fortune

5   **Frank Brito:** Dale L. Walker, "New Mexico's Last Rough Rider," *El Paso Magazine* (June 1973): 7–11; and Frank C. Brito compiled military service record, NARA.

6   **"In those days":** As quoted in Janet Lovelady, ed., *Rough Writings: Perspectives on Buckey O'Neill, Pauline M. O'Neill, and Roosevelt's Rough Riders* (Prescott, AZ: Sharlot Hall Museum Press, 1998), 7.

7   **divide within his family:** Corinne Roosevelt Robinson, *My Brother Theodore Roosevelt* (New York: Charles Scribner's Sons, 1921), 29–30; and Edmund Morris, *The Rise of Theodore Roosevelt* (New York: Random House, 2010), 8–9.

7   **"I had always felt that":** *Theodore Roosevelt: An Autobiography* (New York: Charles Scribner's Sons, 1921), 217.

7   **pack small boxes:** Morris, *The Rise of Theodore Roosevelt*, 14.

8   **New York National Guard:** *Roosevelt: An Autobiography*, 229–230; and *Documents of the Assembly of the State of New York*, vol. 4 (Albany: The Argus Company, 1887), 197.

8   **"It was a land of vast silent spaces":** *Roosevelt: An Autobiography*, 93.

8   **"The light has gone out":** TR, *A Most Glorious Ride: The Diaries of Theodore Roosevelt*, ed. by Edward P. Kohn (Albany: State University of New York Press, 2015), 228.

9   **newspaper reports of growing tension:** See, for example, the *Fort Worth Daily Gazette*, July 24 and Aug. 2, 1886. The incarcerated editor was Augustus K. Cutting.

9   **"offering to raise some companies"** . . . **"opportunity that turns up":** TR to HCL, Aug. 10, 1886, in MOR, 1:108.

9   **"If a war had come off":** TR to HCL, Aug. 20, 1886, in MOR, 1:109.

9   **American mail ship *Alliança*:** *The Evening Star*, Washington, D.C., March 15, 1895; and *The Chicago Tribune*, March 16, 1895.

10   **"In the very improbable event":** TR to Levi P. Morton, March 19, 1898, in MOR, 1:436.

10   **"weak and decadent":** TR to William Astor Chandler, Dec. 23, 1897, in MOR, 1:747.

10   **"I am a quietly rampant":** TR to Anna Roosevelt Cowles, Jan. 2. 1897, in MOR, 1:573–574.

11   **Roosevelt and Wood first met:** Hermann Hagedorn, *Leonard Wood: A Biography*, 2 vols. (New York: Harper & Brothers, 1931), 1:138.

11   **Wood's experiences chasing:** See Jack C. Lane, ed., *Chasing Geronimo: The Journal of Leonard Wood, May–September, 1886* (Albuquerque: University of New Mexico Press, 1970). Wood received his Medal of Honor on April 8, 1898, twelve years after his acts of gallantry.

11   **"superb chest":** Owen Wister, *Roosevelt: The Story of a Friendship, 1880–1979* (New York: The MacMillan Company, 1930), 169.

11   **"was inclined to be silent":** Ibid.

12   **"Theodore, you have the mind":** As quoted in Robinson, *My Brother Theodore Roosevelt*, 50.

12   **"widening his chest":** Ibid.

12   **took up boxing:** *Roosevelt: An Autobiography*, 28.

12   **"real tastes were for the rougher":** LW, "Memories of Roosevelt's Spanish War Days," *Metropolitan* (Nov. 1919): 8.

12   **maybe starting a ranch:** John G. Holme, *The Life of Leonard Wood* (New York: Doubleday, Page & Company, 1920), 41.

12–13   **"Many wounded":** *The Evening Star*, Feb. 16, 1898.

13   **breaking windows:** *New York Tribune*, Feb. 16, 1898.

13   **threatened U.S. citizens:** Fitzhugh Lee and Joseph Wheeler, *Cuba's Struggle Against Spain* (New York: The American Historical Press, 1899), 189.

13   **"Blown Up by Spain" . . . "the Food of Sharks":** *The Evening Times*, Washington, D.C., Feb. 16, 1898.

14   **"The *Maine* was sunk by":** TR to Benjamin Harrison Dibblee, Feb. 16, 1898, in MOR, 1:775.

14   **"I don't want to be in an office":** TR to C. Whitney Tillinghast 2nd, March 9, 1898, in MOR, 1:792.

14   **dined with Senator Redfield Proctor:** LW, "Memories of Roosevelt's Spanish War Days," 9.

14   **died from starvation and disease:** "Facts About Cuba: Desolation, Starvation, Sickness and Death, From a Speech by Senator Redfield Proctor, of Vermont, In the U.S. Senate, March 17th, 1898," pamphlet published by the Cuban Relief Committee, TRC-W.

14   **"aroused a spirit of hot indignation":** LW, "Memories of Roosevelt's Spanish War Days," 9.

15   **"[W]e might have ignored cruelty":** Wister, *Roosevelt: The Story of a Friendship*, 56.

15   **Proctor's chilling report:** LW, "Memories of Roosevelt's Spanish War Days," 9.

15   **"was destroyed by the explosion":** As quoted in *The American-Spanish War: A History by the War Leaders* (Norwich, CT: Chas. C. Haskell & Son, 1899), 102. The cause of the *Maine* explosion is debated to this day. Spain's own inquiry determined it was not the result of a mine, but "undoubtedly due to some interior cause." *The San Francisco Call*, March 29, 1898.

15   **referred to them as the "war party":** Ray Stannard Baker, "General Leonard Wood: A Character Sketch," *McClure's Magazine* 14 (Feb. 1900): 374.

15   **"have you and Theodore declared war":** LW, "Memories of Roosevelt's Spanish War Days," 9.

15 **McKinley asked for authorization:** Lee and Wheeler, *Cuba's Struggle Against Spain,* 221.

15 **"The President still feebly is painfully":** TR, 1898 Diary, TRC-H.

15–16 **"the entire land and naval force of the United States":** As quoted in Lee and Wheeler, *Cuba's Struggle Against Spain,* 223.

16 **"I have the Navy in good shape":** TR, April 16, 1898 Diary, TRC-H.

16 **"I want to introduce you to":** TR to Roger Wolcott, April 16, 1898, LW Papers, General Correspondence, Container 26, 1898 Folder 1, LOC.

16 **ten men clamored:** TR, *The Rough Riders* (Charles Scribner's Sons, 1899), 5–6.

16 **Seventy-First Regiment, New York National Guard:** LW, "Memories of Roosevelt's Spanish War Days," 9; and TR, *The Rough Riders,* 6.

16 **General Fitzhugh Lee:** *The Sun,* NY, April 17, 1898.

16 **a false story went over the wires:** *The Dalles Times-Mountaineer,* Dalles, OR, April 23, 1898; *El Paso Daily Herald,* April 20, 1898; and *The Evening Times,* April 19, 1898.

16 **"possessing special qualifications":** S. Doc. No. 105, 58th Cong., 2nd Sess. (1904), p. 229.

16 **Wyoming senator who believed:** *The Arizona Republican,* Phoenix, April 18, 1898; and *Kansas City Journal,* April 22, 1898.

17 **"I believe that the 'cow boys,' ":** *El Paso Daily Herald,* April 20, 1898.

17 **Would Roosevelt accept command . . . ?:** *Roosevelt: An Autobiography,* 218.

17 **appoint Captain Wood:** Ibid.

18 **"I did not wish to rise" . . . "did the work":** Ibid.

18 **"It may be that I am going" . . . "last six months":** TR to Sylvane M. Ferris, April 24, 1898, in MOR, 2:820.

18 **Roosevelt then agreed to accept:** *The Sun,* NY, April 26, 1898.

18 **"Mr. Roosevelt, you have six children":** As quoted in *A Memorial to Theodore Roosevelt* (Albany: J. B. Lyon Company, 1919), 14.

19 **Their conditions were so serious:** Lawrence F. Abbott, ed., *The Letters of Archie Butt, Personal Aide to the President* (Garden City, NY: Doubleday, Page & Co., 1924), 146.

19 **"I have done as much as any one":** As quoted in *A Memorial to Theodore Roosevelt,* 14.

19 **"I know now" . . . "in every family":** *The Letters of Archie Butt,* 146.

19 **"man of unbounded energy and force" . . . "a very high mark":** As quoted in Morris, *The Rise of Theodore Roosevelt,* 644.

20 **"Go right ahead and don't":** As quoted in Holme, *The Life of Leonard Wood,* 45.

20 **Wood promptly planted himself:** *Roosevelt: An Autobiography,* 219.

20 **First U.S. Volunteer Cavalry:** R. A. Alger authorization to raise 1st U.S. Volunteers, April 28, 1898, LW Papers, General Correspondence, Container 26, 1898 Folder 1, LOC.

20 **was calling it "Roosevelt's Rough Riders":** See, for example, the *Charleston Weekly News and Courier,* South Carolina, May 7, 1898.

20 **"The newspapers keep talking about":** Eugene Fuller to LW, New York, NY, May 26, 1898, LW Papers, General Correspondence, Container 26, 1898 Folder 2, LOC.

21 **"This only goes to show":** *The Somerset Herald,* Somerset, PA, May 11, 1898.

21 **"frontiersmen possessing special qualifications":** R. A. Alger Memorandum of April 28, 1898, LW Papers, General Correspondence, Container 26, 1898 Folder 2, LOC.

21 **"Desperate characters":** *The Sun,* April 30, 1898.

21 **"If anyone is going":** *The Arizona Republican,* Phoenix, May 7, 1898.

21 **"because I want to personally":** Miguel A. Otero to R. A. Alger, telegram, April 27, 1898, LW Papers, General Correspondence, Container 26, 1898 Folder 1, LOC.

21   **"only A-1 men would be accepted":** Miguel A. Otero to R. A. Alger, Santa Fe, April 26, 1898, TANM, microfilm r. 139, f. 139.

21   **famed lawman Pat Garrett:** M. A. Otero to W.H.H. Llewellyn, Santa Fe, April 25, 1898, TANM, microfilm r. 139, f. 134.

22   **"started for some selfish":** M. A. Otero to E. H. Skipwith, Santa Fe, April 26, 1898, TANM, microfilm r. 139, f. 147.

22   **"are all extremely anxious":** M. A. Otero to R. A. Alger, Santa Fe, April 22, 1898, TANM, microfilm r. 139, f. 136.

22   **bilingual men:** Ibid.

22   **about five percent:** *The Eagle,* Silver City, NM, May 7, 1898.

22   **"I did not like to include":** M. A. Otero to W. B. Allison, Santa Fe, May 3, 1898, TANM, microfilm r. 139, f. 178.

23   **"tenderfoot cowboys":** As quoted in the *Albuquerque Daily Citizen,* May 4, 1898.

23   **"Roosevelt's cowboy regiment"** . . . **"ever rode a horse":** As quoted in Clifford P. Westermeier, "Teddy's Terrors: The New Mexican Volunteers of 1898," *New Mexico Historical Review* 27 (April 1952): 113–114.

23   **"The members of this so-called":** *The St. Johns Herald,* St. Johns, AZ, May 7, 1898.

23   **"Many of them are not horsemen":** Clipping, May 8, 1898, Spanish-American War News Clipping Collection, Folder 6, "Rough Riders," SHM.

23   **"the working cowboy"** . . . **"great credit to the territory":** Clipping, April 30, 1898, in ibid.

23   **They were miners:** Regimental and company books, company muster rolls, as well as the compiled military service records of individual Rough Riders, provide occupations. The compiled military service records for individual Rough Riders are available online at the National Archives website (www.archives.gov), within Record Group 94: The Records of the Adjutant General's Office, 1762–1984.

24   **"Any chance to get in cavalry":** George Hamner to Henry B. Hersey, May 5, 1898, telegram in Box 10835, Folder 2, Records of the Adjutant General, Collection 1973–019, NMSR.

24   **"If you are first class":** Henry B. Hersey to George Hamner, May 5, 1898, telegram in ibid.

24   **"I am fighting":** As quoted in Dale L. Walker, *The Boys of '98: Theodore Roosevelt and the Rough Riders* (New York: Forge, 1998), 126.

24   **One banner:** Photographs of the troop train with its banners are in the collections of RRM.

24   **According to one Rough Rider:** Undated clipping in Marinel Ash Collection, AC 385, Box 1, Folder 16, FACL.

24   **outlaw Jim Cook:** Cook was convicted in November 1894, for the killing of Sequoyah Houston, a Cherokee deputy. See the *Guthrie Daily Leader,* Nov. 23, 1894, and March 3, 1900; and the *Indian Chieftain,* Vinita, Indian Territory, July 28, 1898.

25   **"Well"** . . . **"There's my hand on it, comrade":** As quoted in *Phoenix Weekly Herald,* Feb. 23, 1899.

26   **Leonard Wood called:** *The Daily Oklahoma State Capital,* Guthrie, OK, May 5, 1898.

26   **having the same firearms:** TR, *The Rough Riders,* 9.

26   **"armed with what might":** Ibid., 36.

26   **precious time to train:** *The Sun,* May 8, 1898.

27   **"that almost every one struck":** *The San Francisco Call,* May 29, 1898.

27   **As for uniforms:** Holme, *The Life of Leonard Wood,* 46.

27   **Model 1884 fatigue:** J. C. Stewart, *Cowboys in Uniform* (Show Low, AZ: Rough Rider Publishing Co., 1998), 4.

27   **"hotter than hell":** As quoted in Alvin S. Fick, "Last of the Rough Riders," *V.F.W. Magazine* (Feb. 1974): 26.

27   **San Antonio, Texas, as the rendezvous:** LW, "Memories of Roosevelt's Spanish War Days," 88; and *Roosevelt: An Autobiography,* 219.

Chapter Two: East Meets West

28   **"for the most part elderly":** *Roosevelt: An Autobiography,* 223.

28   **"Oh, dear!":** Ibid., 226.

29   **more than six thousand:** *Albuquerque Daily Citizen,* May 4, 1898. Thomas W. Hall, the regiment's quartermaster and adjutant, put the number at "about ten thousand." See Hall, *The Fun and Fighting of the Rough Riders* (New York: Frederick A. Stokes Co., 1899), 33.

29   **"We haven't room"** . . . **"all right yet":** As quoted in the *Sun,* May 8, 1898.

29   **raised to one thousand:** TR to LW, Washington, D.C., May 9, 1898, LW Papers, General Correspondence, Container 26, 1898 Folder 1, LOC.

29   **clerks jumped up:** *The Kansas City Star,* May 8, 1898.

30   **"millionaire recruits":** *The Guthrie Daily Leader,* Guthrie, OK, May 18, 1898.

30   **"Gentlemen: You have now":** *Boston Daily Advertiser,* May 7, 1898.

30   **Corbin swore in Roosevelt:** *Alexandria Gazette and Virginia Advertiser,* May 6, 1898.

30   **a physical examination:** Ibid.

30   **"could not recognize his best friend":** Jack Willis, as told to Horace Smith, *Roosevelt in the Rough* (New York: Ives Washburn, 1931), 55.

31   **His constant pestering:** TR to LW, Washington, D.C., May 9, 1898, LW Papers, General Correspondence, Container 26, 1898 Folder 1, LOC.

31   **widely scattered points:** D. W. Flagler to TR, Washington, D.C., May 9, 1898, LW Papers, General Correspondence, Container 26, 1898 Folder 2, LOC.

31   **"I suppose you will be keeping":** TR to LW, Washington, D.C., May 9, 1898, LW Papers, General Correspondence, Container 26, 1898 Folder 1, LOC.

31   **"It will be bitter":** TR to Corinne Roosevelt Robinson, Washington, D.C., May 12, 1898, in MOR, 2:830.

31   **"Yes, they are characters":** *The Arizona Republican,* Phoenix, May 12, 1898.

31   **"There are no outcasts":** As quoted in *San Antonio Daily Express,* May 8, 1898.

31   **"We are not long-haired":** As quoted in *San Antonio Daily Light,* May 7, 1898.

32   **"Once when I was about twenty-one"** . . . **"Had his gun up against my belly":** As quoted in undated news clipping in Marinel Ash Collection, AC 385, Box 1, Folder 16, FACL.

32   **six-month-old mountain lion:** Edward Marshall, *The Story of the Rough Riders, 1st U. S. Volunteer Cavalry, The Regiment in Camp and on the Battle Field* (New York: G.W. Dillingham Co., 1899), 23–24; *Boston Journal,* May 28; and *San Antonio Sunday Light,* May 8, 1898.

32   **"[H]e has been looked at and admired":** As quoted in undated news clipping, Spanish-American War News Clipping Collection, Folder 6, "Rough Riders," SHM.

33   **"gifted dog":** News clipping, May 22, 1898, in Scrapbook of Mary M. Goodrich, TRC-H.

33   **the two mascots played together:** George E. Vincent, ed., *Theodore Miller: Rough Rider, His Diary as a Soldier, Together with the Story of His Life* (Akron, OH: Privately Printed, 1899), 87.

33 **"took leave of civilization":** J. O. Wells, *Diary of a Rough Rider* (St. Joseph, MI: A. B. Morse, n.d.), 5.

33 **"college boys":** Guy Murchie, "Harvard's Santiago Campaign," *The Harvard Monthly* 27 (November 1898): 54.

33 **"a splendid set of men":** Wells, *Diary of a Rough Rider*, 7.

34 **"at a distance of several blocks"** . . . **"mirrors in the valises":** *Phoenix Weekly Herald,* May 19, 1898.

34 **"What do you want the picture for?":** As quoted in *San Antonio Daily Express,* May 13, 1898.

34 **"seem to like the New Yorkers":** Arthur F. Cosby to Frank Cosby, San Antonio, May 27, 1898, Arthur F. Cosby scrapbook, TRC-H.

34 **"You would smile to see":** LW to Louise Wood, San Antonio, May 13, 1898, LW Papers, Personal Correspondence, Container 190, 1898 file folder, LOC.

35 **from the civilian mule packers:** Hall, *The Fun and Fighting,* 26.

35 **their own rubber ones:** Wells, *Diary of a Rough Rider,* 5.

35 **a shoe came flying:** Royal A. Prentice, "The Rough Riders," *New Mexico Historical Review* 26 (Oct. 1951): 266.

35 **"it is almost hell":** Letter of Thomas J. Laine in undated news clipping, Spanish-American War News Clipping Collection, Folder 6, "Rough Riders," SHM.

35 **Roosevelt stepped off his train:** *San Antonio Daily Express,* May 16, 1898.

36 **ordered from Brooks Brothers:** TR to Robert Harry Munro Ferguson, Washington, D.C., April 28, 1898, John and Isabella Greenway Papers, 1860–1953, Arizona Historical Society, Tucson.

36 **black valet, Marshall:** Ibid., and TR, *The Rough Riders,* 60.

36 **"master of the hounds":** *The Times,* Washington, D.C., May 1, 1898.

36 **"a bit slick":** TR, May 16, 1898 Diary, TRC-H.

36 **"tenting with the most remarkable":** Hall, *The Fun and Fighting,* 40.

36 **Roosevelt got right to work:** *San Antonio Daily Express,* May 16, 1898.

37 **"Theodore Roosevelt is only":** Ibid.

38 **opportunities to be ornery:** *The Arizona Republican,* May 19, 1898.

38 **"playing patriotic airs":** *San Antonio Daily Light,* May 16, 1898.

38 **"the eyes of the entire civilized world"** . . . **"that we must do":** Ibid., and Walter Gregory, Troop B, letter in *Phoenix Weekly Herald,* May 19, 1898.

38 **"He looks as though":** William A. Owens, Troop B, as quoted in David L. Hughes, Troop B, "Research Materials for the Rough Riders," Hermann Hagedorn Collection, TRC-H.

39 **made no effort to hide:** Hall, *The Fun and Fighting,* 41.

39 **"was the greatest 'mixer' ":** Albert Loren Cheney, *Personal Memoirs of the Home Life of the Late Theodore Roosevelt* (Washington, D.C.: The Cheney Publishing Co., 1919), 6.

39–40 **"Not a bit of it"** . . . **"broke my glasses":** As quoted in "Hunted with Roosevelt," *The Macon Telegraph,* GA, Oct. 29, 1898.

40 **"We took a shine":** Ibid.

40 **"The men always do their best":** As quoted in Robinson, *My Brother Theodore Roosevelt,* 167.

40 **"the most magnetic man":** Alvin C. Ash to mother, Tampa, Florida, June 10, 1898, quoted in news clipping, Marinel Ash Collection, AC 385, Box 1, Folder 16, FACL.

40 **Uniforms and gear:** Hall, *The Fun and Fighting,* 36.

40 **days without knives and forks:** *The Guthrie Daily Leader,* May 21, 1898.

41   **Blankets finally showed up:** *The Guthrie Daily Leader,* May 16, 1898; and *San Antonio Sunday Light,* May 15, 1898.

41   **As each trooper stepped up:** Hall, *The Fun and Fighting,* 37–38.

41   **found a surprise in his:** Walter Gregory, Troop B, letter in *Phoenix Weekly Herald,* June 2, 1898.

41   **downtown to buy bandannas:** *San Antonio Daily Light,* May 13, 1898.

41   **The coveted Krags:** *San Antonio Daily Light,* May 19 and 20, 1898.

41   **menacing-looking machine guns:** Ibid., and *The Guthrie Daily Leader,* May 21, 1898. The machine guns were the Model 1895, designed by John Browning.

41   **purchased by two older sisters:** Philip Schreier, "Hidden in Plain Sight: Colt Automatics at Santiago," *American Rifleman* (March 2013): 60.

42   **"tear human beings to pieces":** As quoted in the *Guthrie Daily Leader,* May 21, 1898.

42   **"All right, we'll capture":** As quoted in Hall, *The Fun and Fighting,* 46.

43   **Kane got behind one gun:** *San Antonio Daily Light,* May 20, 1898.

43   **Model 1895 Winchester:** *San Antonio Daily Light,* May 28, 1898. Both the Colt machine gun and the Model 1895 Winchester came from the designs of one man: John M. Browning.

43   **"I may not shoot well":** As quoted in Philip Schreier, "Roosevelt's '76: 'The Best Gun for Any Game,' " *American Rifleman* (Feb. 2008): 52.

43   **bunches of twenty-five and thirty:** *The Guthrie Daily Leader,* May 16, 1898.

44   **shipped to them by rail:** Ibid.

44   **Roosevelt purchased two mounts:** TR, *The Rough Riders,* 34 and 60.

44   **"well broken to saddle":** *San Antonio Daily Light,* May 6, 1898.

44   **"hadn't been broke but once"** . . . **"scattered all over Texas":** *Albuquerque Tribune* clipping, 1953, William McGinty file, RRM.

44   **"horses hadn't the slightest idea":** Prentice, "The Rough Riders," 268.

45   **"knocked clean out":** Robert Munro Ferguson, as quoted in Robinson, *My Brother Theodore Roosevelt,* 167.

45   **"take some of the devilishness":** *The Guthrie Daily Leader,* May 18, 1898.

45   **firing their Colts in the air:** David L. Hughes, Hagedorn Collection, TRC-H.

45   **"He was riding a high-spirited horse":** Ibid.

45–46 **"Six hundred horses galloping":** As quoted in *Harvard Crimson,* June 4, 1898.

46   **"Captains will dismount"** . . . **"I will cinch him":** Sherrard Coleman, Troop E, "Research materials for the Rough Riders," Hagedorn Collection, TRC-H.

46   **"Nectar never tasted as good":** Prentice, "The Rough Riders," 267.

47   **reported in the local newspaper:** *San Antonio Daily Light,* May 20, 1898.

47   **"[O]f course an officer"** . . . **"Good night":** LW, Hagedorn Collection, TRC-H. Another version of this exchange between Wood and Roosevelt is found in Thomas H. Rynning, as told to Al Cohn and Joe Chisholm, *Gun Notches: A Saga of Frontier Lawman Captain Thomas H. Rynning* (1931. Reprint. San Diego, CA: Frontier Heritage Press, 1971), 145.

47   **"Nothing doing":** As quoted in George Curry, *George Curry, 1861–1947: An Autobiography,* ed. by H. B. Henning (Albuquerque: University of New Mexico Press, 1958), 123.

47   **lined up to apply for a pass:** *The Arizona Republican,* May 15, 1898.

48   **definition of a martinet:** Hall, *The Fun and Fighting,* 20–23; and Arthur F. Cosby to Charlotte Cosby, Tampa, Florida, June 5, 1898, Arthur F. Cosby scrapbook, TRC-H.

48   **shopping list included:** *San Antonio Daily Light,* May 13, 1898.

48   **the Alamo mission:** *The Arizona Republican,* May 12, 1898.

48   **Colbert, a Chickasaw Indian:** Colbert's father was reported to be one-fourth Chickasaw and his mother one-half Choctaw. See "Rough Rider Colbert," *The Daily Ardmoreite,* Ardmore, Indian Territory, Feb. 27, 1905.

48   **a new cylinder recording:** Benjamin H. Colbert diary, May 23, 1898, typescript, Department of Culture and Humanities, Chickasaw Nation, Ada, OK. The original of this diary is at the Oklahoma Historical Society, Oklahoma City.

48   **a dip at Scholz's Natatorium:** Royal A. Prentice, diary, 102, Royal A. Prentice Papers, Box 1, Folder 12, FACL; and Wells, *Diary of a Rough Rider,* 9.

48   **a small dining establishment:** Hall, *The Fun and Fighting,* 58–59; and *San Antonio Daily Light,* May 12, 1898.

49   **Waldorf-Astoria:** Arthur F. Cosby to Frank Cosby, San Antonio, May 29, 1898, Arthur F. Cosby scrapbook, TRC-H.

49   **"really sick or just tired":** Letter of Paul W. Hunter, Troop D, in the *Guthrie Daily Leader,* May 21, 1898.

49   **cleaned the western boys out:** Prentice, "The Rough Riders," 267.

50   **several hundred "dog tents":** *San Antonio Daily Light,* May 20 and 21, 1898.

50   **"The perspiration simply rolls":** Arthur F. Cosby to Frank Cosby, San Antonio, May 27, 1898, Arthur F. Cosby scrapbook, TRC-H.

50   **hadn't slept in a house:** *San Antonio Daily Light,* May 20, 1898.

50   **"Several glee clubs":** As quoted in the *Guthrie Daily Leader,* May 21, 1898.

50   **put on stag dances:** Walter Gregory, Troop B, *Phoenix Weekly Herald,* May 19, 1898.

50   **"They are now all brothers":** *The Evening Times,* May 26, 1898.

50   **"simply astounding" . . . "fine body of men":** LW to William McKinley, San Antonio, May 22, 1898, LW Papers, General Correspondence, Container 26, 1898 Folder 1, LOC.

50–51 **"I really think that the rank" . . . "sooner the better":** TR to William McKinley, San Antonio, May 25, 1898, in MOR, 2:832.

51   **"a few weak sisters":** LW to Louise Wood, San Antonio, May 22, 1898, LW Papers, Personal Correspondence, Container 190, 1898 file folder, LOC.

51   **"a pitiful failure":** TR to HCL, San Antonio, May 25, 1898, in MOR, 2: 833.

52   **"one of the finest soldiers":** Rynning, *Gun Notches,* 141.

52   **four bullet wounds:** TR, *The Rough Riders,* 17.

52   **"so used to gunfire":** As quoted in R. K. DeArment, "Major Llewellyn: In Good Company," *Wild West* (Feb. 2013): 42.

52   **in charge of the captive Chiricahua Apaches:** Randolph Iltyd Geare, "Historic Swords," *The Chautauquan* 33 (Sept. 1901): 628.

52   **elected him captain of Troop L:** *The Guthrie Daily Leader,* May 15, 1898.

52   **"take him out of the line of promotion":** Ibid.

53   **"tall and lithe":** TR, *The Rough Riders,* 18.

53   **mastery of Indian sign language:** Ibid., 66–67.

53   **an incredible career:** *Phoenix Weekly Herald,* July 14, 1898.

53   **penned realistic short stories:** Lovelady, ed., *Rough Writings,* 23.

53   **"a wild, reckless fellow":** TR, *The Rough Riders,* 17.

54–55 **"Tonight the citizens":** *San Antonio Daily Light,* May 24, 1898.

55   **"one of the largest ever" . . . "hear it last night":** Ibid., May 25, 1898.

55   **"I was in the Franco-Prussian":** As quoted in ibid.

55   **no live rounds:** *San Antonio Daily Express,* May 26, 1898.

55   **under guard in camp:** Hall, *The Fun and Fighting,* 30.

55   **"one of the finest things":** Royal A. Prentice, diary, 101–102, Royal A. Prentice Papers, Box 1, Folder 12, FACL.

Chapter Three: A Perfect Welter of Confusion

56   **Irad Cochran Jr.:** *San Antonio Daily Express*, May 28, 1898; *San Antonio Daily Light*, May 27, 1898; *Houston Daily Post*, May 28, 1898; and *Santa Fe New Mexican Review*, June 2, 1898.

57   **orders arrived at camp headquarters:** *San Antonio Daily Light*, May 28, 1898.

57   **then embraced his friend:** *Houston Daily Post*, May 28, 1898.

57   **"Colonel Wood is exactly":** Henry B. Hersey to Gov. Miguel Otero, San Antonio, Texas, May 12, 1898, TANM, microfilm r. 128, f. 813.

57   **a poker face:** David L. Hughes, Hagedorn Collection, TRC-H.

57   **not yet completely outfitted:** *San Antonio Daily Light*, May 26, 1898.

58   **"They express us stuff we don't need":** TR, May 21, 1898 Diary, TRC-H.

58   **delays were a backlash:** Hall, *The Fun and Fighting*, 13–14.

58   **importance of the machetes:** *San Antonio Daily Light*, May 26, 1898.

58   **960 horses and 192 pack mules:** *The Sun*, June 1, 1898.

59   **loading lasted all day:** *San Antonio Daily Light*, May 30, 1898; and *San Antonio Daily Express*, May 30, 1898.

59   **Each chugging locomotive:** Henry B. Hersey to Gov. Miguel Otero, on train near Texas-Louisiana line, May 30, 1898, TANM, microfilm r. 128, f. 1127.

59   **Inside the coaches:** Hall, *The Fun and Fighting*, 66–67.

59   **Cowboy ballads and rousing:** Ibid., 73–74; and Arthur F. Cosby to Frank Cosby, San Antonio, May 29, 1898, Arthur F. Cosby scrapbook, TRC-H.

59   **"How well we remember":** As quoted in Guy Murchie, "Harvard's Santiago Campaign," *The Harvard Monthly* 27 (November 1898): 55–56.

60   **"A Hot Time in the Old Town":** Hall, *The Fun and Fighting*, 59. The *San Antonio Daily Light* published the program for the concert given by Professor Beck's band in Riverside Park on May 24. Included in the program is a march titled "A Hot Time," which one assumes was based on the popular song.

60   **Young women passed:** Hall, *The Fun and Fighting*, 68–69; and *San Antonio Daily Light*, June 8, 1898.

60   **his mother was waiting:** Colbert diary, May 31, 1898, CNCH.

60   **"There were cheers, music"** . . . **"such an ovation":** E. Guy Le Sturgeon to Eunice Le Sturgeon, May 31, 1898, as quoted in *San Antonio Daily Light*, June 8, 1898.

60   **"All the cost of this war":** LW to Louise Wood, Tampa Bay, June 9, 1898, LW Papers, Personal Correspondence, Container 190, 1898 file folder, LOC.

61   **"[W]hat I want to do is":** As quoted in Vincent, ed., *Theodore Miller: Rough Rider*, 71.

62   **"I almost yelled for joy":** Ibid., 78–79.

62   **Robert Wrenn, William Larned:** *The Sun*, May 31 and June 1, 1898.

62   **a derby hat and dress suit:** Vincent, ed., *Theodore Miller: Rough Rider*, 80.

62   **"Rough! Tough! We're the stuff!":** As quoted in the *Sun*, June 1, 1898.

62   **"grandly picturesque":** E. Guy Le Sturgeon to Eunice Le Sturgeon, June 2, 1898, as quoted in *San Antonio Sunday Light*, June 12, 1898.

62   **"They are mean looking":** Royal A. Prentice, diary, 104, Royal A. Prentice Papers, Box 1, Folder 12, FACL.

63   **African American culture:** Vincent, ed., *Theodore Miller: Rough Rider*, 88.

63   **"Nothing is sacred":** E. Guy Le Sturgeon to Eunice Le Sturgeon, June 2, 1898, as quoted in *San Antonio Sunday Light*, June 12, 1898.

63   **"He had strong ideas":** Hall, *The Fun and Fighting*, 75.

64   **"in a most frightful mix":** LW to Louise Wood, Tampa Bay, June 9, 1898, LW Papers, Personal Correspondence, Container 190, 1898 file folder, LOC.

64   **make a temporary camp:** Ibid.; and Hall, *The Fun and Fighting*, 77–78.

65   **asked the engineer and conductor:** *George Curry, 1861–1947: An Autobiography*, 123.

65   **punched out a restaurant manager:** *Las Vegas Weekly Optic and Stock Grower*, May 7, 1898.

65   **"Captain Curry":** As quoted in *George Curry, 1861–1947: An Autobiography*, 123.

66   **" 'boys' are delighted to find":** Arthur F. Cosby to Charlotte Cosby, Tampa, June 5, 1898, Arthur F. Cosby scrapbook, TRC-H.

66   **"silk stocking troop":** *New York Times*, Oct. 20, 1912.

66   **"has a large number of first rate":** As quoted in Robinson, *My Brother Theodore Roosevelt*, 167.

66   **paid out of their own pockets:** LW, diary transcript, June 2, 1898, LW Papers, Container 2, LOC; TR, *The Rough Riders*, 53; and Walter Gregory, Troop B, letter in *Phoenix Weekly Herald*, June 16, 1898.

67   **"dough boys":** E. Guy Le Sturgeon to Eunice Le Sturgeon, June 3, 1898, as quoted in *San Antonio Sunday Light*, June 12, 1898.

67   **not nearly enough transports:** William R. Shafter, "The Capture of Santiago de Cuba," *The Century Magazine* 57 (Feb. 1899): 613–614.

67   **So only the general:** Lee and Wheeler, *Cuba's Struggle Against Spain*, 363.

67   **take a reduced rank:** John Campbell Greenway, *It Was the Grandest Sight I Ever Saw: Experiences of a Rough Rider as Recorded in the Letters of Lieutenant John Campbell Greenway*, ed. by Charles Herner (Tucson: The Arizona Historical Society, 2001), 18.

67   **"the lions of the camp":** *The Arizona Republican*, June 4, 1898.

67   **"They were afraid":** As quoted in Westermeier, "Teddy's Terrors," 122.

67   **ran out of cash:** Hall, *The Fun and Fighting*, 86–87.

67–68 **"photograph fiends"** . . . **"I know not what":** Ibid., 84–85.

68   **filmed the Rough Riders:** The cameraman's name was William Paley, and his short films are available for viewing on the Library of Congress's website: www.loc.gov.

68   **"contrary to the regulations":** *The Arizona Republican*, June 4, 1898.

68   **required to have a pass:** "Visitors for Roosevelt's Men," news clipping in Scrapbook of Mary M. Goodrich, TRC-H; and Hall, *The Fun and Fighting*, 83.

69   **"Why, you are nothing but":** As quoted in Henry La Motte, "With the 'Rough Riders,' " *St. Nicholas* 26 (July 1899): 731.

69   **"[T]hey had heard of":** LW to Louise Wood, Tampa Bay, June 9, 1898, LW Papers, Personal Correspondence, Container 190, 1898 file folder, LOC.

69   **"Halt, who goes there"** . . . **"afraid of your sword":** La Motte, "With the 'Rough Riders,' " 731.

70   **"It has been a real holiday":** TR to the Roosevelt children, Tampa, June 6, 1898, in MOR, 2:834.

70   **"so enormous that the":** Richard Harding Davis, *The Cuban and Porto Rican Campaigns* (New York: Charles Scribner's Sons, 1898), 49.

70   **breach of military etiquette:** TR to Corinne Roosevelt Robinson, Tampa, June 7, 1898, in MOR, 2: 835; and Richard Harding Davis to Charles Davis, Tampa, June 5, 1898, in *Metropolitan* (July 1917): 53.

70   **swam in the hotel's pool:** Vincent, ed., *Theodore Miller: Rough Rider*, 91.

70   **clubmen took baths:** Richard Harding Davis to Charles Davis, Tampa, June 5, 1898.

70   **"not good":** Arthur F. Cosby to Charlotte Cosby, Tampa, June 5, 1898, Arthur F. Cosby scrapbook, TRC-H.

70   **"Them dudes will have to":** As quoted in news clipping in Corinne Roosevelt Robinson scrapbook, Corinne Roosevelt Robinson Papers, TRC-H.

71   **"awful morning":** TR to HCL, Tampa, June 6, 1898, in MOR, 2:835.

71   **limited to seventy men:** TR, *The Rough Riders,* 55.

71   **"What would be the good":** E. Guy Le Sturgeon to Eunice Le Sturgeon, June 3, 1898, as quoted in *San Antonio Sunday Light,* June 12, 1898.

71   **"I am sorry I cannot take":** As quoted in Curry, *George Curry, 1861–1947,* 124.

71   **"Colonel, I must beg you":** As quoted in *Las Vegas Daily Optic,* Aug. 7, 1954.

71   **"Everybody was excited":** Vincent, ed., *Theodore Miller: Rough Rider,* 95.

72   **"We were too angry":** As quoted in Lovelady, ed., *Rough Writings,* 13.

72   **The captain thrust the Krag:** Vincent, ed., *Theodore Miller: Rough Rider,* 95.

72   **Wrenn's weapon came courtesy:** TR, *The Rough Riders,* 219; and Vincent, ed., *Theodore Miller: Rough Rider,* 95–96.

73   **half of the dog tent:** Wells, *Diary of a Rough Rider,* 23.

73   **Missing from the belt:** Stewart, *Cowboys in Uniform,* 50–51.

73   **much-touted machetes:** Hall, *The Fun and Fighting,* 62.

73   **ordered a dozen pairs:** Will M. Clemens, *Theodore Roosevelt: The American* (New York: F. Tennyson Neely, 1899), 152–153.

74   **A Colt New Navy Model:** The revolver is now part of the collections of Sagamore Hill National Historic Site, Oyster Bay, New York.

74   **gift from some of the employees:** *Alexandria Gazette,* May 10, 1898. The sword is part of the collections of Sagamore Hill National Historic Site.

74   **"No plans; no staff officers":** TR, June 6, 1898 Diary, TRC-H.

74   **getting his men to the siding:** LW, diary transcript, June 7, 1898, LW Papers, Container 2, LOC; and TR, *The Rough Riders,* 57–58.

74   **"We were in columns of four":** Arthur F. Cosby to Charlotte Cosby, Troop Ship *Yucatan,* Port Tampa, June 11, 1898, Arthur F. Cosby scrapbook, TRC-H.

74   **bum breakfast:** Vincent, ed., *Theodore Miller: Rough Rider,* 97.

75   **Wood got the train stopped:** TR, *The Rough Riders,* 58.

75   **pulled off on a sidetrack:** La Motte, "With the 'Rough Riders,'" 732.

75   **"Hallo Teddy! . . . Teddy—Roosevelt!":** As quoted in ibid.; and Harold L. Mueller in collaboration with Chris Madsen, "With the Rough Riders," Feb. 23, 1936, article clipping in collections of RRM. The article probably appeared in *The Oklahoman.*

76   **finally found Generals Shafter:** TR to HCL, Port Tampa, June 12, 1898, in MOR, 2: 840–841.

76   **failed to allot a transport:** Hall, *The Fun and Fighting,* 96; and "Testimony of Col. Theodore Roosevelt," in *Report of the Commission Appointed by the President to Investigate the Conduct of the War Department in the War with Spain,* vol. 5, S. Doc. No. 221, 56th Cong., 1st Sess. (1900), p. 2258.

77   **promptly commandeered it:** *Roosevelt: An Autobiography,* 233.

77   **no one else could get close:** La Motte, "With the 'Rough Riders,'" 732–733.

77   **"What he was saying":** *Roosevelt: An Autobiography,* 234.

77   **"100 in the shade":** Colbert diary, June 8, 1898, CNCH.

78   **"What are you young men up to?" . . . "alive and roaring":** Albert E. Smith in collaboration with Phil A. Koury, *Two Reels and a Crank* (Garden City, NY: Doubleday & Co., 1952), 57.

79   **"Almost died under weight":** Vincent, ed., *Theodore Miller: Rough Rider,* 98.

79   **Wood's Weary Walkers:** Hall, *The Fun and Fighting,* 97.

79   **940 men crammed into the *Yucatan*:** LW, diary transcript, June 8, 1898, LW Papers, Container 2, LOC.

79   **changed the song's words:** Colbert diary, June 8, 1898, CNCH.

Chapter Four: Cuba at Last

80 **more than three hundred pounds:** George Clarke Musgrave, *Under Three Flags in Cuba: A Personal Account of the Cuban Insurrection and Spanish-American War* (Boston: Little, Brown, and Co., 1899), 253.

81 **"Wait until you get further" . . . "before reaching the Gulf":** As quoted in Lee and Wheeler, *Cuba's Struggle Against Spain,* 349.

81 **Shafter learned why:** John D. Miley, *In Cuba with Shafter* (New York: Charles Scribner's Sons, 1899), 33.

81 **"yellow fever season:"** Arthur L. Wagner, *Report of the Santiago Campaign, 1898* (Kansas City: Franklin Hudson Publishing Co., 1908), 31.

82 **no room for drills:** TR to HCL, *Yucatan,* Port Tampa, June 12, 1898, in MOR, 2:841.

82 **Black Hole of Calcutta:** TR to HCL, Port Tampa, June 10, 1898, in MOR, 2:837.

82 **howls of the mascot Cuba:** TR to Ethel Roosevelt, Off Santiago, 1898, in *Theodore Roosevelt's Letters to His Children,* ed. by Joseph Bucklin Bishop (New York: Charles Scribner's Sons, 1919), 15.

82 **"I thought it was a joke":** Prentice, "The Rough Riders," 273.

82 **called it "salt-horse":** Roger S. Fitch diary, June 17, 1898, RRM.

82 **bottles of champagne:** *The San Francisco Call,* July 12, 1898. The Harvard man was Charles C. Bull of Troop A.

83 **the best swimmer:** La Motte, "With the 'Rough Riders,'" 733.

83 **"'rustling' extras":** Arthur F. Cosby to Charlotte Cosby, Troop Ship *Yucatan,* Port Tampa, June 11, 1898, Arthur F. Cosby scrapbook, TRC-H.

83 **Five New Mexico troopers:** *The New Mexican Review,* Santa Fe, June 23, 1898.

83 **"I suppose it is simply":** TR to Corinne Roosevelt Robinson, *Yucatan,* Port Tampa, June 12, 1898, in MOR, 2: 839.

83 **"roughed it all of" . . . "beforehand is trying":** Arthur F. Cosby to Charlotte Cosby, Troop Ship *Yucatan,* Port Tampa, June 11, 1898, Arthur F. Cosby scrapbook, TRC-H.

84 **On Sunday afternoon:** Miley, *In Cuba with Shafter,* 39.

84 **"When Colonel Roosevelt heard":** Wells, *Diary of a Rough Rider,* 27.

84 **taken off the *Yucatan*:** F. Allen McCurdy and J. Kirk McCurdy, *Two Rough Riders: Letters from F. Allen McCurdy and J. Kirk McCurdy* (New York: F. Tennyson Neely, 1902), 1.

84 **Less than six feet separated:** Burr McIntosh, *The Little I Saw of Cuba* (New York: F. Tennyson Neely, 1899), 42–44; Hall, *The Fun and Fighting,* 104; Vincent, ed., *Theodore Miller: Rough Rider,* 101–102; and LW, diary transcript, June 13, 1898, LW Papers, Container 2, LOC.

85 **two Colt machine guns:** Frederick Herrig, Troop K, "Research Materials for the Rough Riders," Hermann Hagedorn Collection, TRC-H; and *Albuquerque Daily Citizen,* June 17, 1898.

85 **The transports carried:** R. A. Alger, *The Spanish-American War* (New York: Harper & Brothers, 78; and Miley, *In Cuba with Shafter,* 44.

85 **Eleven foreign attachés:** Miley, *In Cuba with Shafter,* 45–46.

85 **"I expect to make myself":** Richard Harding Davis to Family, on USS *New York* off Havana, April 26, 1898, in *Metropolitan* (July 1917): 50.

85 **William Randolph Hearst:** John C. Hemment, *Cannon and Camera: Sea and Land Battles of the Spanish-American War in Cuba, Camp Life, and the Return of the Soldiers* (New York: Appleton and Co., 1899), 65–66.

85 **Stephen Crane:** Stephen Crane, *The War Dispatches of Stephen Crane,* ed. by R. W. Stallman and E. R. Hagemann (New York: New York University Press, 1964), 134–137.

85–86 "Today we are steaming . . . "a world movement": TR to Edith Roosevelt, *Yucatan*, Gulf of Mexico, June 15, 1898, in MOR, 2:843.

86   That plan, conceived in: Alger, *The Spanish-American War*, 46–47.

86   holed up in Santiago's: Ibid., 48.

86   virtually untouchable: TR, "The Fifth Corps at Santiago," in Lee and Wheeler, *Cuba's Struggle Against Spain*, 638.

87   Shafter's task: Miley, *In Cuba with Shafter*, 17.

87   pedestrian seven knots: McCurdy and McCurdy, *Two Rough Riders*, 1.

87   burial at sea: Oscar G. Wager, Troop A, "Research Materials for the Rough Riders," Hermann Hagedorn Collection, TRC-H. The owner of the accordion was Charles E. "Happy Jack" Hodgdon, and there are contradictory accounts regarding his rather memorable instrument. Another trooper, Thomas P. Ledwidge, Troop E, claimed that Happy Jack was "quite musical" and carried his accordion through the San Juan fight. David Hughes also remembered Hodgdon as always having his accordion with him and playing various tunes in camp at night. Roosevelt mentions Happy Jack three times in his *The Rough Riders* and once in his diary but says nothing about an accordion. The Ledwidge and Hughes accounts are in Hagedorn Collection, TRC-H.

87   Rough Riders drilled: TR to Corinne Roosevelt Robinson, *Yucatan*, Gulf of Mexico, June 15, 1898, in MOR, 2:843.

88   "in case of retreat" . . . "charge through it quickly": As quoted in *The Oklahoma State Capital*, July 6, 1898.

88   best soldier in the regiment: TR, *The Rough Riders*, 18.

88   "Capron's training and temper": Ibid., 67.

88   had to stop eating: Hall, *The Fun and Fighting*, 105.

88   "The cans were opened and": Prentice, "The Rough Riders," 273.

89   "simply poured money": Vincent, ed., *Theodore Miller: Rough Rider*, 104.

89   swells finagled their way: Ibid.

89   "One not having experienced": Ibid.

89   "All the men have lost flesh": Arthur F. Cosby to Jim [?], *Yucatan*, at sea, June 17, 1898, Arthur F. Cosby scrapbook, TRC-H.

89   How Wood and Roosevelt: Wood does not mention the food shortage on board the *Yucatan* in his letters, diary, and later published accounts. Roosevelt does not mention it in either his *The Rough Riders* or his autobiography. However, in his "The Fifth Corps at Santiago," prepared for Fitzhugh Lee and Joseph Wheeler's 1899 history of the conflict, he writes, "The travel rations were good, except in two important instances." Those instances involved canned beef that was essentially inedible, not enough vegetables, poor water, and no ice for the men. It should be noted that there seems to have been plenty of food, and of a healthy variety, at the officers' table.

89   flown by the *insurrectos*: Colbert diary, May 31, 1898, CNCH; Arthur F. Cosby to Jim [?], *Yucatan*, at sea, June 17, 1898, Arthur F. Cosby scrapbook, TRC-H; Wells, *Diary of a Rough Rider*, 29; and McCurdy and McCurdy, *Two Rough Riders*, 5.

89   "At night we looked at": TR, *The Rough Riders*, 65.

90   "the mysteries which lie": Ibid., 67–68.

90   "If, by risking his life": Ibid., 68.

90   two life insurance policies: *The Border Vidette*, Nogales, AZ, July 21, 1898; and the *Florence Tribune*, AZ, Oct. 1, 1898.

90   Colonel Wood marveled: LW, diary transcript, June 20, 1898, LW Papers, Container 2, LOC.

90 **he had seen in Montana:** TR to Corinne Roosevelt Robinson, Troop Ship near Santiago, June 15, 1898, in MOR, 2:844.

91 **"I feel that I am where":** Wells, *Diary of a Rough Rider,* 30.

91 **About midday, the *Yucatan*:** Vincent, ed., *Theodore Miller: Rough Rider,* 113.

91 **Worried that a severe gale:** Colbert diary, June 21, 1898, CNCH.

91 **a waterspout:** Ibid.; Hall, *The Fun and Fighting,* 108; and McCurdy and McCurdy, *Two Rough Riders,* 5.

91 **Late that afternoon:** Colbert diary, June 21, 1898, CNCH.

91 **wanted Shafter to attack:** Shafter, "The Capture of Santiago de Cuba," 617; and Alger, *The Spanish-American War,* 85.

91 **Cuban force of one thousand men:** Miley, *In Cuba with Shafter,* 57.

91 **the *Yucatan*'s cooks:** Prentice, "The Rough Riders," 273–274.

93 **Orders called for each man:** General Orders No. 18, Headquarters 5th Army Corps, June 20, 1898, LW Papers, General Correspondence, Container 26, 1898 Folder 1, LOC.

93 **at least sixty pounds:** Letter of Edward W. Johnston, Troop D, in *The Oklahoma Leader,* Aug. 4, 1898.

93 **the booming of gunboats:** Colbert diary, June 22, 1898, CNCH.

93 **This was a feint:** Miley, *In Cuba with Shafter,* 57.

93 **"The valleys sent back":** Wells, *Diary of a Rough Rider,* 31.

93 **scribbled in his diary:** Colbert diary, June 22, 1898, CNCH.

93 **of the Eight Infantry:** Musgrave, *Under Three Flags in Cuba,* 264; and TR, "The Fifth Corps at Santiago," in Lee and Wheeler, *Cuba's Struggle Against Spain,* 647.

93 **mounted *insurrectos* galloped:** Miley, *In Cuba with Shafter,* 66.

94 **defenders had evacuated:** Ibid.

94 **not nearly enough landing boats:** TR, *The Rough Riders,* 70.

94 **Shafter had set up in advance:** Alger, *The Spanish-American War,* 92–93.

94 **his black Cuban pilot:** Ibid.; *Roosevelt: An Autobiography,* 234; and Hall, *The Fun and Fighting,* 112.

94 **"like a flock of sheep" . . . "we could help it":** *Roosevelt: An Autobiography,* 234.

95 **six to ten feet at a time:** George Hamner, *With the Rough Riders,* ed. by Ann Stevens Delk, Jean Bradley Hamner, and Selena Hamner Delk (Kensington, CA: Adelk Publications, 1996), 8.

95 **quickly fling their carbines:** Hall, *The Fun and Fighting,* 113.

95 **spent the afternoon diving:** Marshall, *The Story of the Rough Riders,* 66.

95 **slipped on the wet planking:** Ibid., 66 and 76; *The San Francisco Call,* June 25, 1898; Hall, *The Fun and Fighting,* 113; and TR, *The Rough Riders,* 71. All the primary accounts differ in some particulars on how these two soldiers died. Miley, in his *In Cuba with Shafter,* 69, says the bodies were not recovered until "some days later." Buckey O'Neill was recommended for the Medal of Honor for his efforts to save the men. See Joseph Wheeler, *The Santiago Campaign, 1898* (Boston: Lamson, Wolffe, and Co., 1898), 75.

95 **large silk American flag:** La Motte, "With the 'Rough Riders,'" 832–833; Marshall, *The Story of the Rough Riders,* 67–69; Hall, *The Fun and Fighting,* 113–114; and *The Arizona Republican,* March 26, 1911.

96 **"Yell, you Arizona men":** As quoted in the *Arizona Republican,* March 26, 1911.

96 **"My Country, 'Tis of Thee":** Colbert diary, June 22, 1898, CNCH.

96 **"No! No! We are":** Hamner, *With the Rough Riders,* 8.

96 **One woman from:** Hall, *The Fun and Fighting,* 116.

96 **"They were a motley":** Wells, *Diary of a Rough Rider,* 32.

96   "a crew of as utter": TR, *The Rough Riders*, 75. Perhaps the vilest description of the Cubans is found in John H. Parker, *History of the Gatling Gun Detachment, Fifth Army Corps, at Santiago* (Kansas City, MO: Hudson-Kimberly Publishing Co., 1898), 78.

96   to live off the land: Colbert diary, July 1, 1898, CNCH.

96   "all imbued with confidence": Letter of George E. Truman, Troop B, in undated clipping, Spanish-American War News Clipping Collection, Folder 6, "Rough Riders," SHM.

97   "after all, they kept": Hall, *The Fun and Fighting*, 121.

97   Thick jungle grew: TR, *The Rough Riders*, 75.

98   smoked Yankees: Ibid., 145.

98   Back in Florida: Edwin Emerson, "The Negro as a Soldier," *Collier's Weekly*, Oct. 8, 1898, 10. The white citizens of Tampa were in fact openly hostile to the black soldiers, the racial tensions finally erupting into a bloody riot the night before the Fifth Corps embarked for Cuba. See Gary R. Mormino, "Tampa's Splendid Little War: Local History and the Cuban War of Independence," *Magazine of History* 12 (Spring 1998): 40–41; and the *Portsmouth Daily Times*, OH, June 14, 1898.

98   Colonel Wood instructed: Wells, *Diary of a Rough Rider*, 32.

98   made chicken soup: Royal A. Prentice, "The Rough Riders," *New Mexico Historical Review* 27 (Jan. 1952): 30.

99   "I may some day": Colbert diary, June 22, 1898, CNCH.

99   welcome soft bed: Wells, *Diary of a Rough Rider*, 32.

99   man-crushing boa constrictors: Royal A. Prentice, "The Rough Riders," *New Mexico Historical Review* 26 (Oct. 1951): 275–276.

99   "At that time, the weight": Royal A. Prentice, "The Rough Riders," *New Mexico Historical Review* 27 (Jan. 1952): 30.

99   Cubans showed them: Marshall, *The Story of the Rough Riders*, 71–72; and Wells, *Diary of a Rough Rider*, 33.

99   offloading of the horses: Shafter, "The Capture of Santiago de Cuba," 619; Hall, *The Fun and Fighting*, 125; and Miley, *In Cuba with Shafter*, 70.

100   "Roosevelt, snorting like" . . . "die from starvation": Smith and Koury, *Two Reels and a Crank*, 59.

100   "Stop that goddamned": As quoted in ibid.

100   at a moment's notice: Marshall, *The Story of the Rough Riders*, 76–77.

100   occupied that morning: Miley, *In Cuba with Shafter*, 71–72.

100   a brief skirmish: Wagner, *Report of the Santiago Campaign*, 51.

100   sought a commission: *The San Francisco Call*, April 29, 1898.

101   "a regular game-cock": TR, *The Rough Riders*, 76.

101   At 1:30, the order: Marshall, *The Story of the Rough Riders*, 77.

101   only allotted eighteen: La Motte, "With the 'Rough Riders,'" 834.

101   the mistake of saying: Ibid.

101   thoroughbred Kentucky mare: Marshall, *The Story of the Rough Riders*, 77.

101   "wrath was boiling": Ibid., 78.

102   "land legs" back: Hall, *The Fun and Fighting*, 125.

102   "McGinty is a little": Arthur F. Cosby to Charlotte Cosby, Transport *Yucatan*, June 15, 1898, Arthur F. Cosby scrapbook, TRC-H.

102   "a better stepper on": As quoted in James H. McClintock, Troop B, "Research Materials for the Rough Riders," Hermann Hagedorn Collection, TRC-H.

102   started out four men abreast: Vincent, ed., *Theodore Miller: Rough Rider*, 115.

102   "At last we could stand it": Wells, *Diary of a Rough Rider*, 34.

102   **"Boys, this won't do":** As quoted in the *Indianapolis Star,* Jan. 8, 1922.

102   **"It was then we realized":** Wells, *Diary of a Rough Rider,* 34–35.

103   **Shafter intended for:** Report of William R. Shafter, Sept. 13, 1898, in *Annual Report of the Major-General Commanding the Army to the Secretary of War, 1898* (Washington, D.C.: Government Printing Office, 1898), 151; Alger, *The Spanish-American War,* 102; and Miley, *In Cuba with Shafter,* 82.

103   **clearly designated Lawton's:** Shafter, "The Capture of Santiago de Cuba," 620.

103   **summoned Wood:** LW, Las Guásimas typescript, LW Papers, Container 2, LOC.

103   **tropical rainstorm:** TR, *The Rough Riders,* 78; and Prentice, "The Rough Riders," 31.

103   **noticed Captain Capron standing:** LW, Las Guásimas typescript, LW Papers, Container 2, LOC.

104   **"We decided that nothing":** Ibid.

Chapter Five: Vultures Overhead

105   **"It was dark as pitch":** Wells, *Diary of a Rough Rider,* 35.

105   **split their blankets:** Ibid., 36.

105   **"smell powder":** Ibid.

106   **have some "fun":** Colbert diary, June 27, 1898, CNCH.

106   **assembled for roll call:** Wells, *Diary of a Rough Rider,* 36.

106   **barely got onshore:** *The War Dispatches of Stephen Crane,* 155.

106   **six hundred feet up:** Marshall, *The Rough Riders,* 91.

106   **"Delicate bugle calls":** Ibid., 92.

106–107   **"The information had leaked":** LW, Las Guásimas typescript, LW Papers, Container 2, LOC.

108   **many jungle birdsongs:** TR, *The Story of the Rough Riders,* 87.

108   **four troops each:** Ibid., 81.

108   **If all went according to plan:** LW, Las Guásimas typescript, LW Papers, Container 2, LOC.

108   **"reconnaissance in force":** Report of Brigadier General S.B.M. Young as quoted in Wheeler, *The Santiago Campaign, 1898,* 25.

108   **"Boys, the Spaniards are":** As quoted in the *Sun,* July 17, 1898. This comes from an interview with First Lieutenant John R. Thomas, Troop L.

109   **body of a Cuban:** *New York Daily Tribune,* July 17, 1898; and *The Evening Star,* July 20, 1898.

109   **"Silence in the ranks":** Marshall, *The Story of the Rough Riders,* 96.

109   **"Load chambers and magazines":** Letter of John G. Winter, Troop F, in *San Antonio Daily Express,* July 22, 1898.

109   **"were totally unconcerned" . . . "New Mexican town":** TR, *The Rough Riders,* 87.

109   **"Great Scott!" . . . "been lately cut":** Marshall, *The Story of the Rough Riders,* 99–100.

110   **"Colonel," . . . "sight of the enemy":** As quoted in TR, *The Rough Riders,* 293.

110   **less than five hundred men:** Ibid., 85.

110   **sounded oddly different:** Hall, *The Fun and Fighting,* 135.

110   **Then they saw them:** Wylie Skelton, Troop L, letter in *Indian Chieftain,* July 14, 1898; Tom Isbell, Troop L, letter in *Guthrie Daily Leader,* July 25, 1898.

110   **Tom Isbell:** *The Butler Weekly Times,* Butler, MO, Sept. 1, 1898; *Indian Chieftain,* July 14 and 28, 1898; and *Guthrie Daily Leader,* July 25, 1898.

111   **"hell opened" . . . "right at me":** As quoted in the *Butler Weekly Times,* Sept. 7, 1899.

111   **Troops F, D, and E:** Marshall, *The Story of the Rough Riders,* 104.

111   "jumped up and down" . . . "in civic life": Ibid.

111   But Roosevelt had little idea: *Roosevelt: An Autobiography*, 236.

112   173-grain Mauser bullets: Garry James, "Las Guásimas 1898," *Guns & Ammo* 56 (July 2012): 49.

112   "like 'zzzzz-eu' ": Marshall, *The Story of the Rough Riders*, 119.

112   "Then it dawned on": *Roosevelt: An Autobiography*, 237.

112   "They haven't hurt" . . . "smashed my specs!": As quoted in Clemens, *Theodore Roosevelt: The American*, 153.

112   "Scatter out to the": Ibid., 231.

113   "Give me your gun": As quoted in *New York Times*, June 27, 1898.

113   taking more hits: TR, *The Rough Riders*, 106.

113   felt like pinpricks: Raymond Spear, "The Wounded of Roosevelt's Rough Riders," *Medical News* 73 (July 9, 1898): 40.

114   through his torso: *The Evening Star*, July 20, 1898.

114   "Let me see it out": As quoted in *New York Daily Tribune*, July 17, 1898; and the *Sun*, July 17, 1898.

114   "Old boy, you've got": As quoted in "How Ham. Fish Met His Death," in *Hero Tales of the American Soldier and Sailor* (Philadelphia: Century Manufacturing Co., 1899), 85.

114   "I would follow him": As quoted in the *Evening Times*, July 9, 1898.

114   "The sun was just": "How Ham. Fish Met His Death," 85.

114   "I am wounded" . . . "And I am killed!": As quoted in the *Evening Star*, July 20, 1898.

114–115   "The same bullet" . . . "you hit hard?": As quoted in "How Ham. Fish Met His Death," 85.

115   Thomas refused: *The Sun*, July 17, 1898.

115   even when dismounted: Marshall, *The Story of the Rough Riders*, 112.

115   "The volley firing of": LW, Las Guásimas manuscript, 1898 diary folder, Container 2, LOC.

115   "if we had been hit": As quoted in Spear, "The Wounded of Roosevelt's Rough Riders," 40.

115   "Don't swear": As quoted in TR, *The Rough Riders*, 95.

115   The Icebox: Alger, *The Spanish-American War*, 109.

115   insurance policy: Marshall, *The Story of the Rough Riders*, 115.

116   "There they are" . . . "near that glade": As quoted in TR, *The Rough Riders*, 91.

116   220-grain bullets: Garry James, "Las Guásimas 1898," 48.

116   Riders had the range: TR, *The Rough Riders*, 91.

116   left eye and ear: Ibid., 92.

117   hold their fire: Ibid.

117   "I don't know what": As quoted in the *Sun*, July 17, 1898.

117   Troop K's guidon: TR, *The Rough Riders*, 94; *The Milwaukee Journal*, November 2, 1898; and Marshall, *The Story of the Rough Riders*, 106–107.

117   "I was in a mood": TR, *The Rough Riders*, 94.

117   regretted wearing the saber: *Roosevelt: An Autobiography*, 238.

118   It was a miracle: TR, *The Rough Riders*, 97.

118   Captain James McClintock's: "Captain McClintock Interviewed in Los Angeles," news clipping, Dec. 24, 1898, in Spanish-American War News Clipping Collection, Folder 6, "Rough Riders," SHM.

118   the damn packers: Hall, *The Fun and Fighting*, 141; and Frederick Herrig, Hagedorn Collection, TRC-H. In an account written years later, Bill McGinty stated that one of the mules became frightened by the gunfire, broke loose, and ran back down the

trail. See *Oklahoma Rough Rider Billy McGinty's Own Story,* ed. by Jim Fulbright and Albert Stehno (Norman, OK: The Arthur H. Clark Co., 2008), 22.

118 **the extreme left of the line:** LW, Las Guásimas manuscript, 1898 diary folder, Container 2, LOC.

119 **"[I]t isn't fair":** As quoted in La Motte, "With the 'Rough Riders,'" 836.

119 **"looked like a butcher":** LW, Las Guásimas manuscript, 1898 diary folder, Container 2, LOC.

119 **retrieved five men:** LW to Adjutant General Henry Corbin, Santiago de Cuba, March 28, 1899, in James Robb Church Medal of Honor File, AGO 80012, Box No. 597, RG 94, NARA.

119 **kneeling beside a downed:** *The Evening Star,* June 27, 1898; and the *Sun,* July 7, 1898. Another man who performed heroic duty with the wounded that day was Private George Burgess of Troop D. See Marshall, *The Story of the Rough Riders,* 128–132.

120 **"You're taking me . . . killed my captain":** As quoted in Davis, *The Cuban and Porto Rican Campaigns,* 154–155.

120 **"After some grumbling":** TR, *The Rough Riders,* 93.

120 **Henry Haefner, a miner:** Ibid., 92–93. The compiled military service record for Haefner states that he was wounded at Las Guásimas and "died in field Hospital same day."

121 **"was heaving with short":** Davis, *The Cuban and Porto Rican Campaigns,* 156.

121 **the New Testament:** This New Testament, along with manuscript condolence letters from Theodore Roosevelt and Richard Harding Davis to Dawson's father, was sold at auction by Swann Auction Galleries on April 14, 2015.

121 **"It's no use" . . . "can do now":** As quoted in Davis, *The Cuban and Porto Rican Campaigns,* 156–159.

121 **"Colonel, I have":** As quoted in LW, Las Guásimas manuscript, 1898 diary folder, Container 2, LOC.

122 **"quick, desperate rushes":** Davis, *The Cuban and Porto Rican Campaigns,* 149.

122 **"By the right flank":** As quoted in letter of John G. Winter, Troop F, in *San Antonio Daily Express,* July 22, 1898.

122 **"[T]he breath left my":** Ibid.

122 **"beating them back":** LW to Louise Wood, Sevilla, Cuba, June 27, 1898, LW Papers, Personal Correspondence, Container 190, 1898 file folder, LOC.

122 **Bacardi rum distillery:** Musgrave, *Under Three Flags in Cuba,* 268; Davis, *The Cuban and Porto Rican Campaigns,* 164; and TR, *The Rough Riders,* 98.

122 **grabbed a Krag:** TR, *The Rough Riders,* 98.

122 **"And yet, by jing":** As quoted in the *Sun,* July 7, 1898.

123 **"I sprang up and":** TR, *The Rough Riders,* 98–99.

123 **"The Spaniards naturally":** Davis, *The Cuban and Porto Rican Campaigns,* 169.

123 **"I see them":** As quoted in Rev. Peter MacQueen, "With Wheeler and Roosevelt at Santiago," *Leslie's Monthly Magazine* (Nov. 1898): 19.

123 **"I had not the faintest":** *Roosevelt: An Autobiography,* 238.

124 **beyond the buildings:** Vincent, ed., *Theodore Miller: Rough Rider,* 119.

124 **"the extreme heat created":** Prentice, "The Rough Riders," 31.

124 **Wood had been killed:** TR, *The Rough Riders,* 99.

124 **Tom Hall had panicked:** *New York Times,* Nov. 11 and 18, 1899.

124 **Wood's dying message:** John Fox Jr., "With the Rough Riders at Las Guásimas," *Harper's Weekly* (July 30, 1898).

124–125   **"Our Adjutant, Hall":** Arthur F. Cosby to Frank Cosby, Camp near Santiago, Cuba, June 27, 1898, Arthur F. Cosby scrapbook, TRC-H.

125   **approximately 7:20 A.M.:** Hall, *The Fun and Fighting*, 145.

125   **too played out:** LW report of June 25, 1898, in *Annual Report of the Major-General Commanding the Army to the Secretary of War, 1898* (Washington, D.C.: Government Printing Office, 1898), 344.

125   **reinforcements from Siboney:** General Wheeler had sent a request for reinforcements at 8:30 A.M. See Alger, *The Spanish-American War*, 110.

125   **"Every one says":** LW to Louise Wood, Sevilla, Cuba, June 27, 1898, LW Papers, Personal Correspondence, Container 190, 1898 file folder, LOC.

125   **"Have we won?" . . . "good fight":** As quoted in LW, Las Guásimas manuscript, 1898 diary folder, Container 2, LOC.

125   **locate the bodies:** LW to Louise Wood, Sevilla, Cuba, June 27, 1898, LW Papers, Personal Correspondence, Container 190, 1898 file folder, LOC.

125   **"Colonel, isn't it Whitman":** As quoted in TR, *The Rough Riders*, 105.

125   **Later, Roosevelt concluded:** Ibid., 284.

126   **"My first impulse":** McIntosh, *The Little I Saw of Cuba*, 82.

126   **"It would be just":** As quoted in the *Evening Star*, June 30, 1898.

126   **"first picture taken":** McIntosh, *The Little I Saw of Cuba*, 87.

126   **"Hello, Marshall!" . . . "find it handy":** As quoted in *The War Dispatches of Stephen Crane*, 158.

126   **written his report on the fight:** Davis, *The Cuban and Porto Rican Campaigns*, 163.

127   **Crane not only carried:** *The War Dispatches of Stephen Crane*, 158 n. 3; and Musgrave, *Under Three Flags in Cuba*, 269 n. 1. Crane's good deed of submitting Marshall's dispatch later cost him his job with the *New York World*.

127   **firing his revolver:** Marshall, *The Story of the Rough Riders*, 116.

127   **"I knew every other":** Charles Belmont Davis, ed., *Adventures and Letters of Richard Harding Davis* (New York: Charles Scribner's Sons, 1917), 255.

128   **General Wheeler endorsed them:** Wheeler, *The Santiago Campaign, 1898*, 36.

128   **make him a captain:** Davis, ed., *Adventures and Letters of Richard Harding Davis*, 255.

128   **"It appeared to be foolish":** Smith, *Two Reels and a Crank*, 64. Smith says this episode occurred during the Battle of San Juan Hill. However, as he only describes one fight of the Rough Riders, and as he claims to have landed in Cuba with the regiment, it is more likely he was at Las Guásimas. I admit his recollections are rather questionable, and it's possible he wasn't at either engagement. None of the footage he said he took in Cuba has survived.

128   **a Spanish captain:** James H. McClintock, Troop B, letter in *Phoenix Weekly Herald*, July 28, 1898; and Harman Wynkoop, Troop E, letter in *Santa Fe New Mexican*, July 21, 1898.

128   **"We can't understand":** As quoted in letter of Edward W. Johnston, Troop D, *The Guthrie Daily Leader*, July 26, 1898.

128   **"In battle with the Cubans":** Letter of George E. Truman, Troop B, undated news clipping, Spanish-American War News Clipping Collection, Folder 6, "Rough Riders," SHM.

128   **more than forty were wounded:** Figures for the wounded vary considerably.

128   **"It was enough to choke":** As quoted in the *Sun*, July 7, 1898.

129   **Captain Allyn Capron:** This episode is from an interview with William H. Brumley, Troop G, who was the guard, in undated news clipping, Hamilton Fish Jr. file, RRM.

Chapter Six: Road to Santiago

130   **except Captain Capron:** Fox, "With the Rough Riders at Las Guásimas." The bodies of Capron and Hamilton Fish Jr. were brought back to the United States in July by Nicholas Fish. See the *Evening Times*, July 9, 1898.

130   **Funeral call came:** Colbert diary, June 25, 1898, CNCH.

130   **"At the head of":** Fox, "With the Rough Riders at Las Guásimas."

130   **read from the Bible:** Ibid.; Letter of John G. Winter, Troop F, in *San Antonio Daily Express*, July 22, 1898; and Wells, *Diary of a Rough Rider*, 40.

131   **Transmission time from Cuba:** "In Direct Communication," *The Times*, July 12, 1898.

131   **"Lieut. Col. Roosevelt's" . . . "a gallant blunder":** *The War Dispatches of Stephen Crane*, 159–160.

131   **painted Las Guásimas as an ambush:** Richard Harding Davis, "Two Hours of Severe Fighting," *The San Francisco Call*, June 26, 1898.

132   **"they had been ambushed":** James Alfred Moss, *Memories of the Campaign of Santiago. June 6, 1898–August 18, 1898* (San Francisco: Press of the Mysell-Rollins Co., 1899), 27.

132   **"a plain standup fight":** As quoted in the *Sun*, July 17, 1898.

132   **"The Spanish let our advance":** Letter of Thomas W. Pemberton, Troop B, in undated news clipping, Spanish-American War News Clipping Collection, Folder 6, "Rough Riders," SHM.

132   **the number was around four thousand:** Writing his mother shortly after the battle, Arthur Cosby offered the four thousand figure, writing that "their [the Spaniards'] book gives that number." General Young's official report of the engagement cites the "Cuban military authorities" for the four thousand figure. See Arthur F. Cosby to Charlotte Cosby, In Camp near Santiago, Cuba, June 24, 1898, Arthur F. Cosby scrapbook, TRC-H; and Young's report in Wheeler, *The Santiago Campaign, 1898*, 27.

132   **no more than six hundred:** Stephen Bonsal, *The Fight for Santiago: The Story of the Soldier in the Cuban Campaign from Tampa to the Surrender* (New York: Doubleday & McClure Co., 1899), 92.

132   **correct number was 2,078:** Herbert H. Sargent, *The Campaign of Santiago de Cuba*, 3 vols. (Chicago: A. C. McClurg & Co., 1907), 2: 62. Sargent got his figures from inquiries made in 1903 to the Spanish government. See Appendix A in vol. 3 of his work.

133   **"[I]f it was a skirmish":** Marshall, *The Story of the Rough Riders*, 122.

133   **ordered to withdraw:** Sargent, *The Campaign of Santiago de Cuba*, 2:55–57 and 69; and Bonsal, *The Fight for Santiago*, 92.

133   **victory's primary accomplishment:** McIntosh, *The Little I Saw of Cuba*, 89–90.

133   **"it seems to me":** As quoted in the *Florence Tribune*, Florence, AZ, July 2, 1898.

133   **"The fight was a perfect":** Fox, "With the Rough Riders at Las Guásimas."

133   **"I had often wondered":** Samuel McLeary Weller to Florence and Cyrus O. Weller, near Santiago, Cuba, June 29, 1898, Budner Roosevelt Collection, Box 1, Folder 10, DL.

134   **"It proved to the men":** Shafter, "The Capture of Santiago de Cuba," 621. Shafter was also in the "no ambush" camp.

134   **things they hastily abandoned:** McCurdy and McCurdy, *Two Rough Riders*, 8; and LW, Las Guásimas manuscript, 1898 diary folder, Container 2, LOC.

134   **"Wood sauntered around":** Letter of Edward W. Johnston, Troop D, *The Guthrie Daily Leader*, July 26, 1898.

134   **"did look too nice":** Frederick Herrig as quoted in the *Macon Telegraph*, GA, Oct. 29, 1898.

134   **"We can get new skin":** Ibid.

135   **"Didn't I tell you":** As quoted in Frederick Herrig, Hagedorn Collection, TRC-H.

135   **"I am personally in":** TR to Edith Roosevelt, Camp 5 miles from Santiago, June 27, 1898, in MOR, 2:845.

136   **very clear instructions:** Wheeler, *The Santiago Campaign*, 246–247, and 254.

136   **rooftops of Santiago:** Wells, *Diary of a Rough Rider*, 43.

136   **Spanish blockhouses:** Hall, *The Fun and Fighting*, 164.

136   **The merry bunch:** TR, *The Rough Riders*, 109; and Davis, ed., *Adventures and Letters of Richard Harding Davis*, 253.

136   **"our friend":** Samuel McLeary Weller to Florence and Cyrus O. Weller, near Santiago, Cuba, June 29, 1898, Budner Roosevelt Collection, Box 1, Folder 10, DL.

136   **Wood and Roosevelt declared:** Marshall, *The Story of the Rough Riders*, 159.

136   **"lived literally from":** Hall, *The Fun and Fighting*, 154.

137   **"Why, Colonel":** As quoted in *Roosevelt: An Autobiography*, 252.

137   **"[L]ast evening we got":** TR to Edith Roosevelt, Camp 5 miles from Santiago, June 27, 1898, in MOR, 2:845.

137   **"Hamner's coffee mill":** George P. Hamner manuscript, 1952, George P. Hamner file, RRM.

137   **bacon and hardtack:** McCurdy and McCurdy, *Two Rough Riders*, 12.

137   **canned peaches:** Samuel McLeary Weller to Florence and Cyrus O. Weller, near Santiago, Cuba, June 29, 1898, Budner Roosevelt Collection, Box 1, Folder 10, DL.

137   **cramps and diarrhea:** John Bigelow Jr., *Reminiscences of the Santiago Campaign* (New York: Harper & Brothers, 1899), 86.

137   **carrier for yellow fever:** Letter of Frank Donaldson, assistant surgeon, Aug. 6, 1898, in *The Philadelphia Medical Journal* (Aug. 13, 1898), 309; and Wells, *Diary of a Rough Rider*, 44–45.

138   **"Mango Abe":** Hamner manuscript, George P. Hamner file, RRM.

138   **with cool limeade:** Hall, *The Fun and Fighting*, 168.

138   **"The juice of this":** Bigelow Jr., *Reminiscences of the Santiago Campaign*, 86.

138   **"With a pipe the soldier":** Davis, *The Cuban and Porto Rican Campaigns*, 176.

138   **sold for two dollars:** Ibid.

138   **dried horse droppings:** Davis, ed., *Adventures and Letters of Richard Harding Davis*, 253.

138   **boil their water:** "Testimony of Col. Theodore Roosevelt," 2262.

138   **canteen full of warm:** Bigelow Jr., *Reminiscences of the Santiago Campaign*, 85.

139   **"It rains every day":** Davis, ed., *Adventures and Letters of Richard Harding Davis*, 253.

139   **Krags began to rust:** Parker, *History of the Gatling Gun Detachment*, 106–109.

139   **Hamner dug a hole:** Hamner manuscript, George P. Hamner file, RRM.

139   **a temporary tub:** Bigelow Jr., *Reminiscences of the Santiago Campaign*, 97.

139   **resorted to scribbling:** Hemment, *Cannon and Camera*, 133–134.

139   **Arthur Cosby mailed:** These items are pasted into the Arthur F. Cosby scrapbook, TRC-H.

139–140   **"These are powder filled":** Samuel McLeary Weller to Florence and Cyrus O. Weller, near Santiago, Cuba, June 29, 1898, Budner Roosevelt Collection, Box 1, Folder 10, DL.

140   **a hard lead core:** *Medical and Surgical Therapy, Vol. 5, Bones and Joints*, ed. by Surgeon-General Sir Alfred Keogh (New York: D. Appleton and Company, 1918), 135. My thanks to Dr. James Bailey for providing me with this reference.

140   **"The Mauser bullets":** TR, *The Rough Riders,* 122. In the *Evening Star* of July 21, 1898, Army surgeon Lieutenant Colonel Chas. Smart stated, "The fact is, the Mauser bullets used by the Spaniards . . . make what surgeons call a 'humane wound.' They drop the man at the time he is struck and take him from the firing line; but if they do not kill him then and there, he gets well."

140   **"garden spot of Cuba":** McCurdy and McCurdy, *Two Rough Riders,* 11.

140   **"Have seen no":** Arthur F. Cosby to Frank Cosby, Camp near Santiago, Cuba, June 27, 1898, Arthur F. Cosby scrapbook, TRC-H.

140   **"nearly wild to":** Samuel McLeary Weller to Florence and Cyrus O. Weller, near Santiago, Cuba, June 29, 1898, Budner Roosevelt Collection, Box 1, Folder 10, DL.

140   **"If I go under":** Letter of Edward W. Johnston, Troop D, *The Guthrie Daily Leader,* July 26, 1898.

141   **"all, officers and men":** TR, *The Rough Riders,* 112.

141   **"a light as large":** Colbert diary, June 27, 1898, CNCH.

141   **"They seem greatly":** Vincent, ed., *Theodore Miller: Rough Rider,* 127.

141   **"The Cuban insurgents":** Arthur F. Cosby to Charlotte Cosby, Camp near Santiago, Cuba, June 30, 1898, Arthur F. Cosby scrapbook, TRC-H.

141   **taken the rations:** Hall, *The Fun and Fighting,* 151; and Wells, *Diary of a Rough Rider,* 40.

141   **keep all Cubans out:** Vincent, ed., *Theodore Miller: Rough Rider,* 128; and Wells, *Diary of a Rough Rider,* 43.

141–142   **"[T]here is no specious":** *The War Dispatches of Stephen Crane,* 163.

142   **picks and shovels:** Vincent, ed., *Theodore Miller: Rough Rider,* 129–130.

142   **a novel raffle:** Hall, *The Fun and Fighting,* 157.

142   **Capron refused to accept:** Ibid., 174. In a double tragedy for the Capron family, Allyn Senior died on September 18, 1898, from typhoid fever contracted in Cuba.

142   **"looked like he could carry":** Wells, *Diary of a Rough Rider,* 44. Miley states that Shafter visited the camps on the afternoon of June 27. See *In Cuba with Shafter,* 100.

142   **"maddening":** TR to HCL, Camp 5 miles from Santiago, June 27, 1898, in MOR, 2:846.

142   **"I do not care a damn":** As quoted in E. J. McClernand, "The Santiago Campaign," in *The Santiago Campaign: Reminiscences of the Operations for the Capture of Santiago de Cuba in the Spanish-American War, June and July 1898* (Richmond, VA: Society of Santiago de Cuba, 1927), 11. For Shafter's side of this episode, see "Shafter Turns on His Critic," *The Salt Lake Herald,* Oct. 31, 1898.

143   **Los Cerros del Río San Juan:** Edwin Emerson, *Who Got There First? Regulars or Rough Riders on San Juan Hill?* (Whittier, CA: Roosevelt Rough Riders Association, 1948), 3.

143   **ranch house or villa:** Hamner, *With the Rough Riders,* 23.

143   **bobbing up and down:** Davis, *The Cuban and Porto Rican Campaigns,* 180.

143   **why Shafter did nothing:** Ibid.

143   **hoped he could advance:** Miley, *In Cuba with Shafter,* 98–99.

144   **"would make a very short":** Hemment, *Cannon and Camera,* 76.

144   **"chances are we will":** Samuel McLeary Weller to Florence and Cyrus O. Weller, near Santiago, Cuba, June 29, 1898, Budner Roosevelt Collection, Box 1, Folder 10, DL.

144   **"generation had passed":** TR, "The Fifth Corps at Santiago," in Lee and Wheeler, *Cuba's Struggle Against Spain,* 651–652.

144   **"If [Brigadier General Adna]":** Davis, ed., *Adventures and Letters of Richard Harding Davis,* 254.

144   **"Everything is moving":** Wells, *Diary of a Rough Rider,* 45.

144   **staff officer rode up:** Davis, *The Cuban and Porto Rican Campaigns,* 188. Roosevelt says

the Rough Riders struck camp "about noon," but Wells, in his diary, has 3:00 P.M. as the time when they received their marching orders, with "only thirty minutes to break camp." See TR, *The Rough Riders*, 113; and Wells, *Diary of a Rough Rider*, 45.

145 **Most everyone expected:** Hagedorn, *Leonard Wood: A Biography*, 2: 157.

145 **blue-eyed George Roland:** TR, *The Rough Riders*, 108.

146 **only enough mules:** Ibid., 113.

146 **General Shafter's marching orders:** Davis, *The Cuban and Porto Rican Campaigns*, 188.

146 **"Every few minutes":** TR, *The Rough Riders*, 114.

146 **observation balloon:** Wells, *Diary of a Rough Rider*, 46.

146 **"an experimental toy" . . . "infinitely better":** TR, "The Fifth Corps at Santiago," in Lee and Wheeler, *Cuba's Struggle Against Spain*, 650–651.

147 **"Look out, Colonel":** As quoted in Prentice, "The Rough Riders," 33.

147 **regiment reached El Pozo:** TR, *The Rough Riders*, 114.

147 **had marched six miles:** Wells, *Diary of a Rough Rider*, 45.

147 **"I suppose that":** TR, *The Rough Riders*, 115.

147 **they ate it up:** Roger S. Fitch diary, July 1, 1898, RRM.

148 **"It was a fine sight":** TR, *The Rough Riders*, 116.

148 **a threat to Shafter's right flank:** McClernand, "The Santiago Campaign," 16.

148 **All three divisions:** Shafter, "The Capture of Santiago de Cuba," 619–620; Hall, *The Fun and Fighting*, 179; and ibid., 17. Richard Harding Davis, Shafter's harshest critic (other than Roosevelt), claims that Shafter's plan actually called for the capture of El Caney on July 1 and then the assault on San Juan Heights by his entire command on the following morning, July 2. See Davis, *The Cuban and Porto Rican Campaigns*, 194.

148 **About thirty minutes later:** Miley, *In Cuba with Shafter*, 107.

148 **"No. 1 . . . load! . . . prime!":** As quoted in Hemment, *Cannon and Camera*, 147.

148 **abandoned their units:** W. C. Brown, "The Diary of a Captain," in *The Santiago Campaign: Reminiscences of the Operations for the Capture of Santiago de Cuba in the Spanish-American War, June and July 1898* (Richmond, VA: Society of Santiago de Cuba, 1927), 299.

149 **"I was quietly writing":** Colbert diary, July 1, 1898, CNCH.

149 **"all collapsed and":** Lewis Maverick, Troop K, "Research Materials for the Rough Riders," Hermann Hagedorn Collection, TRC-H.

149 **"It was thoroughly evident":** Frederic Remington, "With the Fifth Corps," *Harper's New Monthly Magazine* 97 (Nov. 1898): 968.

149 **an awful bump:** Hall, *The Fun and Fighting*, 182; and TR, *The Rough Riders*, 118.

149 **"That's the first one":** As quoted in the *Sun*, Aug. 3, 1898.

149 **crest of the hill:** William Sanders to Helen Sanders, near Santiago, Cuba, July 19, 1898, Sanders Collection, TRC-H; and TR, *The Rough Riders*, 118.

150 **"Must stop":** Vincent, ed., *Theodore Miller: Rough Rider*, 133.

Chapter Seven: A Bully Fight

151 **several frustrating halts:** TR, *The Rough Riders*, 117.

151 **their heavy packs:** Royal A. Prentice, diary, 110, Royal A. Prentice Papers, Box 1, Folder 12, FACL.

151–152 **"The shriek of the":** Roger S. Fitch diary, July 1, 1898, RRM.

152 **"huge, fat, yellow":** *The War Dispatches of Stephen Crane*, 176.

152 **dragging the balloon:** TR, *The Rough Riders*, 120; and Hemment, *Cannon and Camera*, 145.

152   **"It was one of":** LW, diary transcript, July 1, 1898, LW Papers, Container 2, LOC.

152   **half mile to the right:** TR, *The Rough Riders*, 119–120; and Hall, *The Fun and Fighting*, 188.

152   **It was now 11:15 A.M.:** H. J. Whigham, "One of the Glorious Deeds of the World," *Chicago Tribune*, July 13, 1898.

152   **Tom Hall, to put a stop to it:** Hall, *The Fun and Fighting*, 189.

152–153   **"We could hear the":** David L. Hughes, Hagedorn Collection, TRC-H. There were actually two men in the balloon's basket: Lieutenant Colonel George Derby and Lieutenant Joseph Maxfield.

153   **behind the First Brigade:** Samuel S. Sumner to TR, San Francisco, CA, May 11, 1905, in *Roosevelt: An Autobiography*, 267.

153   **like Spanish guerrillas:** Hall, *The Fun and Fighting*, 190.

153   **a sunken road:** TR, *The Rough Riders*, 120; and Hall, *The Fun and Fighting*, 193.

153   **dubbed Kettle Hill:** According to George Clarke Musgrave, the hill was known locally as Marianje. Musgrave, *Under Three Flags in Cuba*, 298.

154   **"The Mauser bullets":** TR, *The Rough Riders*, 121.

154   **simple rope swings:** David L. Hughes, Hagedorn Collection, TRC-H.

154   **"There was no hiding":** Davis, *The Cuban and Porto Rican Campaigns*, 208.

155   **like a havelock:** Ibid., 217; and George Kennan, *Campaigning in Cuba* (New York: The Century Co., 1899), 99.

155   **"Boys, this is the"** ... **"in the future":** As quoted in Hemment, *Cannon and Camera*, 180.

155   **"See here, boys":** As quoted in the *Evening Times*, Aug. 5, 1898.

155   **"constitutionally opposed":** Letter of Joshua D. Carter, Troop A, in *Arizona Weekly Journal-Miner*, Prescott, July 27, 1898.

156   **"Both Col. Wood and":** Report of Brigadier General S.B.M. Young as quoted in Wheeler, *The Santiago Campaign, 1898*, 30.

156   **"Captain, a bullet is"** ... **"that will kill me":** As quoted in TR, *The Rough Riders*, 123–124. For Arizona Rough Rider accounts confirming O'Neill's now-famous last words, see the letter of James D. Raudebaugh, Troop A, in the *Coconino Sun*, Flagstaff, AZ, July 23, 1898; and the letter of John Hall, Troop B, in undated clipping, in William O. "Buckey" O'Neill Vertical File 3, SHM.

156   **Frantz heard a sharp crack:** "Captain Frantz Tells of the Death of O'Neill," *The Herald*, Los Angeles, Oct. 27, 1898.

156   **A spot of blood:** Letter of James D. Raudebaugh, Troop A, in the *Coconino Sun*, Flagstaff, AZ, July 23, 1898.

156   **"He never knew what struck":** Letter of Joshua D. Carter, Troop A, in *Arizona Weekly Journal-Miner*, Prescott, July 27, 1898.

157   **"[H]e fell with two holes":** Letter of James D. Raudebaugh, Troop A, in the *Coconino Sun*, Flagstaff, AZ, July 23, 1898.

157   **"If I had all the lead":** Letter of Daniel L. Hogan, Troop A, in the *Coconino Sun*, Aug. 6, 1898.

157   **"Teddy is as brave":** William Sanders to Helen Sanders, near Santiago, Cuba, July 19, 1898, Sanders Collection, TRC-H.

157   **"I wish they'd let":** As quoted in the *Evening Times*, Aug. 5, 1898.

158   **yet another messenger:** TR, *The Rough Riders*, 124.

158   **"I was tempted several":** Oscar G. Wager, Hermann Hagedorn Collection, TRC-H.

158   **"He done that to me":** As quoted in Jacob A. Riis, "Roosevelt and His Men," *The Outlook* 60 (Oct. 1898): 292.

158   **"What in hell has":** As quoted in Nicholas A. Vyne, Troop G, "Research Materials for the Rough Riders," Hermann Hagedorn Collection, TRC-H.

158 **"Move forward and support"**: As quoted in TR, *The Rough Riders*, 125.

159 **"my 'crowded hour' "**: Ibid., 126.

159 **"Are you afraid to"** . . . **"cover was killed"**: Ibid., 127.

159 **"Well, come on!"** . . . **"Forward, March!"**: Hall, *The Fun and Fighting*, 194.

159 **left of the sunken lane**: TR to Captain E. D. Dimmick, In Camp Near Santiago de Cuba, July 31, 1898, in *The Santiago Campaign: Reminiscences*, 421.

159 **"I . . . told him that it wouldn't"**: Cliff D. Scott, Troop D, "Research Materials for the Rough Riders," Hermann Hagedorn Collection, TRC-H.

160 **through line after line**: TR, *The Rough Riders*, 128.

160–161 **"Then I am the ranking"** . . . **"let my men through, sir"**: Ibid., 129–130. Roosevelt also wrote of his encounter with Captain Dimmick in a letter to Dimmick dated July 31, 1898, cited above.

161 **"The cheer was taken up"**: Henry Anson Barber to TR, Cambridge, MD, March 27, 1902, Theodore Roosevelt Papers, LOC.

161 **"Rough Riders going to"** . . . **"ahead of me"**: As quoted in letter of William E. Dame, Troop E, *Santa Fe New Mexican Review*, July 28, 1898.

161 **"E Troop to the front"**: As quoted in Sherrard Coleman and Thomas P. Ledwidge, both in Hagedorn Collection, TRC-H. See also Coleman letter in *Santa Fe New Mexican Review*, Aug. 11, 1898; and the account of this same incident by Private Daniel Ludy, "Rough Rider Home," *The Topeka State Journal*, Sept. 5, 1898.

161 **"I most positively assert"**: Thomas P. Ledwidge, Hagedorn Collection, TRC-H.

162 **"That one came close"** . . . **"I was needed"**: George P. Hamner manuscript, 1952, George P. Hamner file, RRM.

162 **"The top of the hill sputtered"**: Arthur F. Cosby, "A Rough Rider Looks Back," typescript, TRC-H.

162 **"never failed to fall"**: Marshall, *The Story of the Rough Riders*, 118–119.

162 **a single Mauser bullet**: Arthur F. Cosby, "A Rough Rider Looks Back," typescript, TRC-H; Arthur F. Cosby to Charlotte Cosby, Field Hospital, Siboney, July 2, 1898, Arthur F. Cosby scrapbook, TRC-H; James Rankin Young, *Reminiscences and Thrilling Stories of the War by Returned Heroes* . . . (Chicago: Providence Publishing Co., 1899), 192; and analysis of A. F. Cosby's wounds by Dr. James Bailey, author's collection.

163 **latched on to Roosevelt**: TR, *The Rough Riders*, 124–125.

163 **"What do you mean by"**: As quoted in Henry P. Bardshar, Troop A, "Research Materials for the Rough Riders," Hermann Hagedorn Collection, TRC-H. The lieutenant who bawled out Bardshar and who was later killed was either First Lieutenant William H. Smith or First Lieutenant William E. Shipp, both of the Tenth Cavalry and both killed on Kettle Hill.

163 **rang like a bell**: David L. Hughes, Hagedorn Collection, TRC-H.

163 **a wire fence**: TR. *The Rough Riders*, 132.

164 **"Did I tell you"**: TR to HCL, Santiago, July 19, 1898, in MOR, 2:853.

164 **"[I] will say that myself"**: Frederick Muller to Edward C. Bartlett, Santiago de Cuba, July 25, 1898, Box 1, Folder 13, Bartlett Papers, Coll. 1960-003, NMSR.

164 **"our guidon, which was carried"**: Letter of Sherrard Coleman, Troop E, in *Santa Fe New Mexican Review*, Aug. 11, 1898.

164 **Legitimate claims, he said**: TR, *The Rough Riders*, 133.

165 **"Obviously the proper"**: Ibid., 134.

165 **"be sure you have it"** . . . **"He never even kicked"**: David L. Hughes, Hagedorn Collection, TRC-H.

166 **"Didn't I order"**: As quoted in ibid.

166   **commendations for bravery:** Report of TR, Trenches Outside Santiago, July 4, 1898, in Wheeler, *The Santiago Campaign*, 79. See also Bugbee's compiled military service record, NARA.

166   **"He seemed to be enjoying":** David Marvin Goodrich to Mary Valinda Miller, Camp Hamilton, Santiago de Cuba, August 5, 1898, typescript in Scrapbook of Mary M. Goodrich, TRC-H.

166   **"The Spanish machine-guns":** As quoted in TR, *The Rough Riders*, 135.

166   **"It's the Gatlings, men!":** TR, "Preface," in Parker, *History of the Gatling Gun Detachment*.

167   **most advanced version:** Ibid., 20.

167   **ordered a cease-fire:** TR, *The Rough Riders*, 136.

167   **"Now by God, men!":** Mathew F. Steele to Stella Folsom Steele, July 10, 1898, as quoted in *MHQ: The Quarterly Journal of Military History* 14 (Spring 2002): 62. See also "Roosevelt Swore in Battle," undated clipping in Arthur F. Cosby scrapbook, TRC-H.

167   **"For God's sake":** As quoted in TR, *The Rough Riders*, 293.

167   **"Lie down, boys":** As quoted in Jeff Heatley, ed., *Bully!: Colonel Theodore Roosevelt, The Rough Riders & Camp Wikoff, Montauk, New York, 1898* (Montauk, NY: Montauk Historical Society, Pushcart Press, 1998), 159.

167–168   **"[T]here was really no possible":** TR, *The Rough Riders*, 137.

168   **"Well, it was a ticklish":** As quoted in Heatley, ed., *Bully!*, 159.

168   **"Every S.O.B. of us":** As quoted in George P. Hamner manuscript, 1952, George P. Hamner file, RRM.

169   **"He doesn't know that"** . . . **"call for a charge?":** Henry P. Bardshar, Hagedorn Collection, TRC-H.

169   **"[E]ven while I taunted":** TR, *The Rough Riders*, 137.

169   **"my mother had accused":** As quoted in the *Sun*, Aug. 29, 1898.

169   **ran over to General Sumner:** Samuel S. Sumner to TR, San Francisco, CA, May 11, 1905, in *Roosevelt: An Autobiography*, 267; and TR, *The Rough Riders*, 137.

170   **"I said goodbye to Thede":** David Marvin Goodrich to Mary Valinda Miller, Camp Hamilton, Santiago de Cuba, August 5, 1898, typescript in Scrapbook of Mary M. Goodrich, TRC-H.

170   **"I'm going, Harry":** As quoted in Vincent, ed., *Theodore Miller: Rough Rider*, 135.

170   **"It was the grandest sight":** Greenway, *It Was the Grandest Sight I Ever Saw*, 36.

170   **"just a mob that went up":** As quoted in the *Santa Fe New Mexican*, June 1, 1971.

170   **"ungodly war-whoop":** Riis, "Roosevelt and His Men," 290.

170   **"Holy Godfrey, what fun!":** As quoted in Henry P. Bardshar, Hagedorn Collection, TRC-H.

171   **"There were a good many":** Roger S. Fitch diary, July 1, 1898, RRM.

171   **confiscated his bugle:** Greenway, *It Was the Grandest Sight I Ever Saw*, 36. The bugle is now part of the Rough Rider Memorial Collection in the City of Las Vegas Museum, New Mexico.

171   **approximately 2:30 P.M.:** Report of Brigadier General S. S. Sumner, Fort San Juan, Cuba, July 6, 1898, in *Annual Report of the Major-General Commanding the Army to the Secretary of War, 1898* (Washington, D.C.: Government Printing Office, 1898), 371.

171   **oozing blood and brain:** TR, *The Rough Riders*, 138.

172   **"This last charge was":** Wells, *Diary of a Rough Rider*, 50.

172   **between three hundred and four hundred:** Robinson, *My Brother Theodore Roosevelt*, 174.

172   **"hold the hill":** TR, *The Rough Riders,* 140.

172   **about thirty of his troopers:** Roger S. Fitch diary, July 1, 1898, RRM.

172   **right into the city:** Hall, *The Fun and Fighting,* 199.

172   **bullet between the eyes:** Wells, *Diary of a Rough Rider,* 50.

172   **buzzed three or four inches:** Ibid., 51.

172   **down to thirty cartridges:** Vincent, ed., *Theodore Miller: Rough Rider,* 135 n. 1.

173   **three Spanish officers:** Wells, *Diary of a Rough Rider,* 51.

173   **several black troopers:** Roosevelt identified the black troopers leaving his line as members of the infantry. However, Presley Holliday, a sergeant in Troop B of the Tenth Cavalry, who was present, said it was not infantrymen but troopers of the Tenth Cavalry. See his April 22, 1899, letter as reproduced in Edward A. Johnson, *History of Negro Soldiers in the Spanish-American War, and Other Items of Interest* (Raleigh, NC: Capital Printing Company, 1899), 65.

173   **"Now, I shall be very sorry"** . . . **"he always does!":** TR, *The Rough Riders,* 145.

174   **"[Y]ou won't have to"** . . . **"with you, Colonel!":** As quoted in Johnson, *History of Negro Soldiers in the Spanish-American War,* 65.

174   **"Everyone who saw":** Presley Holliday, quoted in ibid.

174   **"he never expected to have":** Kennan, *Campaigning in Cuba,* 144.

174   **later, he would credit:** TR, *The Rough Riders,* 143 and 146.

174   **They shouted gleefully:** Ibid., 146.

174   **"Colonel Wood orders you":** As quoted in Parker, *History of the Gatling Gun Detachment,* 142.

175   **"[W]hy didn't God make":** As quoted in letter of Matt T. McGehee, Troop G, in undated clipping, Marinel Ash Collection, AC 385, Box 1, Folder 16, FACL.

175   **"Theodore moved about in":** Robert Munro Ferguson, as quoted in Robinson, *My Brother Theodore Roosevelt,* 174.

175   **officers' mess still cooking:** Letter of John D. Honeyman, Troop A, in *San Antonio Daily Express,* July 28, 1898; and TR, *The Rough Riders,* 149.

175   **"like it was chocolate cake":** Colbert diary, July 2, 1898, CNCH.

176   **"By George, sir!":** George P. Hamner to The Editors of *Life,* Hollywood, FL, Aug. 27, 1952, in George P. Hamner file, RRM.

Chapter Eight: The Siege

177   **"emphatic protest":** *Roosevelt: An Autobiography,* 243.

177   **"it would be far worse":** TR, *The Rough Riders,* 148.

177   **Fever or not, there was:** Lee and Wheeler, *Cuba's Struggle Against Spain,* 409.

177   **Wheeler waited until:** Joseph Wheeler endorsement, July 10, 1898, in *Annual Report of the Major-General Commanding the Army to the Secretary of War, 1898* (Washington, D.C.: Government Printing Office, 1898), 372; and Wheeler, *The Santiago Campaign,* 272.

178   **"cost us much prestige"** . . . **"a severe day":** Wheeler, *The Santiago Campaign,* 277.

178   **"and while a dear old":** LW to Louise Wood, In front of Santiago de Cuba, July 15, 1898, LW Papers, Personal Correspondence, Container 190, 1898 file folder, LOC.

178   **"Well, General":** *Roosevelt: An Autobiography,* 244.

178   **"Had I disobeyed the":** As quoted in *The Letters of Archie Butt,* 112.

179   **"As we went silently back":** Wells, *Diary of a Rough Rider,* 52.

179   **good at chasing moonshiners:** *New York Times,* June 17, 1910; and *The Evening Star,* Feb. 5, 1891.

179   **"it would be worth as much":** As quoted in *Atlanta Constitution,* Sept. 11, 1902.

179   **"[H]e cooked some of the":** As quoted in *Washington Post*, Oct. 21, 1905.

179   **Bardshar secured one of:** TR, *The Rough Riders*, 154.

180   **believed were "two heads":** Wells, *Diary of a Rough Rider*, 53.

180   **"A perfect hail of bullets":** Ibid., 54.

180   **killing or wounding five:** TR, *The Rough Riders*, 155.

181   **left his studies:** *Biographical Sketches of Distinguished Officers of the Army and Navy* (New York: L. R. Hamersly, 1905), 230; and Fortescue obituary, *New York Times*, April 22, 1952.

181   **as an extra orderly:** TR, *The Rough Riders*, 152.

181   **the greatest secret:** Edward J. Renehan Jr., "A Secret Roosevelt," http:// historynewsnetwork.org/article/1877.

181   **grabbed Carr's canteen:** Wells, *Diary of a Rough Rider*, 54.

182   **"He presented a sickening":** Ibid., 55.

182   **"My God! I am shot!":** As quoted in ibid.

183   **Playing dead, Wells:** Ibid., 56.

183   **"To realize what war":** William T. Sherman to Ellen Sherman, June 26, 1864, in *Sherman's Civil War: Selected Correspondence of William T. Sherman, 1860–1865*, ed. Brooks D. Simpson and Jean V. Berlin (Chapel Hill: University of North Carolina Press, 1999), 657.

183   **bodies without heads:** *The Peoples' Voice*, Norman, OK, July 29, 1898.

184   **"with arms in slings":** John Fox Jr., "Santiago and Caney," part three, *Harper's Weekly* (August 6, 1898).

184   **carrying or helping the wounded:** Hemment, *Cannon and Camera*, 192.

184   **never unloaded:** Report of James R. Church, Camp Wikoff, Long Island, Sept. 10, 1898, in *Report of the Commission . . . to Investigate the Conduct of the War Department*, vol. 8, 479.

184   **large tarpaulins stretched:** Richard C. Day, Troop L, "Research Materials for the Rough Riders," Hermann Hagedorn Collection, TRC-H.

184   **as many as four hundred:** Vincent, ed., *Theodore Miller: Rough Rider*, 137.

184   **"Jack, I can stand to see":** As quoted in Hemment, *Cannon and Camera*, 186.

184–185   **"the other scenes of the":** Ibid., 187.

185   **"worked like Trojans":** James Burton, "Photographing Under Fire," *Harper's Weekly* (August 6, 1898).

185   **Miller, still clinging to life:** Vincent, ed., *Theodore Miller: Rough Rider*, 136–137; and David Marvin Goodrich to Mary Valinda Miller, Camp Hamilton, Santiago de Cuba, August 5, 1898, typescript in Scrapbook of Mary M. Goodrich, TRC-H.

186   **wrote his mother:** Arthur F. Cosby to Charlotte Cosby, Field Hospital, Siboney, July 2, 1898, Arthur F. Cosby scrapbook, TRC-H.

187   **"his hand bandaged" . . . "find in this fight":** Fox Jr., "Santiago and Caney," part three.

187   **moved into position:** Miley, *In Cuba with Shafter*, 116; and Hall, *The Fun and Fighting*, 200–201.

188   **cramped pits for ten hours:** Roger S. Fitch diary, July 2, 1898, RRM.

188   **they ran like hell:** TR, *The Rough Riders*, 162.

188   **"Wait, I'll go with you" . . . "depending on you":** As quoted in Billy McGinty, "A War Story," typescript in William McGinty file, RRM.

188   **the wet liquid:** Ibid. Roosevelt tells this story in his *The Rough Riders*, 162–163.

189   **A heavy rain:** Miley, *In Cuba with Shafter*, 124; and David L. Hughes, Hagedorn Collection, TRC-H.

189   **"It looks real funny":** Colbert diary, July 2, 1898, CNCH.

189   **"kept up in their trees":** TR, *The Rough Riders*, 171–172.

190   **"tall, sinewy, handsome":** Ibid.

190   **Proffitt still carried it:** "Recovered His Revolver," clipping, Spanish-American War News Clipping Collection, Folder 6, "Rough Riders," SHM.

191   **"Sir, you said not to take":** As quoted in David L. Hughes, Hagedorn Collection, TRC-H. Hughes is the only source for the account of Goodwin and the unnamed Buffalo Soldier.

191   **total of eleven snipers:** TR, *The Rough Riders*, 172. Roosevelt's July 4 report to Colonel Wood stated thirteen snipers had been killed. See Report of TR, Trenches Outside Santiago, July 4, 1898, in Wheeler, *The Santiago Campaign*, 79.

191   **General Shafter had been ill:** *Correspondence Relating to the War with Spain*, 2 vols. (Washington, D.C.: Center of Military History, 1993), 1:74.

191   **"general view of the":** Report of William R. Shafter, Sept. 13, 1898, in *Annual Report of the Major-General Commanding the Army to the Secretary of War, 1898* (Washington, D.C.: Government Printing Office, 1898), 155.

191   **a journalist later revealed:** McIntosh, *The Little I Saw of Cuba*, 130.

192   **"San Juan was won by":** As quoted in Davis, *The Cuban and Porto Rican Campaigns*, 218.

192   **an early evening meeting:** Shafter, "The Capture of Santiago de Cuba," 624; Miley, *In Cuba with Shafter*, 124; and MacQueen, "With Wheeler and Roosevelt at Santiago," 20.

192   **Roosevelt ran past Crockett:** TR, *The Rough Riders*, 174.

193   **lie down in a skirmish line:** Colbert diary, July 2, 1898, CNCH.

193   **"[I] tell you the black boys":** Letter of John Hall, Troop B, in undated clipping, in William O. "Buckey" O'Neill Vertical File 3, SHM.

193   **"tramping up and down":** Parker, *History of the Gatling Gun Detachment*, 162.

194   **"I chanced to get half":** Colbert diary, July 2, 1898, CNCH.

194   **"In one way or the other":** Henry P. Bardshar, Hagedorn Collection, TRC-H.

194   **"They were hanging to":** Davis, *The Cuban and Porto Rican Campaigns*, 250.

194   **Paris Exposition Universelle:** Roosevelt's promise was mentioned in a letter of William F. Palmer, Troop D, excerpted in the *Albuquerque Daily Citizen*, July 25, 1898.

194–195   **"Dear Cabot: Tell the":** TR to HCL, Outside Santiago, July 3, 1898, in MOR, 2:846.

195   **"you can hold your present":** As quoted in Alger, *The Spanish-American War*, 177.

195   **"Fall Back Shafter":** Cliff D. Scott, Hagedorn Collection, TRC-H.

195   **The booming of big guns:** Wells, *Diary of a Rough Rider*, 59; and Colbert diary, July 3, 1898, CNCH.

195   **"it was better to die":** As quoted in Wheeler, *The Santiago Campaign, 1898*, 291.

196   **José Toral y Vázquez:** Toral had assumed command of the Spanish forces at Santiago after Lieutenant General Arsenio Linares y Pombo was wounded during the Battle of San Juan Heights.

196   **The demand was a ploy:** McClernand, "The Santiago Campaign," 34–35.

196   **One of the regimental bands:** Shafter, "The Capture of Santiago de Cuba," 625.

196   **extended the truce:** Miley, *In Cuba with Shafter*, 130.

196   **improve their earthworks:** Walter J. McCann, Troop B, "Research Materials for the Rough Riders," Hermann Hagedorn Collection, TRC-H.

196   **a commanding knoll:** TR, *The Rough Riders*, 190.

197   **"It was the most powerful":** Parker, *History of the Gatling Gun Detachment*, 164.

197   **there was no food:** Frederick W. Ramsden, "Diary of the British Consul at Santiago During Hostilities," *McClure's Magazine* 11 (Oct., 1898): 589.

197–198   **"The sight is truly pitiful"**: Letter of Sherrard Coleman, Troop E, in *Santa Fe New Mexican Review*, Aug. 4, 1898.

198   **86 killed and wounded**: Report of TR, Trenches Outside Santiago, July 4, 1898, in Wheeler, *The Santiago Campaign, 1898*, 78. Roosevelt would later revise this figure to eighty-nine killed and wounded in his *The Rough Riders*, 155.

198   **"The great heat prostrated"**: Ibid.

198   **The enemy's numbers**: TR, *The Rough Riders*, 156–157; and Sargent, *The Campaign of Santiago de Cuba*, 2:99–100 and 129–130.

199   **"The Spaniards have been"**: Letter of Arthur Hudson, Troop E, in *Santa Fe New Mexican Review*, Aug. 4, 1898.

199   **"the most conspicuous gallantry"** . . . **"needless risk"**: Report of TR, Trenches Outside Santiago, July 4, 1898, in Wheeler, *The Santiago Campaign, 1898*, 80.

199   **disappearing to the rear**: "Tom Hall's 'Fun and Fighting'—A Rough Rider's Version," *New York Times*, Nov. 11, 1899; and "Neither 'Fun' Nor 'Fighting' for Him," *New York Times*, Nov. 18, 1899.

199–200   **"Salute! Why don't you men salute?"** . . . **"get out, the better"**: As quoted in Charles A. Wilson, Hospital Corps, "Research Materials for the Rough Riders," Hermann Hagedorn Collection, TRC-H.

200   **"Hall went completely"**: Ibid.

200   **talk of a Medal of Honor**: Richard Harding Davis dispatch, July 4, 1898, undated *New York Herald* clipping, "Dashing Bravery of Rough Riders," in Arthur F. Cosby scrapbook, TRC-H.

200   **"If there is another battle"**: Samuel McLeary Weller to Florence and Cyrus O. Weller, In camp with the American army on the battlefield in front of Santiago de Cuba, July 6, 1898, Budner Roosevelt Collection, Box 1, Folder 10, DL.

200   **"making medicine"**: Letter of Joshua D. Carter, Troop A, in *Arizona Weekly Journal-Miner*, Prescott, July 27, 1898.

200   **"past burial"**: Letter of John Hall, Troop B, in undated clipping, in William O. "Buckey" O'Neill Vertical File 3, SHM.

200   **"We covered up lots"**: Letter of Sibird Henderson, Troop B, in *Arizona Silver Belt*, July 28, 1898.

200   **"We on the firing line"**: TR to HCL, Outside Santiago, July 10, 1898, in MOR, 2:850.

200   **"An unconditional surrender"**: Letter of John Hall, Troop B, in undated clipping, in William O. "Buckey" O'Neill Vertical File 3, SHM.

201   **proposition was not approved**: H. C. Corbin to W. R. Shafter, Adjutant-General's Office, Washington, D.C., July 9, 1898, in *Correspondence Relating to the War with Spain*, 1:119.

201   **especially annoying battery**: TR, *The Rough Riders*, 193–194; and Prentice, "The Rough Riders," 38.

201   **plagued by several problems**: The gun's operator was Sergeant Hallett Alsop Borrowe, and he detailed the weapon's flaws in a July 14 report to LW in *Annual Report of the Major-General Commanding the Army to the Secretary of War, 1898* (Washington, D.C.: Government Printing Office, 1898), 354. See also Hall, *The Fun and Fighting*, 221.

201   **dynamite gun's shells**: Parker, *History of the Gatling Gun Detachment*, 164; and "The 'Dynamite' Gun," *New York Tribune Illustrated Supplement*, July 10, 1898.

201   **A tremendous explosion**: Prentice, "The Rough Riders," 38; and Davis, *The Cuban and Porto Rican Campaigns*, 285–286.

201–202   **terrified Spanish soldiers**: TR, *The Rough Riders*, 194; and Parker, *History of the Gatling Gun Detachment*, 165.

202   **still in the holds**: Wagner, *Report of the Santiago Campaign*, 119.

202   **"A siege without siege guns"**: Hall, *The Fun and Fighting*, 221.

204   **Theodore Miller Edison**: "Joy Mingled with Sorrow," *The Times*, Washington, D.C., July 13, 1898.

204   **large, stained yellow package**: *Guthrie Daily Leader*, July 11, 1898.

204   **"Enclosed find $50"**: As quoted in ibid.

Chapter Nine: The Real Foe

205   **rifled field mortars**: Miley, *In Cuba with Shafter*, 45 and 153; and Parker, *History of the Gatling Gun Detachment*, 166–167.

206   **"I thought I'd let the"** . . . **"not be shot at"**: As quoted in Frederick Herrig, Hagedorn Collection, TRC-H.

206   **ordered to a new position**: TR, *The Rough Riders*, 195.

207   **crisp new uniforms**: Wells, *Diary of a Rough Rider*, 65.

207   **his valet Marshall**: TR to Edith Roosevelt, Camp 5 miles from Santiago, June 27, 1898, in MOR, 2:845.

207   **remove all his sweaty**: TR, *The Rough Riders*, 195.

207   **a tremendous storm**: LW, diary transcript, July 11, 1898, LW Papers, Container 2, LOC.

207   **"Oh! how disagreeable"**: Colbert diary, July 12, 1898, CNCH.

207   **began firing their weapons**: Ibid.; LW, diary transcript, July 11, 1898, LW Papers, Container 2, LOC; and Wells, *Diary of a Rough Rider*, 65.

208   **"The water was running"**: TR to Ethel Roosevelt, Camp near Santiago, July 15, 1898, in *Theodore Roosevelt's Letters to His Children*, 16.

208   **wrapped him in dry blankets**: TR, *The Rough Riders*, 195–196. Holderman mentioned Roosevelt's early-morning visit in his diary, excerpts of which are found in Verna Stonecipher Fuller, *The Genealogy of Robert Marion Fuller, Sr.* (CreateSpace Independent Publishing Platform, 2014).

208   **signed the commission**: Roosevelt's commission is part of the collections of the Theodore Roosevelt Birthplace National Historic Site.

208   **"Kane turned up every"**: Parker, *History of the Gatling Gun Detachment*, 181–182.

208   **"I am as strong as a"**: TR to HCL, Outside Santiago, July 10, 1898, in MOR, 2:851.

209   **"fully 60 percent of the men"**: Frank Donaldson to *The Philadelphia Medical Journal*, In the Camp of the Rough Riders, July 12, 1898, in *The Philadelphia Medical Journal* 2 (Aug. 13, 1898): 308.

209   **men were consuming quinine**: Ibid.; and Frank Donaldson, "Physical Condition of the First United States Cavalry (Rough Riders) at Date of Mustering Out," *Medical News* 73 (Oct. 15, 1898): 490.

209   **"All of us took a tablespoon"**: Prentice, "The Rough Riders," 42–43.

209   **"there was nothing else"**: Dudley S. Dean to Charles Sanders, Boston, MA, Aug. 20, 1898, Sanders Collection, TRC-H.

209   **some said cowardice**: Charles A. Wilson, a member of the Hospital Corps, recalled that "Dr. La Motte was not much better than Adjutant Hall." Charles A. Wilson, Hagedorn Collection, TRC-H.

209   **also suffering from malaria**: TR, *The Rough Riders*, 200.

209–210   **"It is simply astounding"** . . . **"worth the sacrifice"**: Frank Donaldson to *The Philadelphia Medical Journal*, In the Camp of the Rough Riders, July 12, 1898, in *The Philadelphia Medical Journal* 2 (Aug. 13, 1898): 308.

210   **it seldom came to them**: Report of Sherrard Coleman, Camp Wikoff, Long Island,

Sept. 10, 1898, in *Report of the Commission . . . to Investigate the Conduct of the War Department*, vol. 8, 481–482.

210   **cowboys gathered up:** TR, "How We Captured the Blockhouse on San Juan Hill," in *Hero Tales of the American Soldier and Sailor* (Philadelphia, PA: Century Manufacturing Co., 1899), 207; and Prentice, "The Rough Riders," 39–40 and 42.

210   **Henry Alfred Brown:** *New York Times*, Aug. 22, 1898; and *The Washington Times*, Oct. 27, 1906.

210   **"could settle a Spaniard":** Fox, "With the Rough Riders at Las Guásimas."

210–211   **"But do you know" . . . "don't get off the horse!":** As quoted in *Roosevelt: An Autobiography*, 253.

211   **"God put it down there":** As quoted in Henry P. Bardshar, Hagedorn Collection, TRC-H.

211   **a shipment of tobacco:** Hall, *The Fun and Fighting*, 210.

211   **Kane received a package:** MacQueen, "With Wheeler and Roosevelt at Santiago," 26.

211   **"the most popular man":** McCurdy and McCurdy, *Two Rough Riders*, 31.

211   **"I think a square meal":** Letter of Daniel L. Hogan, Troop A, in the *Coconino Sun*, Aug. 6, 1898.

211–212   **"Colonel, this man" . . . "to the guardhouse":** As quoted in MacQueen, "With Wheeler and Roosevelt at Santiago," 23.

212   **"[Our] men must have" . . . "you bet we'd go":** As quoted in ibid., 28.

212   **not to cheer:** Wells, *Diary of a Rough Rider*, 67.

213   **finally agreed to surrender:** W. R. Shafter to H. C. Corbin, Playa, July 14, 1898, in *Correspondence Relating to the War with Spain*, 1:142.

213   **a pretty good haul:** TR, *The Rough Riders*, 201 and 274.

213   **"This is a red letter":** Wells, *Diary of a Rough Rider*, 68.

213–214   **"The horrors of war!":** Letter of Sherrard Coleman, Troop E, in *Santa Fe New Mexican Review*, Aug. 11, 1898.

214   **one-sided trades:** MacQueen, "With Wheeler and Roosevelt at Santiago," 24.

214   **Roosevelt soon forbid:** TR, *The Rough Riders*, 197.

214   **carried the elderly women's bundles:** Ibid., 197–198; and Thomas P. Ledwidge, Hagedorn Collection, TRC-H.

214   **"The Almighty would":** As quoted in TR, *The Rough Riders*, 198.

214   **At 11:45 on July 17:** Colbert diary, July 17, 1898, CNCH.

214   **regimental bands playing:** Wells, *Diary of a Rough Rider*, 68.

214   **"What's the matter with":** As quoted in the *Wichita Daily Eagle*, Aug. 23, 1898.

214   **"As I glance down":** Wells, *Diary of a Rough Rider*, 68.

215   **"By George, men, you":** As quoted in MacQueen, "With Wheeler and Roosevelt at Santiago," 28.

216   **"The boys certainly made":** Colbert diary, July 17, 1898, CNCH.

216   **123 Rough Riders reported:** Report of TR, Santiago, July 20, 1898, in MOR, 2:859.

216   **only 275 were on:** "Roosevelt's Care of His Men," undated clipping, Arthur F. Cosby scrapbook, TRC-H.

216   **bunks in their tents:** TR, *The Rough Riders*, 202.

216   **"made us look like tree-dwellers":** Nicholas A. Vyne, Hagedorn Collection, TRC-H.

216   **"made little difference":** Prentice, "The Rough Riders," 42.

216   **"Do you think they":** As quoted in Rynning, *Gun Notches*, 184.

216   **"Had fried tenderloin":** Roger S. Fitch diary, July 22, 1898, RRM.

216   **tried to buy a machete:** Wells, *Diary of a Rough Rider*, 71.

216 **delivery of back mail:** Ibid.; Colbert diary, July 24, 1898, CNCH; and McCurdy and McCurdy, *Two Rough Riders*, 28.

217 **"Where are you today":** As quoted in Joe L. Todd, " 'Softened as into a Dream': The Letters of Robert B. Huston, Oklahoma Rough Rider," *The Chronicles of Oklahoma* 76 (Spring, 1998): 10.

217 **Very few of the Rough Riders:** Samuel McLeary Weller to My Dear Sister, In camp with the Cavalry Division of the American Army four miles northeast of Santiago de Cuba, July 20, 1898, Budner Roosevelt Collection, Box 1, Folder 10, DL; and *Oklahoma Rough Rider Billy McGinty's Own Story*, 52.

217 **"We had coffee served":** Royal A. Prentice, diary, 117, Royal A. Prentice Papers, Box 1, Folder 12, FACL.

217 **"She being the first American":** Colbert diary, July 24, 1898, CNCH.

217 **water hole:** *Oklahoma Rough Rider Billy McGinty's Own Story*, 48.

218 **" 'Sharks,' says the colonel":** As quoted in Morris, *The Rise of Theodore Roosevelt*, 690. Morris identifies Lieutenant John Greenway as the officer who swam to the wreck with Roosevelt and also the narrator of this story, but in a letter to his mother of July 31, 1898, Greenway clearly states he passed on the invitation to visit the harbor, choosing to remain in camp. See Greenway, *It Was the Grandest Sight I Ever Saw*, 40–41. Roosevelt gives a much tamer version of the swim in his *The Rough Riders*, 214.

218 **There were rumors:** Colbert diary, July 15 and 20, 1898, CNCH.

218–219 **"My Dear Mr. Secretary":** TR to R. A. Alger, Santiago, July 23, 1898, in MOR, 2:859–860; and the *Times*, Washington, D.C., Aug. 5, 1898.

219 **"as bad as ever" . . . "hardly stand":** Wells, *Diary of a Rough Rider*, 71.

219 **"the hospitals and ground":** Greenway, *It Was the Grandest Sight I Ever Saw*, 40.

219 **once the fever cases:** R. A. Alger to W. R. Shafter, War Department, July 28, 1898, in *Correspondence Relating to the War with Spain*, 1:185.

219 **"Of course, the malarial" . . . "I earned it":** TR to HCL, Santiago, July 31, 1898, in MOR, 2:862.

219 **secretary and a typewriter:** TR to Patty Selmes, In camp near Santiago, Cuba, July 31, 1898, John and Isabella Greenway Papers, 1860–1953, Arizona Historical Society, Tucson.

220 **"I wish I could give you":** TR to A. J. Dawson, In camp near Santiago de Cuba, July 31, 1898, private collection.

220 **"as rapidly as" . . . "many troops away":** R. A. Alger to W. R. Shafter, Washington, D.C., Aug. 2, 1898, in *Correspondence Relating to the War with Spain*, 1:196.

220 **yellow fever epidemic:** W. R. Shafter to H. C. Corbin, Santiago de Cuba, Aug. 2, 1898, in *Correspondence Relating to the War with Spain*, 194.

220 **they turned to Roosevelt:** *Roosevelt: An Autobiography*, 246.

221 **"I don't want to take it":** As quoted in ibid. Shafter's version of the round robin and Roosevelt's letter is much different. See his "The Capture of Santiago de Cuba," 629–630.

221 **his own detailed report:** W. R. Shafter to H. C. Corbin, Santiago de Cuba, via Haiti, Aug. 3, 1898, in *Correspondence Relating to the War with Spain*, 200–202.

221 **"If we are kept here":** As quoted in the *Evening Star*, Aug. 4, 1898.

221 **replied to Shafter's recommendation:** Alger, *The Spanish-American War*, 264–265.

222 **"Your letter is received":** As quoted in the *Times*, Washington, D.C., Aug. 5, 1898.

222 **"Everywhere they are":** Undated news clipping, Box 11, Rough Riders, RRM.

222   **"as gross a violation"** . . . **"the author's prospects":** *New York Times* as quoted in the *Evening Star*, Aug. 6, 1898.

223   **"Every mother of us":** Letter of Emma H. Brainard, New York, Aug. 7, 1898, undated, *New York Herald* in Arthur F. Cosby scrapbook, TRC-H.

223   **"the only thing I want":** TR to HCL, Santiago, July 31, 1898, in MOR, 2:863.

Chapter Ten: Crackerjacks in New York

224   **"canary coats":** *The Sun,* Aug. 21, 1898.

224   **"warm-climate uniforms":** "The Boys in Drab," *The Sun,* May 2, 1898; and Stewart, *Cowboys in Uniform,* 9.

224   **"I am so thin":** Wells, *Diary of a Rough Rider,* 73.

225   **credited Roosevelt's letter:** Hemment, *Cannon and Camera,* 236–237.

225   **"All the boys are delighted":** Roger S. Fitch diary, Aug. 4, 1898, RRM.

225   **sixty thousand Spanish soldiers:** Sargent, *The Campaign of Santiago de Cuba,* 1: 83.

225   **tossing the old ones:** Wells, *Diary of a Rough Rider,* 74; and Roger S. Fitch diary, Aug. 7, 1898, RRM.

225   **"made in the year one hundred":** Royal A. Prentice, diary, 121, Royal A. Prentice Papers, Box 1, Folder 12, FACL.

225   **Roosevelt riding at the:** "Rough Riders Sail for Home," *The North American,* Philadelphia, Aug. 8, 1898.

225   **paymaster soon appeared:** Roger S. Fitch diary, Aug. 7, 1898, RRM; and Wells, *Diary of a Rough Rider,* 74.

226   **Third Cavalry's band played:** Colbert diary, Aug. 8, 1898, CNCH; and Wells, *Diary of a Rough Rider,* 75.

226   **Five sick Rough Riders:** "Rough Riders Sail for Home," *The North American,* Philadelphia, Aug. 8, 1898.

227   **a history of the Rough Riders:** TR to Robert Bridges, Camp near San Antonio, Texas, May 21, 1898, in MOR, 2:832.

227   **happy to share it:** TR, *The Rough Riders,* 215.

227   **"I would like to bid":** Colbert diary, Aug. 6, 1898, CNCH.

227–228   **"On shore this was not":** TR, *The Rough Riders,* 217.

228   **"He never recovered":** Ibid.

228   **"Twas quite a sad":** Colbert diary, Aug. 12, 1898, CNCH.

228   **"I am happy to take my":** Ibid., Aug. 14, 1898.

229   **"Nearly all my men":** As quoted in the *Milwaukee Journal,* Aug. 15, 1898.

229   **"Will you be our"** . . . **"to command it":** As quoted in Heatley, ed., *Bully!,* 63.

230   **about fifteen troopers:** Ibid, 66.

230   **brought their first meal:** *The Sun,* Aug. 16, 1898.

230   **"they were on American":** As quoted in ibid.

230   **fresh fruit, eggs, and milk:** Heatley, ed., *Bully!,* 159.

230   **two large packing cases:** *The Sun,* Aug. 16, 1898.

230   **These men had suffered:** Marshall, *The Story of the Rough Riders,* 53–54.

231   **"We want to see Teddy!":** As quoted in "More Troops for Montauk," undated clipping in Arthur F. Cosby scrapbook, TRC-H.

231   **About halfway, they were:** Edwin Emerson Jr., "Life at Camp Wikoff," *Munsey's Magazine* 20 (Nov. 1898): 260.

231   **five- to ten-day furloughs:** *The Sun,* Aug. 20, 1898; and "Rough Riders Besieged," undated clipping in Arthur F. Cosby scrapbook, TRC-H.

231   **"What a pity you boys":** As quoted in McCurdy and McCurdy, *Two Rough Riders*, 44.

231   **"We could not spend a cent":** Colbert diary, Aug. 19, 1898, CNCH.

232   **"simply immense, the finest":** Royal A. Prentice, diary, 127, Royal A. Prentice Papers, Box 1, Folder 12, FACL.

232   **Futurity horse race:** *The Sun*, Aug. 24, 1898.

232   **a raucous crowd:** Ibid., Aug. 21, 1898.

232   **"It was all perfectly clear":** Robert Bridges, "Theodore Roosevelt as Author and Contributor," *Waterloo Evening Courier*, IA, Oct. 27, 1921.

232   **six articles at $1,000:** Morris, *The Rise of Theodore Roosevelt*, 722.

232   **"Col. Roosevelt will accept"** . . . **"conversation was politics":** *The Sun*, Aug. 21, 1898.

233   **Lieutenant William Tiffany:** *The Sun*, Aug. 24 and 26, 1898; and undated clippings on Tiffany's death and funeral in Arthur F. Cosby scrapbook, TRC-H.

233   **Roosevelt remained convinced:** TR, *The Rough Riders*, 216.

233   **Colbert became so ill:** Colbert diary, Aug. 25, 1898, CNCH.

233   **"in a well-developed state":** As quoted in "Rough Rider Taken Ill," *New York Times*, Aug. 22, 1898.

234   **case of J. Ogden Wells:** "Harvard Man's Experience," undated clipping in Scrapbook of Mary M. Goodrich, TRC-H.

234   **"No condemnation"** . . . **"the Red Cross":** Letter of Paul Hunter, Troop D, in the *Guthrie Daily Leader*, Aug. 30, 1898. See also "Story of Horror," *El Paso Daily Herald*, Aug. 26, 1898.

234   **established a kitchen:** *The Sun*, Sept. 3, 1898.

234–235 **"Well, we will make it a trifle"** . . . **"not mention me":** As quoted in "In Memory of 'Willie' Tiffany," in undated clipping in Arthur F. Cosby scrapbook, TRC-H. Roosevelt sent money in late July to five wounded Rough Riders in the post hospital on Governors Island. See "Col. Roosevelt's Largesse," *The Times*, July 29, 1898.

235–236 **"I want to see Col. Roosevelt":** This delightful story, which was published in the Oct. 15, 1898, issue of the *New-York Commercial Advertiser*, is reprinted in Heatley, ed., *Bully!*, 218–220. Neither Roosevelt nor McGinty mention the episode in their reminiscences.

236   **soon be mustered out:** *The Sun*, Aug. 27, 1898.

236   **a favorite Roosevelt pastime:** Ibid., Aug. 28, 1898.

237   **"I'd let my sisters ride":** As quoted in the *Evening Star*, Sept. 10, 1898.

237   **The contest took place:** TR, *The Rough Riders*, 226–227.

237–238 **"once mounted a tornado":** *The Sun*, Aug. 31, 1898.

238   **"whether most to wonder":** TR, *The Rough Riders*, 227.

238   **"Nice little horse":** As quoted in the *Times*, Sept. 4, 1898.

239   **"Colonel! I'm glad to"** . . . **"Colonel, I will":** As quoted in the *Sun*, Sept. 4, 1898.

239   **"Three cheers for the President":** Ibid.

239   **"I'm proud of these boys":** As quoted in ibid., Sept. 1, 1898.

240   **"What they will do after":** As quoted in ibid., Sept. 4, 1898.

240   **"It would be a rather ridiculous":** As quoted in ibid., Sept. 5, 1898.

240   **Roosevelt asked McGinty:** *Oklahoma Rough Rider Billy McGinty's Own Story*, 71.

240   **"I hope to be as great":** As quoted in ibid.

240   **Alice Lee asked Frank Brito:** Walker, "New Mexico's Last Rough Rider," 11.

241   **the regiment's mascots:** TR, *The Rough Riders*, 221–222.

241   **oranges and tea:** *The Sun*, Sept. 5, 1898.

241   **"great success"** . . . **"about a hundred":** As quoted in Heatley, ed., *Bully!*, 315.

241   **surrender their trusty Krags:** TR, *The Rough Riders*, 219. Robert Wrenn's Model 1895

Winchester he used in Cuba is now part of the collections of the Theodore Roosevelt Birthplace National Historic Site.

241   **souvenir peddlers invaded:** Emerson Jr., "Life at Camp Wikoff," 268.

242   **"Boys, you all have bought"** . . . **"Bully for you, Tony!":** As quoted in Bradley Gilman, *Roosevelt: The Happy Warrior* (Boston: Little, Brown, and Company, 1921), 154–155.

242   **final bucking contest:** Emerson Jr., "Life at Camp Wikoff," 268.

243   **"pure bloods and half-breeds":** TR, *The Rough Riders*, 228.

243–244   **"a very slight token"** . . . **"governor of New York!":** *The Sun*, Sept. 14, 1898.

244   **"I made Pollock, the Pawnee":** As quoted in the *New York Tribune*, Sept. 14, 1898.

244   **$120 in pay:** *The Sun*, Sept. 14, 1898.

244   **"Colonel, we men present":** As quoted in "Passing of the Rough Riders," *The County Record*, Kingstree, SC, Sept. 22, 1898.

245–246   **"Shields, there is no one"** . . . **"that's all I'll say":** *Roosevelt: An Autobiography*, 250–251.

246   **ladies' headwear:** *The Sun*, Aug. 31, 1898.

246   **"This is the golden eagle":** As quoted in the *Sun*, Sept. 17, 1898.

247   **auction of the regiment's horses:** *The Evening Times*, Sept. 21, 1898; and "Sale of Army Broncos," undated clipping in Arthur F. Cosby scrapbook, TRC-H.

248   **"all sorts of funny tricks":** *The Sun*, Sept. 26, 1898.

248   **visit the White House:** "President Sees Rough Rides," undated clipping in Arthur F. Cosby scrapbook, TRC-H; and "Yells in the East Room," undated clipping in Marinel Ash Coll., AC 385, Box 1, Folder 16, FACL.

248   **"We are going home":** *The Evening Times*, Sept. 21, 1898.

Chapter Eleven: Children of the Dragon's Blood

249   **Roosevelt had testified:** "Roosevelt on the Stand," *The Evening Star*, Nov. 23, 1898.

250   **More than eight thousand officers:** Sargent, *The Campaign of Santiago de Cuba*, 2:130.

250   **"I don't ask this as a favor":** TR to HCL, New York, Dec. 6, 1898, in MOR, 2:892.

250   **"gallant and meritorious":** *The Evening Times*, Jan. 4, 1899.

250   **infuriated unnamed friends:** Ibid., Jan. 5, 1899.

250–252   **"showing he performed"** . . . **"before Santiago de Cuba":** As quoted in *Topeka State Journal*, Jan. 9, 1899.

252   **"We gather from Mr. Alger's":** *The Times*, Jan. 9, 1899.

252   **"is indignant at what it is":** TR to HCL, Albany, Jan. 12, 1899, in MOR, 2:909.

252   **"that infernal medal":** TR to HCL, Albany, Jan. 19, 1899, in MOR, 2:919.

252   **"every act of the officer":** "Burr McIntosh's Lecture," *The Evening Star*, April 22, 1899.

252–253   **"If the Colonel was looking":** As quoted in Musgrave, *Under Three Flags in Cuba*, 270.

253   **When the final names:** *The Sun*, June 11, 1899.

253   **hadn't performed any actions:** "Did But His Duty," *The Cedar Rapids Evening Gazette*, April 12, 1899. The requirements for the Medal of Honor, as issued in a statement from the War Department's Board on Brevets, are found in the *Daily Record-Union*, Sacramento, CA, Jan. 8, 1898.

253   **"Algerian point of view":** *The Times*, Jan. 6, 1899.

253   **formed a veterans association:** "New Social Military Order," *The Sun*, Sept. 1, 1898.

253   **their first reunion:** The reunion was covered extensively in the press. See *El Paso Daily Herald*, June 26 and 27, 1899; *Albuquerque Daily Citizen*, June 26, 1899; *The Houston Daily Post*, June 25, 1899; *Topeka State Journal*, June 26, 1899; and *The Arizona Republican*, June 25, 1899.

253   **the bronze medal:** *The Sun*, Sept. 12, 1898; and *Albuquerque Daily Citizen*, Oct. 31, 1898.

253   **governor Miguel A. Otero:** Miguel Antonio Otero, *My Nine Years as Governor of the Territory of New Mexico, 1897–1906* (Albuquerque: The University of New Mexico Press, 1940), 64. In this volume, Otero characterizes Roosevelt as little more than an egomaniac and publicity hound at the Las Vegas reunion. It is well to remember that Roosevelt chose not to reappoint Otero as territorial governor when his term expired in early 1906.

254   **Roosevelt got a medal:** This medal is currently on display in the Theodore Roosevelt Museum at Sagamore Hill National Historic Site. See also "Medal for Gov. Roosevelt," *The Sun*, June 26, 1899.

255   **"Dick, I sincerely hope":** As quoted in Nancy Green McCleary, "Notes and Documents," *New Mexico Historical Review* 24 (Jan. 1949): 65.

255   **into its third printing:** Charles Scribner's Sons advertisement in *New-York Daily Tribune*, May 20, 1899.

255   **"[I]f I was him I'd call":** *Harper's Weekly* 43 (Nov. 25, 1899): 1195.

255   **"I regret to state":** TR to Finley Peter Dunne, Albany, Nov. 28, 1899, in MOR, 2:1099.

255–256   **"one of the most thrilling":** *New York Times*, May 20, 1899.

256   **"children of the dragon's blood":** TR, *The Rough Riders*, 298.

256   **Cassi blew his trumpet:** *The Evening Times*, Oct. 25, 1898; and "Rough Riders to Aid Roosevelt," *New-York Daily Tribune*, June 27, 1900.

256   **mounted honor guard:** "Rough Riders Arrive," *The Evening Star*, March 2, 1905; and "Thousands Cheer the President," *The Washington Times*, March 5, 1905.

256   **"I certainly love all my boys":** As quoted in *New-York Daily Tribune*, June 19, 1910.

256   **translating every word:** "Teddy Greets Indians and New Mexicans," *The Arizona Republican*, Sept. 19, 1912.

256   **Armijo boy's baptism:** "Acted as Sponsor," *The Albuquerque Daily Citizen*, May 7, 1903; and TR to John Hay, Oyster Bay, Aug. 9, 1903, in MOR, 3:557.

257   **"The President is engaged"** . . . **"against a Rough Rider":** As quoted in Gilman, *Roosevelt: The Happy Warrior*, 160.

257   **"as if we were the parents":** TR to Bellamy and Maria Storer, Oyster Bay, April 17, 1901, in MOR, 3:58.

257   **"Dear Colonel: I write you":** As quoted in ibid.

257   **the shooting was rooted in:** "Killed His Sister-in-Law," *Bryan Morning Eagle*, Bryan, Texas, Sept. 18, 1900; and "Asesinó á su Cuñada," *La Voz del Pueblo*, East Las Vegas, New Mexico, Sept. 22, 1900.

257   **"I draw the line at":** TR to W.H.H. Llewellyn, Oyster Bay, April 15, 1901, in MOR, 3:54.

258   **sentenced to ten years:** *The Anaconda Standard*, Anaconda, MT, May 12, 1901.

258   **"For the sake of the regiment":** TR to W.H.H. Llewellyn, Oyster Bay, July 13, 1901, in MOR, 3:118.

258   **"This incident has tended":** W.H.H. Llewellyn to TR, Santa Fe, Feb. 20, 1903, Theodore Roosevelt Papers, LOC.

258   **Otero pardoned Brito:** *Albuquerque Morning Journal*, June 29, 1905.

258   **a long crime spree:** "A Rough Rider and a Senorita," *Denver Evening Post*, Oct. 5, 1899; and *Denver Evening Post*, Oct. 13, 1899.

259   **reached out to Roosevelt:** Edward G. Collier to TR, Canon City, Nov. 26, 1902.

259   **"Assuredly he is no angel":** James H. McClintock to TR, Phoenix, AZ, Dec. 11, 1902, Theodore Roosevelt Papers, LOC.

259   **a letter from the president:** TR to The Board of Pardons, Dec. 19, 1902, ibid.

259 **wrote McClintock again:** TR to James H. McClintock, Oyster Bay, July 8, 1903, ibid. This letter is misdated 1902.

259 **on December 10, 1903:** Parole Record, Colorado State Penitentiary, vol. 2, p. 140, Colorado State Archives, Denver.

259 **Darnell's boss fired him:** "The Killing of Darnell," *El Paso Daily Herald*, Feb. 21, 1899.

259–260 **"See you again, old man" ... "will get you anyway":** As quoted in "A Bad Man Bites the Dust," *Phoenix Weekly Herald*, Feb. 23, 1899.

260 **"Tom was dead when":** George Roland to Roger Fitch, Deer Creek, Diamond A Ranch, New Mexico, March 28, 1899, George Roland file, RRM.

260 **two eagle feathers:** Helen W. Ball, "The Pawnee Rough Rider," *The Midland Monthly* 10 (Nov. 1898): 453.

260 **in the Fine Arts Department:** "An Indian Artist," *The Outlook* 52 (Dec. 7, 1895): 992.

260 **"Christian gentleman":** Ball, "The Pawnee Rough Rider," 453.

261 **signed a contract:** "Dozen of Rough Riders," *The Wichita Daily Eagle*, March 8, 1899.

261 **"vivid, truthful, thrilling":** Wild West Show advertisement in the *Evening Star*, April 8, 1899.

261 **paid $50 a month:** *Florence Tribune*, March 4, 1899.

261 **"the fever was in his veins":** "One Good Indian," *Daily Record-Union*, March 26, 1899.

261 **a replica San Juan Hill:** *Oklahoma Rough Rider Billy McGinty's Own Story*, 95–96.

261 **341 times in 132 towns:** George H. Cook, compiler, *Route-Book, Buffalo Bill's Wild West, 1899* (Buffalo, NY: The Matthews-Northrup Co., 1899), 50.

261 **"excellent in every respect":** "Colonel Cody's Rough Riders," *The Times*, April 16, 1899.

262 **Army surgeons claimed:** "Shot on Firing Line," *The Indianapolis Journal*, April 6, 1899.

262 **leg would be amputated:** "Edward Marshall Loses a Leg," *New York Times*, July 30, 1899. Lorrin Muxlow of Guthrie, one of the Rough Riders who had helped carry the wounded Marshall off the battlefield, was in the Cody show, and Marshall sought him out for what was an emotional reunion. See "Buffalo Bill's Wild West," *The Times*, April 19, 1899.

263 **entered the sanitarium:** Jennie Dunbar Hall's application for a widow's pension, National Archives. My thanks to Nancy Samuelson for her notes from Jennie's application.

263 **the help of Frank Hayes:** Hayes admits assisting "poor old Tom Hall" in a 1926 inscription in a first edition copy of *The Fun and Fighting* in the Theodore Roosevelt Collection, Widener Library, Harvard.

263 **got her divorce:** "Tom Hall Divorced," *The North American*, Jan. 11, 1899.

263 **"in a position to partake" ... "abhorrence and contempt":** *New York Times*, Nov. 18, 1899. Cosby's letter is in the issue of Nov. 11.

263 **He died ten months later:** "'Tom Hall' Dead," *New York Times*, Aug. 25, 1900.

264 **dead in his garage:** *Benton Harbor News-Palladium*, Benton Harbor, MI, Dec. 17, 1928.

264 **a trio of close Michigan friends:** Ibid., April 29, 1944.

264 **received a package:** "Death of a Hero," undated clipping in Scrapbook of Mary M. Goodrich, TRC-H.

264 **"stands in the midst":** Vincent, ed., *Theodore Miller: Rough Rider*, 178–179.

265 **recommendation from Roosevelt:** TR to H. C. Corbin, Santiago de Cuba, Aug. 2, 1898, Arthur F. Cosby scrapbook, TRC-H.

265 **"Too far from where" ... "following its colors":** Edwin Emerson to Robert Denny, New York City, Sept. 3, 1948, Edwin Emerson file, RRM.

265–266 **"I have asked for so many favors":** TR to W.H.H. Llewellyn, Oyster Bay, July 13, 1901, in MOR, 3:118.

266 **"how it paid to belong":** "How It Paid to Belong to the Rough Riders," *San Antonio Light*, April 8, 1908. See also "Rough Riders Win Offices," *The Sun*, March 25, 1906; and Broughton Brandenburg, "The Rough Riders Ten Years Afterward," *The Evening Star*, Feb. 9, 1908.

266 **Daniels's colorful history:** TR, *The Rough Riders*, 25–26.

266 **Daniels pressed Roosevelt:** Robert K. DeArment and Jack DeMattos, *A Rough Ride to Redemption: The Ben Daniels Story* (Norman: University of Oklahoma Press, 2010), 107–108.

267 **persuaded Governor Brodie:** Ibid., 127.

267 **"Perhaps [Roosevelt] . . . thinks":** As quoted in ibid., 136.

267 **"I have learned from sad":** Colbert diary, Aug. 5, 1898, CNCH.

267 **He was investigated:** *Chickasha Daily Express*, Chickasha, Indian Territory, Sept. 9, 1903; and *The Daily Ardmoreite*, Aug. 26, 1903.

267 **scandal involving Chickasaw:** *The Daily Ardmoreite*, June 29, 1905; and *The Chickasha Daily Express*, June 29 and July 25, 1905.

267 **indicted for fraud:** "The Chickasaw Warrant Frauds," *The Daily Ardmoreite*, June 24, 1905.

267 **acquitted in federal court:** *The Daily Ardmoreite*, Oct. 11, 1908.

267 **left the Republican Party:** "Ben Colbert Follows Teddy," *The Daily Ardmoreite*, Sept. 4, 1912.

267 **volunteered in World War I:** "Two Rough Riders Are Writing Books on Lives," *Las Vegas Daily Optic*, Aug. 7, 1954.

268 **Oklahoma veterans' home:** Michelle Cooke, "Benjamin H. Colbert: Legacy of a Chickasaw Rough Rider," *The Journal of Chickasaw History and Culture* 11 (Fall 2008): 44.

268 **printed a full page:** See, for example, the *Valentine Democrat*, Valentine, NE, Nov. 3, 1904; and *The Weekly Register*, Point Pleasant, VA, Nov. 2, 1904.

268 **"did not see a Spaniard" . . . "imaginary Spaniards":** Ibid.

269 **newspaper blamed Remington:** "Mr. Remington's Man on Horseback," *The Sun*, April 26, 1908.

269–270 **"The San Juan Block House":** As quoted in Lawrence F. Abbott, *Impressions of Theodore Roosevelt* (Garden City, NY: Doubleday, Page & Co., 1922), 202.

270 **"remains a high point in":** "The Rough Riders Ride Again," *Life* (Aug. 25, 1952): 43.

270 **"That's the grossest":** George P. Hamner to the Editors of *Life*, Hollywood, FL, Aug. 27, 1952, George P. Hamner file, RRM.

270 **perpetuated by historians:** See, for example, Brian W. Dippie, *The Frederic Remington Art Museum Collection* (Ogdensburg, NY: Frederic Remington Art Museum, 2001), 120; and Peter R. DeMontravel, *A Hero to His Fighting Men: Nelson A Miles, 1839–1925* (Kent, OH: The Kent State University Press, 1998), 332.

270 **"peculiarly dependent upon" . . . "fair to expect":** TR, *The Rough Riders*, 143.

270–271 **"Has Col. Roosevelt":** *The Broad Ax*, July 30, 1904.

271 **"No officers, no soldiers":** As quoted in Johnson, *History of Negro Soldiers in the Spanish-American War*, 68.

271 **gone on a shooting spree:** Harry Lembeck, *Taking on Theodore Roosevelt: How One Senator Defied the President on Brownsville and Shook American Politics* (Amherst, NY: Prometheus Books, 2015), 35–36.

271 **discharges for 167 men:** Ibid., 130.

271 **"These comrades of the":** As quoted in "Roosevelt Hotly Answers Senate," *Los Angeles Herald*, Dec. 20, 1906.

272 **"was a man of many and strong":** Gilman, *Roosevelt: The Happy Warrior*, 127.

272 **an entire cavalry division:** TR to Frank Ross McCoy, Oyster Bay, July 10, 1915, in MOR, 8:947.

272 **"which sums up the beauty":** As quoted in MOR, 8:1193 n. 2.

273 **"The thought that his country":** James E. Amos, *Theodore Roosevelt: Hero to His Valet* (New York: The John Day Company, 1927), 66–67.

274 **snobbishness and jealousy:** Jack C. Lane, *Armed Progressive: General Leonard Wood* (San Rafael, CA: Presidio Press, 1978), 221–222.

274 **"This is no time for differences":** As quoted in Amos, *Theodore Roosevelt: Hero to His Valet*, 67.

274 **blood clot had detached:** *New York Times*, Jan. 7, 1919.

274 **in the large trophy room:** *New York Tribune*, Jan. 9, 1919.

274 **"To my way of thinking":** Willis, *Roosevelt in the Rough*, 18.

275 **silver-mounted rabbit's foot:** *Sculptor in Buckskin: The Autobiography of Alexander Phimister Proctor*, ed. by Katharine C. Ebner, second edition (Norman: University of Oklahoma Press, 2009), 186.

Epilogue

276 **"our highest military decoration":** A video and transcript of the Medal of Honor ceremony is available online at www.c-span.org/video/?161885-1/medal-honor-ceremony.

276 **In 1996, Congress passed:** Barbara Salazar Torreon, "Medal of Honor: History and Issues," Congressional Research Service Report, Aug. 18, 2015, 11–13, https://fas.org/sgp/crs/misc/95-519.pdf.

277 **legislation to award Roosevelt:** The bill was HR 2263.

277 **submitted a formal request:** *The Awarding of the Medal of Honor to Theodore Roosevelt, Hearing Before the Military Personnel Subcommittee of the Committee on National Security*, House of Representatives, 105th Cong., 2nd sess., Sept. 28, 1998 (Washington, D.C.: U.S. Government Printing Office, 1998), 7.

277 **determined that Roosevelt's actions:** Ibid., 10; and "Congress Votes Medal of Honor for Colonel Theodore Roosevelt," *Theodore Roosevelt Association Journal* 22 (1998): 2.

277 **"the same standard of merit":** As quoted in *Congressional Record*, Oct. 21, 1998, 27594.

277 **army solicited the public:** "Army Invites Public Submissions for Medal of Honor Award Recommendation for Theodore Roosevelt," U.S. Army News Release, #99-024, March 18, 1999.

277 **Cohen forwarded to Clinton:** *Congressional Record*, June 13, 2000, 10603.

277 **"TR was a larger-than-life":** Video and transcript of the Medal of Honor ceremony at www.c-span.org/video/?161885-1/medal-honor-ceremony.

278 **the only two members:** Rough Rider George G. McMurtry, Troop D, received the Medal of Honor for his heroics as commander of a battalion that was cut off and surrounded by the Germans in the Argonne Forest in October 1918.

278 **"I regard the fact":** TR to Ralph Emerson Twitchell, Sagamore Hill, Nov. 12, 1911, Box 8472, Folder 91, R. E. Twitchell Collection, 1959-209, NMSR.

INDEX

Note: Page references in *italics* indicate photographs and their captions.